African Whiteboy

Ian Watson

Buchanan Books

BUCHANAN OF ARGYLL

BBC

Trafford Publishing

Buchanan Books

Cambridge, Fort Lauderdale

Editor-in-Chief: J. Edwards
Production Editor: M.E. Cairns
Editorial Assistants: Bevan W. Watson,
Katherine A. Reid

Author's Note: In a gesture of privacy the names of some persons in this story were changed. Acknowledgments: The cover painting of Madiba is based on an African National Congress (ANC) photograph. Thanks for help and direction are extended to Helen Atsma, Little, Brown and Company, Publishers.

Note for Librarians: A cataloguing record for this book is available from Library and Archives Canada at www.collectionscanada.ca/amicus/index-e.html
ISBN 1-4120-8093-2

Printed in Victoria, BC, Canada. Printed on paper with minimum 30% recycled fibre. Trafford's print shop runs on "green energy" from solar, wind and other environmentally-friendly power sources.

TRAFFORD
PUBLISHING™

Offices in Canada, USA, Ireland and UK

Book sales for North America and international:
Trafford Publishing, 6E–2333 Government St.,
Victoria, BC V8T 4P4 CANADA
phone 250 383 6864 (toll-free 1 888 232 4444)
fax 250 383 6804; email to orders@trafford.com
Book sales in Europe:
Trafford Publishing (UK) Limited, 9 Park End Street, 2nd Floor
Oxford, UK OX1 1HH UNITED KINGDOM
phone 44 (0)1865 722 113 (local rate 0845 230 9601)
facsimile 44 (0)1865 722 868; info.uk@trafford.com
Order online at:
trafford.com/05-3090

10 9 8 7 6 5 4 3

This book is dedicated to
Stella & Jack Suberman.

Writer Stella
— *When It Was Our War* and *The Jew Store* —
and
English Professor Jack
are both still engaged in
teaching me how to write.

"He is walking history, one of the most extraordinary people of all times. The day has finally arrived. It's the interview of my lifetime." So said Oprah Winfrey. Her moving conversation with Nelson Mandela, in November 2000, inspired me to begin this narrative. It had long been prompted by my students and friends who, even as I write, continue to ask about my former life in Africa and how I came to be living in the United States.

My saga offers a tribute to
Nelson Mandela
for his brave stand against the forces of evil,
and for his unembittered graciousness at the
time of his triumph.

It honors the memory of the late
Sir John Knill,
my professor at the Royal School of Mines,
a man of lasting influence on my life.

Nkosi Sikelel' iAfrika!
May the Divine One bless Africa!

CONTENTS

[NOTE: For photographs that illustrate this book, please see:
www.africanwhiteboy.com]

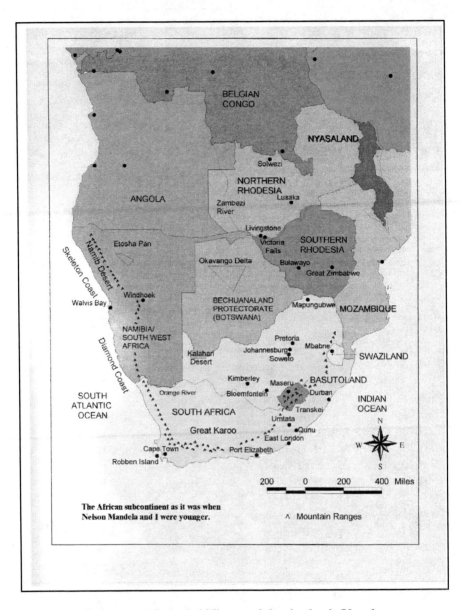

Southern Africa in the Colonial Times of the Author's Youth.

[Sketch map prepared from GIS data.]

A LOST UTOPIA

I recently returned to Africa. It had been more than forty years since I first fled my native land, more than four long decades since the Sharpeville massacre, that dark moment when I decided that I could no longer tolerate the agony of living with *apartheid*. Still, though I had found cherished freedom, and a long-fought-for new home in magnificent America, emotionally I had never strayed far. Africa, if you were born there, clings to you and does not easily let you forget her.

And so I had been lured back, mainly to see family and friends. But on this visit, with democracy once more in place, I responded to her evocative call by promising myself something different, something special, a safari into an absorbing corner of the old continent that I had left as a war zone.

As our party came together, I found myself in a group of twenty-four that was largely comprised of Afrikaner kin, my wife's extended family by marriage, amongst them *Boers,* farming folk, whose ancestors had fought a war against members of my British lineage — the Boer War of 1899-1902.

The deep wounds of that hostility had not healed easily, if at all, and I was aware that the grandparents of many Afrikaners my age had sympathized with the Germans in World War I; in fact, one of my safari companions mentioned that his *pa,* his father, had actively backed the Nazis in the Second World War. This was not unexpected information, for it was common knowledge that a profusion of radical Afrikaners had defended, if not embraced, the rival platform. Indeed, *apartheid* politicians, including Prime Minister Vorster, were interned during World War II for openly supporting the enemy. Still, this long-enduring animosity towards the British was a tough revelation to come to grips with face-to-face, because on my side of the clan both my father-in-law and my dad had served in uniform for the Crown, and under their imperial influence we had fiercely championed the cause of the Allies. Moreover, when — shortly after the war — *apartheid* showed its ugly face, our families had resisted it with a vengeance.

But our opposition had been futile. As I grew up, anti-British feelings and racist sentiments persisted, and it was the National Party politicians and public who projected these uncompromising points of view who became my adversaries, and whose attitudes forced me to abandon South Africa.

However, at this moment I chose to forget all that. We were on what was turning out to be a fine trek into the *gramadoelas,* the true undiluted *bundu,* the distant backveld, presently camping in the remote wilds of Kaokoland, in Namibia — old *Kolonial Deutsch-Südwestafrika.* In this still lost utopia of sacred fires, trance dancing, and ancestor-spirit worship, I found that I could sit around the campfire, with the old familiar stars of the southern sky above me, and talk and laugh and joke with these folk as if the past did not exist. Amiability was the prevailing mood, and it occurred to me that though a former generation of Afrikaners had initiated and lost a protracted battle to enforce racial segregation, their offspring were coming to terms with the result. There was, of course, still a strong element of denial, but they, in general, were doing better than I was at coping with what went before.

The trip had been all I had hoped for, a relive, if only a brief one, of a uniquely African outdoor life that I had left behind with feelings of nostalgia. We had made our way north through settlements with 'O' names — Omaruru, Otjiwarongo, Outjo, and Okaukuejo — and then bumped along a trail close to Etosha Pan. This, the dry skeleton of what was once — 14 million years ago — an inland sea, is a wildlife area bar none. We rounded a blind corner shortly before sunset, and skidded to a stop. *Ongeyama!* Lion! But it was an urgent whisper of *"renoster"* that caught my ear. Unlike a lion, a rhino can flip a 4x4. She approached us slowly from a waterhole. Then suddenly she snorted and, with her head lowered, bore down on us. I slammed the gear stick and retreated. But she veered off; a mock charge.

*O*n a later morning I awakened in my vehicle-top tent to the rustle of three young Himba driving long-horned cattle through thorn trees. They recognized our safari leader, Jan Joubert, and shyly made their way to a fire still burning from the previous night.

These bushveld semi-nomads were, as always, wondrous to behold, and I gazed at them with pleasure. I had spent several years prospecting for diamonds along the Skeleton Coast and inland, and knew a little about the Himba — that, for example, their hairstyles reflected their age, sex, and social status — and I stared now at two pre-adolescent boys with exotic forward-jutting *ozondatu,* pigtails. They were clad about the waist in pleated animal-skin skirts, but despite an early morning chill all three were baretopped. The third Himba, a tall girl as statuesque as a young giraffe, had hair hanging in strands that were tightly braided, wrapped, and smeared with clay, fashioned in a way that showed she was of marriageable age. How alive I felt to see them again, wild people with keen instincts, and survival skills all but lost to us in the modern world, fiercely proud of their accomplishments and traditions. It brought back to me the raw enchantment of my motherland.

Jan extended them a greeting, and a silent invitation to warm themselves at the fire. A quiet conversational exchange slowly emerged in a native language, and although I could not begin to understand any part of it, it was clear from its intimate tone that Jan held these herders, young as they were, in high esteem, and that the respect was mutual.

They were possibly the offspring of a wealthy elder — there were tribesmen in the region with more than a thousand head of cattle, and Jan would certainly have appreciated the deep knowledge of husbandry required to maintain a herd that size. The Himba are intelligent but unassuming, and animated despite their shyness, and possess a calm earthy demeanor with none of our flamboyant show, or frantic hurry.

*H*imba-like in many of his ways, Jan Joubert, to me, was Oom Jan. 'Oom,' an Afrikaans term, translates literally as 'uncle,' but is also used beyond the family to convey endearment and respect, generally by a younger person for someone much older. I was Jan's senior, but because of the superior wilderness knowledge he brought to our safari group, I invariably addressed him as Oom Jan, and he accepted this without protest.

I had been forewarned that Oom Jan and other members of my brother-in-law's family were extraordinarily proud of their past, and no doubt wanting to impress on me their version of history, Jan drew me close around the campfire for conversation. I guessed what this would touch on in the circumstances of a frowned-upon runaway like me, reproach, a slap on the wrist, certainly politics, and something of the differences between the ethnic and racial groups. *"Kom sit by my,"* Oom Jan said, beckoning me to an empty chair. Then, mellowed by a stiff *dop* of his Klipdrift brandy, he began: *"Ek is 'n Afrikaner jy weet,"* I am an Afrikaner you know, "and we Afrikaners have done more for Africa and its people than any other white men."

I knitted my brow, offering a mild objection to his claim of the Afrikaner as Africa's foremost champion. "And what about the British?" I asked him. I had no intention of stirring a serious debate, but I was more than interested in what he might have to say. I had long known that Jan could have written an authoritative book on the African struggle, and was familiar with his contributions to the native — black African — peoples, particularly those in Namibia, one of South Africa's neighboring countries.

In my wife's family the story had often been told of how, as a high-ranking government conservation officer in South West Africa, Oom Jan had helped the Himba, lobbying for simple hand-pumps to extract water from their bore holes instead of those powered by engines — well-meaning foreign aid gifts that were constantly in need of fuel, parts, and repairs. We also knew him to have been instrumental in helping them establish an eco-tourist camp to secure some precious hard currency. And aware of the spiritual reverence in which these ritualists of dusty Kaokoland held the pristine Epupa Falls, we were acquainted with Oom Jan's protests against building a hydroelectric power scheme on that untamed reach of the mighty Kunene River, a project that would have submerged their sacred cataracts.

The Himba appreciated his efforts, and a local headman had given Oom Jan some land in the valley of the Hoarusib River near Purros, a place that attracts game from the surrounding thirstland. I saw this *"ongeëwenaarde woesteny,"* as one of our party referred to it, this unrivalled gem of unspoiled nature, while Oom Jan and I stood one morning on top of a *kopje* watching broad-footed desert elephants feed in the linear oasis of trees that snaked along the water's edge below. He proudly pointed out the boundaries of his property, the river, a tall tree to the northeast, a... It was prime real estate, extensive and spectacular in its beauty. *"Kosbaar leegte,"* valuable land, I offered Oom Jan. "The perfect spot for a fly-in hunting lodge."

In return I received a lesson in ecology. "Cut down trees for an airstrip?" he exclaimed in horror. "The Himba cherish their wilderness resources," he added sternly. "They build small fires to conserve wood. And they themselves do not hunt the wild animals of their region, so much do they respect them. How could I possibly not follow their good example?"

I swallowed hard and looked out again to the far horizon. Oom Jan's *verlate woestynwêreld,* his secluded private patch of this vast desert-world, merged with the open spaces; there was no fence around it.

*T*hat evening I broached the subject again. "And what about the British?" I desperately wanted an acknowledgement, if only some miniscule feedback, that my forefathers might also have contributed something to the welfare of the indigenous African peoples.

Oom Jan spat out his answer. "The English? The bloody *Rooineks?* No, I don't think so. No!" He turned to face me, to kill, or at least draw off my challenge. His eyes changed to the sparkle of a canny old fireside politician. "Only two good things ever came out of England," he said, with a side step, "rugby and the Land Rover." He paused, and then pressed his advantage in the same witty vein, "And I'm not so sure about the Land Rover."

I fought it, but I had to smile for I recalled that we'd had trouble with the vaunted British vehicle just that day. Still, I did not let his humor divert me from trying to make my point. "So the Afrikaners did it all?"

Oom Jan set aside my sarcasm with a confident, *"Ja, dis reg."* Yes, that's right.

I was surprised to find myself slightly annoyed, and was slightly annoyed with myself for being so. Nevertheless, I drew a breath and drove a spur. "And what about *apartheid?*" I asked.

His countenance clouded, and he waved his large hand in a gesture of dismissal. *"Apartheid,"* he said, "was less than fifty years of our history."

*Y*es, it was less than fifty years, but years of torment and distress, unremitting pain, an all but half-century of such horror that even after so long in the States the blood and guts of it still followed me like a black hyena.

As I left the fire circle and returned to my tent, I thought back on a life of turmoil. But although rage-filled and tragic, it had not all been bad — it had not been without humor, or inimitable characters, or leaps of grand adventure. My mind drifted to my childhood.

Part 1

AFRICA'S MAGIC MEMORIES

Son of a Railroad Man

Whenever I reflect on my youth, trains crowd my first lighthearted thoughts. I grew up with magic memories of Africa, snaking my way across the veld behind gargantuan steam engines. One of my earliest recollections is that of awe as I stole a glimpse at two thundering behemoths that were dragging us up the Hex River Valley — the *hex*, the witch. They were of monstrous size and power, and each bellowed like a livid ogre.

There was a rhythm to their roar that registered in my gut, and called on me to peep in their forbidden direction. I resisted at first, in anguish. Then there was a long, shrill, luring whistle, like the cry of a loon, and my burning curiosity overcame my fear. As if compelled by a spirit beyond me, I turned my head for as long as I dared and stared in wide-eyed wonder. Two angry hippopotami ran, despite their weight, and as they strongly hustled onward these colossal beasts belched billowing clouds of steel-gray smoke into a sapphire sky.

Steam locomotives were all that existed on the iron roads between cities, and we were told that if we ever looked forward while underway red-hot cinders would burn our eyes out. However, impending blindness was not my immediate source of alarm. My apprehension at that moment stemmed from the fury my father might unleash on me at the mere suspicion of disobedience; he seldom spared the rod in matters concerning our safety. And, as it turned out, my trepidation was not unfounded. While I briefly gaped at the mighty Garratts a heavy hand descended on my miserable right ear, and the hiss that accompanied the action added insult to my injury — "You stupid little sod!"

Each Christmas period, summer in the southern hemisphere, most Whites had a break from work, and our family took a long exploring train journey. The main reason for this was that my father worked for the railroad and received an annual free pass. And from his celebrated references to what our various train adventures would have been priced at, if we had had to pay for them, it became clear to my sister and me that the further — 'farther' my grandmother said we should say — we traveled the more we saved. At the end of each trip we could count on seeing Pop's straight teeth flash with a satisfied smile. "I'd hate to think what a bloody trip like that would have cost," he would crow in a gloating gush of pleasure.

"It wasn't that he was cheap," I reasoned in a conversation with my sister when we were older. "He just hated to squander a privilege."

"No," Joy laughed. "In many ways he was just plain cheap."

Over the years we journeyed to the most remote corners of South Africa, to railway outposts that were not even marked on the map. And although Joy and I failed to see the purpose of many such destinations, we took some pride in the fact that my dad invariably knew people in these Godforsaken settlements, albeit a stationmaster or a signalman.

The South African Railways had arranged, bit by bit, reciprocity with their counterparts in neighboring countries, and this provided us with access to Portuguese East Africa, now Mozambique; the Bechuanaland Protectorate, Botswana; and old German South West Africa, present-day Namibia, a place that later would enchant me with her many secrets.

We also traveled into the Rhodesias, now the countries of Zimbabwe and Zambia, to visit the magnificent Victoria Falls on the great Zambezi River. "In 1855, when John Roebling was completing one of his famous bridges across a gorge near the Niagara Falls," my dad exclaimed over the wheel-noise of our dining car, "David Livingstone came upon his much higher African cascade, the largest curtain of falling water in the world." After fifteen years of exploration, Livingstone, a Scot — from just north of where my grandfather was born, we were told — was the first European to witness its grandeur. He described the falls, Pop affirmed, as "the most wonderful sight" he had seen in Africa.

This was typical of the information my dad fed his American tourists, and us. He worked for the Publicity and Travel Department of the South African Railways and Harbours, the 'Tourist Office,' as we knew it. In fact that is how he met my mom when she, a student nurse, consulted him about a scenic route to Walvis Bay, where her aunt lived, and he persuaded her to go instead to Scottburgh, a beach town on the opposite side of the country where, unbeknown to her, he had arranged to spend his own summer vacation.

Pop was a great charmer, and one of Mom's oft-told tales was about two "elderly American ladies," as she referred to them, who had wanted to adopt him. Before departing from South Africa they gave my parents an elaborately carved chest they had purchased in Hong Kong. It was one of my mom's most treasured possessions, and always occupied a high spot in our homes. Pop had met the wealthy sisters while serving as tour-train manager, his best-loved duty, on an excursion to the Kruger National Park, a side trip to their world cruise on the *Empress of Britain*.

My dad prized all his foreign tourists, but especially "the Yanks." And my Granny Watson laughed when she recalled how he, as a younger man, had always gone out of his way to entertain them. "He was constantly digging into books by local authors," she said, "and talking to the Natives, searching for little pearls of information with an interesting twist to them. He was like Mulunga," she smiled, "the old storyteller on the mines, a connoisseur of African trivia and reminiscences."

Pop, as we ultimately became aware, tested his material on us. He had two voices, his "tour-guide voice," as Ga — my mom's mom — christened it, and his "ordinary voice," as Joy quickly ad-libbed. "The Natives had long known of Livingstone's find," Pop began now in his tour-guide voice, "as *Mosi o Thunya*, the Smoke that Thunders." He waited for our attention. "And like many African names, this was a very descriptive one. For from a distance," he explained, "the spray of the falls looks just like smoke. And when you walk towards them," he went on, "you hear their thunderous roar long before you see them."

"*Mosi o Thunya,*" Joy repeated, quite accurately.

"Yes," Pop snorted, amused. "But Livingstone decided to rename them after his Queen." He told us that this noble gesture had undoubtedly secured Dr. Livingstone's aristocratic burial in Westminster Abbey, a considerable honor, he declared, for a Briton. "But when he died," Pop continued in the gruesome detail he knew young children thrived on, "his trusted Native guides made sure that his heart remained in Africa. They cut it out," he said, "and buried it under a tree in his dearly loved Rhodesia."

Joy scrunched her face. "And what about the rest of him?"

"The rest of him they shipped to London."

"So half of him was buried in England and the other half in Africa? I've never heard of a thing like that."

Pop tried to keep a straight face. He was clearly entertained, but no doubt equally impressed — I know I was — by how quickly she had put it all together.

It was at the beginning of the new — 20th — century, Pop told my mom as we rumbled on towards the falls, that Africa became the place in vogue for the adventurous rich of foreign society, a sought-after retreat of mystery and intrigue. "In Africa they found their roots," he said, "and rekindled their primordial past on the savannas where man first evolved."

His antiquarian lore was lost on me; then again, it was not intended for us kids. We were supposedly asleep. "You must catch up on your rest, my darlings," my mom had advised us, "for a big day ahead." But I, usually with a gift for slumber, was much too excited even to doze, and lay on my bunk wide awake, imagining Livingstone's mighty waterfall.

Pop continued in a quiet voice as we sped on, speculating in hyper detail on an earlier generation of tourists from abroad. They took pleasure in being witness to the primitive way of life of the 'noble savage,' he supposed. They fulfilled dreams of treading in the footsteps of mighty chiefs and famous explorers. They basked in the charm, the drama, the unrefined energy of a truly exotic continent. They emulated royalty by journeying along paths paved with diamonds and gold. They experienced the drugged romance of unusual safari encounters and remote camp sites in the backveld.

Pop was the enthusiastic talker in our family, Mom the enduring listener. Although born overseas — her grandparents were German Jews — my mom had spent practically all her life in Africa. Yet Pop often treated her like a new arrival, telling her all sorts of things that she was probably well aware of. But she weathered his onslaughts with serenity and grace.

He would go on and on, as he was doing now, about the reasons, as he saw them, for tourists first wanting to visit the Dark Continent. Wealthy travelers of old, he construed, were drawn to a land that differed vastly from their own. They craved this world of the past, he recited as if on stage, with its kaleidoscope of unspoiled nature, "this God-given refuge," he liked to call it, that remained relatively untouched by the meddling hands of industrial man.

While Mom bore the brunt of my dad's tour-guide rehearsals, Joy and I were not exempt. "Many like Theodore Roosevelt and Ernest Hemingway," he told us the next day, "satisfied a passion to hunt in a bushveld teeming with the greatest diversity of wild animals on the planet. Only in old eternal Africa," he observed, "could these privileged outdoorsmen still find, in a natural setting, the glory of the legendary Big Five." — the lion, the leopard, the buffalo, the rhino, and the elephant.

Our reactions to Pop's mention of the acclaimed hunters, apparently, lacked the required zeal, for Mom quickly interjected with an ego boost, exclaiming that our well-informed father knew of every famous American who had ever visited our country.

Later that day he told us how fortunate we were to be living in Africa; and when Joy asked him why, he said because we could see it all "for free. My foreign tourists may have pots of money," he noted, "but it still costs them a fortune!" His frequent remarks on the merits of 'free,' had once prompted Ga to jest on the possibility of a "Jewish streak" in him. He had chuckled, but Mom, embarrassed, had asked Ga please to shush.

"And above all," Pop lectured on, "there were those who set their hearts upon that most-prized jewel, that vista of primitive fury you'll see today, that breathtaking leap of the raging Zambezi." Although Joy and I struggled to follow his language, his drama was infectious, and we were all for hearing more. Joy wanted to know if anyone had fallen over the edge of the falls. But he digressed to the history of the railways, the topic closest to his heart. "So many foreign celebrities expressed interest in our queen of waterfalls," he said, "that Rhodes saw the potential for a special train."

Cecil John Rhodes, an Englishman, was one of our family's great heroes. He had come to Africa to search for diamonds near Kimberley, and before long, Joy and I had been assiduously informed, he had owned every diamond mine worth owning.

During the Boer War my Granny Watson was in the Siege of Kimberley with Rhodes, and she loved to tell of it. "I don't know what Cecil Rhodes had to eat," she would scoff, "but the likes of us survived on soup. 'Siege soup,' we called it. It arrived in buckets at the town square, and we bought it for a tickey a bowl." A tickey, derived from the Malay word *tiga*, three, was the old three-penny piece — worth about a nickel.

"Having already secured his fortune," Pop related now, "Rhodes was searching for a way to make a broader mark on history. And his proposed extravaganza to the falls," Pop said, with an extra arch on his eyebrows, "was just the thing." He noted that Rhodes had astutely recognized that the upper echelon of the well-to-do, those he had targeted for his railroad odyssey, would travel only if they could do so in the luxury they were accustomed to. "You don't leave a world-class cruise ship," he said, shaking a finger at us, "for a thirteen-hundred-mile train trip, unless you've heard a thing or two about the train. You don't."

With this point made, Pop disclosed that Rhodes approached his brilliant engineering friend, Sir Charles Metcalfe, and asked him to design a train with all the comforts of an ocean liner. Rhodes impressed on Sir Charles that in addition to luxury and speed, a given, the train needed a colonial snob appeal that would attract the rich and famous.

"It must have cost a lot," Joy commented shrewdly.

Pop glowed. "It did," he acknowledged, "and the Yanks are always asking me how much."

I asked him if the train had ever actually been built — a train with all the comforts of a ship was beyond me.

It was clear from his expression that he also liked my question. "Yes," he replied with a grin, "it was built, and started service in 1902. That was six years before I was even born."

Joy asked if it was called the *Blue Train*.

No, he replied, that came later. This train, he said, was named the *Train De Luxe* to start with, but soon came to be known as the *Zambezi Express*. He went on to tell us that it was pulled by one of the most powerful steam engines of the times, and quickly gained a reputation for being the most luxurious train in the world.

Our less-luxurious train jerked from a stop at a siding, and we twisted to the window with a start. But Joy's eyes immediately returned to Pop. "The *Zambezi Express*," she echoed; she wanted all the details.

Pop obliged — at length. The coaches, he narrated, were paneled with rare woods and filled with fancy gadgets. An elegant dining car boasted cuisine that matched the very best served in Victorian hotels. "And the buffet car," Pop said, "was even fitted with a wine cellar." This, he explained, was built into the coach under-frame, and accessed from the galley via a trap door. Card playing was much in fashion at the time, he said, so the designers included a large and exclusive card room. "It had every convenience one enjoys on a *Union-Castle* liner," he noted smugly, "but in miniature."

And other amenities of this "steam-train *Versailles*," as he would sometimes proudly call it, included a smoking saloon, an expansive reading room, and a comprehensive library. "In the rear coach was an observation platform with comfortable armchairs," he said, "where her passengers of fortune could pass their time snoozing after big meals, or ..."

"...observing the show of passing African scenery," my mom broke in with a smile, "while drinking tea from pots kept hot by hand-knitted woolen tea cozies." She, it appeared, knew his patter backwards. But he immediately protested, saying that the "tea cozies bit" had been my grandmother's creation, a suggestion for spicing the train up a notch for the story benefit of his American tourists. "Unfortunately," he smiled, "I've learned that most Americans don't know what tea cozies are."

*I*n contrast to those many famous travelers of old, our undistinguished family journeyed to the Victoria Falls on a train that bore little resemblance to the *Zambezi Express,* or to the other special trains that Pop worked on. Yet in the young minds of my sister and me, ours was no ordinary conveyance. As our parents were served wine by dignified saloon staff in uniform, and we slurped soup selected from a long menu with impressive French words, we imagined that we were following in the footsteps of wealth and royalty, and that our simple railway journey had all the majesty of a truly grand adventure.

When we first saw it, the Zambezi River formed the border between the two Rhodesias. Both countries were under British rule, and a Union Jack — the British ensign — that we spotted as we approached the falls clearly broadcast this fact. Our first sight of the waterfall was close to the Devil's Cataract. Here a section of the river has bitten into a weak zone in the rock mass to tumble headlong into a chasm, "nearly twice the drop of the Niagara Falls," Pop reminded us. "That 'twice-the-Niagara-height' thing," Joy would snicker years later, "was his most-used remark, by my count, for trying to impress his Yankee tourists."

Pop had purposely not prepared me for it, and the titanic steel bridge that soared high across the gorge completely took my breath away. Rhodes had personally selected its location, my dad claimed, not for the engineering-geological convenience of its site, but because he wanted his distinguished passengers to have a first breathtaking glimpse of the falls from his train. "Rhodes wanted them to stand agape at what they saw," he said, "to be awestruck by their thunderous roar and, if the wind was right, to be in coaches washed by swirling cascades of spray." His clear objective, I gath-

ered in looking back, was to have his elite tourists identify these unforgettable falls with his railway. It certainly worked for me.

The Victoria Falls Hotel, with its Edwardian architecture, was reputed to be amongst the finest in Africa. The Royal Family had been there
only a year before us, and Joy asked all sorts of questions about what Princess Elizabeth — she was not at all interested in Margaret — might have
done on her visit. Although quite young, she was well aware that Elizabeth
would one day be Queen.

As a special treat we were taken to the Hotel for dinner, and there I
unintentionally made a mark on our family history by ordering a boiled egg.
To my acute embarrassment, Pop, in his often rough-and-ready way, repeated the story to his friends on countless occasions. "Take him to the best
hotel in the world," he would say, "and when they ask him what he wants,
he orders a bloody boiled egg. Stupid little sod!"

Some fifty-three years later I received an e-mail from my nephew,
John, saying that he would be visiting Lusaka on business, and very much
hoped he could get down to the Victoria Falls Hotel to see where I had ordered the boiled egg. It was a story that, as Joy said, "traveled well through
the generations," especially if you had known my dad.

We donned our raincoats at the falls, and Pop was in his element
guiding us along muddy footpaths for spectacular views. Then he had us
board a boat and we were taken upstream.

"The Zambezi flows through several countries," my dad said. "But
the Natives fish and barter along the river as if borders don't exist. And best
of all," he cheered, "nobody bothers them."

We admired flame trees, and waved to unclothed children playing at
the water's edge, near mud huts on the banks. Mom lifted Joy to better see a
lady, "grinding corn by hand, my darling. I'm glad I don't have to do it." She
turned to Pop. "They still respect the old ways," she smiled.

"They have no choice," he shrugged. "I'm always intrigued by the
fact that here on the river, only a few miles from the train, nothing much has
changed since Livingstone's time."

Joy asked if, once upon a time, the Natives had had their own name
for the river, just like they did for the falls. "*Mosi o Thunya,*" she articulated
again. Pop grinned and said that yes they did. In the vicinity of the falls, he
told her, the Zambezi was known as the *Lwambay,* the Great River. In Portuguese East Africa, he said, it was called *Kwamo,* the River of Great Floods.
He went on to mention that African tribesmen of old knew neither its
source, nor its outlet to the ocean. "Even today," he noted, "the people here
pay little attention to what occurs beyond their stretch of the river. Yet, to
their credit," he added, enlarging his eyes for emphasis, "they follow the
time-honored tradition of not taking more fish than they can eat, or trade, so

their neighbors downstream don't go hungry. As Mom puts it," he smiled, "the Natives still respect the old ways."

Pop turned his head and pointed to some fishermen not far from us. "Now these are people I respect," he said. "They might not face ocean storms, but hippos are worse than sea monsters, and a hungry croc can easily snatch a man from his dugout."

Joy asked what a dugout was, and he explained, steering her gaze to one. "It's a hollowed-out log," he informed her, "and it's very tippy." I ungraciously learned the truth of this some years later, when using one for stream-sediment sampling — searching for copper.

The shadows were already long when we returned and disembarked. We thought we were done for the day, but Pop took us back to the falls. The colors changed at sunset, he insisted. "Most of my tourists are on the older side," he expressed, "and can't manage all I'd like to show them." But he showed us, walking even my mom to a standstill.

Joy asked to see the tree where Livingstone's heart was buried, but Pop, reminded of the name, went on again about the famous man, telling us that he had been a doctor by training, and that this not only had endeared him to the Natives, it had saved his own life when he was once mauled by a lion. He put a screw into a broken bone, Pop choked, then stitched up his gaping wounds. But Livingstone at heart, he said, was a missionary, and his main reason for exploring the Zambezi was to open the African interior to Christianity.

I questioned this information with a blank look.

"Well, if he could find the river to be navigable," Pop clarified, "other missionaries could travel from the coast by boat." It was a lot easier than walking, he made clear.

"Walking," Joy broke in, her face showing fatigue, "did Princess Elizabeth have to walk this far?"

The Royal Visit

When Joy was out of earshot, I heard Mom whisper in an amused tone to my dad. "The Princesses are much too important to walk as far as she has." But the reality was that Joy was not the only one impressed by royalty, we all were. Hailing from the Isle of Man — my grandmother had married an Englishman — a British island in the Irish Sea, my mother had an excuse for being an ardent royalist, but my father had been born and bred in Africa. Nevertheless, like many of his countrymen of English descent, he was often mocked for being 'more English than the English.'

In looking back one can see why Afrikaners, like Oom Jan, made fun of us — and despised our arrogance — for there was no doubt in the mind of anyone with English blood, including my father, that Englishmen were superior. And if we, as children, were not always directly told so, we assumed it by the inference of a host of daily reminders. At that age, even on the train, I wore a dressing gown that displayed a badge of a large Union Jack under which was imperiously inscribed: "There will always be an ENGLAND." And we, in one of England's proud possessions, thought then that nothing would ever change. Our besotted foreign Englishness showed in everything we did. A Christmas meal served in our compartment, for instance, would see us pause before eating, and then, to the accompaniment of wheel-clatter on the tracks, all proudly singing the words of the British National Anthem.

In those days it never dawned on me to think that I owed allegiance to anyone other than King George VI. I was overwhelmed by the fact that he thought my country sufficiently important to embark on an extended visit to it in 1947, and I was honored beyond all measure by his gracious reference to South Africa as, "one of our imperial family of nations."

I saw the King in person, and was enormously impressed by his stately appearance. He had served in the Royal Navy at the famous Battle of Jutland, still often dressed as a naval officer, and my memory of him in full uniform is vivid — a starched white jacket with gleaming brass buttons, colored war ribbons, and a cap low on his forehead.

The Royal Family was a symbol of the British Empire and, at that time, the single most celebrated family in the world. It was also, Pop noted, the wealthiest. And it followed that the royal visit to South Africa was an especially momentous occasion for a family of displaced British souls like my own. We followed their every move on radio, and on the many newsreels we saw at the cinema, or 'bioscope,' as we referred to it. There was no television in South Africa in those days — in fact, the *apartheid* government, which would soon censor the airwaves, kept TV out until 1975 — so the highlights of the weekly news were shown in a series of shorts before the main feature. During big events, like the royal visit, or a cricket test match, we were taken to the *bioscope* regardless of what was showing. The primary purpose was to see the news cuts. We left if the advertised picture was 'not suitable.'

When allowed to stay we kids were always sad when the film ended, however poor it had been. Joy often cried and I would look for her silent tears in the raised lights as we stood dutifully to attention while the Anthem was played, "God save our gracious King ..." That was how the movies ended in those days, in British parts of Africa.

When the *White Train* — especially built for the Royal Family — was dismantled, Pop went to great lengths to acquire the bathtub that had been used by King George VI. He installed it at considerable cost in our house, and always thought of it as one of his better purchases. He did not use it much, as he preferred the shower. He just liked having it. Nor was he at all concerned about the extra money the dwelling might fetch if he ever came to sell it. Once he had procured the tub, he promptly buried, in an old tin trunk, the paperwork that proved its authenticity.

However, amongst his pleasures was to show the King's bath to un-suspecting visitors and, if asked, elaborate on the many details of the *White Train*. He also knew much about the 4,000-mile royal journey.

*T*he royal visit to Basutoland, now Lesotho, was the topic of one of my fa-ther's most colorful stories, a saga he had no doubt painstakingly polished for his tourists. This "rainy rooftop of the subcontinent," as he called it, was an African kingdom set high in the Drakensberg. A product, in the distant past, of active volcanoes, these otherworldly 'Mountains of the Dragon' de-rived their name from Native myths that ferocious, fire-breathing saurians lived there. The combination of legend, lightning, and thunder that echoes between precipitous peaks, discouraged intruders, Pop said, and helped af-ford these forbidding highlands their natural protection.

The railroad did not run into mountainous Basutoland, and Pop ex-plained that the *White Train* was stopped at the nearest approach to Maseru, seat of the British Commissioner. Thousands of Basutos descended from the adjacent alps and crossed the border to meet the train. They had come to see the Great White King. "As Baroness Karen Blixen writes, in *Out of Af-rica*," he would say, " 'Natives, have very great ideas of kings and like to talk about them.' " But it was the pair of smoking Garratts, Pop insisted, that seized their immediate attention.

Then, as if by magic, his story went, the King's black car appeared, a fitting contrast to the chalk-white train. He described it as a "half-convertible," and said that as it moved off and steadied at a royal pace, it was fallen upon by the hordes of Basutos riding hardy mountain ponies. These skilled horsemen soon organized themselves into a magnificent cavalcade, he smiled, that proudly followed the royal car into the capital. And there, the regent of the Basuto nation, Mantsebo Seeiso, "a noble lady," he portrayed her, welcomed the Royal Family.

The climax of this grand gathering, Pop pronounced, was when the King decorated this illustrious Basuto Queen with the M.B.E. — Member of the British Empire. His Majesty also presented medals to her soldiers who had served with distinction in World War II, not long ended.

Although Pop did not suspect it, he would never again witness any-thing like the scene he had described. The Empire was about to shrink, and we with it. Royalty would not visit South Africa again until 1995, when President Mandela reintroduced the country to the British Commonwealth, and Elizabeth, then Queen, took part in the celebration.

Part 2

THE TRANS-KAROO

Panting Cheetahs

As a youngster, like I said, Africa, to me, was trains, and I knew a lot about them. The first exclusive train to run the 999 miles from Pretoria — across the Karoo — to Cape Town, was the *Union Limited*. This sumptuous express began service in 1903. It was renamed the *Blue Train* in 1939, to rival the select *Train Bleu*, which journeyed between Paris and the Côte d'Azur in the south of France. It remains the *Blue Train* today, and still outdoes itself in pampering its passengers.

With blue coaches, cream stripes, and embellished coat of arms — showing a springbok and a gemsbok supporting a quartered shield — and a cream color to its decorative roof, the train of my day presented an eminently distinctive bearing. Pop told me that to hold out the intense heat of the Great-Karoo sun, the windows of its opulent dining car were once tinted with real gold, and that elegant private sleeping accommodations contained en-suite bathrooms with floors of the best Italian marble and fittings plated with 24-carat gold. He had no qualms about referring to it as "the best train in the world" — a similar reference to the old *Zambezi Express* — and although he had not then traveled on the *Orient Express*, or some of the world's other prestigious trains, he simply could not imagine anything better than his *Blue Train*.

Unfortunately, our family free pass did not extend to the lavish 'Train Bleu.' That imposing train was reserved for the elite. It carried affluent foreign tourists, and local financial giants like Sir Ernest Oppenheimer who had assumed the De Beers diamond fortune from Rhodes, and members of the country's parliament who met for half the year in Cape Town and the remaining half in Pretoria.

When we journeyed between our home in Johannesburg, and Cape Town, which we did each year to visit my grandmother, it was on the *Trans-Karoo*. The standards even on this lesser train were surprisingly high, as they were at the time on all main-line trains in South Africa.

Pop's pass entitled us to a spacious private compartment, and this was fitted out like the cabin of a well-appointed yacht. At night our accommodation converted to a sleeper. Our parents slept on the lower berths, and we got the uppers where I, afraid of falling, slept as close as I could to the bulkhead. To my disgust, Joy, two years younger, showed no such fear.

On the extended journey of the *Trans-Karoo*, steam locomotives were changed or added at frequent intervals. To combat the steep passes that led to the top of the Great Escarpment, Pop explained, a second engine was needed for the pull. And on the downward journey, the trains were again double-headed to secure the necessary braking power.

It was our custom to walk to the front of the train and observe the shunting ritual that accompanied each engine change. We would hail the drivers who my father often knew and, if time permitted, we would cautiously climb up into the cab to shake their hands. It was sweltering up there, even in cold weather, and the hairy, half-clad drivers and their mates sweated like panting cheetahs after a chase. They smelled and dripped perspiration on us; they were deaf from the constant engine noise, and shouted a great deal; and their friendly barks were punctuated by drawing snorts to clear black coal dust from their throats. They spat a lot.

To entertain us a fireman might begin furiously shoveling coal into the flames of the firebox. The whole scene was intimidating for a child as timid as I was at that age, and it reinforced my dreaded fear of hell. And having been in the cab of a steam engine once, I would gladly have called it a day had not Joy always insisted on scrambling up into that grisly inferno each time the opportunity presented itself. As it was, pride dictated that I follow her and even mimic her enthusiasm.

On one occasion my dad called to a toothless driver and asked him if he would mind having his photograph taken with us.

The burly man blinked down at Pop. *"Ja, Meneer Watson, maar wag net 'n oomblik, asseblief."* Yes, Mr. Watson, but please wait just a moment. He then tore across the footplate, blabbering. When he returned he was sporting a full set of false teeth he had borrowed from his fireman. *"Nou ja,"* he grinned, highly pleased. Joy and I clambered up into the cab to join him.

Whilst the train was underway Pop liked to sit at the window-seat that faced forward. This enabled him to look ahead and be the first to spot anything of interest. To reserve his perch he invented the story that Mom preferred to sit with her back to the engine. He stated this so often that she herself almost came to believe it. I was somewhat puzzled by her strange whim, as I regarded it, but as a child I never thought to question her on it. Years later, after my father had died, Joy told me that she had eventually approached Mom on the matter and learned the truth.

From his forward-looking vantage point Pop might announce "mine dumps ahead," or some such message, and we would scramble over to the window to see.

The Great Karoo, now semi-desert, was once a tropical forest where dinosaurs roamed. "We know this from the fossil record," Pop stated with tour-guide assurance. And it was also known, from correlations based on geological mapping, that the Karoo, in the distant past, lay near the center of the supercontinent Gondwana, with Antarctica a short distance to the east, and South America, in rotated form, joined just to the west.

Today the landscape consists of endless arid plains, but our train journeys across these were never tedious. Pop told us stories that he himself would interrupt by pointing and shouting, "jackal," "dik-dik," or "springbok." We would dive over him to look, and if we were lucky we might see a herd of graceful gazelle moving in a cascade of resilient movements, with random members of the group *pronking*, as it is called, in stiff-legged elastic leaps, high above the others. Pop said that the springbok was the favorite prey of the planet's fastest animal, the cheetah, and had developed a variety of behavioral patterns to distract its attention.

We also loved to see troupes of long-stepping ostrich. These largest of living birds are flightless but, according to my dad, they can hurtle along at more than 30 miles an hour. This impressed us. But we were very disappointed when he dispelled as myth the fanciful belief that, when cornered, an ostrich will stand and bury its head in the sand. On the other hand, he informed us that ostrich chicks, which cannot slip away from danger as quickly as their parents, will often fall and lie limp on the ground, pretending to be dead. We were somewhat appeased by that.

We searched in vain for Joy's favorite animal, the wildebeest, or *gnu* as the African San people knew it for its *gnu*-like snort. Her preoccupation with this unlikely beast stemmed, no doubt, from its child-pleasing name, and its use to illustrate the letter 'G' in her treasured alphabet-book that she brought along on train trips. She was smarter and a far better student than me, and I recall that when I was struggling to read my first schoolbooks, she could recite my lessons by heart, merely having heard me agonize repeatedly over them with my long-suffering mom.

Early travelers to the Karoo were greeted by abundant wildlife. Natural springs fed water-holes that supported the herds. However, in times of need, Pop disclosed, antelope could smell ground — underground — water and dig for it. And predators like the lion, he informed us, could survive for long periods without water, sustained by the blood of their prey.

Karoo Kopjes

As sheep farmers intruded into the Karoo, Pop said, the wild herds diminished in size, and the Cape lion retreated to the refuge of the high sentinels — hills — that dot the veld, the famous African *kopjes*. Sadly, the last lion was sought out and shot. A similar gory fate befell the Karoo cheetah. And the last recorded kwagga, a breed of zebra, my dad lamented sadly, disappeared in my grandfather's day.

And in a shrinking wildlife domain, *kopjes* served not only as the last refuges to predators, these were also the final bastions of the all-but-vanished San nation, the "Bow and Arrow Men," as Lawrence Green called them in *Strange Africa*, a book my mom frequently mentioned. The San, more often referred to by Whites — and by themselves, at least those I have met — as Bushmen, were amongst the first residents of Southern Africa. "Their hunting and gathering lifestyle," Mom said, "was established long before white people ever thought of visiting the subcontinent. And their paintings, my darlings," she added, "are amongst the finest treasures of Africa."

I am still interested in Bushman rock art, but to find it I have often had to travel far, typically led by people like Oom Jan down precipitous boulder-strewn trails, one could hardly call them roads, to sites that required arduous climbing, or squeezing into crevices and caves. But it has always been worth it. For although the scenes are similar, wild animals and scenes of the hunt, each masterpiece is unique.

The art I have seen exists either as petroglyphs, engravings that have been chiseled into the joint faces of outcropping exposures, or as paintings on a similar canvas. Paints may be made from such naturally occurring materials as zinc, iron oxide, and kaolin. These are ground to a powder and mixed with wild honey to create colors of yellow, ochre, and white. My mom and I tried it, and it worked. However, the early Bushmen, no doubt, had their own superior formulae, because some paintings of the type I have seen in Namibia date to more than 20,000 years before present, yet their colors remain vibrant.

The eland, my favorite of rock-art subjects, is held sacred by the San, and is the focus of much of their work. A card in the South African Museum notes that, in 1873, J.M. Orpen, expanding his research on a hunter-gatherer mode of existence, posed a question to a wise old Bushman named Qing, 'Where is the trickster deity, Kaggen, the creator of the eland?' And Qing replied wryly, 'We do not know, but the elands do.'

My friend Kat — who I introduce more fully in a later chapter — had Bushman blood, and also possessed their sharp wit, animal-like instincts, and uncanny bush sense. His small stature, and color, a type of Asian yellow, were also typical.

"The history of the San is a lesson in adaptation," my mom said. She explained how Bushmen had successfully adjusted to a host of environmental changes, like climate, "only to fall victim to the evil of man," as she put it. She went on to describe how Whites and hostile Africans had invaded their territories and "hunted them down like rabid dogs." Their persecution, she said, was one of Africa's great tragedies.

Crossing the Karoo by train, in my view, is an enchanting journey. Some *kopjes*, freaks of weathering and erosion, soar skyward in special majesty, and these, according to Lizzie, our maid, were held by "very old Natives" to be the homes of the gods. If this was true, Pop said, the spirits would have had an inspiring view, and witnessed much of the changing history of South Africa. They would have seen great wars between powerful African chiefs, and observed the Afrikaner *Voortrekkers*, in wagons pulled by long spans of oxen, journeying to some Promised Land in the north. At the turn of the century they would have been party to the Boer War, a lengthy battle that brought my grandfather from England, and consolidated British rule in South Africa. Winston Churchill, then also a young man, Pop said, was taken prisoner by the *Boers*, the Afrikaner guerilla forces in that war, but managed to escape. And soon after the war the spirits would surely have cheered adventurous young veterans-turned-pioneers, like my grandfather, in horse-drawn stagecoaches, hurrying to the new gold mines on the Witwatersrand and beyond.

"Home to the gods, but also home to a black devil," Pop smiled, as we whistled through a dusty Karoo hamlet. His reference was to an account he had read of an African highwayman, Murosi, who used a *kopje* to prey on passing traffic. When Cape Government soldiers besieged his position, Pop began, Murosi personally decapitated a captured scout and placed his severed head on a stake where it could be seen from below. The troops were incensed, my dad recounted, and stormed the cliffs. After ghastly hand-to-hand combat, the summit was finally secured. "The troops were exhausted," Pop said, spreading his hands, "but still frantically searched for Murosi. Their rage abated only after they had cut off his head and placed it on the very pole that had borne the skull of their ill-fated companion."

This chronicle, like Pop's account of Livingstone's heart being cut out, was another grisly child-enthraller and, at our request, he narrated it more than once as we steamed by *kopje*s in the Karoo. The parts about the severed heads raised a whimper from Joy with each retelling, and I recall that this, in turn, would send a shiver down my spine. "Three Government soldiers received the VC," my dad always concluded proudly. The VC, Victoria Cross, is a bronze Maltese rood representing the highest award for heroism in the British armed services.

Because of its sparse rainfall and stark nature, the Karoo has not attracted development and not changed much, and trains are still a central feature of its charm. In 1997 there was considerable excitement in Karoo *dorps* along the railroad when President Mandela inaugurated a modernized *Blue Train,* in celebration of the new South Africa. Railway enthusiasts have been hard-pressed to say that it is better, but they all agree, as Pop might have expressed it, "that it has more doodads."

And, today, the gods of the *kopjes* see a *Trans-Karoo* with a slightly lifted face. It is diesel-driven and cleaner, but, to my mind, has less character. However, when I traveled on it recently I was rewarded with an extraordinary surprise. On our approach to Johannesburg I awakened to great noise, and the lovely smell of smoke. I quickly dropped a shutter and, leaning excitedly out of the window, saw a steam engine at the head of the train. It was breathing, this Goliath of steel. It was heavy. It shook the ground and made it rumble. It was vibrant, full of life.

At an unscheduled stop the manager let me run forward to snap a photograph. She — not 'it,' I now saw, on closer inspection — was a Lady. She was *Elsabe*, a ghost from my childhood. She had been lovingly restored to her former splendor. A rush of memories engulfed me, the African panoramas that had passed by my compartment windows, my fascination with the *bundu* where my grandfather had searched for gold, and the wildlife Joy and I had enthusiastically looked for and learned about.

Part 3

THE PROSPECTOR & THE GEMSBOK

The Prospector

I credit my interest in family affairs, in history, and in the natural sciences, to what my parents told Joy and me as we traveled across the African subcontinent on trains. Some of my most cherished memories are of Pop talking about his father, and pointing out the many distant places he had explored as a prospector.

My grandfather, unfortunately, died before I was born, but I had learned so much about him I felt I knew him. He came to South Africa, as I mentioned, during the Boer War, was captivated by the potential for adventure, and stayed on to break new ground in the days when some of the greatest deposits of gold in the world were found there. He was a carpenter by profession, but a prospector at heart.

In those days carpenters made good money on the mines. This was because so much of what enabled the mines to function was fabricated of timber. Carpenters erected the skyscraping headframes used to lower the miners down the shafts and hoist up the ore. They made the tall shaft houses and bracing for the shafts — these provide vertical access to the drifts and stopes that follow the gold reefs in the earth's bowels below. Carpenters built the gigantic frames for the metal stamps that were used to crush the ore, and the sturdy supports used to stabilize the underground workings.

"Your granddad worked hard, saved his wages, then wasted everything on prospecting," his wife, my Granny Watson, often complained. "Gold, 'colour' he called it, consumed him like a drug," she said. "He boasted a knack for sniffing it out," she laughed. "But that nose of his must have been blocked up with a cold for all the time that I ever knew him."

In those early times, gold, in veins, was accessible in outcrop, and prospectors took pride in finding it in odd places. South African author Thomas Bulpin, *Trail of the Copper King,* says it beautifully in the words of one of his characters, French Bob: "The geologist might find the gold where the professors think it ought to be, but the prospector finds the gold where the professors say it didn't ought to be, and that, mon ami, is where it generally is."

"**Y**ou might have thought that people like your grandfather would have been wealthy men," Granny Watson suggested, when we were a little older. But she went on to explain that the financial downfall of harbinger prospectors like my grandfather was that they were addicted to the mere lure of gold. "The excitement of finding it was more attractive to them than the gold itself. It was the lifestyle that they cherished more than the treasure that they found." As a consequence, she said, they repeatedly turned over good claims and spent their profits on new prospects. "That was the existence they were addicted to, and that kept them poor, a charmed way of a life in the backveld that they loved."

"And a good lesson for you kids," my dad offered. "It's far better to be happy than rich."

We thought that to be both was the real answer, but kept that opinion to ourselves. However, we both identified strongly with our grandfather's love of the outdoors.

Things had changed, Pop said, since his dad was a young man, but he made sure that we were taken to places that remained unspoiled, settings that he imagined appeared much the same as when my grandfather had experienced them.

The Gemsbok

*T*he old Africa of my grandfather's day was still to be found in the Bechuanaland Protectorate, and on the edge of the great Kruger National Park. These places remained home to the leopard and the lion, and on the long stretches between stations, when our steam engine was stopped at wayside water towers to quench its thirst, my dad would look about very cautiously before alighting. He would then dash forward from the front car, and have the driver fill his teapot with boiling water. Like all good 'Englishmen' in the colonies, he loved his tea, and he preferred to make it himself.

It was here also that my mom and dad gave us biology lessons. And in later years when I took my own son to Africa and tried to duplicate some of what my parents had taught us, the vivid imagination of a child led him to compare the characteristic recurved horns of the buffalo to upturned braided pigtails. "They look like little Dutch girls," he commented spontaneously of the Cape buffalo. His remark was typical of the many colorful elucidations my sister made at that age.

Our lessons were often in the form of games. Mom would say, "The adult oryx is seldom brought down by predators. Now, my darlings, you look out for one and tell me why."

We would then sit glued to the train window and tirelessly search for a gemsbok, the local term for this majestic antelope. If we were in the Kgalagadi we might spot an entire herd amongst the red Kalahari dunes.

This would set us off frantically endeavoring to sketch them, and wracking our brains to commit annotating notes to our crude drawings.

And while we were preoccupied with this time-consuming labor, our parents would bury themselves in their books. My well-bred mom, especially, was an avid reader, and like Nadine Gordimer's story persona, Mrs. Hansen — who sought out a Swiss newspaper to enjoy on her railroad journey from Cape Town to Johannesburg — Mom spent days before each trip visiting book shops to choose something special.

Eventually, with considerable help, we would come up with some rough art, and words to the effect that the gemsbok was seldom killed because it was tall and strong, and highly skilled at fighting off attackers with its lethal, scimitar-like horns.

Mom would tell us how clever we were, and add something new. What she found most impressive about the gemsbok, she said, was the way it had so perfectly adapted to its arid environment. "It's the animal equivalent of the Bushman," she smiled, explaining that by grazing at night and in the very early mornings, when grasses have their highest moisture contents, the gemsbok could go for extended periods without water. "And also like the San," she told us, "it's a wizard at finding water-storing plants, like the desert cucumber."

Drawing from her medical background, she added that the gemsbok could function perfectly well in extreme desert heat, sustaining an unusually-high body temperature — 113 degrees Fahrenheit, I think she stated. "Most animals," she declared, "would suffer brain damage and die at body heats considerably below that."

"But not the gemsbok," Joy sang, shaking her large head and smiling.

"That's right," my mom confirmed. "And the reason why," she said, "is that the gemsbok has an internal heat-exchange mechanism that protects the brain. This," she asserted, "is facilitated by a panting process that cools an intricate network of blood vessels in the nasal sinuses."

We did not understand it all at the time but, like many of Pop's accounts of African history and geography, we were impressed by the way she told it, and today the gemsbok still remains one of my favorite animals.

And so, as our metal dragon puffed onward, jostling us towards Bulawayo, or some such destination, we learned about the gemsbok, and of how the Namaqua sandgrouse soaks its breast feathers to carry water back to its young, and why the regal lion has white stripes under its eyes to reflect the light of the moon and help it hunt at night. And we were similarly informed about the leopard, the cheetah, the hyena, and the many other wild animals that crowd my magic memories of Africa.

Unfortunately, the magical quality of my recollections would soon be soured by *apartheid* voodoo. But not yet; I still had ahead of me the splendor of the veld.

Part 4

AFRICAN VELD

Schoolboy's Republic

*I*n the days when I was a young schoolboy in Africa, most lads of all ethnic backgrounds spent a lot of time playing in the veld. The veld is the natural environment of virgin grassland — and dispersed trees — that dominates large portions of the subcontinent.

My home was on the outskirts of Johannesburg. This had mushroomed from a mining camp in my grandfather's day, to a fair sized city, and the downside of growth, for youngsters my age, was that open veld was not as readily at hand as in other parts of Africa. Nevertheless, within a short walk of our house there was a stretch of open grassland and spring-fed wetlands, and this provided a sufficient wilderness area to satisfy our recreational needs. It was a place where we, rather than our parents, called the shots, a cherished schoolboy's republic, a milieu where we learned not from books, but from life. I started playing there when I was seven, with a group of neighborhood lads who ranged in age from about six to thirteen. We were all white boys.

Black kids, in an economic separation that existed before *apartheid,* had their own stretches of veld. We had our little tribes, and the Blacks had theirs. But as I was to learn from my prospecting co-worker, Kat, our upbringing, aspirations, and experiences as youngsters, were quite similar — not, as the Afrikaner government would later have it, worlds apart.

*L*ike the young African bird-hunters I had observed from trains, we white kids were also pretty good with slingshots, or 'catties' as we said. We crafted these ourselves, from Y-shaped twig prongs, string, elastic strands cut from old automobile inner tubes, and leather tongues extracted from discarded men's shoes.

Shoes were usually in short supply because my charitable mother periodically bundled up all our old — and not so old — clothes and shoes, and gave these to the church for distribution to, as she said, "the poor Blacks in the townships." This committed me to extreme measures to secure a critical aspect of raw material I needed for my catapults. I remember Pop casting me a quizzical glance one day as I wheeled my bicycle out of the house on my way to school. "What happened to your shoes?"

I swallowed. I could not believe he had noticed. Who on earth would take a second look at a boy's school shoes? I searched desperately for a plausible defense, but there was none. "I cut a piece off for my catty," I responded nervously, and braced for a lively response.

But it was slow in coming. There was only a painful silence, then a bewildered groan. "But those were brand-bloody-new shoes."

"I cut it under the laces," I whispered, trying to ease his pain.

He glared at me in disbelief. "Under the laces, by thunder. I ought to beat the living daylights out of you!"

I nodded. Nothing came to mind to add in my favor. I anticipated another lug across the ear, but Pop merely grunted, then turned abruptly, and I made a thankful escape, pleased for once to be off to school.

There was a knack for effective catty use. This involved placing the "ammo," generally a pebble, in the shoe-tongue, gripping this with two vice-like fingers, then pulling it back as far as one dared stretch the elastic bands. Before releasing, careful aim was taken through the open V of the prong that was held in the outstretched hand. Novices could be counted on to occasionally misfire and hit the hand that held the fork. This was excruciatingly painful. However, even worse than the hurt was the embarrassment of sniggers from boys who had already mastered the art of using the weapon.

We experimented with a variety of ammunition, and my friend Tiaan once had a brainwave. "Maybe we should try real bullets."

There were enthusiastic nods. But where could we get them? Our fathers all had handguns to protect our homes at night from *tsotsis* — black township thugs. However, they kept these carefully locked away in the day-time.

"I know where my old man hides his key," David offered.

"*Lekker!*" Great! Our hope was that cartridges would explode on contact. But this, of course, proved not to be the case.

By a process of elimination we eventually narrowed in on the best ammo, steel ball bearings. But these were hard to come by, so our limited supply was held in reserve for the crack shots in our group. 'Ironies,' as we called them, were issued only on occasions when we were really starved for some wild game.

I never attained the envied ranks of the sharp shooters, but it was not for lack of trying. I desperately wanted to be a good hunter, a Green, a Hemingway, and practiced endlessly, raining stones on telephone poles, street signs, or anything else that would serve as a mark.

Our favorite targets were bottles, scavenged from litter piles at the edge of the veld. Unlike rural Blacks who showed respect for open land, we suburban Whites demonstrated no such deference. While paying African 'garden boys' to keep our own yards in impeccable shape, we had total disregard for the undeveloped countryside. 'Do you still need this?' 'No.' 'Then chuck it in the veld.' Out went surplus building materials, old tires, car parts, and other garbage, onto the pristine savanna. This environmental crime, needless to say, was great for us kids. We salvaged discarded generators for their copper wire, and generally compounded the damage by spreading the junk.

By green-care contrast, a boy in our childhood troop had been told that good hunters never wasted, so we always ate the birds we shot no matter how small. We generally plucked and *braaied* these on the wood coals of an open fire, turning them over with our knives, which we always carried. A pocketknife was standard equipment for a white boy of my age at the time. Sometimes we packed the birds in clay and lit a fire over them in a type of baking process we had learned from the Africans.

There was no big game in the veld near us, so our best trophies were wild geese, or the occasional *dassie*. The latter was our name for the hyrax, an ungulate mammal with a thickset body, short legs, and a rudimentary tail, about the size of a rabbit. We could always count on finding these on a hillside outcrop that we named *Dassies'* Rock. It was a long walk to get there and back, an all-day adventure, and like most wild things *dassies* were difficult to hit with a catty and all but impossible to kill. They posted sentries which would alert the colony at the least sign of danger. Thus to bag a *dassie* we had to work the wind, and stealthily approach them on our bellies. It was far from easy. *Dassies* frustrated predators like the black eagle, far more adept than us, and we most often ended the hunt with scratched arms and legs, black-jacks sticking to our clothing, ticks in our hair, and no *dassie*. But that was the way I preferred it. Cleaning a *dassie* was a squeamish job I neither relished nor even wanted to be around, and eating one was almost as bad.

Years later when I found myself shying away from hunting, I rationalized it with the excuse that I simply did not like taking life — and good aim requires the will to kill. But shooting for the pot was a sport of legend in the remote outdoors where I was subsequently engaged in prospecting, and I often felt I was wasting my place on the continent by not participating in this grand pastime.

The Cattle Peoples

The greatest difference between our experiences and those of African boys in the veld was that, whereas our activities were exclusively play, theirs had a strong focus on work. "I began working as a herd-boy at the age of six," Kat, my *Bas Boy,* Boss Boy — the supervisor of my African prospecting team — told me. This was common. The job involved helping care for the precious animals that constituted the wealth of rural Africans. "Man is not a man without cattle," my friend said. Many items, such as the *lobola,* the offering a Xhosa husband bequeathed to the family of his bride, were traditionally paid for in cattle. In African male circles, Kat let me know with a droll smile, marriage was a costly undertaking.

But the responsibility imposed on a herd-boy in the veld extended way beyond the monetary value of his bovine charge. The cattle peoples of Africa have a spiritual attachment to their animals that is quite unique. They study their esteemed beasts with keen insight. "We name them for the way they are," Kat informed me.

I asked him what he meant by this, and he explained that cattle were a lot like people. Some were "unfriendly," even "haughty," he said, and others were just the opposite. Their names reflected their personalities. "And we made up songs for those we liked best," he revealed with a shy elfin simper.

However, despite this naming ritual, and a lyrical show of affection for their favorites, I have noticed that Africans do not appear to indulge their cattle in the manner we might pamper our pets. Yet they honor them with a variety of elevated practices. It is not unusual amongst the Himba, for example, to see the heads of cattle inscribed on tombstones, and horns stacked adjacent to graves. Kat told me that his father's worst nightmare would have been an afterworld without livestock.

Young herd-boys spent long hours alone in the veld, and often dreamed up ways to ward off boredom. "I learned my first arithmetic," Kat told me, "by counting my father's *nkomo*." — cattle.

I was fascinated by this and wanted to know more. "But surely," I said, "when you had counted them once, you knew how many there were. How much more could you learn?"

He smiled at my naiveté. "I would pretend that some were lost," he explained, "and come up with a number; or that mothers gave birth, and add these to what I had already counted; that some died and departed to *mputu* " — the world beyond — "that ..."

"Okay, I get it," I broke in. I went on to say that I imagined all African boys might have had a similar introduction to mathematics.

But Kat discounted this with a sharp hand-sweep and a melodramatic, "No!" He was about to punish me, in his subtle fashion, for the rude way in which I had interrupted him. His great-grandmother, a Bushman, he said, had told him that her people did not bother to count above more than about four. "There was no need to," he said with a little fleer. "They kept no cattle."

"But what if a Bushman scout saw eland?" I asked, trying to redeem myself. "Wouldn't the hunters want to know how many were in the herd?"

"No," he replied again, with a squint of satisfaction. "They could just say '*maningi.*' That would be fine." *Maningi* meant 'many,' or 'a large number.' I had learned this, and other pseudo-Bantu words, from my *Miners' Companion*, a small dictionary of mainly Zulu and Xhosa elements.

"The Bushmen," Kat said, continuing with his explanation, "would be interested in shooting only one eland, the weakest in the herd." They lived in small groups, he clarified, and a single animal would feed the clan for many weeks. "They would dry the meat, and it would last forever," he added with liberal exaggeration.

I nodded, thinking that that, at last, was the end of our discussion on numbers; I had another burning question to ask him. But I was wrong.

"*Manzi*," he said, referring to water, "was even more important to the Bushman than meat, and there was no way to count that." He was still onto me about my faux pas.

"Couldn't they count it by the gourd, or calabash," I prompted, "or whatever they used to carry it in?"

He smiled indulgently. Like Oom Jan, he invariably reserved a right to the last word. "They carried it in ostrich eggs," he said smugly. "But clans were always moving," he added, "and *manzi* is very heavy. Better to know where to find it, or where *Tsamma* melons grow."

I offered no comment on this, and we sat in silence for a while — I had forgotten my pressing question. There was a crocodile in the river not far from us, and we both kept half an eye on it. Kat stretched, and returned to his boyhood in the veld. "But learning arithmetic and composing songs for cattle," he continued, "often had to be put aside."

And why was that I asked him.

"I had other things to do." He went on to account for his time: he had to attend to the grazing needs of his animals, he said, drive them to the river to drink, and fight off jackals that periodically fell on calves at the edge of the herd. "I had no gun," he sniggered quaintly, "only a slingshot and a *knobkerrie*." — a stout staff with a heavy wooden ball, or bulge, at one end.

We white boys played in the veld only when the weather was good, and then it was a romantic fairyland. But Kat and his friends spent many days there, cold, wet, and shivering. The herds went out daily, and the boys were required to care for them both as a matter of character-building and necessity. "Our fathers," Kat shrugged, "were away on the mines."

His own dad, he mentioned, worked *mgodin*, underground, for many years, even when he was sick. He eventually died of silicosis, a fatal lung condition brought on by the dust from drilling and blasting.

"Did all Xhosa men work on the mines?" I asked witlessly.

"Many did, but not all," Kat replied. Madiba's dad, he said, was from a family of Xhosa monarchs and therefore spared the indignity of going underground.

"He had royal blood?" I asked in surprise.

"Yes," Kat responded, "high descent." All the same, he told me, Chief Mandela did not wish to spoil the prince. "So just like me," he said, "Rolihlahla was put to work."

"As a herd-boy?" I queried.

"Yes," he laughed. "Both I and Madiba were herd-boys."

His reference to Madiba — Nelson Mandela's clan name, which I also adopt out of respect for him — was interesting. When I first met Kat in 1961, Madiba was much in the news. He had just been acquitted of treason and fled abroad, and when I learned that Kat had grown up not far from him, I pumped him with questions. He had not met Madiba, but had a friend who had been at school with him, and so knew a little about him. However, much to my frustration, Kat hoarded this information like gold-dust, and only dispensed one small anecdote at a time. He also, as I would learn, fiercely guarded certain aspects of his own privacy.

*I*n addition to the dissimilar priorities of black and white boys in the veld, work versus play, the day-to-day living conditions of Africans differed substantially from those of Europeans. In contrast to our over-spacious homes, automobiles, and other modern conveniences, and our place in suburbia where most white people lived, the majority of Africans followed a simpler lifestyle in the countryside. They were people of the soil, healthy folk, well away from air-polluting stacks and industrial discharges to ground water. They were tribesmen and women who, without knowing it, practiced organic farming methods, raising hardy crops without chemical fertilizers or pesticides, and rearing animals in fine fettle, free from steroids.

"We lived in a *kraal*," Kat said. He was referring to an undersized African farm. This consisted of several small, but spick-and-span *rondavels*, round houses with domed or center-peaked roofs. An extension of the *kraal* was fenced off with spiked vertical or interwoven horizontal stakes, to provide a safe night area for cattle. Each family attended to its own building needs. "We made bricks by mixing clay with *nkomo* dung," Kat laughed, "and our roofs were nothing more than long grass."

But he, as usual, was thoroughly underestimating the sophistication of their homes. I once helped to thatch a roof at one of our mineral exploration camps, and observed the work firsthand. For a start the 'long grass' had to be carefully cut, bound tightly together with twine, and skillfully packed to make it watertight.

The finer points of construction, of course, varied according to culture and climate. A Himba *kraal*, for example, known as an *onganda* — the term *kraal*, Oom Jan informed me, has an Afrikaans derivation — contains *rondavels* the lower portions of which are often left unplastered. This results in open spaces between the slender sticks that constitute the frame. "It's hardly a shelter at all," I offered in a critical tone.

"Nou ja," Oom Jan endorsed, "but it serves as a sunshade. And it facilitates cross-ventilation to offset the heat of this semi-desert environment, *ideaal vir 'n kombuis of voorkamer."* — perfect for a kitchen or living room. "And when it occasionally rains here," he explained further, "they have full enclosures to move into." He pointed to another tall structure that looked like a *rondavel* perched on stilts. *"Weet jy wat is dit?"* he asked. Do you know what this is?

I shook my head.

"It's a silo," he said, raising his arm to emphasize its height. "It's used to hold food above the reach of wild animals. The Himba know the micro-climates. They move from place to place in search of grazing, and a store like this caters perfectly to their semi-nomadic existence."

"Slim mense," I commented. Clever people.

He smiled at my *rooinek* accent, but nodded assent.

Kat informed me, with a certain amount of pride, that each *kraal* was largely self-sufficient. The economies of African homelands, such as the Transkei and Zululand, he said, hinged on a barter system. "But we needed cash," he complained, "to pay hut taxes, and buy things like *gwayi."* *Gwayi,* tobacco, was perhaps Kat's only weakness. At that time, most Xhosa men, and married women, smoked pipes.

Kat also told me what I already knew from Lizzie, our housemaid, that women too, although less frequently than men, worked away from the Transkei, mostly as domestic servants. Lizzie had lost her husband and needed the — meager — wages we paid her, she said, to put her son through school. Her sister took care of her *kraal.*

I learned, in addition, from both Lizzie and Kat, that many men were polygamous. Kat said that his father had two wives, and Madiba's four.

"How did the wives get along with each other?" I asked.

"Well," he shrugged in a way that implied that my question was a frivolous one. "But life was hard," he said. "When my father was away, my mothers and we *pikinins"* — small children — "did everything."

"You tended the cattle?"

Kat laughed. "Yes," he confirmed, "but that was just the start. We also ploughed the fields, sowed the seed, harvested the crops, and threshed the grain. And don't forget," he added in a lofty tone, "we were not, like you, living in *eGoli."* — Johannesburg. "There was no electricity in the *kraals.* We had to collect dung or firewood to cook." He went on to say that there was also no running water, so families had to bathe and wash their blankets in streams. And on larger rivers like the *Mzimvubu,* home of the hippopotami, his grandmother had told him, they had had to keep a watchful eye on *iMvubu,* the fat ones. "And every day," he offered in addition, "we had to carry *manzi* back to the *kraal."* His mother, he related with a sense of joy, frequently walked barefooted, with his baby sister strapped to her back, him often hanging on her arm, and a huge urn of water, or bundle of firewood, balanced on her head.

"That's absolutely amazing," I commented.

"Yes, *manzi* is heavy," he reminded me, again with his little smug squint. "But she made it look easy. She sang like a finch-lark as she walked."

I could identify with his delight. I had often seen such women in the *bundu*. They possessed the erect postures of queens, and although the ground was rough and thorny they strode as confidently as gazelle. And as to their voices, it seemed to me that every footpath boasted a country girl who was a Myriam Makeba — a *Mamma iAfrika;* she, to my ear, is the greatest of all African folk singers.

African tribes have proud histories recorded over the centuries by word of mouth. "Very little is written," Kat said.

I asked him why that was, and he explained that there were many of the older generation who still could not read.

"Like my grandmother," I smiled, "my Granny Watson."

He was visibly astounded by that, a white person who could not read. And he was further taken aback when I informed him, truthfully, that I believed his schooling had been superior to mine. "Some of your mission teachers had doctorates," I reminded him. "Your education probably differed only slightly," I said, "from that of a boy in England."

"Do you really think so?" he asked with genuine surprise.

I assured him that I did, and explained that my early tuition had been in government schools, from Afrikaners who had never been abroad and had presented us with a *Boer* slant on history.

"Our history had a Xhosa slant," he chuckled, "at least what we learned from our fathers." He gave me some examples, stories of ancestors and legendary chiefs, their hunts, battle encounters, and other notable exploits. "We would imitate them with our own games and adventures in the veld," he laughed. "It was a wonderful learning experience."

'A wonderful learning experience,' indeed. But it was far more than that. Let me illustrate, by briefly skipping ahead, that by their escapades in the veld, and a liberal measure of inbred instinct, Kat and his African friends gained knowledge beyond their years, and in the process became grand masters of the wild.

Part 5

GRAND MASTERS
OF THE WILD

Kat

Digressing from my childhood to make a point — I shall return — I first met Kat in Northern Rhodesia, and worked with him there in mineral exploration. And when I think back on it now, it is difficult to imagine how my white colleagues and I could have managed at all without the intuition and outdoor skills of men like him.

The bushveld there is often dense and has few topographic landmarks, and without our guides we would have been hopelessly lost on an almost daily basis. I was always amazed by their extraordinary sense of geographic orientation; like migrating birds they appeared to be tuned to an inbuilt tracking mechanism.

Over the years I encountered many experienced outdoorsmen, but Kat, despite his diminutive size, was by far the best. Some of our distant ancestors, no doubt, had a sense of nature that matched his, but we city folk, alas, have long since lost a lot of what it takes to overcome the odds against our precarious survival in the remote African wild.

Kat was capable of closing a six-mile geological traverse — an essentially rectangular sampling hike that began and ended at the same location — to within a few hundred paces. His only tools were his measured step and an old army compass. His feats were all the more impressive when one considers that, at some locations, we found ourselves walking a zigzagging course through virtual forest. Moreover, traverses tended to be threaded by streams that had to be crossed at places of convenience. And there were invariably obstacles to circumvent, a swampy wetland, a rogue elephant sniffing the air for intruders, and these called for additional detours and pacing allowances. Furthermore, the concentration of a guide was challenged by constant sampling stops called for by the geologist.

And when it came to halts to hammer outcrops for specimens, it seemed that I was amongst the worst offenders. The Africans had their own names — but no songs — for the Europeans, and in one camp I was known as *Bwana Bula*, an abbreviated form of *Bwana Bula Matari*, the destroyer of rocks. I had no way of assessing whether this was meant as a compliment or an insult, but I strongly suspected the latter.

*T*he only time I saw Kat lose his bearings was as a passenger on a helicopter flight. The incident involved our pilot returning to base camp after delivering samples for assay. He spotted us from above in dazzling veils of rain-washed light. We were crossing a *dambo*, a natural opening in the trees. The chopper landed. "I'm lost," her pilot announced sheepishly.

We nodded sympathetically.

"I ran into fog shortly after leaving town," he complained, "and diverted west." He clenched his teeth; he was shaken. "The next thing I knew, my compass was spinning. I must have run into a magnetic anomaly, somewhere near Mujimbeji."

I locked onto him with a penetrating gaze, my thoughts darting immediately to magnetite. Although copper was king within our concession, his inadvertent find was worth a look at. "Let's go back and check it out," I suggested in a tone of elevated interest.

His reply was a chilly stare and four cold words. "Which way is camp?"

I turned to Kat who reached for his *kasembi*, his homemade axe, which he invariably carried behind his back, with the elbows of both arms curled over its shaft. He held the blade, the sharpened section of an old Land Rover spring, and pointed its slender handle. "That way, *Bwana*."

The airman's face betrayed an entreating look. "Why don't you two call it a day and come back with me?"

We agreed and he lifted the little flying craft, now burdened by our weight, nose-dived it forward, and swept it in a long arc to gain elevation. Once we were safely above the canopy of trees that surrounded the *dambo*, the aviator addressed Kat, "Which way did you say, my man?"

Kat looked down vacantly; in the air he was out of his element and completely disoriented.

The frustrated pilot pivoted to me, but I shrugged hopelessly.

"Damn," he swore and returned to the clearing. Kat alighted and walked some paces from where we had landed. He peered about, perhaps looking at the slant of shadows, then twisted and pointed once more in the direction of the camp. The flier quickly took a bearing, and Kat's face creased in a brilliant smile.

The meerkat, after which Kat was named, stands "barely a foot tall, even on tiptoe" — *Meerkats Stand Tall.* "But if helpfulness equaled height," biologist Tim Clutton-Block says, referring to their social behavior, "meerkats would be giants." We felt the same way about our little scout. And although I sensed that Kat, for his part, had a keen awareness of his high value, he never flaunted it. In fact, as I would learn years later, he kept a lot from me about his service to the white man.

Kat was perhaps twenty years older than me. But if I stood back and viewed him, in silhouette, against a rising or setting sun, I saw a far younger man, almost a boy.

Besides preventing us from being lost in the backveld *kwas* — brush — our African co-workers had unshakeable loyalty, and were as vigilant as shepherds in protecting us. They informed us which wild fruits we could eat and which we should avoid. And when a chopper failed to spot us, they pointed out the grasses and plants, like bracken, that would burn with the thickest and blackest smoke to attract it.

And they exercised uncanny powers in anticipating danger. Having grown up in the quietness of the veld they had super-acute powers of hearing. *"Imisa!"* Stop! Kat whispered urgently to me one day while we were working a prospecting line — he had heard the snap of a distant twig. He stood motionless, scanning the undergrowth for a predator.

And although snakes to a city dweller are silent, Kat could discern the sound of their movement from at least five paces, a critical distance in avoiding a strike. And, like an eagle, he could clearly see what I could barely make out with binoculars.

Aside from providing for my protection, Kat's backveld knowledge gave me a new dimension in observing nature. "I must suggest," he advised me with calm competence, "that you build this bridge higher."

I was engaged, at the time, in the construction of a new access bridge to the airstrip near our field camp. I asked him why.

"Buka!" Look! he said, giving me his crooked little glance, and pointing to some weaver nests hanging from trees along the river.

I looked and shrugged.

"They are building higher this year."

"So?" I said, still unable to make the connection.

"The birds know that the summer rains will be heavier than usual," he said simply, "and that the river will rise above its usual level."

On his advice I modified my plans for the elevation of the bridge. It survived what I later computed to be a 20-year flood, one so severe that it occurs, on average, only once every 20 years.

Madiba

Madiba did not choose to employ his veld-honed inclinations in the direction of African rangers like Kat. However, it has always been my contention that the animal-like instincts he developed in the outdoors played a crucial role in his long-suffering survival. For example, in the perilous years of organizing the freedom fight, he often had to make snap decisions on the people he could trust. "Nature teaches beasts to know their friends," the Epic

Minstrel notes in *The Tragedy of Coriolanus,* and I believe it was an intuition sharpened by nature that helped the wily leader to ferret out the government jackals who attempted to infiltrate his anti-*apartheid* movement.

Furthermore, it was Madiba's veld-bred clairvoyance that kept him alive in that austere prison on Robben Island. Indeed, it was his acute sixth sense, I believe, that prevented him from being swept up by an elaborate escape plan, a trap that was cunningly contrived by the security police. Their devious scheme would have given them a sought-after pretext for shooting him, a murder they were otherwise loath to commit at the time, under the increasingly watchful eyes of the world. It was Madiba's upbringing in the wild that saved him.

We white boys also had our lives shaped by growing up in the veld and, as I have already suggested, there was a lot more common ground than we ever might have imagined as youngsters, between African lads and us.

Part 6

AFRICANS & US

Whiteboy Learning Experience

*I*f growing up in the outdoors served as a valuable learning experience for young Africans, it fulfilled a similar function for us white boys, one that was quite sophisticated when I look back on it.

We referred to the wetlands and eroded ravines near my home as 'the dongas.' And when we were not shooting at things with our *catties*, or otherwise occupied in the veld, we spent hundreds of hours in the *dongas,* building miniature dams out of clay. We got the idea for this from Antonio, whose father was a civil engineer. Born in Italy, Antonio had visited many of his dad's world-wide projects, and we were astonished by what he knew. At that stage of our lives, aside from Antonio and the Potts brothers, none of the rest of us had been out of Africa.

During the dry season when there were no thunderstorms to contend with, our network of dams spread out like beaver ponds. We stocked them with tadpoles and constructed irrigation schemes for farms of small frogs that we referred to as our cattle. We built penstocks into our impoundment structures, let the falling water turn paddle wheels that we fabricated from the tops of old tin cans, and pretended that these were hydroelectric power systems. Our transmission grid embraced model cities, and boasted power lines realistically fabricated of copper wire.

We liked the look of shining copper. "Strip it" was a common instruction to the younger boys in the group, and I spent many hours and suffered countless cuts removing insulation with my pocket knife. If the gauge was too heavy, the task extended to unraveling the twisted strands to secure something closer to the scale of our model layouts.

*W*e also used gleaming copper wire to fabricate one of our most creative structures, a suspension bridge. As would be supposed, Antonio was the project manager for its construction, but I was the proud assistant PM. I was a little older when we built the bridge, and Antonio had me keep a log of the time everyone spent on the construction effort. We computed that the project took almost 300 man-hours to complete. That equated to about a workweek, Antonio said, for our gang of engineers.

"But we've been slaving on this thing since the day before my birthday," Tiaan protested. "That's almost two months."

"Listen," Antonio tried to explain, "some days we only work-a one hour or two; a man-week is-a forty hours."

Tiaan argued further, but Antonio dropped the matter with his hands in the air and a disgruntled Italian mumble.

We named our imposing structure the Brooklyn Bridge, and referred to it informally as the Monumental Bridge. Antonio provided both names. He had visited New York and seen the real Brooklyn Bridge, and reported that his father had described it as one of the world's greatest monuments to civil engineering.

As we neared completion on our version of the cyclopean bridge, we began talking about a grand opening ceremony. But Antonio quickly specified that only a lady could crack the champagne bottle needed to "bring-a it on line," as he said. It was a stalling tactic. He had fallen in love with the project and did not want to see it end. But we second-guessed him on that occasion; we already had a girl in mind, Annatjie — 'Little Ann' in English.

Annatjie was a tomboy and we all thought very highly of her. We persuaded Koos, her brother, to secretly invite her, and sneak her out of the house. Our sisters were strictly banned from the supremely dangerous *dongas*. They stayed at home and played with dolls, or indulged in girls' games with their friends. But Annatjie was more like us. We occasionally let her join in our soccer games, but only as goalie. From seeing her dribble with her dad we suspected that she was better than some of us, and we did not want her scoring and showing us up. We did not have much time for girls in those days. But Annatjie was different.

Annatjie made a great fuss of our bridge. She softly touched things here and there in appreciation, and showed a keen eye for the details of our efforts. After she had undertaken her inspection, we managed to coax someone's pet guinea pig to crawl across the bridge. Annatjie then slipped her hand into an oversized leather glove that we had found on a constructions site — while searching for copper wire — and smashed an old water-filled champagne bottle on a rock that supported one of the towers. "I now declare this bridge open," she announced. Although she was Afrikaans, she spoke perfect English.

Antonio made a short speech.

Annatjie then stood up, raised a hand in the air and graciously proposed a toast: "To the genius engineers who built this bridge." She punched a dainty fist above her head and led us in three hearty cheers, immodestly for ourselves. "Hip, hip," she cried.

"Hooray!" we chorused. There were three, perhaps four rounds of hurrahs. We were intoxicated with our triumph.

Unfortunately our version of the Great Bridge stood intact for less than a day after its opening. It was totally demolished by one of our rival schoolboy factions. We found a cryptic message scratched on a rock in charcoal. It read: "Our compliments, ●"

We were devastated by our loss, but numbly intrigued by this sign-off communiqué, and the next day confronted one of the party's younger members on the school playground. We offered him some money for the tuck shop, and asked him what it meant. He jumped at the bribe. "It's the 'black spot,' the death mark from *Treasure Island*," he whispered.

Hmm...clever, we surmised. We wished we had been the ones to have thought of that.

The loss of our bridge left a black mark on us. Our dams had often been breached, and we had even, on occasion, destructively bombed our own engineered structures. But the bridge was different.

"Don't-a worry," Antonio consoled us. "We'll-a build a new one."

But we never did. We could not stand the thought of a second loss. Antonio had even suggested that we build it in his yard. No one would dare to break in there, he said, not with the dogs he had.

We declined. It wouldn't be the same, we argued, if we weren't in the *dongas*.

"We'll make-a our own *dongas*," Antonio offered desperately.

We felt sorry for him and wanted to tell him the real truth; we were scared to death of his dogs. "They won't-a bite white people," he had often reassured us. But one of his slobbering canines had once jumped up on my back, and my friends had had to beat it off with sticks. It had stood upright, on its hind legs, taller than I was. It had clutched my shoulders with its front paws, and tried to "rape" me as the boys said.

Antonio kept on about a new bridge, and we were tempted to put it on the line. Get rid of those nasty dogs, then we'll think about it. However, we knew that that was not an option. Most households had at least one dog, to scare off would-be burglars. But the other dogs were different. A bite was one thing, but having a dog try to rape you was an indignity that no one was prepared to risk, least of all me, for a second time. However, it was no use trying to explain it all to Antonio. He was just not afraid of dogs, any dogs, not even the half-wild native dogs that accompanied the ox-wagons.

The Ox-Wagons

There was always considerable excitement amongst us kids when the first ox-wagon was spotted. With a team of some sixteen oxen, as far as I can recall, it was a magnificent sight. The wagons rolled in like old wooden sailing ships on a rough sea. Buckets, lanterns, and dripping canvas water-bags swung beneath the carriages. The wagons creaked under their heavy loads, and their iron tires, strapped to expertly-crafted wooden wheels, scoured the roadway.

The black owners, who we recognized from past years, walked alongside their ox-teams, cracking long whips, calling to their animals by name, and whistling shrill orders to the slow-moving beasts. Women sat inside the swaying wagon tents with their babies, but herd-boys, many of them considerably younger than us, scurried along behind their fathers, imitating their calls. And ferocious native dogs, with spiked collars to protect them from jackals in the backveld, tore at leashes hitched to the wagons. We fancied that they would like to have shred to ribbons the neighborhood pets that frantically barked at them from the safety of chain-link fences.

"Now there's a scene from a different time," Pop marveled, waving to a driver as a wagon rumbled past our house, its brakes screeching.

We nodded, but like many of the things he told us on our train journeys, we were not exactly sure what he meant.

Pop had a special respect for the wagon-drivers. He admired all rural Africans, often referred to them as the "black aristocracy" of Africa, and considered them above a new breed of Blacks who now lived, and in some cases may even have been born in squalid townships on the edge of 'European' cities. "See how polite and courteous they are," he would frequently comment after an encounter. "And they know a lot more than us about nature." We were well aware of the fact that anyone who lived close to nature was in a special class in my father's estimation.

When the wagons reached the dirt road at the edge of the veld, the tired oxen sensed that they were nearing the end of the day. They began bellowing and stamping their hooves, and this raised clouds of dust that added to the colorful scene. They voluntarily increased their pace, lifting their heads and sniffing the air. "They smell water," Pop said, turning to us and smiling.

For as long as I can remember the wagons arrived by a route that took them past our house. "They used to come by a different way," Pop said, "but someone bought a parrot that could mimic the whistles of the wagon-guides." He laughed. "You should have seen the confusion."

There were often as many as four wagons outspanned in our stretch of veld. The owners would draw them up in a semi-circle to get shelter from the wind, and camp for ten days or so. They used the wetlands for watering their oxen and doing their washing.

Some sixty oxen wrought havoc with our hydroelectric schemes, but we did not give it a second thought. The annual ox-wagon visits were an interlude of celebration. Our parents bought produce from the Africans, and pooled resources for communal watermelon feasts and *mealie braais*. 'Mealie' was our name for corn on the cob.

We boys begged and borrowed things like tea, jam, and flour from the pantries of our mothers, and bartered our booty for stalks of sugar-cane. Sugar-cane was something of a treat for us. It was not available in the grocery stores or from Sammy — the Indian who visited our neighborhood once a week in his mule-cart, and sold fresh greens to our moms — and we could get it only once a year from the ox-wagons. The Africans, in turn, were more than pleased to exchange their raw cane for our refined products. They were also happy to accept the few beans, onions, and tomatoes that I grew in my own little garden and usually sold to my mom.

While the wagon families were there we attached ourselves to their ranks, and felt as if we were a part of their safari. We watched them tend their oxen, repair their yokes and *trek*-chains, and skillfully weave baskets of grass. And in the early evenings we sat around the edge of their fires sniffing the second-hand smoke of their pipes. They sometimes offered us food, game birds stewed in cast-iron pots, and dumplings steamed on grids above the simmering fowl. It was delicious, and we secretly wished that we could have camped out in the veld with these wagon people. But our parents would not even have begun to allow that. So each day when the sun began to set, and the men reached for their *paraffin* cans to fill their dusty lanterns, we knew it was time to make our sad departures and return home, like sissies, to our moms.

African Moms

*B*esides what African boys learned on their own in the veld, and from their fathers, they also gained much knowledge from their mothers. "Xhosa women are excellent equestriennes," Kat told me, using his mission-school vocabulary, and it was his mother, he said, who taught him to ride. "And moms could also tell stories," he smiled.

Female chronicles, their moms' and ours, broached more gentle topics than those of the men. Rather than severed heads on stakes, theirs were more typically akin to lively fables in which animals could speak and owls were wise. Children's tales with a moral are very popular in Africa, and Lady Margaret Tredgold, a legendary ethno-botanist and expert on African folklore, is of the firm opinion that Aesop's fables had their origins in Africa. Aesop, she says, is a corruption of "Aethop, the Ethiopian."

Whereas the stories that our moms told, or more frequently read to us, were usually bedtime treats, the educational discourses of black women tended to be delivered before evening meals in the *kraals*. Kat's fond recollection was of watching his mother prevail over a three-legged cooking pot on a fire, while she told stories "out of her head," as he put it. She could read but never used a book, he said.

I got the impression from both Kat and Lizzie that the *kraal*, in general, was a serene retreat where the mother prevailed as matriarch, a place where order abounded to a greater extent than within many white homes.

Kat hinted at the fact that black youngsters were encouraged to be seen rather than heard, as the saying goes. And Lizzie often threw her arms up when Joy and I bombarded her with questions, implying that such behavior would have been considered disrespectful in a Xhosa home. And Madiba too made reference to the fact that when he first visited the dwellings of Whites, he was surprised both by the volley of questions that children posed, and by the preparedness of their parents to answer.

Although moms were the *grande dames* of the *kraals*, fathers, Kat said, despite seldom being home, were always the heads of households. Nevertheless, moms had considerable influence. All decisions on his schooling, Kat told me, were made by his mother. And Madiba records in his autobiography, *Long Walk to Freedom,* that at the age of seven, it was also his mother, a Christian, who first raised the issue of him attending a mission school.

One day as we rested in the shade of a giant ant-mound, I asked Kat what he thought was the main difference between black and white mothers. "The fewer toys they allowed us to have," he replied without hesitation.

Timmy's Mom

The fact that Kat even hinted at having been deprived of toys surprised me, because I considered him to be totally indifferent to material things.

When the ox-wagons departed from our stretch of the veld, we would go back to repairing our dams and cities. Oxen spoor were everywhere and looked like bomb craters on our model landscape.

The termites soon knew we were back and building. Their anthills were our borrow pits, and our construction efforts took a heavy toll on their ecology. Like African boys our age, we had somehow discovered that their above-ground colonies were ideal materials to work with, sufficiently impermeable to make our dams watertight and, when wetted, plastic enough to mold into the buildings that made up our towns.

Our most innovative city structure was a coliseum, a small attempted replica of that famous historic landmark in Rome, another of Antonio's ideas. In place of gladiator fights we held contests using bigheaded soldier-ants with large pincers. We patiently drew these from ant holes on long strands of grass. We also promoted special-event fights between scorpions, when we could find them. We put these in heated cans, and probed them with lighted cigarettes to force them to combat. Encounters were so spectacular that we invited some boys from one of our rival bands to witness a battle. They stayed awhile, but one of them said it was cruel and that our group was "no better than a bunch of savages."

Although we pretended to ignore it, the comment surely struck a responsive chord, for when a scorpion later stung one of our members, and someone suggested that it might be God's punishment for our barbarism, we quickly reverted to our less exciting battles featuring army ants.

The events surrounding the scorpion sting began with Little Timmy provoking the venomous creature by trying to pin its body to the ground. He had just overturned a small boulder, spotted it, and his immediate objective was to prevent it from escaping. Unfortunately, he was wearing leather sandals and the petite arachnid must simply have arched its segmented tail upward and injected its lethal tip. The first we knew of the incident was when Tim cried out that he had been "bitten." Our hearts dropped. We ran over to try to help him, but we feared the worst. Timmy stood stark still and gave us the ghost of a smile as we came up on him. But his brave gesture froze when he saw the looks of terror on our faces. He started to sweat. "Am I going to die?" he inquired in a wavering voice.

"No," we lied.

We asked him if he could walk and were relieved when he said he thought he could. We began hurrying him in the direction of his home. He limped, whimpered quietly about pains in his groin and armpit, and complained that his lips were going numb. We knew the poison was taking effect and we urged him on. We badly wanted to get him home. We would never hear the end of it if he expired in the veld.

At a convenient point, not too close to his house, we cowardly let him go on alone. From slunk-down positions in the tall grass we saw his mom open the door for him. We then retreated to a safer distance and kept a silent vigil on the house. An ambulance arrived and left, and Koos said: "Let's *waai!*" — Let's 'blow!' Let's get out of here!

"We'd bloody better," I heard, and we took off in a panic.

We ran through stretches of water to keep our scents from tracker dogs, then hid in a storm sewer near the golf course. Here we began frantically thinking of a likely yarn to tell our parents, and the police. The younger boys like Timmy were our responsibility, and the best story in the world, we knew, would not explain the death of one of them. But we tried. We hung around in agony, rehearsing one lie after another. "Maybe we could say that *tsotsis* chased us," David suggested, "and that Timmy was separated from the group."

However, as the sun began to set, we eventually settled on the truth. It was an accident. Unfortunately, there was no excuse for neglecting to escort Timmy to his door, and explaining things to his mom. "That'll cost us time in clink," Tiaan said.

On our dreaded exit from the safe haven of the veld, David stole a glimpse at Tim's house and called out in exultation, "Hey, there's Tim." We all swung round, expecting to see his ghost. One boy, then two, then all of us began running in his direction. "What happened?"

"Nothing," Little Tim said, shrugging his shoulders.

Just then his mom emerged from the house and strode towards the fence where we stood. "I want to talk to you boys," she cried.

We turned and fled, not even saying goodbye to Timmy.

On the following evening we were gathered before a hastily-assembled committee of parents to apologize to Tim's mom and dad, and listen to a series of lectures about responsibility. We were then banned from the veld for a week, and I knew my mom was pleased about that.

Later, after I had been sent to bed on short rations, I overheard her pleading for me to be permanently forbidden from playing in the veld.

"No,·no, no," Pop responded. "It's good for him! It's toughening him up. Do you want him growing up to be a bloody pansy?"

"Of course not, darling," Mom conceded, "but what about this thing with Little Timmy?"

"They're boys," Pop said in a tone that closed the incident. He was good in that way. He even let us watch the stick fighters.

The Stick Fighters

As youngsters we were always very conscious of toughening ourselves up, and we frequently engaged in stick fighting, an African sport that we learned from the Xhosa mineworkers.

On weekends we frequently visited my cousins, or friends who lived on the mines, and here the veld was every lad's dream. It was spotted with old prospecting adits, rusted boilers, discarded stamps, and antiquated mining equipment of every description. There were all sorts of things we could climb, old mills we could explore, and mountainous mine dumps we could play on.

Children occasionally fell to their deaths from headframes, or from rotten ladders in old stopes, or were drowned in the quick sands of slurry ponds atop the dumps, and we were grateful to be let loose with just a few words of caution — "Yes go, but just be bloody careful!"

We might not have shown it at the time, but we appreciated the trust that Pop extended to us. Having grown up on the mines he knew full well what boys got up to.

To my mom's horror, Pop often related stories of his own youthful exploits on the mines, and his adventures made ours seem trivial. In 1922, in one of the most infamous strikes ever to take place on the new gold mines of the Witwatersrand, my dad smuggled food to my grandfather and other striking workers barricaded in at the mine. Martial law had been declared and gun posts had been set up around the perimeter of the workings. Armored cars and tanks were held on standby at strategic locations, and military aircraft flew reconnaissance flights over the mine buildings. Pop and his companions, then schoolboys, had to creep in like storm troopers, under a cloak of darkness.

"One night," he said, "I accidentally bumped my schoolbag of supplies against a sheet of corrugated iron, and we were shot at."

"And did they get you?"

"No," he smiled. "I don't think they were shooting to kill. They knew we were kids." But that, it appeared, was about the only break they were given. "By the end of the strike," Pop said, "more than 150 people were dead and over 500 injured."

Pop was extremely proud of his dad's stand against worker exploitation. "Your grandfather," he once told us after his annual glass of champagne — he always drank in the New Year, but otherwise described himself as a teetotaler — "was part of mining history."

Joy and I smiled proudly.

He placed his arms around our shoulders. "And don't you forget," he advised us, "to do your bit in life."

"Yes Pop," we answered, wondering what his 'bit' had been — besides helping our grandfather during the strike. But even my precocious little sister was not about to get into that.

On another occasion Pop interrupted a game we were playing, and dragged us clear across the sprawling city, to Pioneer Park in Booysens. There, he enthusiastically showed us our grandfather's name engraved on a memorial plaque celebrating the courage of early prospectors and miners. He read the name aloud: "John Henry Watson."

In later years when I learned in school that it was General Smuts who had ordered the martial law that might have resulted in the deaths of both my father and my grandfather, I approached my dad on the matter. "Skilly," I said, referring to our history teacher, "told us that it was General Smuts who brought the army out against the mine strikers."

He gestured agreement.

"Well, why did you vote for him?" I asked in surprise.

"Consider the alternative," he said. It was an expression he often used. He was silent for a moment, then added philosophically: "Listen, Smuts was a good man, but even good men sometimes make mistakes."

Although my dad, as I said, turned a blind eye on most of our activities around the mines, our exploits were limited by the solidarity of other more-concerned parents. We were strictly forbidden to go anywhere near the locations where the African mineworkers congregated on Sundays to drink their homebrewed beer and engage in stick fighting — like the oxen on Karen Blixen's farm, the miners were not required to work on the Sabbath.

"On no account go there!" a friend's father decreed, shaking a fist in our direction. "Not even the police go near the stick fighters."

"They'll be smoking *dagga*," another dad said, referring to marijuana, "and they'll beat the life out of white kids snooping on them."

These morbid warnings scared us, but we crept up on their gatherings nonetheless, and observed their fights in wonder.

Stick fighting is done with two stout wooden staffs, one held in each hand. The hand that grips the center of the non-hitting stick is heavily bound to protect it from injury; long swaths of cloth are wrapped around both the hand and the staff. This outstretched stick serves as a shield to ward off blows. The other is used for striking one's opponent.

In the way the miners went about it, it was a vicious sport that both thrilled and frightened us. For though the defenses of fighters were remarkable, heavy swipes inevitably found their targets, and open gashes bled profusely, especially from the head. We were astonished that the men even survived some of the cracks leveled at them. Occasionally someone would be knocked cold by a powerful blow to the skull. And although this was rare, there was no escaping being hurt. But the combatants invariably fought on. They were the toughest men we had ever seen.

We observed our first fights from a distant hideout using army binoculars. We thought we were hidden, but with their hawk-like eyesight the miners knew we were there. One day an older worker crept up on us, and scared us half to death with his deep-voiced, "How!"

We swung around with the jitters. But when we saw his broad grin, we swallowed our initial fear and responded with the same alien greeting.

The man walked up to us, clasped each of our hands, in turn, with both of his, and invited us to a closer viewpoint.

We agonized over his tempting offer. Although his Herculean size gave us good cause for alarm, his warm bearing and friendly manner attracted us. We were torn by a mixture of fear and respect. We had never felt hands like his, as rough as granite. But this old man, who we came to know as Willie, turned out to be a gentle giant. He said we made him think of his grandchildren. On the Sundays that we spent with him, Willie was both our commentator and our coach. He told us about the contestants, and explained the fine arts involved in fighting. "Small sticks for small boys," he instructed us.

We did not like that at first. But we came to accept 'small sticks' as perhaps his most useful piece of advice.

In the protective custody of Willie neither the fighters nor the spectators took any notice of us, and this generated a dilemma. On one hand we were grateful for the anonymity. On the other we found ourselves uncomfortably close to the action, where both the intensity of the fighting and the charged atmosphere of the onlookers terrified us. We were also mindful of being the only white people in attendance. Nevertheless, the excitement of the contests was intoxicating, and with an upward spiral in our own fighting skills we kept coming back.

Then, one Sunday, Willie was gone. He had returned to his native Pondoland we were told. No one invited us to stay, so we slunk back to our distant hide-away and things were not the same. In our own fights, however, we religiously stuck to his directives. For one thing we continued to employ light sticks. Thus we were able to enjoy this outstanding contact sport, while limiting our injuries to scratches and welts. Although we craved the scars of the real stick fighters, we knew that serious wounds would have to be explained to our moms. And that was a problem. They tended to overreact to the sight of blood.

Transkei Fosterlings

*S*tick fighting amongst African boys was bloody. Kat once pointed out a healed gash on the side of his head. "I got this as a boy in the Transkei," he said proudly.

The Transkei, frequently mentioned in my story, and a place that will feature in my escape, was a large region of untamed beauty that is now absorbed into the Eastern Cape, one of the nine provinces of the new South Africa. Its original boundaries made it a little larger than the state of Maryland, a little smaller than the Netherlands. It lay between the rugged Drakensberg ranges — 'Mountains of the Dragon' — and the Indian Ocean, and comprised an unspoiled area that, like the kingdom of Basutoland, was reminiscent of an Africa of old. A single road of significance traversed it. Kat lived near this road, but winding paths tramped by generations of feet were all that connected small villages like Mvezo and Qunu, where Madiba was born and spent his early years.

The Transkei region, as implied, is the ancestral home of the great Xhosa nation, and when Madiba and Kat were boys it was shared with only a small minority of other Africans, and a few 'Europeans' — Whites, regardless of where they had been born, were referred to in South Africa as Europeans. These, in the Transkei, included a handful of missionaries, teachers, and officials like magistrates who represented the British rule that prevailed at the time.

Madiba remembers of his early youth that the role of the European in his life was a remote one, and that the existence of white people barely crossed his mind. Kat, on the other hand, lived closer to civilization and frequently saw Whites in the capital. They were friendly, he said. He told me his uncle, then working as a wagon driver, always tipped his hat to them, and he shyly confessed that he felt proud to receive a wave from "all these important people in *Mtata*" — Umtata.

*U*nlike me, both Kat and Madiba were fosterlings. When Kat's father died, his uncle took the young ward under his wing and treated him like a son, and Kat often referred to him as his father. Likewise, when Madiba's father passed away, the care and education of the nine-year-old continued under the acting paramount chief of his tribal clan.

A particular highlight of the royal stripling's new life with the Regent involved the tribal meetings that were periodically held at his residence, the 'Great Place.' Typical agendas addressed political and legal issues, farming matters such as the need to dip cattle, and actions necessary to cope with environmental emergencies such as droughts or floods.

In the highly democratic form of government practiced by the Xhosas, everyone was invited to these meetings and, as Madiba remembered, large crowds converged on them by foot and on horseback.

The first Europeans to witness these gatherings in the 18th century were struck by them. Author Anthony Sampson, in *Mandela,* records the favorable impressions of an early missionary, William Holden, on the wisdom of council speakers; his view was that, in their own rights, they were the equals of British lawyers. Others have likened Xhosa council meetings to those of the early Greeks. The basis of this comparison was an unusually pure premise of political equality.

The young Mandela hunkered for hours at the edge of the tribal gatherings, studying the tactics of the speakers. And the Regent, in turn, responded to the boy's interest by sharing his thoughts on what he considered to be the role of a statesman. His pellucid words of wisdom were still imprinted on Madiba's mind more than sixty years later when he wrote his autobiography. He recorded that the Regent had compared a good leader to a shepherd. He stays at the back of his flock, the old man said, letting curious animals go ahead. The others follow without realizing that all the while they are being guided from behind.

In observing Madiba's subsequent success as a leader there is no doubt in my mind that when things were going well he always led from behind, and let his carefully-selected colleagues take credit for the prosperity. However, when fortunes changed he would immediately step forward. "You take the front when there is danger," I once heard him say with conviction. True to his word, as we shall see, he always did. The lion-hearted leader never flinched in a crisis.

The Unflinching Jew

*A*t the end of the World War II a substantial number of Germans, including high-ranking Nazis, fled their country and, often under false identities, sought refuge abroad. In 1948 when the Nazi-sympathetic Afrikaner party came to power in South Africa, Germans appeared everywhere. They were referred to as 'Nazis' in our largely English-speaking neighborhood, and were generally made to feel unwelcome.

Although my father, a war veteran, had no particular love for the German nation, least of all for the Nazis, my sister and I were expressly told to greet these people, and to be polite if we were spoken to. "And above all," Pop directed, "I don't want you talking about them as Nazis."

This last instruction dismayed us, and my sister was audacious enough to question him on it. "Why not?" she asked.

"Why not?" he exploded. "If you were a boy, I'd tell you why not across your rear end."

Her lip started to quiver and he immediately collected her into his arms. "Sorry, I shouted," he apologized quickly, giving her a kiss on the cheek. "But I want you to listen to me, and remember what I say."

We furrowed our brows.

His message was like a scorpion sting. "There is never, ever, an excuse for bad manners!"

My resolve to be a better person was soon put to the test, and I fear that I failed it miserably. I arrived home from school one day just as a new family was moving in, and I knew from their clothes that they were German.

As I entered our house, I heard my mom's sweet voice from the kitchen. "Darling, is that you? Will you do me a quick favor?"

I said I would, and she appeared bearing a tray of tea and freshly-baked scones. "Would you pop these over to the new neighbors?"

"Gee, Ma," I balked, "they're Germans."

Her look reprimanded me better than anything she might have said.

"Okay, okay," I complained, "but what do I say to them?"

"Say 'welcome to our neighborhood,' " she suggested.

It was a small thing, but at the age of eight it was just not in me to be that good a person. But I did it. I did it for my mom. And I regret that my overriding concern was that one or other of the neighbors, heaven forbid any of my friends, would see me visiting 'the Nazis.'

Of course no one in the neighborhood knew anything about these people. They may have been the former Nazis that people said they were, but they may well not have been. Whatever the case, I knew that Mom was pushed to the limit to be civil, and I noticed that Ga, when she visited us, flatly refused to have anything to do with them.

Where we lived there were three loosely organized cliques of boys who hung out in the veld. These were known as *The Christians*, *The Jews*, and *The Immigrants*. Surprisingly, as I look back on it, there were not many Afrikaners living in our area. Had there been, a fourth group would surely have emerged. As things were, I belonged to *The Christians*. But in our squad we had David, a Jewish boy. And I was technically Jewish, or so Ga said. And we had Annatjie's brother, Koos, an Afrikaner, and Antonio, despite overtures extended to him to join *The Immigrants.*

Although there were only four Germans in the immigrant group — most German families, Pop said, kept their boys away from situations with the potential for being confrontational — they had the reputation for being tough, and we were all a little scared of them.

During one of our encounters in the veld, throwing stones at each other, we heard a hail for a cease-fire.

Our rivals warily approached us, and Hans Otto said he wanted to challenge "the Jew-boy" to a fight that would decide the battle.

Normally we loved hand-to-hand combats, but this one was out of the question. David, we argued, was half his size. We would choose our own contestant for the fight, we said.

No, they objected. It had to be "the Yid."

We firmly shook our heads and were already reaching for stones to resume our skirmish when we heard David's high-pitched voice. "I'll fight," he offered courageously.

We pleaded with him to step down. "He'll kill you," Tiaan yelled.

But David didn't flinch. When the signal was given he ran at the stronger boy, sprang in the air like a monkey, and locked his legs around the head of his antagonist. Both lads fell to the ground, but David clung to his opponent like a barnacle. With his sturdy legs he applied the squeeze of a constrictor snake.

Some moments passed and the face of the bigger boy started to turn dangerously red. His eyeballs bulged, and after two or three minutes the veins in his head appeared as if they might explode.

"Do you give up?" David screamed at him.

The German grunted like a pig, and Koos rushed in and pried the brawlers apart. The big lad gasped, and desperately drew air into his tortured lungs. He wiped the snot from his face, reached up in agony, and placed his hands over his red, burning ears.

"Do you want to fight again?" David screeched, waving a menacing karate hand in the air — we had never seen this side of him.

His victim looked up and shook his head convincingly.

"Okay, but I'll have your Cracker Jack collection," David dictated in a final humiliation. In our African whiteboy circles, I am ashamed to say, we defeated our opponents with dishonor.

Defeat Without Dishonor

*T*he guiding light of his existence as a boy, Kat told me — as he stood on one leg, and clutched the foot of the other behind his back, a stance he commonly assumed — was "Xhosa Christianity." This, he explained, revolved around Christian beliefs that were tempered by the credence given to spirits, tribal customs, the laws of nature, and the powers of the 'witch doctor.' The latter, when I was young, was regarded by Europeans as a pagan oddity. However, in today's more-enlightened world traditional healers are being asked to recommend plants for cutting-edge research on anti-cancer drugs, and to point out edible roots and wild fruits that will help eliminate starvation in Africa. At the present time, as in the past, most African medicine men and women lack formal academic training, but possess a broad base of knowledge passed down through the generations.

A notable aspect of tribal custom and adaptive Christianity, Kat said, related to the honoring of ancestors, those deceased members of the clan regarded, more or less, as 'saints.' Africans, he indicated, had long believed in a Creator God — the Xhosa *Qamatha,* the Sotho *Modimo,* the Bushman *Kaggen* — and a life after death in which the soul was conceptualized as *moya,* literally the 'wind,' but perhaps more appropriately translated, Kat insisted, as the "heavenly wind." Some held that the Supreme Being, the "Divine One," as Kat said, could be approached via the spirits of the dead. But this, he smiled, had a little of the idiom of myth. The more pervasive practice of honoring ancestors, by sacrifice or other rituals, Kat informed me, was a symbolic expression of loyalty to the family, the need to respect elders, and the high value placed on preserving harmony within the clan. Tradition held that discord within a kinsman group dishonored one's predecessors, and brought ill fortune, even sickness, to the perpetrator. The opposite, he said, was also true.

Embedded within their faith, Xhosa beliefs such as these — in being at one with nature and the Earth, in moral codes, and spiritual wellness — posed no conflict to Christian Africans. In fact, in one of our philosophical discussions, Kat implied that many Africans believed that Christian teachings sometimes fell short of their specified objectives. For example, Africans have a heightened awareness of the dignity of man, he said. In Xhosa culture it is a sin to unnecessarily humiliate a fellow human being, even a foe. This message, Kat considered, should be more strongly emphasized in Christian Bible classes. And Madiba recollected, in *Long Walk to Freedom,* that even as a boy he had defeated his opponents "without dishonoring them."

"I am a Xhosa Christian," Kat said, on another day, as we sat under a tree eating honey stolen from wild bees that he had smoked from their hive, "but I also try to follow some of the teachings of Buddha."

"Like what?" I asked.

"Like striving to avoid an impure mind," he replied, and went on to quote one of The Buddha's insights: " 'If the mind is impure, it will cause the feet to stumble along a footpath that is rough and difficult; there will be many falls and much pain. But if the mind is pure, the path will be smooth and the journey peaceful.' "

"That has the ring of Xhosa Buddhism," I commented.

Kat laughed, but on that occasion added nothing further.

Like my white friends and me, Kat, Madiba, and their young African colleagues were born free and grew up free. They had the same great feral joy as us at just being alive. They had their customs and traditions and we had ours, but the rudiments of our lives, even our political and religious beliefs, were not that different. We were all well served by our experiences in the veld, by the eye-to-eye contact we had with nature, and by the wisdom and solid values of our family upbringings. In a perfect world we would have mixed, learned from each other, and pulled together in an integrated society. But even as it was, tending to our own affairs, our basic values were very similar. And if we had been spared from crossing paths with unscrupulous Afrikaner politicians, we might all have gone on to lead relatively trouble-free lives. But that, of course, was not to be.

That Infamous Election Day

In 1948, as I said, the Afrikaner National Party came to power, and on that infamous Election Day I trudged to the home of some mates to get a drink after playing in the parched veld. I was eight. Mr. Potts, the father of my two companions, met us at the door. He had a slender glass of sherry in his hand. He raised it in our direction. "To His Majesty, the King," he toasted.

We kids began to laugh, but smartly clammed when we saw that Mr. Potts was not sharing our mirth.

"Start packing your bags, boys," he announced. "We're moving to Australia."

"Australia?" the two of them sang in unison.

"That's right!" he thundered with feeling.

When I recounted the story at home that night, my dad turned to me in silence.

"Are we going too, Pop," I asked, "to Australia?"

He placed both hands over his eyes, then looked at me again. "No," he responded sadly, "but we probably should be."

Part 7

MY JEWISH GA

A Bloody Yid

I will never forget a day when, at the age of ten, my grandmother announced that I was old enough "to know a few things." She was visiting us, which she did each year to escape the worst of the wet winter weather in Cape Town, and opened the discussion by inquiring whether my mom had ever given me an account of her side of the family.

I asked what she meant.

"Well," she went on, "did she ever tell you where Old-Granny was from?" She was referring to her mom, my great-grandmother, who had died the year before.

"She was from Cape Town," I said.

"No, no," my grandmother disagreed. "That's where you remember her always living, but she wasn't from there at all. Both her and your great-grandfather came from Breslau, in Germany. They were German Jews."

I reacted with an involuntary shudder. She had often made mention of the fact that I was technically Jewish, but I had never quite understood the term, nor how exactly it applied to me. My friend David was Jewish to be sure; he went to shul, and I had been to his brother's bar mitzvah, a very Jewish affair. But I had always thought that I was exclusively Christian. No one ever referred to me as a 'Yid,' or a 'bloody Yid,' as they usually said, not that they did so to David either, at least not after his fight.

I hesitated before asking a dreaded question. "So...so...so am I technically German as well?"

"Not really," Ga said, shaking her head, "at least no more so than the British Royal Family."

I was highly relieved by her reply. And although I was curious, I quickly resolved not to pursue any further this unfortunate matter of my German heritage.

But she continued. "I only wish you could have met your great-grandfather, 'Other-Granny,' as your mother named him." She paused and smiled. "He and your great-grandmother were very cultured," she said, "with a big house full of classical music, old books, and the most marvelous paintings. Jews, in those days, were people of standing in Germany." She talked about the way things were, about the "genteel tone," at the time, of this proud corner of Europe, about my great-grandfather being a connoisseur of

Romanesque and Gothic art, and about my great-uncle being a First Class recipient of the Iron Cross.

Then her expression changed as she went on to tell me how racial and ethnic attitudes had subsequently reversed in Germany, about Adolf Hitler's assault on the Jews, about the barbaric goings-on in the death camps — toddlers thrown alive into pits of burning bodies, she said — and about the gruesome end to the Warsaw uprising in Poland.

"How do you know all this?" I asked with some skepticism.

"Because there are people still alive today who saw what happened, a few lucky survivors. *'Yiddin fashreibt!'* Jews write! they were instructed. And I have read a lot of what they wrote."

I nodded, barely able to absorb the horrors that filled my head.

"There were those who were not afraid of dying," she said. "They knew they'd be murdered and become *kedoshim,* martyrs; they'd seen so many other people die." She paused and wiped a tear from her eye. "Only one thing scared them," she went on, "the dreaded thought of being forgotten. A *Shoah,* millions dead, and no one left to report the Annihilation."

"But why did God let it happen?" I asked, now also in tears.

She shrugged. "Is there a God?" Her eyes pierced mine.

"Yes," I replied in an emphatic tone.

"Those people, my people, also thought so," she said. "And they believed that God would swallow the killers with gaping earthquakes, or strike them dead with jagged lightning bolts. Even the Nazis were afraid at first."

"And what happened?"

"Nothing happened! Nothing at all! So the sadists relaxed and killed more people, men, women, and beautiful children; on sunny days like this, when the little ones should have been out playing."

"But everyone has a conscience," I said. "What about that?"

She gaped at me, surprised by my question. "Killing a Jew," she answered after a moment, "appeared to trouble the Nazi conscience less than yours or mine might do if we stood on an ant."

"But I'm sometimes sorry when I stand on ants," I argued.

"Then a better analogy, a better comparison," she offered, "might be squishing a cockroach. 'Good riddance,' our minds would likely say, and we'd go on to squish the next cockroach, and the next."

I was about to comment further, but we were interrupted. "Hello Ga," Joy called, tripping into the room and presenting our grandmother with a hug. "Can you also tell me about squishing cockroaches?" She and my mom had just returned from shopping.

"Give your mother a hand," Ga said, motioning to me.

My mom was standing at the bedroom door with packages in both hands. "And what have you two been up to?" she asked, her dark eyes flashing.

"Nothing," I replied. "We were just talking about killing Jews in Germany and Poland."

She turned to Ga. "You'll give him nightmares," she scolded.

"*Yiskor!*" my grandmother hissed in a tone that made me jump.

"What does that mean?" Joy asked, also startled.

My mother pursed her lips, and looked down at her feet before speaking. "It means we must remember," she explained in a shrill voice. "We must remember the Holocaust, the killing of the Jews and other innocent civilians in Europe, in World War II. We must remember, so that we can be sure that it never happens again."

"Unfortunately," Ga said, "I fear it happening again, right here in our dear South Africa. That's why we were talking about it."

I had heard her discussing the Holocaust just a week before, with the *Smous*, the Jewish hawker, or "peddler" I think Pop referred to him, who called on us from time to time. Ga had invited him in for tea.

Ceylon Tea

*O*n another day when Ga and I were having tea — actually she was drinking Ceylon tea; I had an egg flip — I posed a question that made her think. I knew this to be the case before she even admitted it, because she looked out, beyond the verandah, and studied our weeping willow prior to answering. And even then her response was preceded by a question of her own. "Have you looked in the dictionary to see what it means?"

"It's not there."

"*Apartheid,*" she said at length, "is really just a word, an Afrikaans word. It translates literally as 'apartness,' or 'separateness.'"

I inclined my head to show that I was listening.

She stared out once more. "But I know what you're asking, and it's making me think." When she spoke again it was in a whisper, half talking to herself. "It's rather an innocuous term," she said, "nothing more than a linguistic quirk."

Now I was really lost, and hard-pressed to stay silent. But she raised a hand and I knew better than to interrupt.

"Look," she said at last in language I could follow, "it's not the word, it's how the government is using it, to make Afrikaners look like the good people, and everyone else, especially the Natives, appear bad."

"But you said *apartheid* means separateness. How does that fit with what they're doing?"

"It's the basis of a philosophy to execute an aim," she answered. "The Nats" — the Afrikaner National Party — "are separating everyone, Blacks from Whites, the black tribes from each other, and even English- and Afrikaans-speaking white people. You've seen how your friends, Koos and Annatjie, were taken from your school and placed in an Afrikaans one. That's a part of it."

"Their parents moved them there," I protested.

"No! Their parents had no choice in the matter. It's happening all over the country. And there are a lot worse things going on as well."

"Like what?" I asked.

"Well, you don't see it much around here, but it's quite common where I live, Whites married to Coloureds I mean. And the government is breaking up these marriages. Even worse, they're splitting up families. Light-skinned kids are being sent to white schools, and darker children in the same family to black schools."

"And who do they stay with," I asked, "these kids?"

"With one parent or the other; Whites in white suburbs. But those the government declare black, now have to live in new areas of their own."

I was confused. "What new areas?" I asked. "The Natives have always lived in the townships."

"Yes," she admitted, "but again that's more of a Jo'burg thing. And the point is that it was never really enforced by law. Coloureds with enough money could live, more of less, wherever they liked."

"Anyway, I don't understand it," I complained. "And I don't see how *apartheid* does all this. You said yourself it was just a word."

"It's the action behind the word," she tried to explain. "It's almost like a code with a hidden message, like the 'black spot,' the symbol your rival school group used. Do you remember telling me about that, about that bridge you built with David and Antonio?" She loved David and Antonio. 'They come from good European stock,' she would say.

I said I did. I remembered 300 man-hours of construction all too well.

"And you recall that in *Treasure Island* anyone who was given the black spot would be killed?"

"Yes," I said.

"Well the black spot for the Jews in Germany was the *Hakenkreuz,* the Swastika. Just seeing it became a message of death. And the Nazis also used words as well, words of deception. Like *endlösung,*" she added after a pause. "It meant the 'end result,' the 'final solution.' It was pretty innocent-sounding, just like *apartheid*. But *endlösung* became the code for killing all the Jews in Europe."

I gulped. "So will the Afrikaner government try to kill all the Natives in South Africa?"

"No," she replied. "But they'll drive them out of places like this. They're already talking about their own 'black spots,' Blacks living in what they say are white areas. There'll come a time, if this mob stays in power, when you won't see too many Natives in cities like Johannesburg. They'll just keep those they need to work on the mines. The rest will be sent back to the Transkei, or Zululand, or wherever the government chooses. South Africa will be a Whites-Only country. Natives will need passports and special permission to work here. And they'll be regarded as *untermenschen,* just like the Jews were in the early days of Mr. Hitler's Germany."

"Oh *ja,* and what does that word mean?"

"It means 'undesirables,' or even worse, 'sub-humans,' " she explained. "And don't use that word, *'ja.'* It's 'yes' when you're speaking English, not *'ja.'* Your grandfather would have had a fit."

"Yes. Sorry Ga. And us, what will they call English people?"

She laughed. " *'Rooineks,'* I suppose, just like the *Boers* referred to the British soldiers in the Boer War, because of their red, sunburned necks. And we'll be trivialized as well, considered unimportant, although not to the extent of the Natives. They're even having their history stolen from them. Do you remember us talking the other evening about Great Zimbabwe?"

Great Zimbabwe

*T*he conversation had begun soon after my dad arrived home from work. Joy and my mom had joined Lizzie in the kitchen to bake a cake for Joy's birthday. I had spent the afternoon playing in the veld, and was lying, dog-tired, on the carpet, when Ga and my dad began talking.

She, for the second time since arriving, had raised the ticklish question of us being placed in private schools. "I'm concerned," she said, "about the propaganda the Nats are dispensing to schoolchildren." She hailed from a family of teachers, and although she had chosen business as a profession for herself, she was very interested in the academic world, and kept a finger on the pulse of what was happening in education. 'A good school,' she often said, 'is the warp and woof of a gentleman.'

"What type of propaganda?" my dad asked.

My grandmother looked at Pop from the corners of her eyes. She knew that he was well aware of the fact that Afrikaner teachers had been placed in English-speaking schools, and that history now had an increasing focus on the Afrikaner. "The early Dutch settlers and the French Huguenots, fair enough," she said, "but the contemporary *Boer* is being projected as the triumphant torchbearer on the continent."

"So," Pop queried, "where does that leave us?"

"With your dear children now learning more about the *Voortrekkers* than about the two Great Wars."

"There's no harm in a little emphasis on South African history."

"Come on Bill," Ga responded. "You know very well what I mean. With the Afrikaner now a national icon, the Englishman in Africa is being relegated to the underdog."

"At least he's deemed worthy of mention."

They exchanged smiles. She knew that he loved playing devil's advocate, and she told him so.

Pop laughed aloud. "It's just that the local school is so handy," he said, "and so conveniently inexpensive."

"If money's the issue…"

"That's very generous of you," my dad interrupted, touching her arm affectionately. "But no. And you'll be pleased to learn that I've been thinking about this school-change thing ever since our last little chat. I'll look into it, I promise."

My grandmother sighed, and appeared hugely relieved. She reached for her needlework and began stitching. "In some ways what bothers me even more," she started on a slight topic departure, "are the lies they're telling black youngsters."

"Lies?" Pop questioned with a spark of new interest.

"Yes, Hansie and Trixie tell me," she said, referring to her sisters, Johanna and Beatrix, both of whom were school teachers, "that the African of the past is being denied even the most mediocre acclaim. He's being projected as a warmonger and a waster, a scoundrel, a transgressor of treaties, a venomous snake in the grass. Africans have no culture, the kids are told, no past achievements, nothing constructive to contribute to this country, and therefore have no legitimate claim to any part of its wealth."

She paused to let Pop comment, but he gestured for her to continue.

"African kids are being informed that their ancestors were little more than troublesome intruders to South Africa. That they had haphazardly migrated from the lower-Saharan north in a move to the subcontinent, they say, which coincided with the arrival of the first Dutch settlers."

"My God, what myth," Pop spat. "Exaggerated myth, if there's such a thing. We've both seen Great Zimbabwe. Do you remember when that was built?"

"In about 1300," she answered, "more than three hundred years before Jan Van Riebeeck landed at the Cape."

"And the Bushmen have been here for thousands of years," Pop added. "Some archaeologists say…"

"But the San aside," my grandmother interrupted, "let me tell you what Hansie says they're onto about Great Zimbabwe. They're telling the kids that it was built by the Arabs."

"By Arabs?" my dad cried. "What about all that work by David Randall-MacIver and Gertrude Thompson? They concluded that all of the Lost Cities were African in every detail."

Ga smiled. "So much for the exhaustive studies of British archaeologists."

"Misinformation," Pop went on after a long silence. "But to tell you the truth, I'm surprised they even mention Great Zimbabwe at all."

"I suppose only because it's too big to hide. Hansie says that in the workshop she attended, the speaker, an Afrikaner, went into detail about its towering walls of finely chiseled stone, its architecturally-inspiring buttresses, and decorative turrets. 'Certainly the work of highly intelligent people,' she said, 'an advanced civilization.'"

"But not African?"

"Of course not," Ga affirmed sarcastically.

Pop shook his head and turned to me. "What do you say about going to a new school?"

"No problem," I replied, raising my head from the rug. Even my young mind was outraged by what I had just heard. Willful deception was bad enough, but robbing children of their proud history, in the manner Ga had related, was more than I could stomach. She had told me about Great Zimbabwe and the other medieval cities of the black kings, and used an atlas to show me their ancient trade routes, merchant thoroughfares that extended as far afield as Arabia, India, and China.

A New School

"I'm going to a new school," I announced as my mom rang a small brass bell and Lizzie appeared from the kitchen bearing a roast. "I hope it's the way *Missus* likes it," she said, then left.

"Which school?" Joy inquired, getting right to the point.

I winced. I could not believe I had not asked. I looked to Ga for a lifeline.

"We don't know yet," she offered quickly. "There's bound to be a good Jewish school within reach."

"A Jewish school?" Joy questioned, turning up her nose.

"It could be a Catholic school," Pop suggested.

"But we're not Catholics either."

"Hush child," my mom prompted soothingly. Like Xhosa mothers she liked accord, and to help ensure it she herself was painfully unassertive, slow even to offer opinions. 'She has an inferiority complex,' I had overheard Ga whisper to my dad on another day. 'It's her German background of course; she'd like to forget it.' Pop had raised an eyebrow. 'And now that the war is over, I suppose it will be her Jewishness that plagues her,' he'd said. 'The bloody Nats are almost as anti-Semitic as anti-Black.'

But as reticent as Mom usually was, except about things like the gemsbok, this occasion proved to be different. She stood tall and spoke up confidently. "I think a Catholic school will be perfectly fine," she said.

My grandmother lit up at her self-assuredness. "I agree," she advanced to support her. "A Catholic school is the obvious choice. I don't know why I didn't think of it in the first place. The Roman Catholics have just recently taken a firm stand against the Nats."

"Are the Nats the Nationalist Party," Joy asked, "or is that a fib?"

"It's no fib," Ga replied, turning to her with a shining look. "And that's a very clever question. Actually, it's the 'National Party,' the 'new' National Party. But a lot of people say 'Nationalist P...'"

"Was there an 'old' National Party?" I interjected.

"Another good inquiry," she acknowledged. "Yes, it's a little confusing. In 1934, General Hertzog's 'old' National Party merged with the South African Party, the old Smuts party, to form the United Party."

"That's our party, the English party?" I submitted proudly.

"Yes," she reassured me. "But remember that though General Smuts was a hero of two world wars, he was born and bred an Afrikaner. And a lot of Afrikaners fought in World War II, and support the United Party." She then asked if my teachers talked much about politics in school.

"A bit," I replied. "The other day Miss Vlok said something about the purified Nationalist Party."

"Yes, the Purified National Party. That's what Dr. Malan, our new prime minister, often refers to it as."

"Tell me again why we don't like the Nats," Joy went on in a very mature voice.

Our eyes twinkled. "Because they're ruining the bloody country, that's why," I offered, repeating what I so often heard at home.

Pop softly clapped his hands, but his spirited face quickly paled and took on a more serious expression. "Ian's right," he acknowledged in response to my comment. "We fought a war to make the world a better place. We bust a gut to ease racial tensions. There were a lot of Native soldiers on our side, all volunteers, and we wanted them to be treated better when they got back. But now the bloody Nats are devouring our good work like parasites, like a swarm of blood-sucking tsetse flies."

"Talking about fighting a war," my mom tendered, "you might like to ask your old tank-corps pal, George, to dinner tomorrow evening. Anneka mentioned that they were sending Tiaan to Marist Brothers College."

The ladies were in the kitchen again, preparing dessert snacks.

George raised his glass. "To your new school," he toasted, extending a warm smile in my direction.

I thanked him and said how pleased I was to have at least one friend going there.

"Yes, and I'm sorry Tiaan couldn't come this evening," he apologized. "He didn't want to miss his violin lesson."

"Do they have music at Marist Brothers?" my grandmother asked, entering the room.

"They certainly do," George replied. "Their whole curriculum is based on a European model, sports and academics alike."

"Good," my grandmother acknowledged. "But our main objective," she said, "is to get away from the political propaganda that seems to be creeping into the government schools."

"Don't tell me about it," George said, raising his eyes to the ceiling.

"And to think that the writing was on the wall right from the start," my grandmother lamented. "All we had to do was read, study the résumés of the Nat cabinet ministers, and take note of their actions."

The three of them shook their heads, and I followed suite.

"The action that augured it for me," George offered after the pause, "was the pardoning of Robey Leibbrandt. No sooner were the *Jaaps* in office than he was out." George was referring to the government's release of a wartime traitor. He had trained in Germany as a saboteur, then returned to join the *Ossewa-Brandwag,* an underground organization that was dedicated at the time to undermining support for the Allies. Veterans like George and my dad branded Leibbrandt and his henchmen, 'The Rats.'

"What did he do?" I asked.

"While our men were being mobilized for the front," Pop roared, "sods like him were signaling German U-boats that troop ships were about to sail. I'd like to have put a bayonet through his gullet!"

"Me too," George asserted harshly. He turned to my grandmother. "And you're right, Regina," he added, "about taking note of the actions of our new leaders. Leibbrandt's release said it all!"

"And that's when I should have left," Pop groaned, adjusting his glasses, "moved to Australia, or taken the Old Lady back to the Isle of Man."

"Well it's too late now," the other vet chortled. "You can't get your money out. The race is over, and The Rats have won!"

While we all laughed at this, I waited expectantly for Ga to comment on what Pop had just said about returning to the Isle of Man. I was old enough to gather that she had desperately wanted us to emigrate as soon as the ill-omened election results had appeared, to reunite with her English side of the family. I remembered the frantic phone calls from Cape Town, and how upset my mom had been.

But Ga was far too diplomatic to broach the matter now. Instead she returned to the discussion of Leibbrandt's acquittal. "Releasing that Nazi," she said angrily, "was a sharp slap in the face for all South Africans, Black and White, all of us who supported the struggle for freedom."

"Yes," George agreed, "and talking about Natives and Nazis, did you hear on the news this evening that Doctor Verwoerd has just been appointed Minister of Native Affairs?"

"Oh no," my grandmother wailed, placing a hand over her face. "I've dreaded the day I'd hear this."

"*Die Pofadder*," my dad expounded, using a moniker often branded about in our English-speaking circles. A *pofadder*, puff adder, is a hog-nosed African snake.

"Yes, and I fear his poisonous venom," Ga spat, responding to Pop's prompt. She turned to George. "I'm not sure if I told you that Julie, my old mom, bless her soul, predicted that Doctor Verwoerd would be our next prime minister. She always saw him as the immoral strategist, the instigator and enforcer of *apartheid*. She said he made her flesh crawl."

"And rightly so. I can tell you for a start," George said, "that like that Leibbrandt rat, *Pofadder* has also spent time in Germany, studying all the wrong things of course."

"I believe you," Ga responded. "Julie told me that she'd heard from a reliable source that he'd supported letting Nazis in, and at the same time strongly opposed Jewish immigration to South Africa."

"Yes, I've also heard that said," George agreed, "and a lot more, like inappropriate remarks to students when he was a professor. 'Quite out of line,' Anneka told me. You know that she was a *Matie*?" — a *Matie* was a student at the University of Stellenbosch, where Dr. Verwoerd once taught.

Ga nodded. "Yes, you've mentioned it."

Anneka, Joy, and my mom came in from the kitchen, and we all sat down to dinner.

"Another toast," George proposed, "to Marist Brothers College."

"*Prost*," my grandmother cheered, lifting her wine glass in my direction. "To Tiaan, Ian, and the Brothers."

Part 8

BOXER & BROTHER YANK

Marist Brothers College

Ga saw things in the unambiguous terms of World War II, good versus evil. And in her political world of encroaching evil, Marist Brothers College was good. She had started off by buttressing my mom's intuition on a suitable choice of school, but quickly began reading up on what the Roman Catholic Church was doing to combat racism. She was pleased with what she found, and elated when my learning institution began to turn out even better than she might have imagined.

There was considerable emphasis on sport at my new school and, much to my mother's delight, this put an abrupt end to my ramblings in the veld. And Mom's infectious sanction of my new lifestyle, in turn, added to my grandmother's exuberance.

Pop was just as happy. I had taken up boxing, an endeavor that met with his enthusiastic approval. He had always been interested in it, he said, but had never had the opportunity to pursue it himself. He knew Jack O'Malley, the boxing coach, by reputation, and was in a state of high excitement when I was selected to join his training squad.

And the largely Irish-Catholic brothers, having endured the "tyranny of the Protestant English," as they said, had an identifying sympathy for "the downtrodden Blacks," and fed us a steady diet of *apartheid* disapproval, just what Ga and Pop had wanted of a private school. In fact, the family was so enchanted by my progress that they soon enrolled Joy at the Assumption Convent, Maryvale, a Catholic school for girls.

It was about a four-mile bicycle ride to my new college, and the route took me up Louis Botha Avenue, the main thoroughfare between the downtown area of Johannesburg and Alexandra township, which was not far from where we lived. Madiba stayed in Alexandra as a pre-law student — after graduating from high school in the Transkei — and although I was unaware of it at the time, we had already lived in the same city, and at times been virtual neighbors, for more than a decade. We would ultimately live within a stone's throw of each other for sixteen years.

On my bicycle ride each morning and late afternoon after sport, I was one of a handful of white schoolboys amongst thousands of black cyclists on their way to and from work. A similar large number of township dwellers traveled into the center of Johannesburg by bus. Others, like Madiba, often walked to save their bus fares. Some even strode barefooted, carrying their precious shoes.

From Alexandra to the city center was a good six miles, and it was a tiring ordeal for the older folk. Many cyclists would alight and walk up the twisting hills, sweating in summer. And in the winter it was dangerous flying off the ridge, after work, in the freezing dark.

Almost everyone who traveled my route on a regular basis was aware of bicycle fatalities, so it was an agonizing decision for Pop to allow me to ride at all. Mom had badly wanted me to use the bus. There were no school buses as such, but an excellent 'Whites-Only' trolley service. These electrified versions of red London double-deckers whisked their patrons past the green diesel-spewing hogs from the townships.

Although most of my colleagues traveled in the comfort of the splendid trolley buses, I had protested. "Buses are for sissies," I'd argued. And Pop had agreed. But he had another reason for letting me cycle. I overheard him present it to Ga one evening before dinner. "It gives him a peep," he said, "of how hard life is for the Natives. These kids need to see something of how the other half lives."

And in retrospect, I know I did. But at the time the ride for us was little more than fun and, as Tiaan said, "good exercise." We weaved in and out of the vast stream of cyclists, racing anyone who cared to challenge us. Sometimes on hills, for a dare, we would muscle in amongst the African riders, and cling to the sides of slow-moving trucks. "Two bob says grab a lorry," one of us might yell. This would provide us with a piggyback ride up the steep pass that led onto the crested rise where our school was. My dad had observed the practice and cautioned me against it. "Don't even think of hitching rides on lorries," he'd warned.

As time went on, cycling to school became routine. But it was never easy, especially on winter mornings. It was cold when we left home. However, we had learned from the Africans that a good way to cut the biting wind was to stuff newspapers into our jerseys. And on particularly bitter days, when the ground was white with frost, we turned our school blazers back to front. This looked strange, but was less uncomfortable than one might think. We wore woolen gloves but our fingers still froze, and when our hands thawed in the heat of the classroom the pain was terrible. It was at times like that, that we sometimes wondered how the Africans managed without gloves; and so, in a small way, I suppose that, even as children, we did begin to think about how the 'other half' lived.

When it rained on our way to school we tried to ignore it. We had found that wearing plastic raincoats on the hill climbs was a waste of time; it made us sweat, and the result was a soaking from the inside. Either way, we would sit and, literally, steam in the heat of the classroom, and take flak from the brothers for not using the bus. We, of course, recognized our imprudent choice, but the worse the weather the greater the chance was that someone would ask: "Hey, did you come in by bike today?" And at that age it would have been more than our lives were worth to have had to say no.

*T*he Marist Brothers had run schools in South Africa since 1867. They had three in Johannesburg, and I was at their Observatory campus that we schoolboys referred to as 'Obs.' There were a few lay teachers at Obs, like Mr. O'Malley, who dressed in street clothes, but the majority of our instructors were brothers, and the long monk-like robes they wore, even when coaching us on the sports fields, broadcast their identity.

Unlike the government school I had previously attended, sport was a big issue at Obs. In fact, organized games, the discipline required to master them, and the teamwork, physical activity, and competition associated with playing them were considered to be essential components of our education. And, as in life, we were told, the best players won.

This suited me just fine. But I was surprised to learn, from having overheard a conversation between Pop and Ga, that this sport-oriented philosophy was also typical both of private schools in Great Britain and their colonial counterparts in Africa, including the many mission schools that existed for Blacks. Unfortunately, Pop had said, the future of Healdtown looked precarious. He was referring to a Methodist institution that Madiba had attended. Ga had agreed, saying that the Nats would never put up with its multiracial staff, or the liberal ideas that were taught there. It was a 'crying shame,' she said, the school, founded in 1855, was almost one-hundred years old. 'Well,' Pop had bewailed, 'I guarantee it won't last another hundred, not with *Pofadder* on the warpath.'

Every boy at Obs was expected to participate in at least one summer and one winter activity, and we were all encouraged to play at least one team sport. The ability to contribute successfully to a team, one of the brothers told us, was central to every worthwhile endeavor in life.

Another quality we were supposed to reap from team sports was leadership. Each side had a captain, and it was he, not the coach, who made decisions on strategy during a game. In practices we were all given a chance to be captain.

There was a place to be had on a team, and coaching, for every would-be athlete, regardless of his talent. I played — and showed a particular lack of skill at — rugby, South Africa's national sport. I attributed my poor form, at least in part, to the fact that over my single-season career I was the second smallest boy on the Under 13B team. But being a runt was a lame excuse. My friend Serge DuPont, a boy of even lesser stature than me, emerged as one of our stars.

On the playing fields we enjoyed a spirited mood that was in complete contrast to the often-oppressive atmosphere of the classroom, where strict discipline was enforced by corporal punishment. Out of doors the brothers showed a completely different face, tolerating and even encouraging all forms of merriment, hilarity, skylarking, and horseplay. But although we were fully expected to have fun, we were also strongly encouraged to defeat our neighboring schools at every level of competition. This was especially true of our sister school, Marist Brothers Inanda — the third school in the group was small and did not pose a threat. However, to say that there was a friendly rivalry between Obs and Inanda would have been to grossly underestimate the situation. "In looking back on it now," Tiaan said, years later, "it was more like unrelenting war."

When we played cricket or rugby against Inanda, practically every brother in the school was there to cheer us on. Cricket games were held on Saturdays and took all day. And although matches frequently ended in a draw, typical of cricket, the brothers stayed until the death. If we won, there was great rejoicing. A victory would be announced at assembly on Monday, and individuals who had excelled in the game would be mentioned by name and, if they had earned it, given a prize. There was a subtle form of bribery at play; a century — one-hundred runs — at cricket, for example, fetched a new bat, a much-coveted item. I clocked up a half-century once, and that got me a ball.

The glory of a win against Inanda extended beyond the playing fields and the assembly quadrangle. One could count on a series of honorable mentions by the various brothers who rotated through our classrooms each day to teach us different subjects. It was not uncommon for an instructor to interrupt a class in session with an undisguised comment of praise. A discussion on Lord Tennyson's *Charge of the Light Brigade*, in an English lesson, for example, might be compared to the charge made 'into the jaws of death' by a boy in scoring a try on the rugby field.

A sporting victory could even have the brothers addressing the heroes amongst us by our nicknames — at our school these were common. The fastest sprinter on our track team, for instance, was reverently known as Streak, and his younger brother, also an outstanding runner, was Little Streak. There was Compton, after the great English batsman Dennis Compton, and a host of others. A pet name, once acquired, usually held for all the time that one was at school, and often beyond it.

I was Boxer. This was earned on the merits of my first boxing tournament when I became the featherweight champion of the school. My mom, with her gentle ways, was less than happy about me being branded a fighter, but Pop, half tongue-in-cheek, explained that all boys needed "a means of self-defense."

The boxing club was the only one that met in school hours. So being a member of the fraternity entitled me, on boxing days, to escape from any class in session a full hour before lessons ended. Some of the older boys speculated that Jack O'Malley, our trainer, a big red-faced man, insisted on an early hour for boxing so that he could be home in time to enjoy his sundowner.

The word on Mr. O'Malley was that, as I already knew from Pop, he had once been a boxer of some acclaim in his native Ireland. It was abundantly clear to us that boxing was the focus of his existence. He was totally dedicated to the sport and spent long hours helping boys who were prepared, as he said, "to work for what they wanted."

Jack O'Malley had an artificial leg, but this did not stop him from excitedly hobbling around outside the ring, even when we were only sparring, and shouting instructions to us as we fought. My fond memory of him is in a boxer's stance next to the ropes, jabbing his clenched fists in the air as he carefully corrected our every move with his own shadow-boxing motions.

But in contrast to the patience he extended to his boys in the ring, when it came to exercising his duties of scholastic instruction, Jack O'Malley was a terror. Each morning he would enter the classroom with a lively limp, and cross himself as he moved towards his desk: "In the name of the Father, the Son, and the Holy Ghost." This was our cue to spring from our desks and hurriedly recite the Lord's Prayer. A Hail Mary followed, and while this was being said the non-Catholics — the Jewish boys, a lone Chinese lad in our class, and the likes of me — stood respectfully to attention. After prayers Mr. O'Malley would greet us with a hearty, "Good morning boys."

"Good morning, Mr. O'Malley," we would respond as a body.

If he lifted a cupped hand to his ear, we would enjoy repeating our greeting in vastly raised voices. After that it was all downhill.

The first ordeal of the day was a verbal defense of our homework. Any error invited his beckoning forefinger, and Mr. O'Malley shuffling about like Long John Silver, trying to reach into his right hip pocket for his heavy leather strap. He used this to beat us on the hands. The offending boy would stand stiffly at the front of the class and alternately extend one hand, then the other, for two, four, or six of the best, according to the seriousness of his error.

The boxers in the class, like me, were effectively spared. For a start we were seldom asked questions. And if perchance we were, the queries posed were so easy that we could not possibly get them wrong. Despite this, however, I managed to blunder.

"Sweet Mother o'God," Mr. O'Malley cursed in disgust.

He called me to the front.

"Boxer," he said, "you're a half-wit!"

The class laughed.

"What are you, boy?"

"A half-wit, sir."

The class laughed again.

"Half-wit or not," he continued, "we can't afford to risk the hands of a fighter, can we boy?"

"No sir."

Much to my humiliation, he had me bend over.

Occasionally one of the boys would skillfully sidetrack Mr. O'Malley into talking about boxing, and that would take care of the rest of the lesson. Over the course of time he discussed a large number of history's great men of the ring, legends like Joe Louis and Jack Dempsey. He had seen many of them fight and met several of them in person.

In the process of writing this book I saw Nelson Mandela interviewed by Larry King on American television. When the subject turned to boxing, I recognized a glint in the eye of the aging Mandela that took me back to my old teacher. Madiba, a boxer himself, was still an ardent boxing enthusiast. The names of a number of fighters were mentioned in the interview, and I was delighted to recognize them all. But more to the point, what I gleaned from that fervent TV discussion was that for people like Madiba, and Jack O'Malley, boxing was more than a sport; it was a passion.

It is still hard for me to believe that anyone would have dared to cheat in a test given by Mr. O'Malley. But the story went that he had once sat at his desk reading a newspaper while a quiz was in progress. The paper entirely covered his face, but unknown to the class, so it was said, he had cut a small peephole into the page. When a boy turned to view a neighbor's answer, the lad was confronted by a ghostly voice from behind the barrier. 'Looking for a flogging, Perez?' The boy withered. 'I didn't see a thing, sir,' he gawked. 'Good,' said Mr. O'Malley, and went back to his reading.

The brothers, as implied, were all Roman Catholic. Most of them were Irish, but there were some from other countries, like Germany, France, and the United States.

We had nicknames for the brothers which, naturally, were used only amongst ourselves. However, they sometimes learned of their cognomens and, as may be imagined, were often less than thrilled about them. Our fondly-regarded Brother Yank once gave us an undisguised reprimanding for our choice of his pseudonym. "Damned Yankees are from the North," he sneered. "I'm from the South, from Arkansas."

There were muted scoffs from the class, not so much at his statement, as at the strange way he pronounced his home State. It was the first time we had heard it enunciated by an American; we had always referred to it as 'Are-Kansas.'

"What's so funny?" he asked.

"Nothing, Brother." It was too complicated to explain.

"The original Yankees," he continued, "were the Union soldiers in the American Civil War...Northerners!"

He paused and we bowed our heads in silence.

"My family was on the other side," he pleaded desperately.

We offered our compassionate expressions.

But his name stuck. To us, all Americans were Yankees. That was just the way it was. Moreover, a nickname, once bestowed, was never changed, least of all on a hint from the recipient.

Brother Yank taught us English for a year, and if it was not the most academically-enriching class we ever took, it was certainly the most invigorating. In contrast to the drab styles of many of the other brothers, he made learning fun. "A dog's life," he said on one occasion, discussing speech in the vernacular.

We shrugged.

"You guys ever read about Sad Sack, in the comic books?"

"Yes, Brother," we laughed. Merely having him refer to us as 'you guys' amused us, but to have a teacher reference a comic book in an scholarly context was a pleasure sublime.

"Sad Sack leads a dog's life," he said. "Are you with me?"

"Yes Brother."

"Okay, another idiom: 'a dead man's hand,' or 'a bed of roses?' "

"A dead man's hand!" we all but shouted.

"It's the card hand Wild Bill Hickok was holding in the bar, Aces and Eights I think it was, when he was shot to death in 1876."

And so the classes went, in what seemed to us like a festivity of learning. We acquired information on all that was American, the National Park system, cars, presidents, baseball, and the fact that the United States held half the gold mined throughout history, most of it from South Africa, Brother Yank informed us. We ached to live in America.

I related some of what I'd heard about the States to Pop, and mentioned I might one day like to move there.

"A good choice," he said. "The bloody Yanks are marvelous. We'd never have won the war without them."

*T*he brothers took for granted that every student had some religious affiliation, and each day one lesson period was set aside for "Holy Scripture." Catholics and non-Catholics were separated at that time. The tutoring discourse for a non-Catholic, like me, pertained mainly to general bible study, with considerable emphasis on the Old Testament. This choice of curriculum, we assumed, was mainly for the benefit of the Jewish boys of whom there was a surprisingly large number, including David. His parents, impressed by what Ga told them of my experience, enrolled him the year after Tiaan and I had started.

Aside from this hour of religious instruction, the brothers tried to keep both religion and politics out of the classroom. But both crept in. The 'plight of the African' was commonly compared to the 'predicament of the Roman Catholic in Northern Ireland.' The 'Afrikaner *apartheid* scourge' had a parallel to 'the English Protestant axe.'

"We can only beseech our Holy Mother that here in South Africa the axe does not keep loping off heads for eight hundred years. For eight hundred years it fell in Ireland, boys...eight hundred years."

"Yes, Brother."

"Ireland has offered more than her fair share of martyrs, and I fear that the day will come when our black brothers will say the same thing here. Do ye hear me, boys?"

"Yes, Brother."

"Many an Irishman fought to his death, died for the freedom of Ireland. Did ye ever hear the name Cuchulain, boys, Cuchulain of Ulster?"

"No, Brother."

"More's the shame on ye. More's the shame."

And Brother Yank said it was "a disgrace" that Blacks and Whites were obliged to attend separate schools. "We have the same practice in parts of the States," he informed us, "but that doesn't make it right." He told us that we white boys were as much victims of *apartheid* as black students. "There is a lot you could learn from each other," he said, "and if you mixed more, you'd all be winners."

He was also upset by the money that had been spent on the construction of the Voortrekker Monument. This, a gigantic marble edifice the height of a twelve-story building, had been opened in 1949 to honor those who had taken part in the Great Trek — the Great Journey, a large exodus of *Boers* from British rule in the Cape; it was triggered by the abolition of slavery there in 1834. "Now I'm not saying that a country shouldn't honor its heroes," Brother Yank said, "but surely a hospital, or a library, would have served a better purpose."

The Voortrekker Monument

That night I mentioned what Brother Yank had said, and Pop went off on a rampage, calling the Monument "a monstrosity," and saying that besides being a waste of money, it was "both anti-British and anti-Black."

"And so, my darling," my mom smiled at length, "you'll just have to inform your dear Brother Yank that your father doesn't agree with him."

Ga laughed like a chime at Mom's unusual sarcasm, then went on to support Pop. "You're absolutely right, Bill," she said. "It's little more than a thinly-veiled shrine to *apartheid.*"

We boys decided to see for ourselves and were unexpectedly surprised. It was about a 20-mile bicycle ride to get there, a challenging pedal, and the site, with its commanding view, was an inviting place to stop for lunch. And besides, there was a host of interesting items to see, a spectacular *laager* — a circular battle encampment — of 64 granite ox-wagons, for one. The Monument became a favorite cycling rendezvous, a popular must-do on the schedules we drew up for school holidays.

We even planned one of our excursions there for 16 December, not to celebrate the *Boer* victory over the Zulus, but to check on something we had read. The Monument was designed, it was claimed, so that at noon on that celebration day each year a shaft of light would pierce a hole in the roof. The beam would strike a stone cenotaph that symbolized the resting place of those who had perished in the Great Trek, and sweep across an inscription of allegiance to *Suid-Afrika*. On the day of our visit we pushed our way to the front and waited doubtfully. But sure enough, precisely at noon, it happened just the way it was supposed to.

"It's a miracle," David proclaimed in delight, and everyone about us spontaneously applauded. There were notices everywhere requesting silence, but no one challenged the outburst.

We hung around for a while, and took in some of the festivities. The Day of the Covenant was an occasion that aroused strong emotions in Afrikaners, and everything we heard was expressed in very pious tones. It was all in Afrikaans, of course, but we understood enough to know what was going on. There was much said, on one hand, about God and the heroism of the *Voortrekkers* — the *Boer* pioneers — who brought civilization to the interior. And on the other, there was close to equal time given to the pagan, uncivilized, and treacherous ways of Dingane and the Zulu nation.

We had been taught about the *Voortrekkers* in our history classes at school, and I asked Ga about the brutal murder of Piet Retief, a *Boer* leader, by Dingane, the Zulu Chief.

"Of course, one cannot condone what happened," she said. "But in fairness to the Zulus," she went on, "and history is about impartial facts, one should know their side of the story."

"Their side of the story?"

"Yes," she said. "Prior to the killing of Piet Retief, the *Voortrekkers* had been in Zulu territory without permission. Moreover, Retief had visited the Zulu Chief and placed enormous pressure on him to cede a large tract of land to the *Boers*." She paused to check that I was following, and then continued. "While Retief waited for an answer to his request for new domain," she narrated, "another party of advancing Afrikaners attacked and defeated Mzilikazi, the headman of a neighboring tribe who had refused to grant them territory. At this point Piet Retief sent Dingane a message that many think was inappropriate. We know from God's Great Book, he said, that unwise kings like Mzilikazi are severely punished — not permitted long to live and reign."

Ga paused again. "Now what would you think about a letter worded like that?" she asked, before answering her own question. "Dingane undoubtedly perceived it as a threat. He was prepared to make certain concessions to the Whites, like permitting Christian missionaries to preach the word of God in his kingdom. But this potential settler, who was attempting to use intimidating witchcraft to trick him out of his precious realm, needed to be dealt with. The Zulus were well aware of the white man's greed for new territory," Ga said, and presented me with a statistic to support her point — over a span of some twenty years following the start of the Great Trek, she said, Europeans had almost doubled their area of settlement on the subcontinent.

She went on to tell me that Francis Owen, a missionary, had witnessed the massacre of the Retief party at the royal *kraal,* and told of it. "Dingane, not wanting to surprise the missioner," she said, "forewarned him, and explained his aversion to giving away Zulu land. He stated that in order to hold his dominion intact he needed to slay the visitors, but promised Father Owen that he would not be harmed and should not be alarmed."

I kept looking at her, not daring to interrupt.

"When a convenient moment presented itself," Ga continued, "Dingane gave the fateful order to his *impis,* a command to the effect of, 'Kill the wizards!' " She pointed at me. "He called them wizards, or sorcerers," she said, "and that's why I used the word 'witchcraft' a moment ago." She sat back and folded her arms, giving me a chance to comment.

I was shocked by her interpretation of the event and told her so.

"As I said," she made clear, "I'm not trying to condone the awful action of the Zulu Chief; he had a reputation for violence and cruelty. I'm just giving you a more balanced account of what happened, in the spirit of an historical record." She went on to tell me how the Afrikaner's increasingly one-sided version of past events was being used to spread bitterness between Whites and Blacks, and how our Prime Minister was mixing politics with religion.

" 'Our history,' Dr. Malan says, referring, naturally, to the history of the *Boer,* 'is the greatest masterpiece of the centuries.' And the reason why it's such a *tour de force,* our dear leader tells us, is that, and I quote him again," Ga said, " *'Afrikanerdom* is not the work of men, but the creation of God.' "

Part 9

LAND IN CRISIS

A Brooding Fascist

Although Ga disapproved of Dr. Malan as a leader, she was not afraid of him. "Politicians tend to wear masks," she said, "but at least one has the feeling that he believes in what he says." However, she did fear Dr. Verwoerd. He, now serving as a senator, was already preoccupied with his obsession of separating Blacks from Whites. And as a former professor of applied psychology, Ga related to me on the upstairs balcony of her large Victorian home in Cape Town, he was being very clever in how he went about it.

It had been several years since, on that winter day in Johannesburg, she had first introduced me to the political woes of my country, and now that I was older our discussions had become increasingly sophisticated. But although she employed more advanced notions and language to challenge me, she still stuck to her simple theme of systematically comparing the tragic history of her Jewish side of the family to the affairs of state she now saw jeopardizing my future. She could never forget that all of her kinfolk who had remained in Germany, as well as all but one who had fled to the Netherlands, had died in the Holocaust.

"And just as the Nazis did not immediately start off by killing Jews," she advanced on this occasion, "so the Afrikaner government has given us only a faint hint of where it is truly heading."

To educate myself for our little *tête-à-têtes*, as she referred to them, I had started reading newspapers. But I could never quite find in them the slant she presented. She had the advantage of a European perspective, of having observed, at close range, masters of the art of deception, like Hitler and Mussolini, and she thus had an insight that was lacking in most local journalists. I eagerly nodded for her to continue.

"Dr. Verwoerd argues, and this is very cunning," she said, "that the idea of separateness, he seldom uses the word *apartheid* of late, follows an inherent order of nature, and that all living things are its beneficiaries. Lions cling together in prides, he says, and do not mix with other predators. Similarly, the zebra profits from the camouflage and confusion of the herd, as does the gazelle. In other words, our doctor-professor makes a case for gregarious members of the animal kingdom congregating, but showing no instinctive urge to mix with other species."

I had an inkling of where the senator's shrewd strategy was going as Ga went on to confirm what I perceived his argument to be: that a similar natural pattern of separate development could be traced in human behavior. His contention, she said, was that ethnic similarity was the basis for the formation of hunting and gathering groups, and that these, in turn, were the building blocks for tribes. Nations, the next step in the progression, also evolved along partisan lines in pursuit of protection, economic advantage, and power. Partition held the key to success, and would benefit everyone, Dr. Verwoerd claimed, especially the various African tribes. Distinguished peoples like the Xhosas and the Zulus, he said, would be granted their own homelands. Here their councils would rule, and each tribe would preserve its individual identity.

Ga explained that the "false prophets of *apartheid*," as she referred to the Minister and his colleagues, had made a special appeal to the traditional chiefs and elders, offering to restore their lost wealth, power, and prestige. "At one point," she smiled, "he even attempted to sweeten the pie by promising to liberate Africans from, as he put it, 'the British plot' to turn them all into 'black Englishmen.' "

She went on to say that when presented in this guileful manner, *apartheid* had a certain seductive quality that was not unlike the golden rules of Marx on sharing and equality. She conceded, with lowered eyes, that as a girl she had expressed some interest in Karl Marx's basic dictums on socialism. "However, as so many of us were to learn," she added quickly, "the fantasy of socialist theory did not translate well into the practice of communism." Likewise, she explained, the premise of *apartheid*, formulated on the basis of an, arguably, interesting hypothesis, offered no solution to the racial problems in Africa.

She turned to me. "Do you remember wanting to know what the word a*partheid* meant?" she asked.

I laughed and said that I did.

"Well, do you see now that the unfortunate vernacular is turning out to be little more than a clouded communiqué of fraudulence?"

I nodded and she continued. "It started with a plot to unite the Afrikaner masses," she said. "And now it's spawning promises to lure the Xhosa chiefs into its tentacles. They've been offered the leadership of a so-called independent region, the Transkei, and they're likely to seize it without probing the small print of the bargain." She closed her eyes and grimaced. "This beautiful land is in crisis," she said softly.

"But why do the chiefs believe him?" I asked.

"Because he's believable," she replied. "He can be such a charmer that even I sometimes forget what a brooding fascist he is at heart. He's the classic Jekyll and Hyde of the political arena. And in his Dr. Jekyll hat one would never suspect his dogmatic ideas on racial bias, his sinister thoughts on ethnic cleansing, or his anti-Semitic views. One would not believe that he had a single bad intention."

The Wanderers Club

South Africa might have been a land in crisis, but one would never have known it at the Wanderers Club. Founded in 1888, it was the largest and most prestigious sporting facility in Africa. My dad played cricket, soccer, and tennis there, and when we returned from our summer vacation with my grandmother, he announced that it was time for me to join.

My favorite club-sport was tennis, and with all the help I received there I could not help but become a half-decent player. A senior member, Bill Peters, entered a team of us boys in the men's third league, and this became the focal point of my weekend tennis existence.

Understandably, the vets who lost to us did not exactly relish the experience, and there was soon talk of dropping us from the league. However, Mr. Peters — 'Old Peters,' we called him, although he was probably still in his early forties at the time — saved the day with his silver tongue. He praised the seniors in the most glowing terms. "You're creating future champions," he crooned. "What these boys desperately need is the experience of playing against wily foxes like you."

That appeased them for a while, and Old Peters took advantage of the breather to go to work on us, not on our tennis, but on our manners and qualities of sportsmanship. "I want you praising your opponents' good play," he demanded, "and smiling even when you're losing."

"That's easy," Tim Farquharson beamed under a mop of red hair.

"We'll see," Bill Peters challenged.

He began drilling us relentlessly. "I said smile when you're beaten by a superior shot," he complained to one of my friends a week or two later.

"I was," the offended lad protested.

"No, no, boy. You were grinning like a Cheshire cat. Tone it down. You're playing tennis, for crying out loud, not trying to become an heir to a will."

Doreen Malcolm also helped us. I scoffed when I was first scouted by her, but soon changed my condescending tone when I found my name on a newly-released list of young players to be sponsored by Slazenger. I was to receive two racquets a year, and gut strings, a considerable expense in those days. I was elated.

Like Old Peters, Mrs. Malcolm was a stickler for good manners and tennis etiquette. She also drilled us on the history of the game, and on the champions of former times. "When you start winning tournaments and being interviewed by the press," she said, "I want you saying something intelligent, something that will inspire a new generation of juniors." She took for granted that we were "going places in tennis," as she phrased it, and over tea, to discuss strategy, she occasionally threw in treats like strawberries and cream. "It's a taste you'll appreciate even more at Wimbledon," she would say.

Mrs. Malcolm's son, Keith, was an up-and-coming star several years our senior, so in addition to us younger boys, she adopted a group of players about Keith's age. And, as we were very well aware, two of these, Gordon Forbes and Gordon Talbot, had been sponsored to play in the English summer tournaments. "A prerequisite for their selection," Mrs. Malcolm informed us, "was their good sportsmanship, and their superior knowledge of the history of the game."

Of course one could undertake the pilgrimage to Europe alone. Owen Williams had done it, and he was our hero of heroes. He occasionally played doubles with us, as did all of Mrs. Malcolm's older boys, and over tea with her afterwards we would beg Owen to tell us stories about his trip abroad. He had worked his way to England on one of the ships of the Union-Castle Line, which carried mail, cargo, and passengers between Great Britain and South Africa; very few people flew in those days.

"What did you do, Owen?" Tim asked him.

"Played tennis...most of the time."

"No, no. On the ship?" Tim corrected. It was his working passage rather than his tournament experiences that we were interested in.

"Oh, nothing grand," Owen responded. "I was an assistant to one of the many chefs aboard. A potato peeler if you really want to know."

"A potato peeler?"

"Yes, you'd be surprised how many spuds the passengers chow."

Our expressions revealed our amazement; a special *ou* — fellow — just to peel potatoes. Our minds raced ahead. There must be a thousand jobs on a ship like that. We too could make it. Mrs. Malcolm was no longer our only ticket. There was another way, and Owen was living proof of it.

"If you don't mind me asking," Tim inquired hesitantly, "did they pay you on the ship?"

"Sure," Owen smiled. "Sure they paid me. And they fed me. Free grub; better than you'd eat at home. And what's more," Owen went on, "I arrived in Southampton in pretty decent shape."

We cast him a doubtful look.

"You see, on a ship they keep the potatoes down in the bilge, down below the water line where it's cool. I must have gone down fifteen ladders five hundred times, and carried fifty thousand tubers to the galley. That will give you a little muscle."

Owen, to us, was *Makulu Nkosi,* Big Chief, our foremost tennis idol, and at the Southern Transvaal championships we would draw lots to ball boy for him. Other favorites were Keith Malcolm, Gordon Forbes, and Abe Segal.

*A*be Segal once gave me a racquet. He had just broken a string with one of his big lefty serves. "Goddamn," he cursed aloud. He was a fan of American gangster movies and had no doubt gleaned the expression from one of these. He paused, glaring at his racquet until he was sure he had the crowd's attention. Then, with the flair of a spectator-pleasing gladiator, he tossed it lightly in my direction. "There you are, kid," he shouted with a smile, "use it when you can hold it." It floated high. I jumped in the air to catch it, and the crowd applauded heartily. Abe had been losing, but the incident galvanized the fans in his favor, and his opponent eventually succumbed to overwhelming spectator pressure.

Abe's wooden Dunlop Maxply was the most expensive gift I had ever received from a stranger, and I negotiated permission to go into the locker room after the game to thank him. "I really appreciate that tennis racquet, Mr. Segal," I offered as politely as I could.

"Sure thing, kid," he responded, "but cut that 'Mr. Segal' crap. How old do you think I am?"

"Not that old," I answered, a little unsure of myself.

"That's right," he confirmed with an engaging grin. "I'm Abe, or Abie, see. And this is my buddy, Forbsie." He turned to Gordon Forbes.

"Yes, I know," I said making my escape. "Thanks again for the racquet, Abe...Abie."

"My pleasure, kid. Say, what's your name?"

"Ian," I shouted back, and disappeared with an acute sense of relief. Abe was a little intimidating, one-on-one.

But in company Abe was a sovereign of fun. He had a faithful following, and we Wanderers ball boys, and our tennis-playing friends, like Cookie Hammill, were part of it. When Abe was on the court his entourage loomed large, with his girl, Heather, as cheerleader. And if Abe was king, then Heather, the Golden Girl, was queen. With her long blond hair, healthy tan, and exquisite figure, we younger boys worshipped the ground she walked on. We loved to hear her girlish laugh, giggle I suppose it really was, which she did constantly around Abe.

Abe was at his best when a rain delay gave him a captive audience to entertain, at his leisure, with tales about his and Forbsie's exploits on the European tennis circuit. We'd heard most of his stories more than once, so heaven only knows how often Heather had listened to them, but she seemed to relish them more with each telling.

Gordon Forbes would ultimately write a book about it all, *A Handful of Summers*. And I imagine that the Golden Girl still raises that delightful titter each time she reads it. The late Peter Ustinov did the foreword to Gordon's book, and described Abe as one of a "rare crop of delightful South Africans, plunging about the court like a minor prophet..." Gordon himself was certainly also a member of that "rare crop" Peter Ustinov referred to. And so was Owen Williams, and my close friend, Cliff Drysdale, who subsequently married Gordon's enchanting younger sister, Jeannie.

"Forbsie," Abe would say, "is an animal."

To this, Gordon would raise a surprised face. He knew the routine well. He was invariably the fall guy in Abe's stories, and he played out his part to perfection.

"You share a room with Forbsie," Abe would chant, "you get a surprise show. It's either a nightmare, or a sleep walk. Sometimes it's both. But, believe me, whatever it is, it's horrendous."

"Come on Abe," Gordon would protest, "there's no need to exaggerate."

"I swear to God," Abe would strike back, "with the performance Forbsie gives you, you don't have to exaggerate. It's usually around midnight. You've just got to sleep for a big match the next day; then all of a bloody sudden there's Forbsie, dancing around with a machine gun, or something, shooting at you as if you were a bloody Commie."

If the audience was responsive, as it invariably was, Abe could keep going indefinitely. But he was quick to stop if interest faded. We, in turn, were always at the ready to spur him on if he faltered. "What do you do, Big Abie," one of us might prompt, "with an *ou* like Forbsie, an *ou* who walks in his sleep like that?"

"You could chain him to his bed, I suppose," he would say. "But he'd still be screaming blue murder. There is no way you could sleep. I mean you could…"

"*I* tried to play with Abie's racquet," I remarked to Cookie, "but it was like hitting with a club."

"You're lucky he didn't give you his *tackies*," — his tennis shoes — Cookie said. "Mind you," he grinned, "they'd have fetched a good price."

"A good price?" I queried, forgetting for a minute that I was around his offbeat sense of humor.

"*Ja*, you could have rented them out as barges on the Nile."

I smiled. "Well, talking about money," I said, "I offered Abe's racquet to my dad, for a bargain price."

"And?"

"The grip was too big, even for him."

"Abie must have hands as big as his feet," Cookie went on. "We'll have to check them out next time we see him."

Cookie's brother dated my sister once in a while, and on one occasion Abe lent them his car. They picked it up near empty and topped it off with gas before returning it. At a crucial point in his match the next day, Abe spotted them in the grand stand. "Hey Jacky and Joy," he hollered, "thanks for the petrol!" And, as with the racquet-gift incident, he won the point and went on to clinch the match. He seemed to thrive on what, for most players, would have been a fatal distraction. The winning effect lay in Abe's ability to appear immeasurably cool on big points, and find a way to needle his opponent's concentration rather than his own.

The apartheid boycotts that were to follow, had not yet affected South African tennis, so once a year Ellis Park was alive with a slew of the world's best tennis players, and we, as their ball boys, basked in a glory of our own. Owen Williams would invite us into the players' area once in a while, buy us soft drinks, and engage in some dialogue with us. "Introduce yourselves to Sedge," Owen said on one occasion, nonchalantly waving over the great Frank Sedgman. I was the first to shake his hand.

"Are you also a tennis player?" he asked.

"Yes, sir."

"There's no 'sir' around here, mate," he spat with contempt, and I was reminded of my locker-room interchange with Abe. The Aussies and the Yanks were all like Abe, inviting us youngsters to address them by their first names. We loved it.

"Where do you play?"

"Just around here…" I could not find it in me to add 'Frank.'

"Ever thought of visiting 'Strylia, mate?"

"I'm not sure where that is…" I was on the point of tagging on 'sir' again, but managed to swallow it. While I was silently congratulating myself, I realized that my friends were sniggering.

" 'Strylia, Australia," someone said in a low voice. The prompt was like a sharp poke in the ribs.

"Oh, Australia," I corrected myself. "Yes, I'd love to go there. But maybe I'd like to visit the States first." The words spewed out of my mouth before I could catch them, and there was another round of laughter.

"You really messed that up," Tim commented as we left.

"I know," I admitted. I bit my tongue. But nothing could diminish the warm feeling I had from shaking hands with Sedge. It meant almost as much to me as seeing the King — who, incidentally, was also a good tennis player; in 1926, King George VI, then Duke of York, competed in the men's doubles at Wimbledon.

*N*o one could compare with 'our boys,' Owen, Abe, Forbsie, and Keith, but a number of other players took the time to be courteous to us. The great Pancho Gonzales exchanged high fives with us, his ball boys, after one of his games and, much to the spectators' delight, gave us each a Coke from a portable refrigerator he had wheeled out onto the court. At the time he was part of Jack Kramer's professional tour, a "tennis circus" Pop called it, with a format that called more for entertaining than winning. And with match-ups between such colorful masters of the game as the Panchos — Pancho Gonzales with his big serve and overhead, and Pancho Segura with his two-fisted forehand — it certainly responded to its mission.

We ball boys put out for our favorites; besides those mentioned, the Americans, Art Larsen and Vic Seixas, and Roy Emerson who, if Peter Ustinov had been introducing a book about Australian players and not South Africans, would certainly have been included with top honors. And Jaroslav Drobny who advised us, in his thick accent, that "theenking" on the court was more important than "heeting de cover off de ball." Too many players, he said, and especially juniors like us, tried to overpower their opponents rather than outthink them. In 1954 'Drob,' as his friends called him, followed his own advice, defeating fellow tactician Ken Rosewall to win Wimbledon. He was thirty-two at the time, 'Muscles' Rosewall only nineteen.

Although we knew that there were better players than our boys, we were proudly aware that they were respected throughout the tennis world for their colorful personalities and good sportsmanship. They would move on to become a significant threat in Davis Cup events, and enjoy their fair share of wins in the big tournaments. In 1962 Abe and Forbsie would reach the doubles final of the French Open, losing to Manual Santana and Roy Emerson. Cliff Drysdale would be ranked number four in the world in 1965, and five times in the world's Top Ten. And in 1968 Cliff would have the best win of his career, beating favorite Rod Laver in the U.S. Open.

In 1974 South Africa would win the Davis Cup after Australia, with less than her best team would lose to India, and the United States, under similar upsetting circumstances, would be unexpectedly defeated by Colombia. India would refuse to play the final against South Africa because of her *apartheid* policy, and for the first time in the seventy-four year history of the Cup, the competition would be decided by default.

We played at Ellis Park ourselves, in the Southern Transvaal Juniors, and that was an experience of unparalleled excitement. Cookie and I would meet at the beginning of each tournament and immediately exchange sweaters for good luck. He and Ray Weeden dominated my age groups, the under-fourteens and, as time passed, the under-sixteens. There were fierce battles, small bets, and cheering groups of players. Parents were not a big feature of tournaments in those days. They were busy working, or tending home, and that was the way we preferred it.

A half century later I still revel in the game, and some of my best friends are still my tennis buddies — Jim McGuire, a friend of Sedge, who lured me into the academic world to make up an afternoon foursome, and got me interested in Australia; Jack Kracke, an engineering genius who re-coded the computer models in the text book I wrote on hydrology; John Benn, already in his eighties, tennis-smart and trim, a world champion in his age group; and a rogues' gallery of other interesting characters.

I also still greatly enjoy visiting tennis and cricket clubs in my travels, and on a recent trip to my old country I popped in on the tennis section of the Wanderers. In the enlightened atmosphere of the new South Africa I expected things to be very different. But on the day that I was there nothing much seemed to have changed. The tennis section still appeared to be exclusively white. Africans were mainly into soccer and road running, so I suppose I should not have been too surprised. But I was.

I knew that there had been some very good black juniors in South Africa. I was also aware that black tennis great, Arthur Ashe, and his friend, Stan Smith, also a Wimbledon and U.S. singles champion, had done much to promote black juniors in South Africa. And to top it all, Madiba was a fan of the game and a keen player himself.

But as discouraging as the situation appeared to me, I knew of one success story, that of Mark Mathabane, a protégé of Owen Williams and Stan Smith. Mark entered the tennis world from the poverty of Alexandra, where Madiba had eked out an existence as a student. He received coaching from Keith Brebner, a school friend of mine at Marist Brothers College, and then moved steadily up the ranks.

Mark was the first Black that I was aware of, to apply for membership to the Wanderers Club. In his fine book, which he called *Kaffir Boy,* the American equivalent of 'Nigger Boy,' he recorded his wonder at entering the "palatial" clubhouse and walking past shields honoring club members over the one-hundred years of its existence. Mark described his meeting with the club president as cordial, but his application was premature; *apartheid* regulations at the time made it impossible for him to join.

Subsequently, with the considerable help of Stan Smith, Mark won a scholarship to a college in the United States. After graduating he wrote the title referred to above, and dedicated it, in part, to Stan Smith and his wife, Marjory, a Princeton graduate.

The Ingcibi

Whereas my transition to young adulthood occurred at the Wanderers Club, unpunctuated by a bar mitzvah, or any other such initiatory ritual, this was certainly not the case for tribal African boys like Kat and Madiba. Their change of status, their move from villages in the veld to urban schools, and their exposure to a broader cross section of African culture, began with their ceremonial circumcision. This was interesting, for although its physical aspect involved no more than the removal of their foreskins, its spiritual face embraced all that contributed to a successful *rite de passage.* The formalities included the isolation of boys from their home environments, and their in-depth tutoring by wise elders to prepare them psychologically for manhood

— their responsibilities to the clan, the need to honor their ancestors and preserve cultural traditions.

To provide relief from the more serious objectives of the observance, one of the pre-circumcision assignments set for the adolescent gathering was to dream up an imaginative stunt, a prank of sorts. Knowing that far-reaching concessions were made for circumcision shenanigans, Madiba's group organized the theft of a pig, enticing it quietly from its sty by sprinkling a path of homemade beer. Kat, in the similar style of a sixteen year old, followed his group in absconding with the horse of the *ingcibi* — the circumcision master — then sending him a meal of goat with a message to the effect that it was horse meat. However, with the deed done, panic swept through their ranks, Kat told me, and they informed the old man of their deception and where he could find his precious horse. The *ingcibi* laughed and said that they should have kept their clever hoax a secret.

With somber preparations and frivolous larks completed, tribal elders roused the boys at dawn on the appointed circumcision day, and led them to the river for a procedural bathe. This symbolized their spiritual cleansing, and promoted much excited babble. However, when the pageant began the boys were nervous. Kat said he was in dread of the telling moment when the *assegai* would descend on his penis. What if his courage failed him? What if the old man's aim was misdirected?

As tribal drums echoed to a beating crescendo, the *ingcibi* began systematically working his way down the line of boys. They sat spread-legged on their faded red blankets. Lost in a time warp of noise and anxiety, they countered fear with fatalistic resolve. Cringing, cowering, or any other sign of weakness would bring disgrace.

Kat saw the master approach and stoically braced himself for the inevitable. When the *ingcibi* drew nearer, he said, he tried to move his mind into a trance. Suddenly the ritual leader loomed large before him. Their eyes met. A deft hand rose. The *assegai* flashed briefly in the sun, then fell.

At that same pivotal moment, Madiba said, in *Long Walk to Freedom*, that he had the sensation of fire shooting through his veins. He instinctively looked down and saw a perfect ring that had been his attached foreskin. In searing pain he drove his chin to his chest. But in the next fleeting instant he recoiled, and lifting his head jubilantly to the sky, he roared "*Ndiyindoda!*" — I am a man!

After the function the 'boys,' now regarded as young men, were body painted from head to foot with a wraithlike white paste. This, an extension of the observance, emblematized their purity, Kat said, in entering the adult world. As darkness fell on the circumcision day they were called on to turn in early. This left them alone with their pain to meditate on the day's events. But they were quietly awakened again at midnight and led out into the eerie shadows to bury their foreskins. Symbolically, Kat told me, they were laying to rest the last memories of childhood.

The young men remained at the seclusion lodges until their wounds healed. Then a grand closing celebration was held and they received several head of cattle, some goats, and a few sheep. "I and my friends thought we were very rich men," Kat said, as he turned to me and smiled with a self-depreciating little sneer.

Before making their departure from the sacred circumcision place, the dwellings they had stayed in were set alight. This was meant to sever a last link with the past. And although it was forbidden to look back, Madiba said that he could not resist. His compulsive act of disobedience reminded me of my own in the valley of the *Hex,* when I had turned my head to steal a glance at the steam engines that pulled our train. But, unlike me, Madiba was spared a smack across the ear. He was now a man.

Of the twenty-six boys in Madiba's circumcision class, he alone, he said, was not groomed for a career on the mines. In fact the Regent repeatedly lectured him against ever thinking about digging for "the white man's gold." But, like both Kat and me, Madiba would also eventually be snared by the mystique of the mines.

"After my circumcision," Kat said, "I continued on at my church school." His school, like all British mission schools for Africans, was committed to strengthening the religious beliefs of Native members of the Empire, providing them with a sound educational base and, ultimately, securing for them a qualified vote — possible at that time. Similar to Marist Brothers, discipline at Kat's school, I gathered, was ironclad but fair, and sporting activities formed an integral part of his curriculum. Kat liked soccer, he said, and *kennetjie,* a type of tip-cat, the latter more of a game than a sport.

Madiba changed to a boarding school, and the Regent accompanied him there and introduced him to Reverend Harris, the school principal. As he had been carefully briefed to do, Madiba firmly shook his hand. It was his first touch of a white man. He was sixteen.

Sixteen

I remember well the age of sixteen, because it was the last time I visited my beloved Ga in Cape Town. We, the immediate family, had enjoyed yet another of our epic train journeys, then boarded the *Trans-Karoo* to spend Christmas and what remained of the summer with her. Pop piggy-backed our car on the train that year and, with Ga as guide, we toured the historic city and did some memorable drives around the Cape Peninsula.

In looking back the mystical element in my character tells me that she must have had a premonition of her death, because she took us to all the places she loved and had her fondest memories of. One was a former family home, *Mount Pleasant*, a small farm on the slopes of Devil's Peak. She showed us the foundation ruins — that section of the mountain had since been declared a reserve — and said how much she wished she could spend some time again at the farmhouse on the Isle of Man, older but still intact, where, she reminded us again, my mom had been born. "I can clearly remember your mother," she laughed, "as a pretty little Manx girl."

We traveled along the shores of False Bay, past Muizenberg with its beautiful old train station and sweep of beach washed by a thousand waves. We passed the Posthuys, an old lookout station and post office. Recorded on a map published in 1697, it was, my grandmother said, the oldest European building still standing in South Africa.

We stopped at the small seaside cottage of Cecil John Rhodes, the place where he died at the relatively young age of forty-nine. Rudyard Kipling, Ga's favorite writer and poet, had spent many pleasant hours trudging along Muizenberg beach with Rhodes, she said, and exchanging a multitude of ideas with him about the state of the British Empire. Kipling wrote a moving poem to honor the memory of his great friend. He named it, 'The Burial.' Ga quoted the words of its ending:

> The immense and brooding Spirit still
> Shall quicken and control.
> Living he was the land, and dead,
> His soul shall be her soul.

Further into the False Bight, as seamen of old knew it, we slowed through Kalk Bay, home to a colorful fishing fleet, but once the site of a large whaling station. We enjoyed tea in Simon's Town, the South Atlantic base of the Royal Navy for well over a century, and then ambled on towards Cape Point where, today, penguins may outnumber people amongst the granite boulders that scatter the shoreline.

We visited Hermanus, widely regarded as the best land-based whale-watching spot in the world, where Ga told Pop that he ought to think seriously about relocating from Johannesburg, "that hotbed of trouble," she called it. "You stay up there, Bill," she warned humorously, "and one day you'll wake up dead. Come to Cape Town," she offered, ever-generous to the end. "My home is your home."

Part 10

ASSEGAI

Tsotsis

*B*ack at home again, Pop came a lot closer than he ever might have thought to 'waking up dead.' And it changed our lives. I had taken to bed with a high fever, and Pop came into my room in the early hours one morning to check on me. Unlike my mom, he was a light sleeper.

While bending over to feel my forehead, he saw a flash of light through the drawn curtain — my bedroom was at the rear of the house with its outlook onto a small verandah and 'servant's door' as we called it. Pop quietly returned to his room and retrieved his old service revolver from under the bed. He then tip-toed to my window, and slowly drew back a corner of the drape. There were three *tsotsis* at the door, presumably trying to pick the lock. Just then one of them struck another match to see what he was doing. To avoid detection my dad leaned to one side, but evidently must have made a sound, he said, because the next thing he saw was one of the men with his arm drawn back like a javelin thrower, ready to launch his *assegai,* the deadly flinging version, a slender ebony spear with a sharp metal tip. Pop fired a single shot and the *tsotsi* fell. I awakened screaming, and Mom came running to my room overwhelmed by dread, thinking, as she later stammered, that Pop had mistakenly shot me. She had read of such accidents and detested having firearms in the home.

By the time Pop looked outside again the *tsotsis* had fled, dragging away their injured companion. But the man who had been hit was eventually caught. Two days later Pop saw in the newspaper that someone from nearby Alexandra had admitted himself to Baragwanath, a Native hospital; the man said he had been shot in a gambling incident. Ballistic evidence, and fingerprints on the spear he had left behind, revealed him to be the *assegai* man.

On hearing the news my grandmother was onto Pop like a demon. Long-distance telephone calls were expensive and, outside of business, uncommon at the time, but Ga called Pop several times, urging him to bring the family to Cape Town.

He resisted at first, and I was pleased. The shooting had scared me to be sure. The bullet-hole had been left in the window, "as a warning to others," Pop said. But, unfortunately, it had the unintended effect of unsettling me, a daily reminder of the near break-in, and who knew what beyond that. However, I had no wish to abandon my school friends, a new girlfriend, and the lifestyle I had grown used to at the Wanderers Club. Leaving, to my mind, was unthinkable.

A few weeks later, news of our impending departure took me completely by surprise. Pop announced it unexpectedly at the dinner table. "It's time for us to sell our house and move from Jo'burg."

"To Cape Town?" Joy exploded with glee.

"To Uitenhage," he corrected.

"Uitenhage," she pouted in disgust, "I've never heard of it."

I asked, with similar aversion, where it was, and was told it was in the Eastern Cape, near Port Elizabeth.

I inquired whether we had ever been there, and Pop said no.

My jaw tightened. "Boy, I can just imagine what a dump it must be." Memories flashed through my mind of some of the awful railway towns we had traveled to, and Uitenhage could be worse. It had not even merited a visit.

"And when do we go?" Joy might have preferred to have been off to Cape Town, or East London, or any of a dozen other places that she had visited in the progress of our extensive train travels. But any move posed an element of excitement to her. She was optimistic and resilient, and had none of my disparaging reservations.

"In July, when school beaks up."

"Can I stay, stay on as a boarder at Obs?" I pleaded.

Pop shook his head.

"What about moving in with Tiaan? Aunt Anneka said I was always welcome." The words splattered out in a desperate rush.

"No!"

"*Ag*, please Pop," I implored. "I'll go nuts without the Wanderers. You said yourself it was your life. I feel the same way. And it's only a year and a half 'til varsity, and then I'll have to move again."

"Listen Son, I'd like to say yes," he said. "I know how you feel. But we stick together as a family on this one."

I asked why. I was desperate.

"Let me tell you a few things," he said taking me by the arm and showing me into my bedroom. Joy followed, but was told to run along and see if she could help her mom. "Ian's in trouble," I heard her confide as she swept into the kitchen.

When we were alone, Pop continued. "I don't want you talking about this to your friends, but things are changing, and changing quickly. You know it from what your grandmother has told you. The country's not the same as it was just a few years ago." His voice dropped to a whisper. "You're old enough for me to tell you that there could be a war here, a civil war. And it could be sooner than anyone thinks. And Jo'burg could be the first battleground."

I stood in silence, unable to take it all in. My mind spun with stubborn hostility. "No, I won't go!" I blurted. "I'm sixteen, I ..."

Pop gently squeezed my arm. "I understand how you feel. I've lived here all my life and I could also cry." But this was a call, he said, that he could not compromise on, a decision that was in the best interests of the family. He promised to make it up to me.

He paused to let me speak again, but there was nothing more to say.

He extended his hand and I shook it. But I was far from happy.

I received a long letter from Ga before we left, sympathizing with me, but saying that in the long run our move was for the best. She told me that Pop had tried to get a transfer to Cape Town, but that this had failed. And she said that if I chose to attend *Ikeys* — the University of Cape Town — she would be happy to have me stay with her.

She went on to discuss political issues and, in particular, preparations for what she referred to as a 'Freedom Charter.' It had been inspired by Z.K. Matthews, she said, an African professor who had returned with the idea after a sabbatical in the United States. The Charter, she went on to explain, was to be a South African equivalent of the American Declaration of Independence. It would document the basic principles for a democratic country of the future. Rusty Bernstein, a Jewish architect who she had met, she mentioned proudly, had been given the task of sparking the process. She enclosed a typed extract of his idea-soliciting call:

> We call the people of South Africa Black and White —
> Let us speak together of freedom!
> Let us speak of brothers without land, and of children
> without schooling.
> Let us speak of taxes and of cattle, and of famine.
> Let us speak of freedom.
> We call on the miners of coal, gold and diamonds.
> Let us speak of the dark shafts, and cold compounds
> far from our families...
> Let us speak of freedom...

And besides Matthews and Bernstein, she wrote, there were other smart people supporting it, for a start, Ruth First, a liberal journalist. 'I know her and her mom quite well,' she penned. She also listed Bram Fischer, a lawyer, Rhodes Scholar, and Afrikaner — she underscored the word 'Afrikaner' — and Zulu Chief, Albert Luthuli, 'a brilliant man,' she said. She went on to state that it might be the beginning of something big, a united multiracial, multiethnic front against the Nats.

Ga ended her letter by saying that for the first time in recent years she sensed some hope for the country, but urged me, nevertheless, to get my university education and then think of moving abroad. England, she said, would be her choice. But my Jewish Uncle Martin, she wrote, insisted that America was the place of the future. 'In the meantime,' she said, 'study your *If*.' I had found it framed and hanging on my wall when we returned home after seeing her off, not long before, on the Trans-Karoo.

Kipling's poem and Ga's letter were my last keepsakes from her. She died soon after writing to me. My mom flew to Cape Town for her funeral. It was her first time in an aircraft; her journey to South Africa had been by ship.

Damn! Damn! Damn! Damn!

Although I knew it had to be, it was a sad day for me when our train pulled slowly out of Johannesburg's modern station. I imagined that I would be back soon. I had no way of knowing that beyond a summer, and another even shorter visit, it would take more than four decades for me to return, and that even then I would just be passing through, visiting a few old friends. Nor could I predict that this was just my first in a series of flights to freedom.

It was the first time that *apartheid,* so to speak, had directly affected me, and as small as the inconvenience was I could not help but resent it. I sat and stared at the changing scene beyond our compartment window as we distanced ourselves from my city of gold, the only place I thought I could ever be happy in. I was distraught and I quietly cursed, "Damn! Damn! Damn! Damn!"

Part 11

POLITICAL OUTRAGE

Varsity

I graduated from high school at Muir College in Uitenhage, the town we had moved to, and my first year at university, the University of Natal, 'varsity' as we referred to it, was in 1959. It was also my first real awakening to the stab of South African politics. And it brought home the fact that one tends, by and large, to ignore political injustice until one is a victim of it, or has some aspect of it rubbed in one's face.

We stood about, talking in mixed tones of nervousness and excitement. It was a muggy, tropical, Durban day, and we were eager to start. I was about to take part in my first anti-*apartheid* march.

Although I was proud to be on the spot at last, the mood was tense, and I felt a nagging guilt in the pit of my stomach. Pop had issued me a warning of much the same character as Mr. Sidelsky had delivered to Nelson Mandela when he had first started working for the Sidelsky law firm. "If you get into politics…you will end up in jail." Madiba had been studying at the time, but also working to earn a little money and gain some experience. He had subsequently graduated, set up the first black law firm in Johannesburg, and all but forgotten what his old boss had said. But Sidelsky's words came back to haunt him when, after dabbling in politics, he was charged with *Hoogverraad* — High Treason. His warrant had sprung on him unexpectedly, like a leopard from a ledge.

Now, as the Treason Trial dragged on — in all 156 people had been accused of betrayal, including 23 Whites — I knew in my heart that I was doing the right thing, little as it was, an anti-government demonstration, a mere token of resistance, like ticks on a jackal's back, a small annoyance. Nevertheless, I was on edge, keenly aware of how vindictive the Afrikaner administration had become. What my great-grandmother had predicted had come to pass; Dr. Hendrik Verwoerd was now prime minister, and tensions were running high. Protest, irrespective of its peaceful format, was increasingly being regarded as a crime.

Conflicting thoughts plagued me. Pop worked for the government — the railroad was government-controlled — and he was paying for the better part of my studies. And although he detested the politics of the time, he did not want me trifling with them. In his optimistic way he still thought, hoped, that at some point Great Britain would intervene and put things right. "If only Churchill was still prime minister." I had overheard him say it to my mother on a least a dozen occasions.

Lost in thought I sensed a new movement, and looking up my gut suddenly knotted. Security policemen were calmly ambling down our line, photographing us. "What are they doing?" I hissed in outrage.

"Watching you, compiling records, making sure you don't get a passport." He said it all with Gothic relish, an older boy, perhaps twenty.

I asked him what he meant.

"It's low-tech, but it's effective. They've got your photo. They match your name. You apply for a passport. Denied!"

I glared at him. "For what reason?"

"They don't need a reason. Gospel! A friend of mine was just turned down. He'd been accepted to LSE, and now he can't go. What's more, he's been called up for the army."

I asked him what LSE was.

"London School of Economics," he replied.

"And that's it? He can't go?"

"That's it. Take my oath, the *ou* is devastated."

Denied a passport, called up for the army; it had not crossed my mind. My thoughts whirled. Ga's wishes for me to move abroad would be inconsequential. My face fell. "So they've taken my photo," I scowled, "but how do they get my name?"

"They've got spies in every *res*," the politically aware senior explained, referring to the college hostels where we boarded.

I clenched my jaw to indicate that I was listening, but I was distracted and acutely uneasy. The march had begun and the air was filled with provocative chatter. But all I could think of was losing my passport. I certainly had not bargained on that when I'd elected to join the rally. In my demented state spectators began to take on the faces of surveillance men, and I felt as if I had a large Cape buffalo's eye tattooed on my forehead.

*T*he same year saw political demonstrators shot to death in the city — we saw bloodstains on a wall where the shootings had occurred — and a further student march to protest that.

And at about that time, in the African township of Cato Manor, on the outskirts of Durban, a crowd of women gathered to protest the fact that they were no longer being permitted to make *tshwala* — beer — for their men. Instead, the government, with an eye to control, had opened municipal beer halls and dispensed with the old tradition.

I had tasted the African home-brew.

"It's *kaffir* beer," the dark-skinned lady said. "Are you sure you want to try it?"

I assured her that I did.

She poured me a glass. "See what you think," she smiled.

I sipped it slowly. Its base was maize, I guessed. It was not what I was used to, but not unpleasant, more like gruel than beer and no doubt a lot more nutritious.

"The white man's beer is thin," she noted, reading my thoughts.

I indicated agreement, acknowledging both its body and its kick.

But now the microbreweries were being closed, and the ladies robbed of their livelihood. The government halls should be done away with, the women protesters insisted. They were irate, but not militant. It was hardly an issue worth risking their lives for. Besides, many of them were young mothers with small babies wrapped to their backs.

But the police were not about to have their time wasted by a gathering of women, albeit more than a thousand of them. They issued an order to disperse, and when this failed to materialize they led a charge into the crowd. I observed the assault from a distance and saw, within a dust-filled frenzy, policemen brutally beating women with heavy wooden batons, and lashing at them with *szamboks* — whips. Ladies crouched with outstretched arms pleading for mercy. The whole incident was not a massacre, but it distressed me and gave me nightmares. I had seen it, and that made it more real to me than other far-worse incidents that I had only heard of, or read about.

*I*n those troubled times there were armored cars posted along the ridge that our campus was built on. The college buildings faced part of the city, and beyond it, the bay, a large natural harbor where we rowed and sailed. But behind the ridge, on the inland side, were African and Indian townships.

We stopped one day on our return from the yacht club, and spoke to an army boy no older than ourselves. He and his companion were sitting on their vehicle, their legs dangling through an open turret. A machine gun mounted on a tripod pointed ominously in the direction of a small squatter community in a shantytown below. "*Hoe gaan dit?*" How're you doing?

"*Goed, dankie,*" he replied, indicating that things were fine, a standard superficial response.

"*Hoe lank gaan julle-ous hier bly?*" I asked, inquiring how long they were going to be there.

"Till it's done," the soldier responded, switching to English.

"That's not so *lekker,*" my friend, Ian Knight, offered in a voice of condolence.

"*Wragtie,*" he smiled, "especially for a *plaas jaapie.*" His words indicated that this was certainly no place for a farm lad like himself.

"Are you *ous* PF?" Ian asked, wondering if they belonged to South Africa's permanent army.

"No, Citizen Force." This meant that they were conscripts, like we would be — fewer and fewer were escaping the draft. The soldier paused, stroked an immature moustache, and then added, "I can tell you though, some of the PF *ous* are real cases."

"Worse than the cops?"

He and his companion looked at each other and laughed. "I don't think so, *maat*," — mate — "no one could be worse than the bloody cops, at least the security *ous*." But he thought better of what he had just said and added, "Not all of them are bad, *jy weet*."

"*Hulle is …*" the second lad broke in diffidently, then fell silent. His face was deep. A beret covered most of his short blond hair, and his khaki shirtsleeves had been rolled up well above the elbow. "Look," he said, "I wouldn't want their job, but the security police are a bunch of arseholes. They stuff up everything; then they expect us to bail them out. We've got a foot patrol down the cliff right now, talking to the *kaffers*, trying to tell them that we're not the cops, and that we don't want to shoot them. But if we have to, we will."

"*Ja, maar sal julle rerig skiet?*" Ian's question challenged them on the reality of actually pulling the trigger.

The army boys looked at each other. Their faces were grim, but there was no hesitation in their response. "If they give us a hard time, threaten us, attack us, we'll shoot them!" The blond boy gave us a bent smile of helplessness. "*Ons sal hulle moet skiet*, finished and *klaar!*" We'd have to shoot them, there's no other way!

Rocking the Boat

*L*ater that year, 1959, Prime Minister Verwoerd shook out a further line of reefs. He officially balkanized the country, bringing into existence eight *Bantustans* — African Homelands — and effectively reserving the rest of South Africa for Europeans. When I heard the news my thoughts went straight to Ga. She could not have called it closer.

"His rationale," my dad said, "was his apparent success in dealing with the Transkei." Pop quivered his head in disgust, and said that he supposed the Prime Minister had had to say something to cover his flank.

Within the newly established territories, Pop explained, the government had been far less liberal — than in the Transkei — with its allocation of space. "Under his new Act," he raged on, "some seventy percent of the population will be confined to less than fifteen percent of the land." He raised his hands in disbelief. "It's a total demographic blunder. But the amazing thing about it all," he seethed, "is that the stupid sod" — Dr. Verwoerd — "could have got away with this entire flaming thing if he just hadn't been so bloody greedy. You'll see though, that what he's trying to do will come back to bite him; you mark my words. The Natives can't stay alive on what he's giving them."

And, as time moved on, the gist of what Pop had said would turn out to be right. The small *Bantustans,* with their scant resources, would become shabby pockets of poverty, incapable of supporting the large influx of displaced persons. Ultimately QwaQwa would have a population density of some 750 people per square mile. This compared to less than 10 persons per square mile for South Africa as a whole. Africans would react violently.

But that was all still in the future. For the present the Prime Minister's handiwork resulted in approximately two thirds of the Blacks in the country suddenly finding themselves living in areas designated for Whites. Under the new law — "the fine-sounding," Pop said, "Bantu Self Government Act" — these 'homeless people' would have to relocate to the new *Bantustans.* Grand *apartheid* had been born.

Apartheid could now be said to exist in three parts. Part One, 'petty *apartheid,*' revolved around civil rights, an annoying array of regulations pertaining to, for example, which park bench one could sit on, which bus one could travel in, and where one might be granted, or denied, access to a restaurant, or school. Part Two, 'Nazi *apartheid,*' as Ga had christened it, focused on the denial of political rights to non-whites. And now, with the introduction of the eight *Bantustans,* a third prong had come into being. Dr. Verwoerd had taken a quantum leap, underscoring his message to Blacks in true Hitler tradition: You might have been born here, but you don't belong here!

The Extension of the University Education Act, which followed, sealed his message: Regardless of how talented you are, you are no longer welcome in our white university system. You can attend a perfectly good institution in your new Homeland.

This was a momentous setback for the 'English-speaking' universities like my own, where considerable effort had gone into trying to achieve a more balanced racial mix. At the University of Natal, for example, 21 percent of our population was made up of non-white students.

As Ga and Pop had often discussed, when she was alive, Dr. Verwoerd's assault on African education had started with a spearhead of attacks on mission schools. Ga's point, as mentioned, had been that the — then — senator particularly resented the *"laisser-faire* ideas," as she had often referred to them, that were presented to black mission schoolchildren. She had quoted the disparaging words of one of Dr. Verwoerd's addresses that, she insisted, said it all:

> If the native in South Africa today, in any kind of school in existence, is being taught to expect that he will live his adult life under a policy of equal rights, he is making a big mistake…There is no place for him in the European community above the level of certain forms of labour.

"That's him in his Mr. Hyde mode," Ga had complained. "His language on sensitive issues like this is stripped of even courteous disguise. It could alienate, irretrievably, all hopes for the future."

Pop had concurred, numbly, and encouraged her to continue.

"The government chooses to ignore the fact," Ga had stated at the time, "that Africans are being extremely well educated in mission schools, and have the potential for making significant contributions to the educational, social, and economic progress of the country." She had presented, as an example, Professor Matthews, whose academic credentials, she said, included a master's degree from Yale University.

"And you go back fifty years," she had added to emphasize her point, "you had men like Seme." She was referring to Pixley ka Isaka Seme. I remembered her saying that he had been raised at an American mission station in Natal, gone on to obtain a bachelor's degree from Columbia University in New York, then studied law at Oxford University in England. On his return to South Africa, after being called to the British bar, she had told me, he was one of four to found the African National Congress (ANC) — Madiba's political party that ultimately came to power in the post-*apartheid* era.

Pop had agreed with Ga on the preeminence of mission scholars. "You just have to look at the leadership of the ANC in recent times," he said, "well educated, well dressed, conservative and respectful."

"Yes," my grandmother had smiled. "And I recall Tilly saying that they were the same way in their homes, portraits of the Royal Family in their studies, and a keen interest in British sports like tennis and cricket."

Ga and Pop had gone on to discuss Dr. Alfred Xuma, who had become president of the ANC in 1940, and led the party when Madiba first joined it. He was a medical doctor who also had studied in the United States. "His political agenda was modest," Ga said, "but he made some notable gains."

Pop agreed. "He did what he could. He respected authority, and when he backed down, it was always with dignity."

Ga had turned to me. "In the relatively favorable racial climate that prevailed before *apartheid*," she'd explained, "the last thing the African aristocracy wanted was to have their leader begin rocking the boat."

The Mines

That summer, while the Afrikaner government was raising Cain, I went off to the mines. Our program required that we gain practical experience, and the gold mines around Johannesburg paid students well. They were keen to look us over, and if we "shaped up," as Pop put it, recruit us when we graduated.

Part 12

eGOLI

Crossing the River

eGoli — City of Gold — Johannesburg, where I was born and raised, where Kat worked for a number of years, and where Madiba started on the mines, moved on to became a lawyer, and spent many exciting years as a freedom fighter, was, in those days, a florid third-world metropolis that had no equal. And although I had lived there for so long, I saw a different side of it, perhaps something closer to its true character, when I returned to work there for three months as a student.

In the half-century since gold was first discovered there, it had grown from the frontier town that my grandfather was familiar with, into the cosmopolitan sprawl of stark contrasts that I got to know better that summer. Plush high-rise buildings stood within sight of decrepit homes that were little better than tin sheds. White men, their holsters covered by finely cut suits, rubbed shoulders on the sidewalks with Africans dressed in blankets and carrying *knobkerries*. Rambling street markets existed near elegant department stores. And it would not have been considered irregular for a jeweler selling world-class diamonds to be located alongside a sawdust-floored butcher shop displaying the carcasses of full-sized animals hanging from meat hooks.

And even with *apartheid* approaching a new high, David, who was now studying business at Wits — the University of the Witwatersrand — and a close friend, Mark, from his martial-arts class, took me to multiracial night clubs where creative black music and explosive dancing beguiled me. It was as heady a time as my exposure had been to stick fighting, and looking about in one *shebeen* I half expected to see Pondoland Willie.

Away from the city-center gold mines dominated the scenery. Each mine displayed its hard-won history, twisted heaps of timber and steel that I remembered as a boy. And from the ruins had grown magnificent new head-frames, and mountain-like tailings dumps that rose ever-higher above the veld, competing, it seemed to me, with the scattered *kopjes* of the Karoo. But these vast surface expressions of the mines, like ant heaps, belied an even greater network of activity underground, one that revolved around a frantic search for treasure. This, as I came to appreciate, lay carefully hidden, embedded in rock a mile and more beneath the city. It was the same bounty that beckoned pioneers like my grandfather, the magical glitter of gold. It bewitched Madiba and Kat for a while, and cast a lasting spell on me.

We summer students were given an orientation, and told a lot of what we already knew from our professors. Gold-bearing conglomerate was originally mined in outcrops at the surface, but easily-accessible reefs had long since been picked of their hoard. The mineralized veins dipped underground, our briefing instructor said, so to find new gold geologists were forced to go deeper and deeper. And this committed us, he stated, to the innards of our planet, to deal with the fierce heat of the earth's core and with intense confining pressures that created dangers of rock burst and collapse. "You'll be underground next week," he added with savor.

Mining in general is a profession of superlatives, the richest, the most difficult to work, the deepest, and the most dangerous. And mining in *eGoli* was all of these. I soon observed first-hand that it was hard and perilous work for a geologist like I hoped to be, and white miners, but it was even more exhausting and full of risk for the tribal Africans who performed the bulk of manual labor at the face.

The face is the vertical rock section exposed at the working end of a drift — tunnel — that is constantly in the process of being advanced deeper into the gold-bearing reef. This is where the bulk of the action occurs, a highly energized station for those who like it. But for those who are doing it just for the money, it is the gateway to hell, a wet and claustrophobic cavity of deafening noise, spinning steel on rock, a dangerous place. And although I could hardly imagine it, in my grandfather's era, so I was told, mining conditions were even tougher. The drills then were more thunderous and much heavier, and worst of all they were 'dry.' These 'widow-makers,' as the old miners called them, sent rock chips flying out like bullets and churned up dense clouds of dust, an environmental nightmare that had men constantly coughing and hacking, and even, Granny Watson said, spitting blood.

Equipment had improved over the years, but the basic procedure involved in hardrock mining, as I was quick to learn, remained much the same. When the scream of the drill died at the face, charges were set in a carefully designed pattern of boreholes. The miners then retreated and waited for an earth-tremoring blast. When most of the dust of the explosion had settled, tons of broken rock had to be mucked out and hauled to the surface. Then, at the mill, the ore was crushed, and the gold extracted in a series of metallurgical processes. This cycle of drilling, blasting, mucking, and recovery, was, and still is the guts of hardrock mining, repetitive and exhausting.

However, the mining profession is not all horrific. It has an exciting and challenging edge to it, in that each shift tries to exceed an assigned quota of ore and thus secure a much-sought-after bonus. And even production is not entirely about money. It brings psychological rewards. Crack teams enjoy the adoration of their colleagues. "We reign as kings," an English-immigrant shift boss proudly told me in a bar one night.

With employees coming from so many different places, communication is generally in a simple mining tongue known as *Fanakalo,* and what little I got to know of African languages — more than forty are spoken on the mines — was embraced by it. *Fanakalo* originated, I found out, when immigrants from India came to Natal, now KwaZulu-Natal, to work in the sugarcane fields, and were obliged to learn English and Zulu at the same time. It soon spread and adapted itself to the mines where it offered an effective means of dialogue between the multi-ethic workers, essential to increasing efficiency and preventing accidents.

Diego, a Portuguese engineer I met that summer, had picked up *Fanakalo* before English or Afrikaans. "It seems crazy, but it makes sense," my college friend, Pete, said. *"The Miners' Companion"* — *Fanakalo* dictionary — "has only about 2,000 words." Diego could call for a *dayiman mtshin,* a diamond drill, or a *bobojan spanela,* a monkey wrench, but not for jewelry, or a wedding ring. There were no such words in *Fanakalo,* no need to communicate that far up the commercial ladder of gold.

When Kat first started on the mines he was following in the footsteps of both his father and his uncle, but against their advice. And as a rookie, he remembered, he had had strong feelings of dread. He knew the risks that mining involved. A hint of his anxiety, he said, was expressed in a miners' song. He sang it to me one day when we were out mapping and, at my request, wrote some of its words in my field book:

In crossing the river I become a new man,
Different from the one I was at home.
At home I was safe.
But now I am on this side,
I am in a place of danger
Where I may lose my life at any time.

Madiba also started with foreboding; like Kat he had ignored the advice of his elders. But he remembered that when the *Induna* — the Headman — at Crown Mines offered him employment, he had trembled with glee, scarcely able to believe his good fortune. And notwithstanding the stories of wonder he had heard over the years about the mines, what he observed with his own eyes was a revelation to him. Like me, he could not believe the scale of operations, the complexities of design, and the dedication of the men who worked there. On his first payday his exuberance reached fever pitch, and the thought crossed his mind that if he had not squandered his time studying, he could, by then, have been a wealthy man.

Mining Geology

In eGoli the primary task of a geologist is to find and predict how best to work the gold-bearing reef. The basis of this challenging augury is the intensive mapping of geologic phenomena, and the continuous interpretation of mapped data. This commences before the mine even exists.

We heard a lot about diamond drilling, core logging, and mining design from our geology professors. In a lecture that comes to mind I recall Professor King asserting: "The greater the factor of safety built into the design, the more expensive the mine. So an optimal design, from the standpoint of an owner, is one whereby the mine collapses, of its own accord, the day after all the gold-bearing ore has been extracted."

In my mind's eye I can clearly see my instructor stepping away from the podium, blowing into his hands, then posing an inevitable question. "Now, gentlemen," he asked, "is this a true statement?"

Lester King's inquiries were not rhetorical. He required us to say something, and to avoid looking like the class fool an answer needed to be laced with a thread of intelligence. We sat and sweated.

When it was clear that no one was volunteering an opinion, he selected someone at random, me. "Okay, Mr. Watson."

"Could you please repeat the question, Prof?"

My class companions quietly chuckled.

Professor King had a student do the honors, but added: "We are talking philosophically, Mr. Watson, about fine-tuning safety factors in design, and the impact of design on economics."

"Well Prof., I say you can't fine-tune on safety, sir. Everything must be as safe as it can be, so it doesn't collapse and kill the miners."

Professor King lifted his hand to his chin. "Mmm...What do you think, Mr. Aitken?"

"I think what Watson said is true, Professor. You can't kill the miners just because you're trying to save money."

"Bravo, I am delighted to have you thinking, class." He paced around the front of the lecture room. He had our attention and he knew it. He let the silence hang until we could bear it no longer.

"Is Watsie right?" someone blurted in a tone of encouragement.

Prof. pointed a bent finger. "He's right and he's wrong," he spat.

We looked at him perplexedly.

"The point is that we are not trying to kill the miners, or anyone else, least of all ourselves! On the other hand, there is no such thing as ultimate safety. Everything we plan has an element of risk. If we tried to design a mine to the standards we address, say, to the foundations of a power plant, or a dam, it would cost more to extract the gold than the gold is worth."

Suddenly the air in our lecture room felt less close, as a fresh breeze of comprehension wafted into our collective consciousness.

He went on. "We have to cut a few corners. Make it as safe as we can, but we must also turn an economic profit. That is what mining is about. That's where our skill comes in." His expression changed to a sneer. "Any Cousin Jack could create a safe mine if cost was not a factor."

He searched the room making eye contact with each of us. "See," he said at length, "the mining game is a balancing act between risk, on one scale, and profit on the other." He paused. "My original point — that we target the mine to collapse the day after the ore is extracted — is, of course, a hypothetical one. No one can call it that close!"

He puckered his brow, waiting for some reaction. Then, apparently satisfied with the interest that we appeared to be showing, he continued. "You will be out there in the real world before you know it, and you will be pressed to the limit to maximize profits. But on no account let yourself be pushed into a venture you disagree with. Better no mine at all than one that fails!"

If it is a case of "no mine at all," he said, the geologist starts again, searching for a better prospect. On the other hand, if the blueprint is sound the operation gets underway. A shaft is sunk to the ore body, and mining commences. Now, once more, the geologist dictates. "But his quarry is evasive," Prof. King cautioned. "On most gold mines the reef thickens and thins, following a tortuous path, sinuous and circuitous, thinning perhaps to nothing, and then exploding to riches."

At some locations, faults — planes or zones across which there has been rock displacement — were the preferred pathways of mineral-bearing fluids in the distant past, Prof. told us, and these were the very places where the gold was to be found. In other areas, faults occurred subsequent to the injection or deposition of the gold, and these displaced the mineralized reef, throwing the miners into a panic. "The geologist must then scramble," Professor King went on, "to predict the direction and movement on the fault, to relocate the gold."

"If you're right and put them straight back on the money, they think you're God," an old *eGoli* mining geologist grunted, on the same topic, that summer, "and they start believing everything you say, and that's bad."

"And if you're wrong?" Pete led on.

"If you're wrong," said our philosophizing geo-companion, sipping his brandy, "the shit hits the fan. They don't believe anything you say. And that's worse."

"*I* can tell you a few things about mining," Lester King offered on another occasion, "and teach you some theory. But most of what you will need to know you will learn on the job, mapping in the field."

"Can you just tell us how we find gold, Prof?"

"You unearth it by intuitive reasoning, my good man. You have to feel your way back in time, to the origin of the rock that is most likely to contain it. When you've interpreted its history, you can predict where to find it, if it's there. It's something like a doctor unraveling your family health history to establish your predisposition to a potential ailment."

A student raised his hand. "Can you give us a case-study, please Professor, of finding gold."

"Certainly," he said. "If you're in the San Juan Mountains of Colorado, for example, in the United…"

"In the United States," the boy interrupted, wheezing in disappointment. "Please Prof. We wanted to know where to look for it in South Africa." He might well have added, '…today, if possible!'

Professor King ignored him. He knew quite well what we were after, but he was not about to be tricked into presenting it to us on a platter. We were going to have to listen and think. He pointed to a spot on one of the many geological maps that adorned the walls of our classroom. "In the San Juans," he said, "we are journeying back some 70-million years, to the Late Cretaceous Period, near the end of the age of the dinosaurs. That is when the parent sediments of the region were deposited, in an enlarged arm of a protohistorical Gulf of Mexico."

Professor King was talking like one of his textbooks, and no one was taking notes. We knew from deliberations in the past that he was simply making the point that geology was a complicated business, but that all the secrets we needed to know would reveal themselves to us, as he always implied, through our "diligent observations in the outdoors."

"In the San Juans," he went on, "there were outflows of lava and doming during a period of volcanic resurgence. And when the dome collapsed we had the formation of the Silverton and Lake City Calderas. A caldera, as you remember, is a collapsed volcano."

We employed a variety of mannerisms to communicate that we were following what he was saying.

"Then, about 25-million years ago, the area experienced its key event, the injection of granites and mineralized ores, gold and silver, into preexisting fractures and faults. So, if you are prospecting for gold in Telluride — where, incidentally, you will want to stay and do some hiking, or skiing after you have found it — you simply feel your way back through this geological history. *Quod erat demonstrandum!*"

There was a ripple of muffled laughter from the class.

"Did I say something to amuse you, gentleman?"

"We think your *QED* was a little premature, Professor. Can you give us a few more details, please?"

He smiled, then expanded his explanation. "By observing outcrops you will clearly see by that your original sediments have changed as a result of the heat of the volcanoes, the simple process of metamorphism. So your country rock, or gangue, will consist of metasediments and volcanics. The gold is hydrothermally injected into this complex. It migrates through the rock mass as a hot fluid. But where does it go?"

We caught our breaths, and began searching again for a response.

But for once he answered his own question. "It follows the path of least resistance. It moves into the cracks in the rocks, the high-angle fractures and faults that typically radiate out from the center of a caldera. Near the surface the pressure decreases, the fluid cools, and the gold is deposited. It's like scale accumulating on the inside of a boiler."

He showed a twisted smile, as if recalling, with pleasure, a real search in his distant past. "If it's in-situ gold you're after, find a fault with a brecciated zone and blast your way into that. If it's placer, remember that the gold leached from veins is heavy. Find a reach downstream of the deposit. See where the slope changes and the flow velocity, the carrying power of the river, decreases. That's where you'll find gold, in potholes on the riverbed."

He was quiet for a moment. He guessed that we were dreaming of soon-to-gain riches, of gold nuggets clinking in our pockets. He was right. "In any event, sample the fluvial sediments," he advised. "Look for gold in your prospecting pan." He frowned. "And by the way," he rasped contemptuously, "if you have a new pan, throw it on the fire."

'On the fire, Prof?' we mimed in silent surprise.

Our quizzical faces made him laugh. "A black and pitted pan is what you want. The pits hold the gold, and the black helps you spot it."

We were into it now, ready to go prospecting at the first opportunity. All we needed was a deposit a little closer to home. "What about finding gold in Jo'burg, Prof?"

"Johannesburg. Now here we have a much older part of the world, gold eroded out of the ancient mountains of Gondwanaland." Professor King paused and glanced at his pocket watch. "I'll talk about gold again, tomorrow perhaps. Read up on the Witwatersrand System. Discuss it before we meet. Good-day gentlemen!"

The Black Miners

Mining, like fishing, is one of man's most honorable occupations. Despite modern machinery, excavating hundreds of miles of tunnels through hard rock remains excruciatingly difficult and dangerous physical work, and the miners I met that summer, and in my later life, were rugged men, amongst the finest characters I have known. But I am afraid that, like Vincent van Gogh, I cannot find it in me to say the same good things about the owners of mines. With exceptions, of course, they have a history of being devious in their management style, and of exploiting the men who work for them. The great Dutch artist compared the lot of the miners of his time to slaves — they had very little say in controlling their destiny; van Gogh had just been on the French border helping mining men who had been injured underground.

The mining brokers of Europe were known for compromising safety standards, and spurning the goals of unions, to say nothing of the havoc they wrought on the environment. But in fairness to owners, as Professor King often said, making a mining venture a profitable business is no easy matter, least of all on the Witwatersrand where the ore is virtually unbreakable, low grade, and exceptionally deep.

Nevertheless, the companies were greedy, and Madiba was quick to see it. It was only "cheap labor," he said, that made the white-owned mining houses so wealthy. The miners tried to negotiate better salaries, but had no bargaining power because of the persistently high rate of unemployment amongst Blacks, and the fact that both owners and government periodically conspired to exploit the situation by employing workers from neighboring countries, like Mozambique and Namibia.

"What's the pay of white miners, compared to Blacks?" I asked.

"It depends on their jobs," a shift boss replied. "It probably varies from about ten to one, to sixteen to one; a lot better for Whites."

Besides low wages, black miners had to deal with segregation, and although petty *apartheid* did not extend underground — there is no sense of color in what amounts to a war zone — they suffered, nevertheless, by being a product of the system. For example, Blacks could not, as mentioned, bring their families from the *kraals* to live with them, and as a consequence were forced to stay in what Kat described as army barracks with concrete bunks. "*Aziko mfazi*," he laughed. No females.

But despite everything, Xhosas, Zulus, Sothos, and countless newcomers from other rural tribes flocked to *eGoli* to seek their fortunes on the mines. They were naïve, but fired up with expectation. And many of them were sufficiently well educated to challenge the political authority of the white man. Things were about to happen. The continent was about to face 'a wind of change.'

Part 13

THE STATES MY DREAM

A Wind of Change

I returned to college after my summer stint on the mines, and early in 1960 the British Prime Minister, Harold Macmillan, finalized plans to visit a number of African countries, including South Africa. In an address to parliament before he left, he mentioned a number of European colonies that were negotiating independence at the time, and compared Africa to a placid hippopotamus about to be stirred into action. In his subsequent speeches in Africa he referred to "a wind of change" that was sweeping through the continent.

The British leader's words did not bode well for those wanting to preserve a status quo in Africa, let alone for the Afrikaner who seemed intent, as Mr. Macmillan noted, "on elevating segregation into a doctrine." According to research by Anthony Sampson, for his book *Mandela,* the Prime Minister told a close colleague that he was dismayed by the imprudence of radical Afrikaners for trying to manipulate a separation of the races by legislation. If they had not made an ideology of it, he explained, they would almost certainly have achieved what they wanted with few "concessions." The economic gap between Blacks and Whites would alone have achieved a practical separation, he said. Of course, Prime Minister Macmillan concluded, it was essential that they "accept" the well-educated African.

But when it came to dealings with Africans, the word 'concession,' Pop said, however small its connotation, was not in Dr. Verwoerd's vocabulary, and anything remotely resembling 'acceptance' was far removed from his political agenda. He could not even find it within himself to muster a token gesture of goodwill by arranging for his important visitor to meet, as he had requested, some leading black politicians. Mr. Macmillan was clearly disappointed, and then further frustrated when, under diplomatic pressure, even the garden party given by the British High Commissioner, Sir John Maud, turned out to be an all-white gathering.

With the unfulfilling way the visit had gone, Dr. Verwoerd was in dread of the speech the Prime Minister was scheduled to deliver before leaving; he expected it to be scathing. But, as it turned out, the British leader was more than polite. He praised the country for some notable achievements. However, his voice was firm when he stated that there were certain aspects of South Africa's policies that made it impossible for Great Britain to continue to support her in the Commonwealth.

*M*adiba and his colleagues were pleased with Macmillan's speech, mild as it was. Anthony Sampson, in *Mandela,* noted that some thirty-five years later, Madiba, then President of South Africa, addressed the British Parliament with words that were modeled, in part, on what Macmillan had said all those years earlier. Mandela, Sampson said, even recalled an old political cartoon that had portrayed the British Prime Minister after his forbearing speech. It had a caption-quote from Julius Caesar:

> O! pardon me, thou bleeding piece of earth,
> That I am meek and gentle with these butchers.

Sharpeville Massacre

*W*hile I basked in the political comfort of a sheltered shore, in largely English-speaking Natal, stormy weather continued to batter the Transvaal. The Treason Trial had entered its fifth suffocating year, and the protagonists on both sides of the drama were exhausted. Prosecutor Oswald Pirow — he had once described Adolf Hitler as "the greatest man of his age" — was dead. And although this made things considerably easier for the accused, they had not celebrated as they might have. They were too tired.

Away from the courthouse, the African National Congress (ANC) and the newly-formed Pan Africanist Congress (PAC) did battle for control of the freedom fight. The ANC had recently conducted two successful boycotts, one against the Afrikaner tobacco giant, Anton Rupert; Africans simply stopped smoking his brand of cigarettes. Second on their blacklist was the potato crop; potatoes were predominantly grown by *Boers.*

This Gandhi-styled rejection strategy was successful, and powerful in the fact that the police could do nothing about abbreviated shopping lists. However, removal-of-patronage efforts were quickly upstaged by a war PAC leader Robert Sobukwe began to wage on pass laws — these were regulations, reminiscent of the old slave days, requiring Africans to carry documents that were constantly in need of update by employees and petty government officials. The ANC had initiated a protest against pass laws, with mixed results, and the PAC pledged to make their efforts work.

Sobukwe was determined to unleash a more militant campaign, and rashly pledged that by 1963 he would eliminate white rule in South Africa. His confidence was inspired by the tone Macmillan had set on his tour. The British leader had not only acknowledged that things were changing in Africa, he had hinted at the fact that his government would support such changes. That portion of his message had been provocative.

On 21 March 1960, Robert Sobukwe and some one-hundred followers set passbooks aside and courted arrest. They urged backers around the country to follow their lead. Unfortunately this led to tragedy at Sharpeville, an African township near Johannesburg. Here several thousand So-bukwe supporters gathered in the vicinity of a police station. The mood of the protestors was described as jovial, David wrote to tell me, but a small faction of the crowd, he said, antagonized police by hurling stones at them. David speculated on what had followed.

The police chief looked on with mounting anxiety as the crowd grew larger by the hour. His dark thoughts gathered like squall clouds, and at some point his mood flashed to anger. It was time for the *kaffers* to be taught a lesson, the chief decided, to be shown who was in charge. He briefed his men. At his call they were to open fire and shoot to kill. There was not to be the usual order to disperse, or a volley of warning shots. '*Verstaan julle?*' he cried. Do you follow me?

It was a barbarous order, but his men indicated that they under-stood, and took up their positions. It happened quickly after that.

'*Gereed!*' Ready! He let the echo die. '*Skiet!*' Shoot!

A volley of fire rang out, and the demonstrators were completely taken by surprise. Some fell where they were shot. Then gritty chaos rippled through the crowd. Those nearest to the police turned and ran. They were unarmed and could offer no resistance. People scrambled for what little cover they could find. Women and children huddled, bleeding, behind dead bodies. It was total mayhem. But the police kept shooting with impunity, expanding carnage into a bloodbath, an appalling massacre.

When a cease-fire was eventually called for, many limped off with bullets in their bodies. More than four hundred lay seriously wounded. Sixty-nine were dead, many shot in the back as they tried to flee. David, his side-kick, Mark, and some other left-wing student friends had been on the fringe of it, uncomfortably close to the action.

*T*he world was dazed. President Eisenhower was in shock. This was not the work of terrorists — that would have been bad enough — but of the police, public servants whose global charter it is to protect people. The United Na-tions Security Council convened and censured the Afrikaner government. The Johannesburg stock market went into a tailspin. The ANC called a Day of Mourning to protest the atrocity. Madiba and Albert Luthuli burned their passbooks as a token of respect for the dead and wounded. In Cape Town a student leader led a demonstration march that grew to more than twenty thousand. It remained peaceful, but tensions ran close to breaking point. In Durban we had our own much smaller student protest.

Talk of revolution was in the air, and English-speaking South Afri-cans initiated a new wave of emigration. David began to think about leaving Wits and moving to New Zealand. He had an uncle there and could proba-bly transfer his credits, he said. And although I was not ready for it, I knew that it was also time for me to go.

On 9 April 1960, less than a month after the massacre at Sharpeville, a disgruntled white farmer drew a service revolver at the annual Rand Easter Show, and shot Dr. Verwoerd at point-blank range. His death would almost certainly have triggered political change in South Africa. However, the gunshot was not fatal and the leader recovered, convinced that divine providence had played a hand in his survival.

A Plan for Flight

Many African dissidents, fearful of more Sharpeville-type terror, fled. Oliver Tambo, Madiba's boyhood friend and business partner, was one of these. He illegally crossed the border and picked his way north to Dar es Salaam. From there he moved on to London where he remained in self-imposed exile for the next thirty years, conducting ANC business from abroad.

Only one good thing came of Sharpeville, Pop said, it hastened the end of the Treason Trial. Judge Rumpff, unruffled by government intimidation, focused on the remaining thirty defendants — under mounting world pressure, charges had been dropped against the others, men like Professor Matthews and Chief Luthuli. The Judge announced that he and his colleagues had reached a unanimous verdict: 'NOT GUILTY.'

Fearing re-arrest, Madiba did not join his companions in the post-trial celebration. He did not even return home. Instead, he disappeared into hiding. He now knew that the passive Gandhi form of political protest he had followed for so long would not deliver the knockout punch he needed. And so, with the encouragement of a corps of rebellious party members, and white activists like Rusty Bernstein, he began structuring a military wing, separate from the ANC. This was given the name *Umkhonto we Sizwe,* The Spear of the Nation. It was the dawn of a new dimension in the freedom fight, a stepping up to the next level.

As Madiba prepared to thrust his spear into white power, I too sought a new course of action. Plans for my escape started on a small hiking adventure. "I've got to get out," I complained to my friend, Pete Aitken.

We were on vacation from university, enjoying a ten-day ramble down a portion of the Transkei shore, not far from where Kat and Madiba had grown up. Some pals and I, all from the same college residence, had hitch-hiked down the Natal coast to Port Edward. Here we had crossed the large Mtamvuna River on a pont, a ferry of sorts used in Africa on low-trafficked roads where it was not cost effective to construct a permanent bridge. Ours was a flat-bottomed pontoon that, as I recall, was capable of carrying two or three cars at a time. We marched down a dirt road, stepped aboard, and greeted the operator in *Fanakalo.* As hinted at, with a long tradition of working in *eGoli,* most Xhosa men understood the tongue.

"Molo!" I hailed. Good day!

"Molo baasies," the ferryman replied cheerfully, mixing *Fanakalo* and Afrikaans. This was typical. His words conveyed politeness. However, within the context of *apartheid* one might read into them subservience. *'Baas'* meant 'master,' or 'boss,' and *'baasie'* 'young boss.' He had used the plural in addressing us, 'Good day young masters!'

"Dubula," Pete sputtered, raising his eyes to the sky. He was alluding to a clap of thunder we had heard on our approach.

The tall Pondo looked up and shook a finger at the heavens. *"Tula!"* he said. Be quiet!

We applauded his good-natured humor. *'Hamba pambili lo manzi, jabulisa?"* we asked. May we cross the river, please?

"Upi ngolovan?" Where is your car? He used the word employed on the mines for an 'ore car,' but we knew what he meant.

"Aziko ngolovan," Pete blinked. No car.

He shrugged in a way that let us know we were an odd group.

But we rationalized that it might have been one of the few times he had experienced white folk crossing the river without motorized transport.

He cast off the ropes that held us to the bank. *"Siz! Bamba ntambo,"* he called with an engaging smile. Help me! Grab the line. He braced himself and began to pull on a long chain.

We reached for the links, and the big scow slid slowly from the bank. Then, as the flow of the river caught her, she gave a short down-current lurch and began to tug on the stout steel cable that stretched across the river.

Once underway, she moved with surprising ease. We were soon on the Transkei side where our operator tied up, chancing that his next traffic would be from that direction.

We extended him a small tip and one of our precious sandwiches.

He graciously accepted both with a soft handclap and a bow.

It was starting to rain. We dug in our backpacks for our anoraks, and noticed that the Pondo had no protection. *"Aziko bantsh?"* Pete inquired. No coat?

He gave a shrug that seemed to say, 'Who cares about a little rain?'

We could not help him. To keep our packs as light as possible we were carrying only the bare minimum. We did not even have sufficient food for our journey. We planned instead to fish and trade.

We waved farewell and struck out on an already muddy trail along the river. We would not be on anything resembling a road again until we reached our destination at Port St. Johns. This was a journey of some sixty miles as the crow flies, but perhaps twice that distance by the winding shoreline route that we would follow.

Well into the hike I tried again. "I've got to get the hell out," I repeated.

Pete still appeared to ignore me. "There's a river down there," he announced from the crest of a bushy rise, "a pretty big one. We'll have to build some sort of a raft to get across that."

"A raft? You've got to be kidding."

"For our backpacks," Pete bristled. "Have you ever tried to swim with a pack on your back, mate?"

I smiled weakly.

"I think it's the Mtentu," Pete muttered, changing the subject.

"The Mtentu?" Goum challenged. "I thought we'd already crossed the Mtentu."

"It really doesn't matter, mate," Pete returned in a rankled tone. All he had was a sketch map, and he was a little touchy about being questioned on our exact whereabouts. "You won't miss your bloody wreck," he snapped at Goum. Goum's sole purpose for doing the hike was to visit the site where the famous old *Grosvenor* had foundered.

We resumed our walk, scrambling down the slope. Pete cast an eye in my direction. "Get out of where?" he asked.

I stared vacantly at him.

"You said you had to get out," he prompted.

"Oh," I said, collecting my thoughts. "Out of the country," I added quickly, pleased, at long last, to have his attention.

"Out of the country where?" he persisted.

I told him that the States was my dream.

"And when, may I ask, do you plan to leave?" His voice held an edge of sarcasm.

"Christmas vac," I heard myself reply, referring to our year-end vacation, our long summer break.

"But you won't have graduated, mate."

I said that I could not wait that long.

"You can't wait that long? Well, I've got news for you; you can't get a decent job either. You'll be a dropout, mate, a bloody dropout!"

He was quiet for a while. The slope had eased, but the bush was thick, and with no footpath to follow we each picked our own way down in an uneasy silence. "If it wasn't for this States thing of yours," Pete said, "I suppose we could head up to Nigeria. I hear they're looking for bums like us to train as drillers." He cast a doubtful glance at me, and then added in a more inviting tone, "Big boodle in oil drilling!"

Money was not the issue, I told him naively. "I thought I'd just like to go sailing for a start."

"Sailing? Sailing on what? Have you been smoking *dagga,* mate? Puffing on the old *ntsangu* pipe? Hallucinating? Your dad has a yacht, mate, a private yacht, just waiting to take us to Miami?"

"Not on our own boat, you dimwit. As crew!"

"Crew?" His expression changed and I sensed some hope.

I slapped at an insect. "I saw an ad in the newspaper last week," I said, "a Durban-based yacht named *Cariad,* hundred-and-twenty-five footer, looking for crew to charter in the Seychelles."

We trudged on for a while in silence.

"Suits me, mate," he said eventually, but without much conviction.

I waited for the 'but,' and it was not long in coming.

"But you know what scares me? Telling my old folks, mate. They're likely to have a blue-arsed fit."

We paused as a flock of seabirds dived over us, heading for the ocean. "We can always say we're just doing it for the summer."

Pete took readily to that. "*Ja!* That'd be good. I suppose we could say we were on a geological excursion, or something. Collecting data for a thesis," he spontaneously rattled on, "like Darwin on the *Beagle.*"

"We'll go for it then?"

"I'm game if you are, mate."

"It's a deal," I concluded, happily shaking his freckled hand.

*I*t took nearly an hour to find driftwood and assemble two crude rafts, and by that time it was well into the afternoon. "I'm not getting my clothes wet again," Pete stated flatly. "I'm going in *kaalgat.*"

"And what are you going to say to those ladies over there, when you come out bare-bummed?" Goum pointed his stick across the river.

Pete swung around. There was no one. "Even if there was, mate," he crowed with false bravado, "I wouldn't give a tinker's toss."

"Oh *ja?* Well, the piranhas are going chew your knackers off!"

We knew full well there were no piranhas, but we had seen a school of what looked like barracuda in one shallow river mouth, and I, for one, was running a little shy. So despite a cooling afternoon breeze, Butch and I reluctantly decided to give our clothes another drenching. The others stripped down and were soon pushing into deeper water. We joined them in kicking and one-arm paddling behind the two small rafts that held our packs.

A surprise awaited us, the current. But as luck would have it, we had forded on a flooding tide. A stiff ebb-flow might have caused us to part with our rafts, and carried our packs out to sea.

Goum was the first out, off and running like one of his cavemen ancestors. We snatched our packs and chased after him, across an untouched stretch of beach. He stopped and turned abruptly. "What do you say to this?" The spot he had chosen was a raised sandbar, nicely protected by scrub and trees.

"Isn't it a bit too early to stop?"

Goum grilled the dissenter. "Ask me after a game of touch rugby."

That did it. Besides, we had already walked five hours that day.

"**D**on't you just hate to leave a place like this?" someone asked as we gathered our belongings the next day.

"*Ja!* It's not everywhere that you can catch fish, and there's firewood to cook with. And the weather clears."

"*Ja*, and take a *goof"* — a swim — "before you leave. Did you see me and Watsie out there surfing? We had some great rides." Pete and I, keen body surfers, had splurged and brought swim flippers. This had meant sharing a tent, but that single hour had already made it well-worthwhile.

"Hey Watsie and Goum!" Butch hailed us from behind.

"What's the story?" Goum asked as we stopped and turned.

He snapped a photograph of us. "That's a great shot!"

I puffed my chest.

"Not of you, *boykie,* the scenery." It showed a good two-day hike ahead of us. "And besides your two ugly mugs," he said, "there's not another person to be seen. That's what I really like about it."

Goum had been fiendishly smoking his *goum* — his pipe, after which he was nicknamed — and he and I had been talking, not taking much notice of what was about us. But now we turned once more and admired the desolate stretch of coastline. Small waves broke in an inviting sandy cove ahead of us. It was bounded, at its far end, by a line of rocky outcrop. Beyond that there was white water again. Then, in the distance, several small bays cut a zigzag line between the rolling grassy slopes of the beautiful Transkei, and the brooding waters of the Indian Ocean.

Pete thrust his chin in my direction. "How can we ever leave a country like this, mate?"

I sighed and admitted that it was going to be tough.

Then suddenly we were upon it, the rusty remains of a winch, a relic of one of the costly attempts to salvage the riches of the *Grosvenor.* "Gold coins!" Goum exclaimed, wound-up.

"I hear that Khotso, the old witchdoctor, has a nice collection." Butch was referring to a traditional healer who lived in the area. Rumor had it that he would occasionally be paid for his herbal medicines with coins picked up by tribesmen hiking along the coastline like we were. It was said that he had put out the word that old medallions could buy the very finest healing ingredients.

"Maybe we can trade for a couple."

"A gold coin for an Indian-market torch; I don't think so, mate."

We had exchanged goods like flashlights, tobacco, and small radios, for *mealies,* fruit, and even a chicken. But everyone in Africa, even in remote places like this, knew the value of gold. And although they probably lacked a good grasp of what collectors would pay for treasure, the locals had seen the many salvage attempts on the *Grosvenor* and surely suspected that the old coins had a premium value.

"According to Matthews," Pete said, referring to one of our geology instructors, "if there's gold around, it will be in one of those low-energy pools, just like heavies in a natural alluvial deposit." He pointed to some potential traps in the wave-swept rocks below the rusted winch.

I agreed and said I was going down to take a look.

Goum glowed with excitement. "Someone said that one of the salvage *ous* dredged pools just like these, and pulled up hundreds of Venetian ducats, gold-star pagodas, a small fortune."

The *Grosvenor* had sailed in the days when the British East India Company was at its height. On her ill-fated voyage from India, in 1782, her cargo manifesto had listed bullion and other precious items. But treasure seekers whispered of an even greater prize, the golden peacock throne of Persia that had gone missing. It was held to be worth more than five million British pounds.

Knee-deep in water, we heard a shout. "*Hey,* check this out!"

We dropped what we were doing and scrambled up from the beach.

"It's the entrance to an old tunnel," Butch cried as we approached.

"Is that all?" Goum croaked.

It was not the peacock throne, but it was interesting enough. We knew that at least one attempt to reach the wreck had involved trying to blast a passage through the bedrock that underlay the bay, and then lead it up into the wreck. This, we imagined, involved advancing a shaft under compressed air from a lock — the air pressure holds out the water — a technique well within the reach of a good mining man. But the tunnel venture, Goum had read, ran short of money before the treasure could be reached.

Normally, for a treasure-seeking operation like this, one would simply use a suction dredge, with pumps or an airlift to remove the sand that covered the ship. But the *Grosvenor* had gone down too close to the shore, and no salvage vessel could operate in the breakers that constantly rolled in. So one ingenious scheme after another had been tried. One crew hung offshore, then darted in on a stretch of calm weather, Goum said, and blasted the site. A ship's cannon was retrieved, and a number of gold coins. But rough seas drove them off before they could find more.

Goum had done a fair bit of research on the *Grosvenor*, and I asked him if there had been any survivors from the wreck.

"It's a curious story," he replied. "Out of more than one-hundred people on board, fewer than twenty drowned. The rest reached the shore, probably right here where we stand. But then…"

"Then what?"

"Then the second part of their trouble started. To find Europeans they had to decide whether to walk north, some 400 miles, to reach LM" — Lourenco Marques, a small Portuguese settlement in Mozambique — "or *trek* almost twice that distance to the Dutch colony at Cape Town."

"So they went north," I offered, trying to speed-up the story.

Goum sniggered. "Actually, they went south. They'd heard reports of former wreck-survivors on this coast who had chosen LM and run into trouble with unfriendly tribes."

"So what about our *ous*? Did they make it?"

"Only a few; a good number of them died along the way. And some apparently fell behind and took up with the Xhosas. They say there are still Natives along the coast with light skins and blue eyes."

Butch jumped on him. "Blue eyes? Not blue eyes, surely."

Goum shrugged defensively. "That's what an old boozer told me once in a South Coast pub."

Khotso Sethuntsa, 'the witchdoctor' as Butch had chosen to call him, had a seaside cottage along our route, and we were anxious to meet him. It was said he was a millionaire, and there were all sorts of stories about him that we wanted to confirm. One was that he had gone into a car dealership and paid in small-note cash for a new Cadillac. Another was that he had some twenty wives. We think that we met two of them when we visited his get-away home, but we had been too embarrassed to ask. We had offered to deal our goods for food, but the ladies gave us what we asked for, and politely refused what we had to offer. The doctor was away they said.

"I wish I'd had the nerve to ask them if they were his wives," Pete complained as he sat munching on a sandwich of avocado and litchi.

"You should have," Goum said, reaching for his drink. We had brewed some herbal tea from Khotso's pantry, 'Bushman's tea,' as we called it. It was made from the fermented needles of the *Rooibos* plant, and known for its astringent taste and salubrious healing power — it is rich in antioxidants. Goum raised a metal mug of the steaming crimson liquid. "To Khotso and his women," he toasted.

"You're going to miss this, you know!" Pete smiled at me.

I smothered a choke, and asked about his reaction.

"I'm not leaving, mate. I mean I might sail somewhere and spend a while there, but I'll come back. This is home for me."

"But what if you find somewhere nicer?"

"There's no place nicer. And even if there was, this'd still be home."

"Well home to me," I said, "is where I don't have to worry about having my passport snatched, where there's freedom, and where the government is doing something constructive for its citizens."

"You want to know something, mate? You're going crazy!"

"And you, my friend, have lost your ability to think rationally. That's what *apartheid* has done to you."

"No, mate, that's not true! Home is home. Your country is your country. You don't just run away and think that everything will be fine. You don't! You only have one home, mate, and that's where you were born and raised. Your countrymen are your family. And you don't leave them when things aren't going exactly the way you'd like them to!"

We met up with Ian Knight and some other friends who could not get away when our hike had started. We crept gingerly along the high cliffs of Waterfall Bluff. We bathed in freshwater pools from which water cascaded into the sea. We continued to tramp along isolated beaches. We did more surfing and fishing, and indulged in some further intermittent bartering with the Africans who lived along the shore. And when we reached Port St. Johns on the Mzimvubu River, home of hippos, and gazed up at the bluffs that towered above it, we were sorry, as always, that another small adventure had ended.

But I sensed deep within me a glow of contentment that I had not felt in months. For, despite our differences, Pete and I had settled on a plan of flight. And I still had tennis to look forward to, the Queen's Cup, a big men's doubles event at our off-campus club.

The Queen's Cup

Things were tight and I was about to choke on my serve. We were in the finals and up against two Springboks, former South African Davis Cup players. It was match point. Two upstart college kids were within a point of winning the coveted Queen's Cup. It would be a huge upset.

I raised my left arm and it turned to lead. The toss went wide and I cursed inwardly. But I somehow retained enough composure to catch the ball and not waste the serve. "Sorry!" I shouted to our opponents.

Drysdale sensed my dilemma. He had been weaving at the net like a coiled cobra, ready to strike if the return was loose. At my call he rose from his crouch, and slowly ambled back towards me. Now what?

"Sorry Driz," I apologized. My mouth was dry.

"It's okay," he said, but he kept walking. I thought his approach was to ask if I wanted to play 'American' — what Americans call 'Aussie,' 'Australian.' It involves the net man standing in the opposite box to where he would normally be. We occasionally used it when serving to the right court. Its purpose is to create an element of confusion.

But I was wrong.

"Hey Watsie," he said, his face up against mine, his eyes flashing in the direction of the clubhouse, "take another look at the trophy!"

I did not need to. We had long admired it before coming out onto the court. It was more impressive by far than the prize players received for winning Wimbledon. It consisted of beautiful cast-silver figurines on a handsome mahogany pedestal that stood well over a foot high. The broad base held individual silver shields engraved with the names of famous winners of the past. Before we came out to play Cliff had pointed to a recently-polished blank medallion and whispered, "Watson and Drysdale."

It was a floating trophy that winners held for a year. Two silver beer mugs, donated by *The Old Mug & Jug Inn, Durban,* were to keep. The display stood on a table outside the clubhouse, in clear view of the court where our drama was being played out. I stole another quick glimpse, smiled at Cliff, and my nervousness suddenly disappeared.

"Signals," he said. "Just like the Karoo." He was referring to the match point of a win we had enjoyed as Eastern Province juniors.

"Okay," I acknowledged with renewed determination. Hand signals. It was a good tactic to suddenly throw in a new variable, just one more thing for one's rivals to contend with. He did not say it, but I knew what he was thinking. 'Keep piling the pressure on, Watsie!' It was a Drysdale trademark that I was more than familiar with, a strategy that I would remember as Cliff went on to become a world-class player, a celebrated analyst of the game, and one of the premier tennis commentators for television coverage in the United States.

He went back to the net and stooped, waited while our opponents regrouped, then deliberately extended his left arm behind his back. Following a certain tilted logic, he slowly unclenched his fist. Open hand. He was going.

For the receiver, of course, this was like a game of Russian roulette. If he guessed right he would return down the tramline, the open alley. And although I would then attempt to cover the return, the receiver would have the advantage. On the other hand, if he presupposed that my net man would stay-put and, instead, he crossed, as Cliff intended to do, the advantage was clearly with us.

So the perplexity for our opponents was: would he stay, or would he go? And if he was likely to go, would he dare go on match point?

I served, going for a slow-kicking spin, no bullet. I wanted my first serve in at any cost. The return was a little high. Cliff tore across the net and with a swinging two-gripped backhand, and lots of wrist, put the ball away. He turned to me and, with as much enthusiasm as coolness would permit, hissed in a voice that was barely above a whisper, "Bloody hell, Watsie, we did it!"

Part 14

A SPLASH OF STORMS

Mac & Cap'n John

By the end of that year, 1960, I could take no more. I fell into a depression that was as black and conchoidal as obsidian. Despite every attempt to distance myself from day-to-day politics, I found that there was no escape. I complained a lot and was tiring to be around. I brooded and my studies faltered; my mind was elsewhere. Finally I decided that my family and friends, my tennis, my hiking trips, and all the good things I enjoyed in South Africa were not enough to hold me there. I wanted out.

Fortunately Pete hung by our agreement, and his lively chants became my sole comfort, a rally from my melancholy. "Seychelles, mate. I can't wait." I realized that I should not have had to lean on him, that I should have had the grit to rely on my own initiative, but I could not.

Our final arrangements for joining *Cariad* were made with Mac, the mate. We met him in the yacht club bar where, dare I say, he drank us under the table before ferrying us out to meet owner-skipper John Hardman. "This is Cap'n John," he introduced us.

"How do you do, sir," we stammered, trying not to slur.

Captain John extended a short-fingered mitt and gave us each a mighty handshake. "Welcome aboard, boys." He seemed untroubled by our condition. "I see you spent some time with Mac."

Having placed us in a tight spot, Mac now came to our rescue. "Shall I show them to the fo'c'sle, sir?"

"Yes, thank you, Mr. Mate. And that will be all."

Though we awakened with hammering heads, we somehow made it through a trying first day. Beyond that we soon settled into an existence that could be described as nothing less than leisurely, sanding, varnishing, chipping or painting until noon, a long lunch with Mac, often as not at the yacht club bar, and afternoons of fascinating errands. "Say boys, would you pick up some line," "a part for the generator…"

When things were really slow we might ask if we could do some dinghy sailing.

"Sure, go for it," Mac would say. "You must keep your hands in on that sailing stuff. Yes, by all means go. See you at five."

Every evening at five we stopped whatever we were doing, and took turns at standing by as ferrymen. Like the *Tanka* — the boat people who live aboard their junks and sampans in Hong Kong harbor — Captain John seemed happy to stay afloat almost indefinitely. But the skipper was no recluse. He detested drinking alone, and we were there to bring visitors aboard and ensure that this did not happen.

There was, amongst the captain's friends, a coterie of high-spirited ladies, considerably older than Pete and me, and sometimes even a stretch for Mac. "The Skipper's a magnet for lively old birds," Mac smiled one day, "and most of them are heaps of fun."

Captain John, short and stout, red-faced with a full beard and a mariner's cap, loved his lifestyle. It was, as we soon learned, that of yachts-man-at-anchor. Now one did not need a 125-foot ketch, a five-time winner of the King's Cup, to be an armchair sailor, but why not? He could afford it. And *Cariad's* size and history catered to the image of a wealthy old seadog, moreover, an interesting and adventurous one.

Although the yacht had not moved for a while, it was plain to the visiting ladies that he was fitting out for romantic charters to exotic sun-drenched islands. The boat's writing paper, for example, was embossed with nautical charts, treasure chests, and a beautiful sketch of the yacht under her full closet of cloth. And in the top left-hand corner, prominently displayed, was the Hardman coat of arms. The Captain's girls especially liked that. A subscript told of the old boat having voyaged seven times around the world under sail. And a subtle one-liner advertised: *Cariad for Safe, Exciting Sailing Holidays that are Different.*

Pete and I made good use of Captain Hardman's paper to impress our own lady friends. The engraved address held a special appeal — *On Board The Yacht "Cariad 1" c/o The Point Yacht Club, Durban, Natal, South Africa.* I read it aloud to Pete. "It has a nice ring to it," I commented.

"*Ja,* mate. Certainly packs more pizzazz than T-Willy." — Townley Williams Hall, our college residence.

But even more inviting, we thought, was an inscription on the left-hand side of the letterhead — *Bound For... ... ...* We used the empty space to write, 'The Seychelles,' although, by this time, we already knew it was a lie.

In our small yacht-club world we began to notice other things that would not have been readily apparent to an outsider. For example, that there were others not unlike Captain John, boatyard skippers who were constantly at work on yachts that were long-past readiness for ocean passages. They might have had the look of brine in their veins, but they were landlubbers with no intention of leaving. They were safe in that there was always something more that could still be found to do on a live-aboard sailboat. They liked the security and social life of the yacht club, the praise they received for the potential seaworthiness of their vessels, and the gratitude for help to sailors passing through.

"He might not put out to sea much," Mac said, referring to Captain John. "And you'll hear people around here say that he hits the pots a tad too heavily. But what do they know? You've noticed, of course, that he never drinks till the sun has crossed the yardarm."

"*Ja,* and we'd also noticed," Pete shot back, "that once it has, he makes up for lost time."

Mac dismissed Pete's comment with a wave of scorn. "Be that as it may," he said. As a former British seaman accustomed to his liberal rum ration, he genuinely admired this aspect of moral character in the "Old Man," as he said, not imbibing in the daylight.

Male visitors to *Cariad* generally found their own way aboard, and we often awoke to dinghies dancing happily off our stern. "Things must have heated up after we turned in," Pete smiled on one occasion.

There was always an open invitation for us to join in the revelry. And when we did we were made to feel most welcome, in fact, on occasion, more than welcome. Some of the Captain's female acquaintances scared us, not Mac, of course, but certainly Pete and me.

"I'm afraid, old chap, that I'm not what I used to be," Mac complained one morning, rubbing his tired red eyes.

"Why's that?" Pete asked.

"I can't seem to take more than about three rough nights in a row."

"Try one rough night in a row for me," Pete laughed.

"Yes, I don't know how the Old Man does it."

"You can say that again, mate. And Natal rum at that. And all those raunchy women. It's bloody miraculous."

"Well, tonight we take a breather, old chap."

"An early night, Mac?"

"I wouldn't go that far. But you're right about the local rum. Tonight it will be nothing more than a cleansing beer, or two. Three is my absolute limit."

"We can play snooker," Pete suggested. "That'll slow us down."

A predicable pattern soon settled in, and the interesting thing about it was that a day seldom passed without some mention of 'the Seychelles.' Eventually Pete said the words and I jumped on him. "Look Pete, we're not going to the Seychelles. We're not going anywhere. This Seychelles thing is a pipe dream. We figured that out within a week of being aboard."

"I know," Pete admitted bashfully, "but who cares?"

"I care," I protested. "I want to move, do some serious sailing, leave the country. That's what we had in mind, not so?"

"I suppose. But this is fun. I feel as if I'm already somewhere else. I mean this whole scene is just out of sight. It's what someone like Steinbeck could write a book on. It's the stuff of…"

"It's the stuff of turning into rum-heads," I interjected.

Pete laughed aloud. "So what do you suggest?"

I told him that while he was playing snooker with Mac a night or two before, I had fallen into a conversation with Vivian who was working on *Senta*. "That sixty footer, the German-built ketch," I reminded him. "They're sailing for the States after Christmas."

"*Ja* mate, and we're sailing for the Seychelles?"

"No! No! Theirs is for real! The owner of the boat is a fellow named Archie Snyman, a hotshot lawyer. According to Viv he can't wait to leave."

Pete·raised a hand. "Put a cork in it Watsie! Now you listen to me. They say this Archie *ou* is as arrogant as hell, and that he knows precious little about sailing. That's a bad combination for a start. And besides, he's a bloody *Jaap*," Pete spat, touching on the fact that he was an Afrikaner.

"Oh yes? Well I think that's a load of bull, the sailing part."

"You think so, mate? Let me spill a little more. His secretary is going along on the trip, as cook. She's also clueless about yachts, they say, and probably doesn't know much about cooking either."

"Well, Viv is going, and he's been around boats all his life."

"He's a small-boat sailor, mate, a dinghy man like us! He'd be fine if they weren't leaving the bay."

I argued that Vivian's friend, Gerry, was also a crewman, and that he had sailed to South Africa with Jim Crawford, on *Dirigo II*.

"Oh *ja*. And why didn't Gerry stay on with Jim? He was probably discharged, that's why. Who would volunteer to layover in a place like this? Take yourself, for example, doing your nut to leave. I swear to God, if the *Flying Dutchman* was shipping out you'd be up for crewing on her."

"Look Pete, this conversation is going nowhere. I'm interested in *Senta*. They may not be a bunch of crack yachtsmen, but at least they have a plan. And the States is where I really want to get to."

"Go for it then, mate. Don't let me stop you. But believe me, it won't be easy. You've already been branded a *Cariad* man; and you might not know it, but everyone is scared to death of Cap'n John. They wouldn't dare sign you on, even if they needed you."

Pete's insight fell on me with the impact of a sledgehammer. "Hmm…" I confessed, "that really hadn't crossed my mind."

"You might give it some thought, mate!"

"Listen Pete, I'm sorry I flew off the handle like that. But let's just feel this *Senta* thing out a little further."

"You feel it out, Watsie," he said. "I prefer the scene we have here, at least till varsity starts again. You check *Senta* out."

"No deal," I declared flatly. "Either we both go, or we both stay."

"It's not like that. Look at the facts. I don't have this hang-up about politics, about leaving the country. I don't like the bloody *Nats* any more than you do. And I don't care for what's happening here. But I'm not tormented by it. I don't feel the absolute urge to leave. You go it alone for a change. I'm serious. And no hard feelings."

I searched his face, but it yielded not the faintest trace of animosity. "Are you sure? Is that the way it really is?"

"I swear it on a stack of bibles," he said, raising both hands. "I'll even ask Mac to give you a hand, a crash course on mechanics. You know that Archie is looking for an engineer?"

"An engineer?"

"*Ja*, he has this old auxiliary, a *Gray Marine*. Not worth a tinker's damn, Mac says. He needs someone to keep it running."

"Me?"

"Why not? Mac says if an engine's clean, and it has clean fuel, it will run. Just tear it down and clean it, and get Archie to buy you a big industrial-size filter. Or buy one yourself, mate."

Pete put his skinny hand out and I shook it. "Thanks," I smiled.

"I'll miss you, shipmate," he grinned back.

Tommy Bedford

*M*ac, as usual, was more than helpful. "Ever stripped an engine?"

"Just the one on my scooter," I answered, "a *Lambretta*."

"*Lambretta*. Good little machine."

I smiled with pleasure. "Yes, I've been all sorts of places on it. Last year Tommy Bedford and I went up and down the Garden Route."

"Bedford, the rugby player?"

Everyone into rugby at the time, and that included most white South African men, knew Tommy. He had already represented our province — Natal — and there was much talk in the newspapers about his talent and shrewd approach to the game. So it would come as no surprise when, some two years later, he was selected to play his first of many games for South Africa.

Tommy was a decent tennis player as well, good at field hockey, and an outstanding student. He would go on to become a Rhodes Scholar, and I would keep in touch with him when he was at Oxford, and I was at the Royal School of Mines in London.

Beyond that ancient seat of learning Tommy would return to South Africa and continue to play on the national rugby team — the *Springboks* — through a number of difficult years when the game was riddled with politics. The downward spiral in rugby would begin with Dr. Verwoerd saying that the Maoris, a dark-skinned people on the New Zealand team — the *All Blacks* — would not be welcome in South Africa on an upcoming tour.

Rugby fans worldwide would retaliate, and our boys playing abroad would be spat on, kept awake at night by screaming demonstrators and, for their own protection, forced to play on fields ringed with barbed wire. Tommy would ease the tension by speaking out publicly against *apartheid* and get away with it. He was that good, and the politicians wanted that badly to win at rugby.

In 1969, at the age of twenty-seven, Tommy would captain the *Springbok* side in the second test against the Australians — the *Wallabies* — at King's Park, Durban, his home ground. The *Boks* would win the game 16-9, and the series 4-0, and it would be a proud day for all of us who knew him, and respected him even more as a man than as a rugby player.

Senta

*T*wo days later, with black fingernails, I set off for *Senta*. I felt I could now avoid a blatant lie when I was asked, as I surely would be, what I knew about engines. "What do you think, Mac?"

"Did you see that flash, old chap?" he smiled. "That was you moving onto *Senta,* as engineer, making ready for the high seas."

His encouragement gave me a needed lift. But as Mac took a wide sweep, approached the stern of the handsome yacht and nudged up on a fender, I felt my nerves return.

I recognized the owner at work on the rigging. He already had an eye on us. I hailed him in Afrikaans, *"Goeiemôre, Kaptein."*

He laughed. His English was fluent.

"Permission to come aboard, sir?"

"Come on up. You're from *Cariad 1*, aren't you?"

"Yes Skipper," I replied, looking directly into his strong friendly face. "I'm Ian Watson," I said, extending a hand, "and this is my friend, Pete Aitken." Pete had agreed to join me in testing the waters for needed crewmen. "And I believe you've met Mac," I added, pointing down to the dinghy.

He gave Pete and me a firm handshake and waved a brawny sunburned arm at Mac. "What can I do for you, gentlemen?"

"We heard you might be looking for a couple more hands?"

"That's true, one in fact, an engineer. But you boys are members of *Cariad's* crew."

My heart sank. It was playing out just as Pete had said it would. Sweating inwardly I explained that *Cariad* was not going anywhere, and that we wanted to do some sailing.

He seemed to understand, but pressed on. "Are you seamen?"

"No sir, students, sir. But we love sailing! It's our passion. And your yacht, Skipper, is a dreamboat."

He rolled his eyes and I felt the pain. "Well, you heard what I said," he harped on. "There's one last berth and I'm saving it for an engineer, someone who can keep an engine running, a mechanic perhaps. What do you know about engines?"

"I'm pretty good with small ones, Skipper. And I've learned something of marine engines from Mac." I tried to let him see my hands.

The owner turned to Mac and received a weak nodding smile.

There was a long silence. "Look," he said slowly, with an expression that did not disguise at least some reluctance to sign me on, "you're probably not the man I'm looking for. But we leave in two days, and I like your enthusiasm. I might be prepared to try you, at least as far as Cape Town. However, I don't want any ill-feeling between Captain Hardman and myself."

"No, no, Skipper," I reassured him. "Cap'n John won't mind."

I anticipated further resistance and it came. "I believe you," he offered apologetically, "but I'd like some evidence of his consent. Get a note and you're with us. We sail on the tide, the day after Christmas."

"Yes!" I yelled, and pumped his hand.

He laughed aloud, a good belly laugh with a wholesome peal. He was not that much older than me, but already clearly a man. I could not help but like him.

Mac broke the news to Captain John, and he, to my great relief, could not have been nicer. "You'll love the Yanks," he said.

"You sound like my father, sir."

"I take that as a compliment," he smiled.

"Yes, sir. And thanks Cap'n John, for all you've done for me."

"Not at all, me lad. And if it means anything to you, young man, I think you're doing the right thing. Boys of your age ought to be looking for another place to live."

Within an hour I was on my way back to *Senta*. Archie observed my approach, and in his book, *Call from the Sea,* which chronicled our voyage, he captured my mood with prodigious insight, saying that I hailed him long before reaching *Senta* and that my face was "glowing with happiness." He commented also on my "small kit-bag," a backpack in fact. It held everything I intended to leave with, a seaman's knife with a marlinspike to adjust shackles, my geological compass, a camera, foul weather gear, a passport, a notebook, a goose-down sleeping bag, and some miscellaneous items of clothing. I also carried some traveler's checks, and a small amount of cash. There were strict limits on how much one could take out of the country, but I was nowhere near the limit.

The skipper took me aft and courteously introduced me.

"I know Jan from varsity," Viv said. After two years in South Africa, from the island of Mauritius, his accent was only slight.

Gerard's, on the other hand, had the full-bodied charm of a Frenchman. "We 'ave not meet, but Ah see 'im on *Cariad*," he said to the skipper. He then stepped forward and clasped my hand. "Welcome Yann. We 'ave need of you." He was slightly built, about twenty-four, I guessed, a year or two younger than the skipper. His clear eyes held a smile, but a full beard masked what I took to be a likeable-looking face.

We exchanged some pleasant small talk before the skipper steered us back to business. "Gerry, you show Ian where to stow his kit."

"*Oui*, Skipur."

"And listen, all of you. I want the rigging done today. Tomorrow is a rest day…in any case, it's Christmas. There's no need to tell you not to celebrate too much, you'll feel it when we hit the open sea. And tomorrow, everyone back aboard by 19:00. We sail the next morning."

*M*ore people than I had expected gathered to see us off. The skipper's parents were there, in tears. Mimi, his wife, was sobbing, and his young son, Philip, still a baby in arms, took the cue from those around him and joined in the crying. But Archie stood firm, independent and restless.

I met Noleen, the skipper's secretary. In his book Archie mentioned that she had "coaxed" him into the purchase of *Senta*, and as I came to know her a little better, I had no reason to doubt this. He described her as "…unpredictable, completely uncontrollable and impulsive." I would find her all of these, but in addition, attractive, humorous, and someone of endless fun to be around.

Pete and Mac did not come aboard. Sentimental goodbyes were not their style. However, they did swing by in *Cariad's* tender to give us a parting wave, and I could not help but feel guilty for deserting them.

The skipper was chomping at the bit to be outward bound, and I sensed his relief when at last we slipped our mooring and started motoring towards the east end of the Bluff.

His family had disappeared as soon as the boatman put them ashore; they had a long roundabout drive to reach the inlet and catch a last glimpse of us leaving.

We came up on the jetty soon enough, and saw them already waiting there. As we neared, Mimi and the skipper's sisters took off running ahead of us. They seemed intent on holding contact to the very last. Mimi carried a camera, and although the skipper surely would have loved a good picture of us departing under sail, a stiff northeaster prevented us from raising canvas until we had cleared the sea buoy.

We felt the first ocean swell lift her bow, and heard the skipper call us to the helm. "We're on the brink of a great adventure," he said, echoing our thoughts. "Good luck to you all."

"And you, Archie," Noleen returned.

He smiled and kept his gleaming eyes on her. "As soon as we round the buoy, run the staysail up. And you, Vivian," he said pointing a finger, "the mizzen. Gerry and Ian standby the main."

Our responses blew off down the wind — "Aye, aye, Skip…"

"Did you get that, Noleen?"

"Yes, Archie."

"Then move it, you rotten crew. Out of my cockpit. Out!"

As we scrambled forward to our stations, Noleen grinned at Gerry and whispered from the corner of her mouth: "It's going to take me a while to get used to all this 'aye, aye, Skipper' crap."

"You get used, *Mademoiselle*," the Frenchman replied in his congenial way, grabbing for a mainsail tie.

I felt *Senta* bite before we had even trimmed the main, and with a few more cranks on our big starboard winch she surged. She dug in and lifted, and a bow wave tumbled out ahead, then another, and another, as she began to speed down the seas, alive as surely as we were.

The skipper gaped over our quarter, and my eyes followed his. His family still stood there, now no more than specks on the end of a lonely pile of rocks. The next time I looked they were lost from sight, and we were alone with nature. "This is great!" Noleen shouted aloud, and I heard the skipper's raucous laughter echo through the rigging.

A Bloody Mutiny

*T*he boat sped on; we huddled together in the cockpit. "Any preferences on watches?" the skipper asked.

"*Ag*, screw the watches, Archie," Noleen rapped, "at least for another hour or so. After all those headaches, we're on our way at last. It's just so much fun to sit around and shoot the shit."

The skipper grimaced, but did not argue, and there was a warm spell of camaraderie. "Okay, Vivian," he said, at the first lull in our chatter, "you take the helm, one-eight-five."

"One-eight-five," Viv repeated.

"Steering sous, Skipur?" Gerry queried. "We don't go too far offshore, *non*?"

"Yes, we're heading out," the skipper confirmed. "I'm hoping that about ten nautical miles will see us in the Agulhas." — the Agulhas current. "We can ride that all the way to Cape Town."

"Cape Town, 'ow far's that?" Viv whispered in my ear.

"Search me," I replied. "It's got to be a thousand miles."

Viv raised his voice for the skipper's benefit. "It seem we are in an 'urry? I thought we 'ave an nice relaxing cruise? Visit Jan and Noleen's 'ome in Port Elizabeth? J-Bay, do some surfing?"

"Maybe, maybe not." Archie's smile held a nip. "Fair wind, we keep sailing. Make hay while the sun shines as we say in the *platteland*."

"But we're not in the country districts now," Noleen protested.

He smirked, but added nothing further.

Presently he set the watches. Noleen and I were assigned the rookie shift, and I turned in early, wedging myself into the starboard quarter-berth in the engine room. We're at sea, I thought contentedly, and that makes me, at last, a sailor. We were heeled over at a good slant and I was below the waterline. I started to think about this, and about an inch of wood, more or less, separating me from the rushing seas. Then, overcome with excitement and fatigue, I fell asleep.

I was awakened with a start by the ship's bell, the general alarm. I hauled myself, half dressed, through the aft hatch and heard Gerry's cry: "The wind 'ave change, Skipur!"

I clawed my way into the cockpit and saw the skipper, his neck extended, peering up into the sails. "We've got to get that main down! What's your heading, Gerry?"

"Two-six-two, two-six-zero, Skipur."

"That's not good," he mumbled. "Standby to drop the main."

"I take the winch?" Viv volunteered.

The skipper thanked him with a slap on the shoulder, and Vivian began crawling forward, reaching for stanchions.

When he at last clutched the mainmast, the skipper screeched, "Hard t' port, Gerry! Get her into the wind!"

We waited until she slowed, righted herself, and we heard the first flap of the sails. The skipper urged us on with a shout. "Let's do it."

Viv released the halyard and began hauling like a madman on the cloth.

"Come on, crew," the skipper called. "Help him pull on that sail — down — down — down — down!"

We fought it stubbornly, with Noleen screaming curses at the wind, and me, the lowly neophyte, proudly helping to secure the many yards of wet canvas.

Without its insane beating, though the squall raged on, things were suddenly much quieter and less threatening. Gerry brought us round, trying for our original heading. But with the wind shift, and much reduced sail, we were off-course and down to four or five knots.

For the moment we did not care. All we wanted was to catch our breaths.

"Check me out," Noleen giggled, hanging her arms out like a mischievous scamp.

"Not bad," the skipper commented, perhaps noticing, for the first time since the alarm, that all she had on was her black underwear.

She stood tapping a bare foot and we raised a cheer.

"Hoot at me?" she challenged. "You should take a look at your bloody selves."

The wind kept moving. "What's it now, sir?" I asked as the skipper checked the compass card.

"Confounded southwester," he groaned, "and freshening."

"Souswest," Gerry repeated, also in a raised voice, "we cannot sail against souswest! Better we run back to Durban, Skipur."

"That'll be the damned day. You want to be the laughing stock of the yacht club? We fight it, by God. There's no going back!"

"We fight it 'ow, Skipur? We cannot sail against such a wind."

"We hove-to!"

"What is 'ove-to, Skipur? Ah do not know what is 'ove-to."

"You didn't hove-to on *Dirigo?*"

"No. Always bare poles in weather like this, and lie to a sea anchor. Jim never say us what is 'ove-to."

"Well, I'll show you," the skipper smiled. He did. And we were soon riding nicely. With her bow held obliquely into the wind she was losing only the minimum of headway. That was a huge advantage over the alternative, dropping all of our sails, or retreating downwind.

The skipper had donned foul weather gear. But we were wet, and by this time shivering uncontrollably. "Let me take the wheel," he offered, glancing at his wrist. "It's almost my watch anyway. You people go below and dry out."

I changed and fell asleep, and the next thing I heard was the skipper rapping on Noleen's bunk. "Hey wake up, Noleen. What's for breakfast?"

"To hell with breakfast! I'll cook, by God, but who will eat? There's a stink of wet wool, or worse. And you're all half dead, the lot of you."

"Oh yes? And what about you? You don't look too good either, a little green around the gills, I'd say."

"I'm not bloody seasick," she swore vehemently. "And don't you go telling the others that I am."

Eventually, to our enormous relief, the storm abated. The wind swung round and, out of danger, we hoisted all the sail we had.

The hours slipped by, and the watches changed with no complications. We continued downwind on a broad reach. The sails were so perfectly trimmed that the helm felt light. *Senta* was all but steering herself. "Double-digit knots. What do you say, Gerry?"

"She sail fast."

"Faster than *Dirigo?*"

"Ah think so."

The skipper's face lit up, and he could not resist the urge to have it repeated. "Do you really think so?"

But at this point Gerry backed off. Archie would be asking next if he was a better skipper than Jim Crawford. "Maybe," he replied, but quickly froze his smile. "No, maybe *Dirigo* 'ave a little more speed. Maybe."

The skipper changed the subject. "How're you feeling, Ian?"

"A lot better. I'm sorry I was seasick when you needed me."

He waved it aside with such graciousness that I was persuaded to verbalize a little gratitude. "You did a good job, Skipper," I said, "of handling her in those squalls. There were some really tight spots."

Noleen punched me on the arm. "Don't tell him that, you nitwit. You sound like his wife. He's a stupid shit, with a head that's plenty big enough as it is."

I saw Gerry gulp and clench his teeth, and his neck muscles tighten. I too sucked in a breath, waiting for the skipper to go ballistic. But all he did was laugh, an endearing guffaw that said, 'she's right.'

*A*fter an early lunch the skipper appeared on deck with his sextant. He stood braced with one arm wrapped around a shroud for support, his instrument in the other. Noleen called out the time, having synchronized her wristwatch with the yacht's chronometer. Gerry stood by with a stopwatch while the skipper, on the brief crest of a wave, swung the reflected rim of the sun to the horizon and shouted "mark!" He then disappeared below, and a short while later we heard him curse. "Damn!"

Gerry checked his calculations, and found them to be correct. But the position he put us at was wrong. Along the coast we could pretty easily check our plots.

"I'll just have to keep practicing," the skipper complained.

Over the next few days, at Archie's urging, Gerry and I also tried the sextant. But as hard as we concentrated, we were eluded both by the stars and by that fleeting shot of the sun at its zenith. The rougher the weather, the worse our sights were. Celestial navigation on a small boat was clearly no easy matter. The constant movement was certainly one factor. Another related to the fact that one could not get up high enough to view a good horizon.

"What do you think, Gerry?" I asked. "I mean nobody aboard can use a bloody sextant. We've got seven thousand miles of ocean to get through. How will we ever make it?"

"*Oui,* better if we can use, but Ah 'ave not worry."

"You're not worried? How can you not be worried?"

"Listen Yann, to Cape Town we 'ave see the coastline, *oui.* So long she are on our right. After, the Atlantic. So long we point near the setting sun, 'is impossible we miss South and North America. Ah am not worry." His body language chanted that it was no big thing. But he decided to put me completely at ease. "Ah don't say this the bloody skipur. But we 'ave can sail without a sextant. We 'ave can sail without a compass. So long we beware the sea, so my father say."

On the following morning we blew out our big genoa, and the skipper decided to layover at East London for a day or two and have it repaired. But it was dark by the time we reached the inlet, and we had no harbor chart. The skipper studied the confusion of lights along the shoreline. "No, this is madness," he concluded after some time. "It would be tricky with an engine. But without one" — we could not get it started — "and no spotlight, and us, inexperienced yachtsmen; forget it!"

We raised such a lament that he was forced to laugh. "You really want to put in here, don't you?"

"Yes Skipper," we responded as a body. We deck apes were tired.

"Okay," he conceded. "We'll move out into deep water, and try again in the morning."

But the weather demons once more conspired against us, this time, ironically, with conditions that under any other circumstances would have been in our favor. Both wind and current slowly drove us south until the lights of East London were barely visible. We hoisted more sail and desperately tried to make up what we had lost. But at daybreak the skipper decided to move on. "Two-one-zero."

Noleen was at the helm. "Two-one-zero," she repeated glumly.

The skipper smiled. "What's the matter, Noleen?"

"Nothing, Archie Snyman. Look at me. I'm brimming with excitement. But if you don't stop at PE, there'll be a bloody mutiny!"

Men in Plain Clothes

The skipper made a landfall at Port Elizabeth, and Noleen, Vivian, and Gerry were elated. But I had mixed feelings about the stopover, remembering, all too well, Pete's apprehension about having to tell his parents that he would be leaving college. The scene on *Senta* clearly did not lend itself to the saga of a Darwin-type geological survey for the summer.

The last time my family had received word of me was from *Cariad,* so I was surprised at Pop's casual tone when he answered the telephone. "Rough trip?" he asked matter-of-factly.

"Do you know where I'm calling from?"

"PE, I assume."

"How did you figure that?"

"It was in the newspaper."

"The newspaper?"

"Yes, a headline caught my eye," he said, and quoted it: " 'Two Students on Yacht to Attempt Atlantic Record.' " He paused briefly. "I was reading the article to your mother," he went on, "saying how pleased I was that you weren't that stupid. Then I saw your name…you can imagine."

I gave an edgy laugh. "When was that?"

"A few days ago."

"But you sounded as if you expected me today?"

"I did. Thanks to my contacts in the good old *SAR & H*" — the South African Railways and Harbours — "I've been in touch with all the lighthouse keepers on the coast. We were about to drive up to East London when it seemed as if you were stopping there."

"I'll be darned," I exclaimed in amazement. "You probably knew more about our whereabouts than we did half the time."

"I wouldn't be surprised," he agreed in a self-satisfied tenor. "I even got a call from the Air Force. Their coastal patrol spotted your boat and tried to make radio contact."

"Unbelievable. Yes, we lost power. Our generator was down for a while, and we couldn't get our engine started. Our batteries eventually went flat."

"We thought it was something like that."

"What does Mom say about it all?"

"We'll talk about that later."

"Well, I mean, is she happy?"

"Happy is hardly the word. She wants me to get a court order to haul you off. You're not yet twenty-one you know."

"So, are you going to?" I asked apprehensively.

"No."

I let out a deep audible breath.

"But that doesn't mean we're not going to try to talk you out of it…By the way, what are your plans for today?"

"The skipper says I can take some shore leave. But I've got to be aboard again tomorrow. The yacht club is having a *braai* for us in the evening. And you're invited. It's New Year. We're sailing again on the third."

"On the third? There's a gale predicted. The Port Captain probably won't let you leave."

"Then we'll leave when we leave. The skipper will decide. Do you know where to find us?"

"Yes. See you shortly. Cheerio."

*B*y the time I got back aboard, two pressmen were just leaving. "You 'ave miss your photo in the newspepper," Gerry reported.

"Oh yes. And where are the others?"

"Noleen 'ave just now gone to 'er 'ouse. Skipur is call 'is wife. Vivian is on shore smoking 'is peep." He turned and pointed over to Vivian who emerged from a cloud of smoke and waved his pipe at me.

"Gerry, do you and Viv want to spend the night at my place?"

"Noleen already 'ave invite us. She come back in one 'our."

"And the skipper?"

"Skipur say 'e stay. Someone come tomorrow for the engine."

"On New Year's Day?"

"That's what 'e say."

"I feel bad about the skipper being here alone."

Gerry shrugged, " 'is boat."

I returned late the next day to find the genoa repaired, and the magnetic switch assembly replaced on the engine starting system. "I got the generator going, but should I have been able to fix the starter motor?" I asked.

"No," the mechanic replied, to my considerable relief. "There's nothing you can do in a case like that, at least not without the parts."

On the following day while we were doing odd jobs, we heard a commotion ashore and, on looking up, heard Noleen call out to the skipper. "Archie! Oh my God, Archie," she cried in a desperate voice, "please help me!"

Viv leapt to the dock, but the skipper ordered him back aboard. "I'll handle this," he growled. He stepped ashore and Noleen tried to grab him.

But two men in plain clothes quickly seized her.

"What's going on?" the skipper demanded in a piercing tone.

"These men want to put me in jail," she cried frantically.

The men held her. One of them flashed a shield at the skipper. "Police," he announced in a thick, threatening accent.

"Well I'm her lawyer," Archie spat, reaching into his pocket. He withdrew his wallet and showed them a card.

"My orders are to remove her immediately," the security policeman barked. There was an expression of malevolence on his face. He changed his grip to her elbow. "Let's go, lady!"

"Never!" Noleen screeched, trying in vain to break loose. "I'd rather kill myself than go with you."

"Calm down, Noleen," the skipper pleaded. He turned. "And you two," he instructed in a bold voice, "take your hands off her!"

Somewhat startled, they let go, but backed down no further. The larger of the duo, a man with cruel slit eyes, slipped his hand into his jacket and the skipper took a step back.

With the prospect of a gun being drawn, Archie's voice dropped a decibel. "Where she goes, I go," he said less aggressively.

"Very well," the man agreed, and they all moved off with heavy steps.

We crept ashore and followed them at a distance. A uniformed policeman picked them up. He jumped out to open the doors, a baton and revolver on his belt, and the five sped off in an unmarked car.

A Forced Departure

The skipper returned later in the day looking wretched. "We sail within the hour," he announced grimly.

"Skipur, the weather..." Gerry gasped, and was about to protest further. But a mask of command caught his eye and froze his words. "Aye, aye," he acknowledged smartly.

The skipper sensed our acute uneasiness. "Noleen joins us again in Cape Town," he promised unconvincingly. "And I'm afraid that's all I can tell you right now."

In South Africa, in those days, one did not ask too many questions about anyone's misadventures with the security police. And besides, Archie was a lawyer and an Afrikaner; we had to trust his judgment on this matter. Perhaps Noleen would be released from custody if we left, and placed under house arrest. Our heads spun, but we had no problem in believing that Archie had somehow struck a deal in her favor.

Nevertheless, the whole incident once again put the fear of God in me. I had considered my passport a sure bet to safe passage, but no longer. What was to stop the police from hauling me off, just as they had Noleen? They had my photograph from at least one protest march. The damage had been done. From their perspective I was clearly a troublemaker. What would prevent me from spilling my guts to the American media? I represented what they most dreaded from traveling student dissidents, bad press abroad. And the United States was a country they least wanted to offend.

So, despite the atrocious weather, I was pleased to be off. I was less of a target on the high seas, I reasoned, well away from pressmen with their cameras and stories — the famous Archie Snyman who, as a student, had been a high-hurdles champion; his dream of a new record for the South Atlantic crossing; his promise to paint South Africa into the history books of sailing; his yacht lost at sea. That newspaper photograph was surely what had triggered Noleen's trouble. I was thankful I had missed it. Any thought of publicity now scared me to death.

I reluctantly phoned my parents, and we said a few hasty goodbyes. Then, steaming with apprehension, we were off into the teeth of what, for our small boat, was a devastating blizzard. We hoisted our small staysail, a storm mizzen, and a reefed main, and with the engine running began hammering our way into tumbling green water. *Senta* jolted, and her timbers groaned as if in sympathy with our depressed morale.

We drove her hard, fighting for every inch of headway, tacking endlessly, working like demons. Breaking seas rolled down on us, and salt spray lashed at our faces. Eventually, after an endless time, we cleared Cape Recife. But we had only reached the edge of Algoa Bay, a gain of negligible account considering the punishment we had taken. And now, without the protection of the headland, conditions worsened. Our backs strained on the winches. We wrestled with the flogging sheets. We were wet, weather-beaten, and exhausted. But we stuck at it, knowing that it stopped us from having to think. For in one way the storm was our salvation. It blurred that forlorn image of Noleen being hauled off so helplessly.

The skipper, a judo expert and fitness guru, seemed tireless. "I was content to battle it out," he wrote.

But as time wore on, we, the crew, began to falter, and used the old boat as an excuse. "You keel 'er, Skipur," Gerry complained. "She break apart. We 'ave to take a second reef."

"No, let her go! She can take it!" His maniacal laugh sounded above the storm, above the screaming wind.

And so, as if to underscore our inexperience, we continued to smash into murderous seas. The wind howled, and the planks creaked painfully as *Senta* pitched and tossed, confronting swell, after swell, after swell. Then a villainous wave, a "big, foaming sea," Conrad wrote in 1897, in *The Nigger of the 'Narcissus,'* "came out of the mist. It made for the ship, roaring wildly, and in its rush it looked as mischievous and discomposing as a madman with an axe." Just such a wave struck us down, and the shock loading on the stays shook our guts and made us tremble. Nothing in our young lives had prepared us for such punishment. The wall of water threw *Senta* on her beam-ends, and every loose thing crashed to leeward.

We clung to what we could while she slowly righted herself, all the while pondering a predicament that grew worse by the minute. Then suddenly our hearts pounded again as two monsters broke the surface through driving spindrift. Recoiling from fright, we saw another, and another. It was a school of false killer whales circling in the darkness, very close.

Threatened by leviathans that could easily sink us, terrors the like of Moby Dick, the skipper crawled below to get his gun.

Gerry followed his retreat from the deck. " 'E's crazy," the Frenchman whispered to me when the skipper was out of earshot. " 'E rip again 'er sail, 'e break 'er mast, 'e sink us. Nobody take a small yacht to sea in weather like this. What you say, Yann?"

I licked my cracked lips, stared mesmerized at the bounding whales, at the phosphorescent light that gleamed along the crests of the bedeviled waves, but thought better of complaining. I was more afraid of the security police than of the sea and her Medusas. "Don't ask me," I shrugged. "What do I know? It's his boat."

"Yes, but it's our lives," Viv protested, wet, cold, and aching. "Gerard is right. This man is insane. I sign off at the next port we reach. Tough it out is one thing, but this is tomfoolery. I leave. For sure, I leave!"

"You leave? What you will do?"

"I go looking for Noleen for a start. I don't believe she will join us again in Cape Town. I don't believe him."

"You are right," Gerry agreed, "we should not 'ave abandon 'er."

I tried to console Gerry. "You don't understand how things work in this country," I said. "You go snooping around, asking too many questions, you'll finish up in detention yourself."

"Ah don't believe," Gerry spat. "Ah..." The discussion was interrupted by more salt water tumbling down the deck towards us. We clung to *Senta* like seaweed.

The skipper had come topsides, but the big fish were gone. Now, below again, braced at the chart table, he scribbled in the log. He mentioned the "raging" storm, the "fantastically high waves" that were "hammering us broadside," and the fact that everything seemed against us. The radio began squawking. The skipper listened, then placed aside his pencil and grabbed for the companionway ladder.

We piped down when we saw him.

"It doesn't look good," he complained, no longer smiling. "I just heard a weather report. It's getting worse. We're putting back to PE."

"Aye, aye, Skipper."

We jumped to it, grappled with sheets and sails, and soon had her about and locked down under a reefed staysail and a storm mizzen. Running with the storm instead of driving into it was like being in a different world. Even the skipper looked relieved. He had hidden it well from us, but he too was exhausted. "I was fatigued beyond all care," he wrote later. "Body and soul seemed scarcely to hang together."

The Cape of Storms

*N*obody laughed in our faces, but back in Port Elizabeth things were less than comfortable. My dad failed to understand why we had deliberately sailed into such a storm in the first place, and rattled on about it, fortunately not when Archie was around. The press was onto us again, turning our misfortunes into *L'Odyssée,* as Gerry said, desperately looking for a scoop on the missing girl. "I seem to spend half my day hiding from those newspaper people," I complained bitterly.

"*Oui,*" Gerry agreed. "They ask me ten time about Noleen."

"I hope you didn't say anything!"

"Ah like to, the bastards police, but Skipur commit me to silence."

But silence did not hold within our own ranks. We were on edge and must have driven the skipper crazy, quizzing him each time he returned from an errand. Eventually, Gerry called on Noleen's parents, but not even they would talk.

And true to his word, Viv signed off. "I saw her go. I saw who took her. And I will get to the bottom of this," he vowed, "I promise!"

This time even the skipper decided to lay low, refusing to speak to the media as we waited out the storm.

And on 10 January 1961 we tried again, slipping from the harbor at first light. Except for a background engine noise and the splash-splash of our wet-exhaust discharge, everything was deathly quiet, so quiet that we were driven to whispering. Then, out of nowhere, a loudspeaker boomed at us. We gasped, startled. But it was no more than a friendly farewell from the signal station. "Weather report favorable. Good luck, *Senta,* and *bon voyage.*"

The wind was now in our favor and things moved like clockwork. But we were also more cautious and a lot smarter. We motor-sailed when we could not make hull-speed — our attempt at the South Atlantic sailing record would start only when we left Cape Town — our minds constantly focused on making headway. I ran the engine every day as the mechanic in Port Elizabeth had suggested, and kept the batteries charged. We scrutinized the barometer, listened more frequently to weather reports, and radioed passing ships for their input. Experienced seamen must surely have a gut feel for pending bad weather, we decided. We kept track of safe havens, Knysna and Mossel Bay, and constantly updated our estimates of how long it would take to reach these. And the skipper kept an hourly log.

Only once did we purposely slow down, for a brief encounter with a school of spirited dolphins. "I haf read," Werner said, "dot der *Strandlopers* haf thought porpoises vere couriers of goot fortune. Unt dot dey haf been sent by a great sea god."

"And my father 'ave say," Gerry added, "that the 'awaiians 'ave think the same thing. Their sea god was name *Kanaloa.*"

"And did you know," the skipper smiled, "that *Strandloper* means Beach Ranger, a name given them by the early Dutch settlers in South Africa? They were really a Khoisan people who chose to spend a good portion of their time along the coast, the beaches and sea cliffs."

"I'm impressed, Skipper," I applauded.

"I'm interested in things like that," he said.

We had two new crewmembers aboard, as different from each other as night and day, Werner, who had first mentioned the *Strandlopers,* a tough young German lad with strong features, a quick laugh, and a rough-and-ready manner; and Johnny, just the opposite, like a Lilliputian, small and delicate, a ladies hairdresser, who the skipper had signed on as chef.

"What do you think of Johnny?" I asked.

"Ah like 'im; 'e's a little strange, but so long 'e can cook."

"The skipper says he was once an army cook."

"*Oui*, that's what 'e say."

We held our breaths as we approached the infamous Cape of Storms. But our streak of luck had run out. We received a gale warning, too late to dart for safety. I felt my stomach sink. As Christopher Buckley so lucidly put it, in *Steaming to Bamboola*, the Cape, for us, was what sailing between Scylla and Charybdis was for Odysseus — "jagged cliffs rising out of chaotic waters," "stiff currents," "and whirlpools," "big whirlpools."

"A Sou'easter," the skipper announced. "But at least it's with us."

By late afternoon the first gusts were upon us and we dropped the main to be ready. The skipper called for an early dinner and set the watches. He had us study the charts and, based on our noon position — he was making phenomenal progress with his sextant — check the dead reckoning courses for the night. "See the lights at Cape Agulhas and Jessie Point. These will give us a fix, and we can make the necessary adjustments. We can check again when we pick up the lighthouse at Danger Point."

"Jees, Skeeper, vot is dot?" Werner asked, pointing his dirty finger to a wreck symbol on the chart.

"The old *Birkenhead*," the skipper replied. "She went down in 1852. More than 400 drowned, mainly British troops."

Johnny was still cooking when we altered course and began heading downwind, rising and partially surfing on the faces of large swells that had started to come up on us from astern. It was exhilarating sailing, but we were hungry. I crawled forward to peek into the galley; the fragrance of frying onions had made my mouth water.

Eventually we heard a voice. "Open up, your dinners are ready."

I dived for the hatch.

Johnny peeped up from the engine room, saw a huge swell looming high above the cockpit and, with an expression of stark terror on his face, screamed, "Look o-o-o-out!"

We swung around. But all we saw was our ensign flying stiffly, as we began to lift some twelve or fifteen feet onto another passing sea. By the time we turned again, Johnny was gone. I surveyed the engine room and saw our banquet spattered around the cabin sole.

"Where are the food?" Gerry called out frantically.

"On the floor," I complained in disgust.

"Pick it up!"

I did so, as quickly as I could, and we wolfed it down before it even got cold.

"Superb!" Gerry cheered, one hand on the wheel, the other showing a raised thumb. "Ah wonder 'ow was taste the gravy?"

*T*wo hours, or so, further into our watch, things began to get desperate, almost beyond fun. The seas had become perceptively higher, and now as we raced obliquely down the waves our bow began to dig. At PE we had lashed two large drums of gasoline to our mainmast shrouds, and their combined weight wasn't helping matters.

"Better we 'ave drop the mizzen," Gerry complained, "Ah am afraid we pitch-pole."

"Pitch-pole? What is that?" I asked.

"Capsize," he explained, "stern over bow." His vivid hand-and-arm movement left no doubt as to what he meant.

"I'll call the skipper," I uttered in alarm.

"*Oui*," he agreed.

The skipper and Werner scrambled up on deck. Werner was wide-eyed, and looked as if he was sleepwalking. "Vhatsdermatter?" he mumbled, while the skipper, very much alert, quickly studied our sails to assess the situation.

"Ah think we drop the mizzen, Skipur. The wind 'ave grown too strong."

"Yes," the skipper concurred readily as he spied our bowsprit dip beneath the water.

We dived for the winch. But although Werner and I put our full weight on it, it would not budge.

"Is there a problem?" the skipper called.

"She's jammed."

"Let me try." But, despite his strength, he was no more successful than we had been.

"Maybe Ah bring 'er in the wind, Skipur?"

"No! No! She'll broach on seas like these. Hold your course."

We waited while he pondered our predicament.

As usual, it didn't take him long. "Ian," he spelled out, in short order, "get the fire axe from the engine room. And Werner, fetch the spare anchor line from the forepeak. We must rig a sea anchor, or at the very least some sort of drag. Come, let me give you a hand."

The two returned within minutes, and awkwardly heaved a heavy coil of manila into the cockpit. "Start streaming this off the stern," he directed, "in a loop. I'll make this side fast. It will slow us down and steady us."

I had no sooner secured my end and paid out the line, than Gerry clapped his hands. "It 'ave do the trick, Skipur, like a tail on a kite."

The skipper might have considered himself an inexperienced yachtsman, but he had a shrewd talent for doing the right thing in a crisis.

"Do you want me to smack that mizzen halyard?" I asked, eyeing the axe that I had fetched from below.

"No, let me first have another go." The skipper had dug up a large wrench, and it was not long before he had the halyard free.

We furled the sail and lashed it to the boom, pulled in the trawl, then went back to the cockpit to enjoy some heavy weather sailing.

Under reduced cloth the bow floated higher as we sped once more down the following seas. The gale was from dead astern.

"This is *Senta* at her best," the skipper offered in animation.

Werner smiled happily. I could smell brandy on his breath. "Jeez Skeeper, dis modderfocker's fast. I neffer haf sail so quick."

"She's got to be doing twelve, thirteen knots at times."

"Dot's right, Skeeper. Unt only mit a fockin jib."

"And a storm jib at that. And by the way," the skipper chided Werner with a slightly annoyed expression, "you might want to start watching your language. We'll have a lady aboard again in Cape Town."

"And she don't like to 'ave anyone swear more than she," the Frenchman quipped.

The skipper let go with one of his chortles. "Well said, Gerry," he bellowed, almost choking on his coffee.

Werner apologized, but the skipper waved it off. "Get some rack."

"Not tonight, Skeeper. I stay by der vheel all der night if I can."

"Ah too, Skipur," Gerry added.

"Well, I can't say that I blame you," the skipper smiled. "I'll be awake, but I'll be writing."

I asked him if he meant writing the log, but he said no, a book, a book about our trip. We looked at each other in astonishment. Then Gerry asked inquisitively: "You will 'ave me in your book, Skipur?"

"Yes, all of you."

"Hell, Skeeper, better I den stop mit sweering."

"And drinking at sea," the skipper said, pointing a finger at Werner.

"It is in English or Afrikaans, you write, Skipur?"

"English," he replied.

We asked him for the name of the book, but he said he had not decided yet. All he could say was that the first chapter was entitled *Ulwandhle,* a Zulu word for 'the sea,' he said. "But no more questions," he begged. "I'll see if Johnny wants to join you."

Johnny did not. He had his head under a pillow. "Those seas scare me, Captain. I think I'll just stay put."

I was also scared, though I did not say it. But for me it was a fear-filled excitement, a breathtaking skim-of-delight, hour after hour of it, my longest surf. There were moments of sheer terror, to be sure, when I thought that we might not rise from the troughs of some of those Cape rollers, when tumbling waves threatened to broach and capsize us, when menacing gusts terrorized us to the point that we expected to be torn from the deck. But we held on tightly, our saltwater-sprayed faces shining in the dim moonlight.

We were pushed off course with almost every swell, and although we tried constantly to correct, we could never be sure of our dead-reckoning line. We simply steered by feel. Fortunately it was a clear night, and we could easily spot the lighthouses — we had learned by then to identify their flash patterns.

But despite our best efforts to hold our distance offshore, we came upon a tortured sea-buoy, its bell tolling insanely on a reef. It scared us half to death, its purpose. We fought our way further seaward, seemingly impervious to fatigue, and in due course we were steering for the light on Cape Point. In the geological past this was the tip of an island off Africa, but now it is joined to the continent and thrusts prominently southward as a peninsula. It is the last land, bar a few scattered islands, before the icy wastes of Antarctica.

Had I been in charge I should have made the conservative choice and sailed into False Bay, to take shelter in Simon's Town. And when the skipper appeared topsides, I stated my case for safety.

"No! No!" he barked into the screaming wind. "Take her round Cape Point."

The thought registered in my mind that he might be doing it for his book. 'Following the tradition of old mariners, we rounded the notorious landmark in a full gale.' But although he mentioned gusts of over 80 knots, he made little of the blustery night, dwelling rather on the "unforgettable impression" of our approach to Cape Town.

'Ulwandhle'

On 20 January 1961 we sailed from Cape Town, parting quietly, as the skipper noted, from that most beautiful of all harbors. And if he had mentioned again what he had said when I had first joined *Senta*, he would have captured my mood accurately, for my face was once more "glowing with happiness."

We had every inch of canvas flying, and by evening we were screaming downwind at fourteen knots. On the following day we logged 244 nautical miles for our 24-hour run, and I knew that I was, at last, beyond the grasp of the security police. For ten long days I had lived with the phobia of being hauled off. So now, like Madiba when he first left South Africa, I also "heaved a sigh of relief" and was "elated" to be away. We were safely into the Trade Winds, and there was no going back. I could relax.

The skipper, for different reasons, shared my euphoria. He was beside himself with optimism, saying that if we could hold that speed we would reach St. Helena in less than ten days. "I visualize," he said, highly excited, "the fastest South Atlantic crossing ever!"

But true to life, not everything could progress that perfectly. The wind let up, and the Frenchman took sick. I awakened one morning and found him at the wheel looking miserable. "How are you?" I inquired.

His reply was worse than I expected. "My teeth itch. Ah don't feel my 'ead. My throat sore me. Ah don't 'ave sleep yesterday night."

And, as we had feared, Noleen had not rejoined us. In her place we had another brunette. "She's got a pretty pair of legs," the skipper had noted for our benefit. But "pretty sticks," as Werner put it, did not cut it. "She's lazy, sonny."

And so, like Napoleon Bonaparte, she too was marooned on St. Helena, our first landfall beyond South Africa. And with her went another new crewman, a big, lazy oaf. He had given some lip, and the skipper had pulled him from his bunk and sent him sprawling against the bulkhead. "Don't you ever speak to me again like that," he had snarled, "or I'll break your bloody neck!"

And little Johnny Swart departed of his own accord at St. Helena. He had continued to cook, but had "not slept a wink," he said. The skipper related Johnny's tale-of-woe to the Governor of the Island, and Lady Hartford, overhearing, offered to set him up in his own salon, provided he did her hair once a week.

Johnny was overjoyed. "And if it doesn't jibe, Captain," he tittered, "I can always leave on one of the Union-Castle mailships, whenever next one comes to St. Helena, three months I think they said."

Part 15

ESCAPE UNDER SAIL

St. Helena

Triomf! Triumph! I had escaped under sail. We had a lot of canvas flying and the ride was exhilarating. Werner leaned back, his face a picture of tranquility. "Hell Skeeper, dot's der life, isn't it, Skeeper?"

"Yes, it's certainly more like I imagined cruising to be." The skipper paused to enjoy a golden sun appear out of the ocean off our starboard quarter. "I had my doubts though, during those hard times in the Indian Ocean. You know, leaving my law practice and all, for that, nothing but storm, after storm, after storm. Mind you, I'm still worried about it, my law firm I mean, whether it will sell. And I'd like to be further ahead on my book. And even now I still worry about money, and about Mimi and Philip, and Noleen, and about whether I did the right thing after all."

"Ach Skeeper, vorry, vorry, vorry. Vhere does it get you?"

The skipper smiled.

"To hell mit your business, Skeeper. To hell mit your book. It's rush, rush, rush. How you can vrite a book about a trip vot you don't properly can enjoy?"

"What do you mean I can't enjoy it?" Both his expression and tone suddenly changed, and now held a hint of irritation.

"I mean you can't properly enjoy it vhen you vorry all der day?"

The German slapped him on the shoulder, and the skipper loosened up. "You know Werner, I envy you, your simple lifestyle, your enlightened philosophy on life. What's your secret?"

"No secret, Skeeper. Just stop mit vorrying and enjoy yourself, like ve do." He turned to us and we nodded, but apparently with less gusto than he was looking for, because he quickly expanded on himself as the example of lightheartedness. "Look at me, Skeeper," he said. "Vot more I need? I haf food. I haf mein bunk. I haf plenty of smokes. Unt I haf me a great adventure. Vhy I must vorry? And vhy, vhen I can haf a life like dot, must I slave in a bloody vorkshop like I used to? You tell me, Skeeper, for vot? For money? Vot money can do for me out here? Unt even on shore, if I haf more money, more people find a vay to take it from me."

The skipper offered him a compromising grin, but would not fully concede. "I'm not so sure about that," he challenged. He turned to the Frenchman. "What do you think, Gerry?"

"*Oui*, Ah agree," Gerry responded thoughtfully. "We are yachtsmen. We don't 'ave be 'ere to worry. We 'ave be 'ere for sailing, relax, and 'ave some fun. When we are at sea, time is not money. If we keep thinking about money, we better 'ave stay at 'ome. And, Skipur, you do too much!"

"Well, Gerry and Werner, I will try to be more like you. My problem, I think, is that I tend to over-schedule, even my free time. But worries, or no worries, I need to spend a few more hours on my book."

"Do it vhen you get back home, Skeeper."

"There will be no time when I get back home."

"*Ja, ja,* Skeeper, ve know. Den better you spend a little time on it. But be sure to vrite vot I just told you."

The skipper disappeared, and I turned to Werner. "Don't you think you were a little rough on him?"

"No sonny, dot's vot he needs."

"Take into account," I said, fixing my eyes on him, "that he's highly-strung, and that people like him always worry. And remember that without his energy and drive, we wouldn't be here right now."

"Vot you mean, sonny?"

"I mean it's his success that is paying for all of this. It was his ambition that got him his own law firm at twenty-whatever. And it will probably be the money from his book that keeps you sailing round the world. He's merely tying to turn this trip into a profitable pursuit. You want my advice? Let him worry a bit."

"*Oui,* and Ah am also worry," the Frenchman put forward.

"Yes Gerry, and what's disturbing you?" I asked.

"What 'e will say about me in 'is book. That Ah am not a seaman. My father, 'e will not be 'appy."

"Your father?"

"Yes, 'e 'ave sail many time around the world, many time Cape of Storms, around Cape of 'orn, Roaring Forties, 'owling Fifties. If 'e will read that Ah am not a seaman. Beware me!"

We laughed.

"You think 'i's funny. Ah 'ave kill the bastard."

"Relax sonny. Skeeper von't say dot you are a bad seaman. But I say you are sometimes so bad as him mit vorry."

"And I am as well," I added.

"Unt vot you vorry, sonny?" Werner asked, turning his attention to me.

"I don't know, South Africa, the politics there, whether I'm doing the right thing in running away from it all, leaving varsity, money, my family, whether I will be able to make it on my own, a million things."

Werner looked me squarely in the eye and I steeled myself for his ridicule. But he was serious for once. "You do der right thing, sonny," he acknowledged, his face tightening to reinforce what he was saying. "I also haf leeft Sous Africa. I haf come der for a new life, but I also cannot stay. And for you is vorser. You get vun day called for der army."

"I'm glad you understand," I muttered, embarrassed about dragging him into my personal affairs. I tried to smile.

But Werner's expression remained solemn. "Mein father vanted to leeft Germany vhen Hitler came in power. But he haf stay until vos too late. He vos caught in der army and must fight for vot he hate."

"Exactly!" I exclaimed. "That was one my greatest worries. Precisely that. The bloody army! Fighting for a cause that I'm against."

"Den you know you haf do der right thing, sonny." He extended a loyal hand and shook mine firmly, and I experienced a surge of support I had not felt since that day on the Transkei coast when Pete had offered to join me in my quest to leave.

*I*t was seldom, if ever, that we saw the skipper completely let his guard down. But Werner's spurring must have had some effect, for he did it at St. Helena. After ridding himself of his unwanted crewmembers, and badgering us to get the boat in order for a visit by Sir Robert Hartford, the Governor, he had been a different person, at ease and animated, quite unlike the skipper we had seen ashore in PE, or Cape Town.

He and Sir Robert had immediately taken to each other, discussing the finer points of sailing, the pros and cons of *Senta's* Bermuda rig, her German construction, and her former history as the visionary private yacht of the Kaiser. And when the conversation had turned to law and the management of the Island, it had been hard to get him away. But he knew better than we did that there was work to be done.

Gerry found us late in the day, scavenging four-gallon cans from shopkeepers to transfer water from the wharf to where *Senta* lay at anchor. "The Governor 'ave send a man to our boat," he announced long-faced.

"Why?" the skipper inquired with concern.

"For invite us to lunch tomorrow, at Plantation 'Ouse."

The lines on the skipper's face changed from apprehension to delight. "That's excellent news," he said. "But you don't look too happy about it. Is there a problem?"

"*Oui*," Gerry responded, "two problem. One, what Ah will wear. And two, 'ow Ah will address 'im."

"You address him the same way you addressed him today."

"But Ah 'ave say nothing to 'im today. Ah was too afraid."

The skipper laughed. "Simply call him 'Sir Robert,' " he advised, "or 'His Excellency.' "

"Sir Robert," Gerry repeated. "And 'er? Ah say 'Lady Robert?' "

This was too much for the skipper, and his bark of mirth appeared to offend the Frenchman. "Sorry, Gerry," he apologized. "Lady Hartford. Address her as 'Lady Hartford.'"

"Lady 'Artford?"

"Yes, that's perfect."

"And what Ah will wear?"

I had been listening politely, but at this point I cut in. "I'm glad I collected a suit in Port Elizabeth," I said.

Gerry's face clouded once more, and I could not believe my tactlessness. "Ah 'ave only a jacket," he lamented. "Maybe Ah will not go."

"Nonsense," the skipper responded kindly. "A jacket is fine."

"But this Plantation 'Ouse, it is a palace, *non?*"

"No, it's no palace. It's just a house, an old house, built in 1791, Sir Robert told me. It's not even all that old by French standards."

"*Oui,*" Gerry replied, lifting his chin proudly, "then Ah go."

Gerry was not the only one to have doubts. Mine surfaced at the Governor's mansion, when I spotted his Elizabethan table setting. "How will I ever know what to eat with?" I whispered frantically, suddenly aware of my profound lack of social graces.

"Just let Lady Hartford lead," the skipper advised quietly. "Do whatever she does. And remember, no talking to the servants!"

It was sound counsel and I passed it on to the others.

We had first sighted St. Helena much as a despondent Napoleon Bonaparte must have, a barren volcanic rock mass jutting steeply from the ocean. However, once one ascends the 699 stairs of Jacob's Ladder, one sees its beauty. And moving inland, things are green and even lush in places. It is a place of beauty, full of fine assets.

"But it's her people who are her gems," the skipper noted.

They were more genial than any I had met. And there were no second-class citizens. By the time Werner pointed this out to me, I had already noticed the perfect racial harmony that existed on the Island.

"Look at these children," the skipper marveled, as a half dozen mixed-race youngsters tagged along behind us, asking us questions, carrying things and doing us small favors, but with shaking heads refusing any small rewards we offered them. "See how spontaneously polite and well-mannered they are."

I mentioned that I was a geology student.

"Oh, you will like it here," a young girl said, reflecting, in her unique way, on the Island's turbulent past. "We have volcanoes all the way up to the mountains."

The adults were the same, wanting us to enjoy their home of fire and fantasy, eager to speak to us, but careful not to intrude on our privacy.

Engagements were subtle. "I was about to have my morning cup o' tea," a shopkeeper announced. "Please join me if you have a minute."

But although they were reserved, once a conversation was initiated they spoke easily and at length, quizzing us in detail about our various backgrounds and, like open books, providing us with all sorts of fascinating information about themselves.

It was immediately apparent that they were extremely proud of their British connections, and of the history of their small — only nine miles by six — piece of real estate. I heard more than once about their hero of heroes, the rather frail, one-eyed, one-armed nautical mastermind, Lord Nelson. How he had lost an eye in the fight for Corsica in 1793, and an arm in a battle off the Canary Islands in 1797. Of how, with his fewer ships, he had sailed onto the enemy coast and taunted Napoleon's fleet still tied up in the harbor. And finally of how, on 21 October 1805, he had engaged and triumphantly defeated the combined French-Spanish armada in the greatest sea battle ever fought, Trafalgar.

"Next time you come, please bring it with you," an old man implored me, his eyes glimmering. "I'd love just to touch it." He was referring to a shanty's fiddle, one of the few heirlooms in my family, that once had been used by a Watson aboard Nelson's flagship. "I cannot believe," he said with adoration, "that you have something from aboard *Victory*." He placed a brown-skinned hand on my shoulder. "A violin," he observed, telling me what I already knew, "is used to give rhythm to the songs the sailors sing when they strain at the capstan to weigh anchor, or heave heavy sails aloft. The tempo lets them push on the bars as one."

"But do you think it really helps?" I asked.

"Yes," he assured me, "the music provides timing and strength."

While I might have anticipated local wisdom on St. Helena's geomorphology, or on her surrounding sea life, or even on Lord Nelson — as an antidote to Napoleon — I was astonished by the knowledge people had of world affairs, and I mentioned this to the skipper.

"They listen to BBC on shortwave," he explained simply.

"Maybe I should also start," I offered seriously. "These people know a heck of a lot more than I do."

"*Oui*," Gerry agreed, "Ah was surprise 'ow much they tell me about Sous Africa, even *aparheid*."

"That's interesting," I noted. "No one mentioned it to me."

Werner raised his eyeballs, and I got the message. But he said it anyway. "Because dey haf know you are Sous African, sonny."

The older folk expressed only one regret. "Over the years," Mr. Benjamin informed us, "we've lost more than half of our population."

The skipper wanted to know why, and was told it was the youth. "They leave for better jobs in England," Mr. Benjamin said.

"And you, don't you feel isolated here?"

"That's the point," the old man smiled. "That's why we stay!"

On our last day we toured part of this remote outpost of the British Empire, and did our re-provisioning in grand fashion, in Sir Robert's car, a stylish black sedan. But one thing went against the grain. Each time we stopped a uniformed chauffeur alighted and, with a courteous bow, insisted on opening the doors for us. "I'm embarrassed by it," I complained mildly.

"Ach, sonny," Werner scoffed, "you are soch a peasant."

We met Jonathan, an ancient tortoise. We visited the house where Napoleon had lived in exile, and saw where, for almost twenty years, his body lay at rest in a tomb amongst Great Norfolk Pines.

"Ah don't think 'e would 'ave like to be remove from this peaceful island," Gerry commented. Not being French we declined to voice our opinions, but I, for one, silently agreed with him.

The Atlantic

*T*here was sadness when we departed St. Helena. However, our next destination was nearby Ascension Island and, born of the same geological parent, the Mid-Atlantic Ridge, we hoped to find a similar paradise. Unfortunately the weather closed in, we could not shoot the sun, and we missed it.

With our reduced crew — seven from Cape Town, now down to four — we were switched to three-hour watches, and at first this posed little hardship. The skipper, with his unbounded energy, volunteered to do the cooking. We had our doubts, but these were immediately dispelled by a hearty breakfast of hot porridge, fresh bread, and fried bacon and eggs. "Hell Skeeper, dot vos better dan vot even can do Johnny."

"*Oui*, Skipur, was delicious. Ah wonder 'ow are doing Johnny?"

"I said, go-go-go, Johnny-Johnny, go-go," Werner sang. And if the words had been right, the tune might have followed.

A German, a Frenchman, an Afrikaner, and an 'Englishman' sounds like the start of a bad joke, one with incompatibility as its theme. But it somehow worked for us. "I feel quite happy with the present crew," the skipper noted in his log, "… and the most important thing is that they all get along like asses in a farmyard."

He conveyed his message verbally in less colorful terms, but the compliment came through and was reciprocated. "A thousand pardon, Skipur," Gerry blurted out of the blue, "that we 'ave fear you cannot find St. 'Elena. Ah think you 'ave navigate so good as Jim." It was the highest compliment he could possibly have paid.

The skipper's smile radiated pleasure — but this time he kept his mouth shut. And although he simply left it at that, he surely must have sensed the new level of respect we had for him. St. Helena was no more than a blade of grass on a rugby field.

We were now in steady South-East Trade winds, and with our mizzen and great mainsail secured to port, and a balancing staysail boomed to starboard, sailing was easy, but slow, six to eight knots. Since we could sail no faster than the wind, the skipper, for the present, was philosophical. We had narrowly missed a record-under-sail for the stretch to St. Helena, and although the skipper did not belabor it, we knew that he was bitterly disappointed. Records were important to someone like him.

As our passage continued, our watches and meals turned to routine, and our little social interactions at sunset differed so little from day to day that we, the crew, gradually began to lose track of time. It was Werner who brought it to our attention. "Vot day ve haf today, Skeeper?"

"Let me go below and check the log."

"No, no. Don't vorry, Skeeper."

"I'm only kidding. What's your guess?"

"*Sondag.*" Sunday.

"Close. Actually, it's Tuesday. Nice to live in a world like yours."

Werner gave him a deflated grin. I could sense him trying to think of a smart-aleck response, but evidently nothing came to mind.

When a sailing vessel, on our course and in our season, approaches the equator, she must pass through the transition area that exists between the South-East and the North-East Trade winds. This is a strip known as the Doldrums, a dreaded place for any craft under sail. It typically exists as a fear-filled band of ocean — 'Der Death Zone,' Werner called it — abounding in calms, but with sudden shifting squalls that can clobber a small boat unexpectedly, and knock her down if she is not braced for it.

One pitch-black night we were smitten by one of these squalls, an assault of such ferocity that we might easily have disappeared without a trace. We were struck suddenly. One moment we were all but becalmed, our sails flapping listlessly, and the next, in pandemonium, we were clinging like limpets to a half-tide rock.

I was on watch and recall that we were overcome with such swiftness that I was helpless to react. I simply grabbed for what I could reach, and held on desperately for life. The blizzard swept over us like the *Orient Express* in a snowstorm, tearing chunks of white water from the ocean and hurling these at us in fury. Hurricane-force winds flogged canvas and sheets, shredding our sail plan and threatening to skin us alive. Blinded by cloth, and lines, and spray, I clung to the tossing deck and thought: This is it! This is the one that kills me! It's just a matter of time, short time, before we are pressed over and swamped, before the cruel Atlantic pours into our open hatches and takes us to the bottom.

However, the next thing I registered was *Senta,* magically taking off. Like a living thing obsessed with her survival, she miraculously began shedding sail. Then, as unexpectedly as the snake-haired Gorgon had come, she was gone, and we bobbed pumice-like in what remained of the turmoil.

I reached up from the deck with dread, straining to see into the bewildering darkness.

Suddenly a voice, a hesitant "Yann?"

My spirits soared. "Gerry!"

"Sonny." Werner.

The skipper: "Whew, I can't believe no one went overboard."

We laughed, but my heart was still palpitating. Gerry crossed himself and mentally I did the same. I cannot remember how long we sat there, grinning superciliously into the night. At some point, without an order, we jumped up, and like fishermen hauling in a net we brought the heavy mainsail inboard. As our eyes adjusted to slightly improved light, we saw that it was torn, but not shredded, as I had thought at first. What had saved us?

We fetched a flashlight and noticed, on closer inspection, that the lower fifteen feet of sail track had been torn from the wooden mast, and this, somehow, had released the brake on the halyard winch.

The sequence that we would piece together later was that a sheet had snapped and let the Yankee jib spill her air. Then, with the sail-track rip, the mainsail had partially let go from the mast, and swept overboard. But still attached, as it was, to the boom and a section of the mast, it had slowed us like a sea anchor. Under her mizzen *Senta* had slowly turned in a wide arc. The aft sail had hardened to a board, and then, with the boat's momentum, put itself aback. "It was that little mizzen," the skipper cheered, "that pushed us like five elephants and brought us up into the wind. Unbelievable!"

"*Oui,*" Gerry agreed. "Senta 'ave save 'erself, and us."

We were more careful after that, drastically reducing sail at nightfall, regardless of the wind. In the daylight things were different; we could see the dark squall lines skulking up on us, and had time to prepare.

"Jim will 'ave use the engine," Gerry whispered, "and break out of this Doldrum. We 'ave plenty of fuel." He pointed in disgust to the big drums on deck that were still lashed, unused, to the mainmast stays.

"You know vhy ve cannot motor, sonny."

"*Oui,* because of the Atlantic record, *non*? 'I's stupid!"

"A record will look good in his book. More money! And the more money, the further you sail around the world."

"Ah suppose," Gerry said, exhaling noisily. "And you, Yann, you 'ave no wish to be a circumnavigator?"

"Not me! I'll stay in the States. That's where I want to be."

"You not go back, ever, in beautiful *Afrique du Sud?*"

"No, I'll never go back! Never!"

And so we labored, hoisting all possible sail for a ghost of wind, and shortening down again when it fell off, sometimes five or six times a day and, in more settled weather, even at night. It was still all about the record. The big main became our enemy, and we cursed each time we were ordered to lay hands on it.

A major sail-change required at least three people on deck, and this meant constantly calling on the help of those off-watch. Prolonged sleep deprivation, the intense heat on the equator, and a constant edge of dehydration led to, in a word, fatigue. It showed in different ways. I was seen mumbling deliriously in my sleep, and making vigorous arm motions, as if wrestling with the helm in a blow. Werner appeared on deck one night, walking unsteadily and raving. He yelled to Gerry at the top of his voice, "Lower der mainsail, sonny!" He then returned to his bunk, and later had no recollection, whatsoever, of the incident.

Another day in the Doldrums saw no wind at all. The sun was a raging tyrant, the sea a tranquil mermaid, not a ripple. We sat under bare poles, immobile. The skipper studied the scene. "I would never have thought that the deep ocean could look like this. It's quite unreal."

"Just what I was thinking," I responded. I was lightheaded, all but panting in the heat.

"Feel like taking a *goof?*" the skipper asked.

His suggestion had the strangest effect on me. It was as if *Senta* had become a part of me, or I of her. I was helpless to tear myself away. I felt a cold, clammy, fainting sweat. "What about sharks?"

"Sharks? There are no sharks out here. We're in the middle of the damned ocean. And anyway, if there were, we'd see them. Let me give Gerry and Werner a call. It's almost lunchtime; they've slept long enough."

Gerry was as hesitant as I was. "Jim say us never to leave your yacht unless land are close in sight."

"I know it's contrary to tradition," the skipper acknowledged, "but I can't resist it. You can join me if you like." He strung some safety lines overboard, one attached to a life ring. Then he was in. Diving gracefully beneath the surface, he popped up on the far side of the hull.

"Vot's it like, Skeeper?"

The skipper raised his goggles. "It's fantastic, truly brilliant!"

"I'm mit you, Skeeper," Werner shouted, and plunged in. He surfaced with a scintillating smile. "It's unbelievable, sonny. Come on in!"

"Ah go," Gerry shrugged against his better judgment.

I was the last in, still thinking about Great Whites.

"What you say, Yann? The water, she are *azure* blue."

"Yes," I agreed readily, my mind racing back to the classroom. "Azurite, a deep-blue basic carbonate of copper, commonly occurring in monoclinic crystals." I recited it aloud.

"Hmm, that's pretty good."

"Thanks Skipper. At least I haven't forgotten everything, yet."

*G*erry said it for all of us. "Thanks God we inventually 'ave clear those damn Doldrum!"

"Yes," the skipper agreed.

"Too bad, Skipur, the record. Yann 'ave say you now receive less money for your book."

The skipper erupted into one of his cascades of deep-throated laughter. "Well at least we got some muscle out of it." He twirled his head to look at his shoulder. "And rugged tans."

A month to the day after leaving Cape Town, we saw our first ship. We had sailed almost five thousand nautical miles. It was our first contact with the modern world since St. Helena. "It is interesting that these old sailing trade routes have been so completely abandoned by steam ships."

"Vhy is dot, Skeeper?" Werner queried.

"In the old days it was all about finding the best winds. Ships sailing from Europe to the west coasts of the Americas, as an extreme example, sometimes had to haul up short at Cape Horn. If they couldn't beat around it, they had to turn and run clear around the world, before the prevailing Westerlies."

"*Oui*," Gerry agreed. "My father also 'ave told me that. They many time come from the other side."

"But these days," the skipper explained, "it's about time and fuel, money, the shortest route."

"*Oui*," Gerry agreed once more, "and very bad for a small yacht like we, if problems ever 'ave befall us. There are no ship to 'elp us."

"*I* was thinking, Gerry," the skipper said, "that we'll be up on the Amazon soon. They say it can be rough there."

"*Oui*, Skipur. My father tell me it depend upon where are the Doldrum, and 'ow deflect the wind."

"Yes, and since the Doldrums were well to the south this year, it seems likely we'll have this northeaster for a while yet."

And that is what occurred. A northeaster persisted, increased in strength, and even moved to N.NE. We were now close-hauled on a dangerous windward shore — the northern coast of Brazil — and taking seas forward of our starboard beam.

We awakened one day to brown water, the Amazon pushing out to sea. Our salt-stiffened main was driving us, and we were cavorting. I asked Gerry if it felt like anything he remembered.

"*Oui*," he offered quickly, "*Afrique*, the first time we 'ave leave Port Elizabeth, a cross sea."

"A similar feel," I confirmed. We again had the current in our favor — this time the South Equatorial — and, as before, the countering wind shortened the seas and made our ride highly uncomfortable.

I shook the skipper to stand his watch, and had the spidery sense of water sloshing beneath his berth. "Do you hear that?" I asked him.

"Yes," he replied. "You might like to pump before you turn in."

"Aye, aye, Skipper," I replied.

But the pump would not respond.

"Try priming it," he suggested, now shouting from the helm.

I tried in vain. I checked the intake. I dismantled the pump and re-assembled it, all to no avail.

"Use the pump on the engine," the skipper ordered.

There was not enough battery power to turn her over.

"Damn! We've been using that radio far too much."

I knew what he meant. Since nearing the coast we had found a frequency operated by the United States Armed Forces. It was such a novelty that we'd had it on almost continuously.

I tried cranking the generator that I had repaired near East London, but that was again frozen solid. "I can't believe they ever installed a generator on deck," I complained for the umpteenth time. "I'll strip her down."

"No," the skipper protested, "it'll take too long. And besides, it's just too wet out here. Bail it!"

"Bail it? How?"

"What do you mean, 'how?' With a bucket, my dear fellow, with a bucket."

I shook the others awake and that is what we did. We bailed the bilge with a bucket. We lifted the sole planks and took turns at scooping, a jug at a time, until we filled the bucket. This we then passed up by chain gang, and emptied it over the side, about forty pails.

"That was quicker than I'd expected," the skipper smiled.

"Dot's vot you sink, Skeeper. You vos at der helm."

We repeated the exercise at sunset, another 160 gallons. "Hell Skeeper," Werner cried frantically, "dot is bad, isn't it Skeeper?"

"It's just the planks working, water seeping in through the caulking. She'll snug up again when the weather lets up. You worry too much, Werner, worry, worry, worry!"

If looks could kill, as the cliché goes, the skipper surely…

The Caribbean

*O*ur passage from St. Helena had taken twenty-nine days, and we were more than ready for a break ashore. Despite our scruffy appearances — we, the deck crew — the Royal Barbados Yacht Club declared us honorary members. They simply bit their lips and let us in, scraggly beards and all. But they drew the line at letting me onto their impeccably groomed tennis courts. "I even offered to play barefooted," I complained to the skipper.

And if we expected the island people to be like those on St. Helena, we were sadly mistaken. In a haphazard section of Bridgetown, the capital, the skipper and I were made to feel, for the first time in our lives, conspicuously white. Werner was onto it in a snap, with a heavy dose of sarcasm. "I sink dis a place you like to open mit a new practice. Vot you say, Skeeper?"

"I don't think so," the skipper disagreed, red-faced. "In fact, I'm beginning to think we might leave tonight."

"Ach, too bad, Skeeper. Me and Jan vos sink to spend a vhile here. Vot you say, sonny?"

I knew I should see the humor in his teases, but somehow I could not, and it took all the self-control I could muster to say nothing.

"Not so nice to be on der odder side of it, hey sonny? Unt dey vos not even know you are Sous African. Imagine if ..."

I cut him off before he could finish. "S-h-u-t up, Werner!"

He slapped his hip and laughed. "I'm glad I vos here to see it, sonny. Dot's all vot I can say."

However, one place did fascinate us, the careenage, harbor to a fleet of inter-island schooners, vessels from a bygone age. These West Indian treasures were, to my mind, the seagoing equivalents of the Arab dhows that trade all the way from the South China Sea to East Africa, places like Mogadishu, Mombassa, Zanzibar, and Dar es Salaam.

The Caribbean sailing fleet, for its part, plies the Windward and Leeward Islands, and the Lesser Antilles. Its sailors are brawny and barefooted, indistinguishable, on sight, from the many African Sinbads who crew alongside Arabs on the lateen-sail dhows. The West Indians speak English of course, but the mariners chat to each other with an accent so strong, it sounds like a different language.

The schooners are hand-hewn — their forerunners were probably Zambezi dugouts — and everything about them is rugged. They carry a compass, but few charts; navigation is predominantly by instinct and eyeball.

"But 'ow you 'ave find a distant island?" Gerry asked.

"We know where it's at, mon," came the unpretentious reply.

To save on the cost of fuel, their auxiliary diesels are sparingly used. We saw able-bodied crews hoist heavy gaff-rigged sails before their boats had even cleared the Bridgetown channel.

*R*eturning to a yacht club cloaked in evening shadows, we gulped down some hot coffee and shipped out in the dark. Our next destination, St. Lucia, was an easy down-wind sail. We approached it as if in a dream, two volcanic peaks towering over a canopy of emerald green, an island set in a fringing sea of turquoise.

Werner was at the wheel with his camera. "Now dot's a bloody island! Unbelievable! Vot you say, Skeeper?"

But the skipper was preoccupied. With the help of a new chart he navigated us round the coast, and we crept into the inlet at Castries, an all-but-landlocked cove reputed to be one of the finest hurricane holes in the entire Caribbean. In our rush from Barbados we were still without an engine, and beating up the narrow channel took all the sailing skill we could muster.

Before we could drop anchor, island children in homemade canoes converged on us. Their boats were laden with fresh fruit and a variety of colorful reef fish. One small vessel caught my eye. It held two good-sized lobsters, crayfish, or *kreef* as we referred to them in South Africa, the spiny two-clawed variety. I poked a finger, and the boys all pointed to themselves. "You," I said, "with the lobsters. No, the lobsters." I made a clawing motion with both hands.

They all laughed.

"What's your name?"

"Michael."

"Yes, Michael, we'll take them bo…"

"Just one," the skipper interrupted in protest.

"Ah not eat it either," Gerry said, drawing up his face.

I looked over to Werner.

"Ja, sonny, ve scoff dot sing easily."

"But listen, Michael, we cannot buy anything now," the skipper cautioned. "Come back when we've cleared the health authorities." He pointed up to our fluttering yellow flag. "Do you understand?"

"Yes, Captain," the boy grinned back respectfully. I could not help but notice that he was polite, but not ingratiating, as a boy of his age and color might have been in South Africa. It was very refreshing.

*A*lan J. Villiers, famed mariner and author, who had sailed aboard a dhow, noted, in *Men, Ships, and the Sea,* that the sailors of these classic boats, on making a landfall, do not rush ashore. Rather, they brew coffee. Only then, after leisurely drinking it, do they leave their vessels, slowly and "with dignity."

Ironically, what brought to mind this self-respecting custom of the dhowmen, was us, remaining aboard for a good hour after anchoring. But that was where the comparison ended. There was nothing dignified about the way we laid into that crayfish. "Werner and Ian polished it off between the two of them," the skipper recorded with much distaste.

After observing us from a distance, he and Gerry moved ashore, and we saw them chatting to the various crews around the basin. Gerry's accent and endearing gambits had a way of breaking the ice. "*Bon jour,*" he would say. "You 'ave an most beautiful yacht!"

We joined them as they were leaving *Enchantress*. "Vot you say, sonny?" Werner asked, placing his hand on Gerry's shoulder.

"Buttons, buttons, everything are buttons. Never Ah 'ave see so many buttons."

"Buttons, vot are buttons, sonny?"

"Push button for weigh anchor, push button for 'oist sail, button to move winch, to trim. Everything are electric gadget."

"Unt you, Skeeper, vot you say, Skeeper?"

"She's beautiful, but she's a toy, definitely not for me. I like the muscle side of sailing. I mean look at us, how fit and strong we are."

"*Oui* Skipur, but Ah think she can move, *non?*"

The skipper narrowed his eyes. "I'll take her on," he said with feeling. "I'll wager that *Senta* can out-sail her, electric winches and all."

*A*fter stretching my legs ashore — I was not going into town after my experience at Barbados — I disassembled the generator, and began wire brushing and oiling parts, piece-by-piece. Despite being in a deck box, the short seas off the Amazon had found their way in and taken their toll.

"Old enemies, engines unt sout water!" A German accent, but it wasn't Werner's.

I turned. They could easily have been mistaken for father and son.

"Dis is Kurt, sonny, an engineer von der ship *Brunseck*. He haf a quick look at our engine."

"Excellent," I cheered, scrambling to my feet.

Kurt went to work. He disconnected the shaft and attached a long crowbar device that he had brought from his ship. First he, then all three of us tried to turn it, but to no avail. "You haf paraffin?" he asked.

"*Ja, ja,*" Werner responded, and soon returned with two gallon cans.

Kurt did some spanner work, then topped off the cylinders. "Ve vait a vhile," he suggested, "haf a couple of biers."

"Ve don't haf got beers," Werner responded. His expression indicated that he was thoroughly embarrassed.

"No biers?" Kurt looked at him in disbelief.

"No beers, no nothing," Werner shrugged apologetically.

"Ach, neffer mind. Ve haf a drink on shore."

We spent a good three hours, but at the end of it the news was bad. "Shot," Kurt reported unsympathetically to the skipper. He ran his eyes lovingly over the lustrous mahogany and oak of *Senta's* interior. "Beautiful German boat," he began in a soft voice that abruptly filled with rebuke. "But get rid of dis!" He turned and pointed at the engine. "Vot you need, Skeeper," he advised in earnest, "is a goot Mercedes diesel!"

It had been a bad day for the skipper. He still had not managed to get a call through to his wife, and now the news about the engine. "We sail at midnight," he announced in frustration.

"What are our next port of calls, Skipur?"

"It's 'ports of call,' " the skipper smiled, beginning to shed his woes. "Actually, the first of our ports of call is Martinique."

"Martinique, *magnifique!*" Gerry cheered. "Martinique are a French island. Ah take you to eat as never you 'ave eat before."

"Thanks, Gerry. Now listen boys, turn in for a few hours of rack. I'll give you a shake when it's time to leave. There's a fresh night breeze. It should be easy sailing."

The next thing we knew it was daylight; the skipper had fallen asleep.

We sailed off our anchorage, dodging yachts that had moved in on us during the night, and were soon joined by a flotilla of small fishing craft with large square sails. Some had more patch than sail, quilts of color. "What a scene," I commented. "It's definitely worth a photograph."

"Yes," the skipper agreed, "picturesque. But imagine if we could have ourselves in it, with the boats and island behind us." This thought must obviously have plagued him, for when we approached Martinique later in the day he asked for the inflatable dinghy to be made ready. He appeared on deck with a large coil of rope, launched the small boat over the stern and jumped into it with his camera, paddles, and flippers. "Let me fall back slowly," he said, and we did. "If I break loose," he called out, "bring her into the wind, and I'll try to come up on you. Just don't let me end up as a castaway!"

As I paid out line Werner winked at me, then hailed into his cupped hands. "Skeeper, shout ven you haf der photos so ve know when to let you go."

"Let me go? Don't you dare let me go!" he screeched.

We lay at anchor off Fort-de-France. The skipper paddled alongside, threw his briefcase onto the deck, and then climbed aboard. "I think I've cleared customs," he smiled, "but I can't say for sure."

I was puzzled by his announcement and asked what he meant.

"Martinique is France," he explained. "Nobody here speaks English. You'll see for yourselves."

"Bon," Gerry responded, his eyes sparkling with anticipation. "Can we go on shore, Skipur?"

"Yes."

"Lunch," he announced, *"à la française; escargot* to start."

*G*erry's lunch was a true culinary delight, and we would have given anything to have stayed on longer at his *le port de Fort-de-France.* But unable, again, to make a telephone call to South Africa — no one had established contact since leaving St. Helena — we pressed on. Aboard now was Patrick McGee, our first American friend. We had met him in a bar. He was looking for a free ride to the U.S. Virgin Isles, some 300 nautical miles to the northwest. "I guarantee you can call from there," he assured us.

He was signed on, and we used the entire passage to shower him with questions. "How ve travel in der States, sonny?"

"Hitch-hike," he advised without hesitation. "Wear those leather shorts, buddy, and people will be fighting to give you a ride."

"Dot sound incredible, sonny! Unt vhere ve sleep?"

"Sleeping is tough," he said. "Expensive. There are no youth hostels in every town. It's not like Europe. I don't know. Carry sleeping bags for sure. Stick to the countryside and you'll always find a spot in a field some-where, at least in the summer. If you get stuck in a city, try a flop house."

"Flop house, vot's a flop house, sonny?"

"You'll find out, don't you worry about that. When the time comes, ask. Someone will tell you."

I was interested in learning about jobs.

"Jobs are a problem. What sort of visa do you have?"

I shrugged and offered to get my passport.

"Don't bother, buddy," Patrick said. "Someone like you won't have a work visa; and no offence. Listen, if you're after half-decent employment — I once worked a great summer on Lake Erie — you've somehow got to get a Social Security number. You'll have to blend in: stay somewhere for a while, get a proper address, join a yacht club, register for a college course." He took a thoughtful draft from his water bottle. "Look," he said, "if you want some serious advice, work in the islands and save some money before you even leave for the States!"

"What sort of work is there in the islands?" I asked.

"Yacht work, buddy! St. Thomas, that's where we're heading, is the charter capital of the world. It's hog heaven! You've never in your life seen anything like the Virgin Isles. They're Shangri-la for bums like us. Skippers are always looking for crews. And you guys, with a story to spin to charter parties, will have it made. You'll really have it made!"

"Do you think so?" I asked excitedly.

"Sure," he confirmed. "And you'll make more in tips than in salary. It'll be better than any gold mine you ever worked on in Africa."

*I*n those days the harbor at Charlotte Amalie — St. Thomas — was not accessible to cruise ships, and this made it a small-boat paradise. Gerry's eyes were bulging. "Ah never 'ave see so many beautiful yacht," he cheered as his gaze swept lovingly over the fleet.

"This is sailing hog heaven!" I said, adopting Patrick's terminology.

He laughed aloud and slapped me. "What did I tell you, buddy?"

*T*he skipper went ashore to clear us, and returned looking grim.

"What 'ave 'appen?" Gerry asked concerned.

"It's bad news for me," he said, throwing a cablegram on the gimbaled table for us to read. It was from Mimi, his wife, informing him that the offer for the sale of his practice had been withdrawn, and that the law society now demanded his immediate return.

"So what you will do, Skipur?"

"I have no choice, I'm afraid. I must go back."

Werner was the first to shake his hand. "Jees, Skeeper. Who now do der cooking?"

The skipper broke into one of his stertorous laughs. It was the last time we would hear it. He had launched us on the greatest adventure of our lives, and we would miss him.

A year later when his book was published, I turned, as was my habit, to the end, and a particular paragraph caught my eye. In it he described his return to South Africa and his sad slip-back into the "monotonous rut" he had been in before his "great voyage," as he called it.

*B*ut for us the "great voyage" continued, albeit in a slightly different direction. Patrick left for the States shortly after the skipper departed, and George and Ben, the owners of boats tied up near us, took us under their wings. "I admire your flight to freedom," Ben said one evening, after I had related a little of my story. " 'Live Free or Die,' is the motto of the state I'm from. You'd fit in well there." Years later I would meet another Ben, Ben Swift, a World War II bomber pilot — his experiences made mine seem somewhat uneventful — and tennis buddy, who reminded me of Caribbean Ben, and who also treated me like a younger brother, perhaps even a son. His wife, Mondessa, had once captained a US ladies' touring tennis team to East Africa and greeted me in *Swahili* when I first met her. *"Jambo,"* she said.

And George, my other Virgin Islands mentor, had built his yacht, *Kukulcan*, in the high Andes, while working there on a hydroelectric project. "I designed her," he said, "to fit onto a narrow-gauge railroad car. It was the only way I could get her to the ocean."

"Ah love 'er," Gerry responded. "You are a genius. Ah would love to build my own little yacht one day."

"She might look a little unusual," George laughed, "but she suits me. And she sails really well. And so does *Kukulcanito*," he added, referring to his cute dinghy that showed similar crimped lines. "You must sail her some time and give me your opinion of her rig."

Evenings brought long conversations, and George, in his inquisitive way, asked us what we had thought of our skipper.

I replied that he was a great chap. "You'd never know he was an Afrikaner," I said.

We asked George, in turn, what he thought of Patrick's idea of us working as charter crew. "Excellent," he responded. "But if you don't mind me saying so," he said, "you first need a bit of a scrub, inside and out. What in the name of God have you been eating?"

"Canned bully-beef, sonny," Werner replied, offended.

"We can take care of that, but first things first, haircuts! Let me introduce you to Jenny, an English rose, the best looking barber on the island. Her helper isn't too bad either." The next day he led us round a maze of wooden walkways where yachts like our own rode at anchor, tied stern-to in order to conserve space. We met Jenny and her young daughter.

Then, looking better than we had in months, George took us aboard *Seaward*, an eighty-five foot schooner, and introduced us to her Norwegian owner. "Chris," George hailed, "I've got your new crew members."

A sinewy little man appeared from the deckhouse. "Chris Lindahl," he said, extending a scarred hand. He then got straight to business. "I thought there were three of you?"

"No sir. Our friend, Gerry, will be staying aboard *Senta* to start getting her shipshape."

"That's commendable, and no problem," he replied. "George said one of you was South African."

"Yes sir, me sir," I volunteered apprehensively.

"You'll be working under a black mate," he said bluntly. "Is that a problem?"

"Nooo…" I blinked. I was so startled by his question that one word was all I could muster.

"Good," he responded. "I have a charter party flying in from Chicago. We ship out on Sunday for a week around the Virgins. We'll feed you well and pay you well, and Florice, my mate, will show you all you need to know."

Gerry jumped on me when we returned to *Senta*. "Yann," he scolded, "Ah am not 'appy with what you 'ave say to George about Skipur."

"What do you mean?" I responded in surprise. "I said he was really nice."

"*Oui,*" he agreed, "but you 'ave say something about an Afrikaner."

"Ye-es," I concurred. "I might have said something about one never knowing he was an Afrikaner."

"*Oui,* exactly! You imply that the most Afrikaners are bastard, and you know that are far from true. 'Is like to say the most German are Nazis. You can say Werner are a Nazi?"

"No," I offered self-consciously.

"Ah-ha! Then beware what you say in America. Me, Ah don't care. Ah say you this for yourself. My father tell me that America are full of German, good German!"

My eyes turned inward, and I could not find it in me to thank him for his excellent advice. He had touched a nerve, and at the time I resented it. But the more I thought about it, the more I knew he was right. And when the full force of his wisdom finally dawned on me, I had a qualm of conscience, and was ashamed and angry that I had missed the chance to express my gratitude. By then Gerry had gone his own way.

Sailing on *Seaward* was as good as it gets. It was difficult to tell who was on holiday, and who were crew. The Halls and the Vances, our first introduction to American families, treated us like precious silver, working alongside us to hoist sails, standing watches for the overnight haul to St. Croix, and inviting us to join them on their various excursions ashore.

One evening we were enjoying a barbeque on the beach. "Let me build the fire, Mr. Hall," I offered. "You and Mr. Vance did most of the sailing today. I'm the one who's getting paid."

He waved my offer aside. "No, this is fun," he insisted. "You run along and talk to Annabel."

Annabel Hall was a college student, about my age, and I was completely infatuated by her. "I'd kill for a tan like yours," she had said, in her flattering way, when she'd first met me. "There was still snow on the ground when we left home."

It was a clear case of 'love at first sight,' at least on my part. I took every opportunity to seek her out, and I was afraid that her parents might object. But they, if anything, encouraged our friendship. We talked for hours about the way things were in the States, college life, music, sport, and a million other things.

However, our conversations were always about America. "You've never asked me much about South Africa," I remarked one evening.

"Because I didn't want to blow it," she replied.

I asked her what she meant. I was unfamiliar with the expression.

"I didn't want to spoil our relationship," she explained. "You see in the States there are two topics of conversation that we are taught to avoid, politics and religion."

"And why would a conversation about South Africa have to deal with politics or ..." The words flew out before I could catch them. "I'm sorry, Annabel," I apologized, embarrassed.

"No apologies necessary," she smiled. "I'm sure South Africa is a perfectly wonderful place, and that the people are nice, and that this whole *apartheid* thing is grossly overstated."

"Well it's not," I replied brusquely, way too brusquely. "It's almost certainly a lot worse than you're aware of."

"You don't have to tell me," she offered, sensing my rising anger.

"Look," I said, "it's just that when I left South Africa I thought I was putting it all behind me, the whole *apartheid* thing. But it has followed me. It's always with me, like a shadow."

"It's in your mind," she suggested.

No, I protested, relating my experience in Barbados, and the way Chris Lindahl had questioned me about working under a black mate.

"Anyhow, you won't find much of that in the States," she assured me. "People will accept you at face value. You'll see."

I bit my lip and waited for her to continue.

"I mean, everyone has heard of *apartheid* of course, but you'll notice how few people know much about it, or even realize that it's particular to South Africa. In their minds it's just an African thing."

"Are you serious?" I laughed. "Americans know everything."

"You'd be surprised," she replied, shaking her head. "We probably have a fair knowledge of Western Europe," she admitted. "But you'll find us very naïve about Africa. You tell people you're South African, and to them you're a novelty, an African whiteboy. They'll ask you what you think of places like Nairobi, and Cairo. You mark my words."

"You're joking," I laughed.

"I might be stretching it a bit," she smiled, "but not much. If you really, really want some advice, I may be able to help you."

"Go ahead," I invited, but with a hint of dread.

However, she kept it light. "Just don't get too hung up on politics," she offered. "With your accent, everyone you meet will ask you where you're from. And you know a few will challenge you when they find out, and make your life a misery."

"So?"

"So don't get sucked in. I wouldn't even say where I was from."

"What do I tell them?" I asked, abashed.

"Say you're British, or something; or even better, Australian. Tell them you're from the beautiful Opal Country."

"Are all your charter parties as nice as that one?" I asked Florice, our mate, after the families had left for home.

"Not quite as great, mon, or even quite as pretty." He winked. "Did I overhear Annabel invite you to visit her in the States?"

"Your sure did, buddy," I laughed. "Think my accent will cut it?"

"Stick to your own accent," he advised, "it's worth money. You hear mine, mon? Got me a lot of tips."

We returned to find *Senta* glistening under a fresh coat of varnish, and with her topsides newly painted. "Jees, sonny, you haf work your death."

"*Oui,*" Gerry admitted. "And 'ow you 'ave enjoy your week?"

We could not bring ourselves to tell him. But it slipped out slowly over drinks, swimming in the rock pools at Virgin Gorda, our hike on St. Johns, the lobsters we had bagged off British Tortola, our night out on the town in Christiansted...

Then, with a lively sparkle, Gerry popped it. "And Yann," he asked, " 'ow you 'ave like work under the black mate?"

I was speechless for a moment. "You might think this strange," I replied, after taking a breath, "but I didn't even give it a thought."

And, no doubt to Gerry's surprise, his question provoked an outburst of elaborate praise for Florice, from both of us, how strong he was, how he could free dive to more than one-hundred feet, how he could shinny up the rigging and scale coconut trees, and of how his grandfather had harpooned whales from longboats off Bequia in the Grenadines.

"Ah am 'appy," Gerry smiled before changing the subject. "Ah 'ave work 'ard so we all three can do charter next week."

"And we have something for you," I said.

He elatedly ripped the envelope open. "American dollar!"

"Werner's idea," I said, "for all that beautiful work you did."

"And 'ow you knew Ah do so much?"

"Ve didn't, sonny, but ve knew you do somesing."

Florice came by later in the day and was equally impressed by what Gerry had accomplished in a week. "I think this one even better than you two. What do you say for yourselves, mon?"

"Gerry is der best, sonny," Werner sang. By this time he had a couple of rums under his belt, but genuine appreciation rang clearly in his tone. "Tonight I pay all drinks for der Frenchman."

"No boys," Florice insisted, "tonight is on me! And what's more, I have a special treat for you. I teach you how to dance, island style."

At dusk Florice led us off to a nightclub on the darker side of town. There we had the time of our lives, and I could not help but smile and wonder what the Special Branch would have had to say about it all. In Jo'burg, with David and Mark, I had observed, but not danced. This step-up was really no big thing, but it was freedom, I thought, and I loved it.

*T*wo more charters and we had enough money to strike out for the United States. "Ve can do it, sonny," Werner claimed gleefully.

"I know we've saved what we said we needed," I protested, "but let's hang around here a little longer."

"But you are der vun, sonny, who keep saying you cannot vait to get to der States."

"I know," I admitted. "But we have it so good here. We've got money, and friends, and all the girls we can handle. And the babes all think that *Senta* is ours. It will never be like this again!"

"Ach, sonny, don't vorry. Ve haf it all again, I promise you."

It was a tantalizing quandary. Gerry had, shortly before, shipped out on a French yacht bound for Tahiti. It had been another round of sad farewells, in some ways even more agonizing than our parting with the skipper. Gerry had been a unifying spirit, and seeing him go was like losing a part of ourselves. We could not bear it. His final handshake tore at my soul. Even Werner, tough as he was, was tearful.

And the Virgins, as Patrick had stated, were truly Shangri-la. But without Gerry's vivacity, his *joie de vivre* — a term the Frenchman had once used to describe the skipper's exuberance — life on *Senta* had changed abruptly. "You're right, Werner," I said at last, "it's time to leave."

*B*y this stage we had learned from scores of people that getting into, and staying in the United States was not going to be as easy as we had at first thought. But we had a plan. Each month 'non-US citizens,' like us, visited British Tortola and received a fresh twenty-nine day stamp to cruise in American waters. With that in our passports, and the visas the skipper had secured for us in South Africa, we felt sure we could at least gain entry.

And George and Ben were also of considerable help. "Tell them Archie will be calling for you in a couple of weeks," George suggested. "You've come on ahead to make arrangements for hauling and refitting."

"Archie will be calling for us where?" I asked.

"Anywhere — Fort Lauderdale. Can you remember that?"

"Yes."

"Then, that's what you tell them. And don't say too much! You guys are a little too friendly. Take care not to talk yourselves into trouble."

Part 16

THE BLOODY NATS

More like a Funeral

"**Y**ou should buy a newspaper sometimes, sonny," Werner said, slapping one into my hand.

"Oh yes. And why's that?" I asked.

"Read unt see," he said, "page three."

I opened it and scanned the small print beneath a headline. It reported that a shift to "full national sovereignty" had been "formalized" in South Africa.

Werner studied my expression. "Vot you say about dot?"

"I'm glad to be away!"

"Vhy sonny? Lots of celebrations, a big party, lots of nice foods unt drinks."

"Not in my house. More like a funeral I'd say. I can just picture my dad, depressed and gloomy, cursing the bloody Nats."

Werner laughed. "Dey say dot only fifty-two percent voted for der changeover."

"Yes, it was close. But you realize, of course, that if everyone could have voted, Blacks as well as Whites I mean, it would have been more like ninety percent against a republic."

"So much as dot?"

"Maybe even more. In Natal, where I was at university, even the white vote was against the proposal. It's a predominantly English-speaking state, you see."

"I don't haf seen dot," Werner noted.

"No, not in this article," I clarified. "The actual referendum was held a while ago, before we left."

"Vell, too bad, sonny. Come, I buy you a drink."

"Two drinks," I responded. "One for my country becoming a lousy Afrikaner republic, and the other for getting our bums kicked out of the British Commonwealth."

"Two drinks. You haf yourself a deal, sonny."

"Isolation. No more Empire Day," I lamented. "Pop will really be devastated about that."

"Vot's dot, sonny?"

"Nothing," I replied. "Just talking to myself."

*T*he next day, still fighting a hangover, I received my first letter since leaving.

"Who haf vrite you?"

"A girlfriend."

"An ex-girlfriend, sonny."

I laughed. "Yes, you would have to say that, wouldn't you?"

"Vot she say, sonny?"

"Nothing you'd be interested in, I promise."

"Ach, come ahnn, sonny."

"It's about African art," I conceded.

He looked at me doubtfully.

"I swear to God. You can read it if you like. She's interested in African art. She says that her hero, Sydney Kumalo, has just been given a government commission for a piece of out-door sculpture. She sees this as a great step forward for South Africa."

"Kumalo is black?"

"Yes."

"So everything now is fine? She thinks you should come home?"

"Yes."

He laughed. "All vomens are der same. I'm glad I don't got a letter."

Part 17

ANECDOTES OF AMERICA

A Time Warp & Precious Gifts

*I*n those days — 1961, I was 20 years of age — there was only a small landing strip on St. Thomas, and flights to and from the Island went through Puerto Rico. From there we flew on to Miami. "Ve made it, sonny."

"Yes," I smiled elated, "thanks to George." We had stuck rigidly to his advice.

"*A*re you sure he's still here?"

"I'm pretty sure." We had been wandering around the campus of the University of Miami, asking everyone we met whether they knew Cookie Hammill, my old South African tennis friend.

"Go to the registrar's office tomorrow," someone advised us. "They'll tell you where to find him."

"Unt vhere ve sleep tonight, sonny?"

"In those pipes that we saw. They're perfect. Keep the rain off, and no one can see us."

Our rooms were large, several-feet in diameter, sewer or water pipes, about to be buried. "Dot's goot, sound like a fishing boat," Werner said. He was referring to the metrical clobber of the diesel-driven pump for the dewatering wellpoints that kept the nearby pipe-trench dry.

*A*nother day, another world. We were sitting in the back of a red convertible, speeding to the beach. "Dot's so great! Vot you say, sonny?"

I slapped his raised hand. "It's fantastic!" I laughed.

"It's unbelievable!"

We were in an explosion of high spirits, exhilarated beyond all measure, seeing everything 'in pink,' as Gerry had once said. We were also in a time warp. I had read of people moving from the sophistication of large cities to rural areas, or traveling to remote countries and feeling as if they had gone back in time. But for us it was just the opposite. On entering the United States we had sprung forward into a new millennium, into an enchanted setting of novel and exciting paraphernalia. In place of a campus filled with bicycles, we were on one crowded with cars, monsters with V-8 engines that sounded like motor yachts, automatic transmissions, fancy convertibles, and even a Corvette, the ultimate icon of fashion, the first one I had ever seen 'in der flesh,' as Werner said.

And later, in Cookie's student apartment, I sat in wonder and, for the first time in my life, viewed television. During an advertisement I reached for a book and found myself gawking at the centerfold in a Playboy magazine, censored material in South Africa. Every turn we took, it seemed, revealed something new and exciting. Even Werner was impressed. "I neffer haf imagine, sonny, dot things can be so different as in Europe."

The next day Cookie led us over to the university cafeteria where we enjoyed lunch with some of the athletes, including football players whose loaded plates were checked by a trainer for calories before they ate.

"I called coach this morning," Cookie smiled. "He wants you to join us tomorrow at practice."

"That's excellent?" I applauded brightly.

"It's a good start. But the problem, as I see it, is that he's already got his players lined up for the season. I don't know what the story is with a late walk-on like you. It's not like home, you know, if you're good enough you're in. It's a complex bloody business here, budgets, academic requirements, tuition waivers…"

After ten days, or so, tennis talks had stalled, and Werner began to murmur about moving on.

"We're on a continent," I said, "that, geologically, is slowly drifting westward. We're moving."

Werner smiled, but the pressure was on.

Cookie sensed a change of mood and started to come up with ever-new ideas to keep us in Miami. But eventually even he accepted the inevitable. Without a scholarship my visa could not be changed, and our twenty-nine days were quickly ticking down.

I had added to my cash reserve and, as in the islands, was sorry to leave my job. I had worked as — what my South African friends would have called me — a 'newspaper boy.' Matt, one of Cookie's American friends, my driver, would stop at the entrance of each of the many ritzy clubs and hotels that lined Miami Beach in the early sixties. My task was to grab a handful of celebrity newsletters and dash in with these, while Matt waited at the curbside or circled the block until I reappeared.

"Where would you like these, sir?"

"Ah, a new boy. Where you from, kid, London?"

"No. South Africa, sir."

"Do you know who's here this week?"

I said that I did not, and he threw out a name, asking if I had ever heard of the person in Africa. "Yes," I lied.

He motioned me to follow him down a walkway, where he quietly opened a door. "There he is," he whispered. "Stay for a while."

"I cannot believe it's him," I played on in a soft voice. "Thank you so much. I'd love to, but there's someone waiting for me outside."

He closed the door again, and we retreated. "Too bad, kid," he said. "Look for me again next time you're here. I'll show you another star. You never know, it might be Frank Sinatra, or Marilyn Monroe." Now that was more like it. I had certainly heard of them, even in Africa.

"Ve leeft tomorrow, sonny," Werner said. "No 'vun more day!'"

But Cookie still had a delay trick up his sleeve. "We'll take you up to Fort Lauderdale," he offered. "It's full of yachts. You'll love it there."

"No, sonny," Werner pleaded. "Ve neffer leeft."

"I swear to God," Cookie pledged, raising both hands. "We'll drop you there. You'll be on your own, hitch-hiking. I promise."

Werner yielded and we drove up a tropical coastline. "This is the beach for Blacks," Matt said, pointing to our right. "Nigger beach."

I gawked in shock, but Cookie's elbow in my side stopped me from saying anything. I turned to see a group of Afro-Americans, no older than us, tossing a football.

We were soon in a small metropolis. "This is great! This is where I'll live one day," I said, pointing to a house on the New River.

Matt shook his head. "On the waterfront? I don't think so!"

"Yes," I confirmed. "I'll have a boat at the bottom of my yard."

"No Iron," he said — in the way he pronounced my name — "in the States things are different. You've got to think of resale value. You don't buy here, on a rat-infested river. Just a few years ago this was all a swamp full of alligators and mosquitoes. You can't get rid of them. They'll come back and eat you alive."

The students dropped us on the outskirts of Fort Lauderdale, on a secondary road — Matt said he thought it was illegal to hitch on the highway — and Cookie left us with a word of advice. "People will stop and spit out the numbers of interstate highways they're heading for. Just remember, even numbers are east-west routes, odd numbers north-south."

We had been there less than twenty minutes when a police car pulled over and backed up on us.

"Jees, sonny!" Werner swore. "Vot ve do now?"

"Just keep your calm," I suggested blindly.

"Okay," Werner gulped.

"Howdy!" the sheriff barked. "Where you guys heading?"

"Atlanta, sir, der Underground, sir."

The officer kept looking down, at Werner's leather shorts. "Lederhosen," he observed. "You're not from here?"

"No, sir, Germany, sir."

The sheriff's face lit up. "The Old Country, I thought so. My grand-father was from Wiesbaden. Ever heard of it?"

"*Ja*, I vorked near der vun time, in Frankfurt."

"I'll be darned. I'd like to take you boys home and introduce you to the wife and kids."

"Thank you, sir, but ve must move on," Werner said, suspicious of our new friend's motive. "Our skeeper vait on us."

"You're on a boat?"

"Yes, sir, a jacht, sir. Ve travel around der vorld."

"You're in luck," he said. "I've got just what you need." He jumped out, opened his trunk — 'boot,' as we called it — and reached for a sheet of cardboard. He proceeded to cut this with a large pocketknife until, satisfied with its size, he began writing on it, in large bold letters: *AROND THE WORLD*.

I stared at it, wondering whether he had intentionally misspelled it to catch the motorist's eye. Mmm, pretty clever, I thought. But I was not about to comment on it, just in case.

"Hold this up for cars to see, or put it on your pack," he said, hand-ing it proudly to Werner.

The radio squawked in his car. "That's me," he said. He gave us each a fond cuff. "Germans," he smiled, "I can't believe it." He jumped into his patrol car and screeched off.

*L*ess than three hours later we were in a Jeep, in a completely different vista, the edge of the Everglades. We had seen sugar cane and swamp, and flights of exotic birds, and gargantuan equipment employed in dredging drainage canals. "It's unbelievable! Bloody mind-boggling," I exclaimed. "I've never seen such huge machines."

"What do you use in Africa?" the farmer asked.

"People," I laughed.

"*Muntumatic,* Africans," Werner joked, but with no disrespect.

"On a job like this you'd probably see five-thousand workers with picks and shovels. A large dam, maybe ten-thousand; a deep mine, fifteen-thousand. I mean, there's some mechanization of course, but it's mainly about people."

"Now to me," the Southerner exclaimed with his eyebrows raised, "that's mind-boggling! Are you sure you're not laying it on to some degree?"

"No," I pledged in earnest. "It's the absolute truth!"

"And I suppose it's the same way with farming?"

"Yes, very similar," I assured him.

He seemed to wrestle with the fact. "I guess it works where labor is cheap," he eventually rationalized with some difficulty. "But what you see here is the future, big machines and high efficiency."

He was quiet for a while as we drove on. Then he began to slow. "This is it," he announced, easing the Jeep to the shoulder.

"Dis is vot?"

"The Lake. You said that's where you were heading."

"I don't see anything," I complained bewildered.

"It's over the dike," he laughed, pointing to a grassed embankment.

"You mean we'll see it from the top of that?"

"You sure will," he verified. His tone held a note of delight.

"Okay," I said with a tinge of uncertainty, "you can drop us here. Thank you very much for the lift."

We found a spot to cross the drainage ditch that blocked us, and scrambled up the steep slope. Then we saw it, crystal glistening in a mist of color, even more brilliant than we had imagined, Lake Okeechobee. It extended like a calm sea to a distant horizon. We could not make out the other side. A cool breeze drifted up on us. "It's beautiful. Ve take a swim unt spend der night here, sonny."

We turned in with nets over our faces to escape the mosquitoes. But the next morning was breezy again, and fine, and we were on the road early. We were still heading north, to Atlanta, as Werner had told the sheriff. It was his choice. Another city on Werner's list was New Orleans, and beyond that Mexico City. "No," I had objected to the latter.

"Ve haf to go to Mexico, sonny, to get new visas. Unt it take all vot is leeft of our twenty-nine day to get der."

His insight ended that debate.

My foremost choice of a southern city was Memphis, the home of Elvis Presley. We had enjoyed our own Elvis in Uitenhage, where I had finished high school. Melville, a close friend of mine, had copied his idol in dress and hairstyle, and could sing every song in the Presley repertoire. And much to our teenage delight, Melville's authenticity extended to the rubber-leg and hip movements that he had learned from Elvis movies. Our parents considered the music radical and the Elvis gyrations vulgar, and they attempted to steer us to the more sedate Pat Boone, and the Boone copycat in our town. But the more they tried to intervene, the closer we clung to Melvis, as we fans referred to Melville, and the more we spent our insufficient pocket money on Elvis records.

Atlanta, in my view, was disappointing, but Werner enjoyed it.

"Memphis next," I cheered.

"Ve do Memphis on der vay north," Werner insisted.

And so for the present, it was south again, towards the Gulf of Mexico. We were hitch-hiking once more, our exclusive mode of travel in the States, tearing along futuristic highways and exceeding all of our best estimates for times of arrival. In Africa, on the long stretches between cities, we might have been driving on 'strips,' as we called them, two thin bands of concrete along the center-line of a sandy road bed. And we were more than happy to have those, pleased to avoid the potholes, the tooth-rattling corrugations, the choking dust, or mud when it rained. The main setback to strips was that there was only one set of them. This meant that traffic moving in opposite directions approached head-on, with each encounter tending to be something of a game of chicken. "This sod won't yield," Pop would swear, veering off at the last second with rasping brakes. "I knew we should have come by train."

And we who were used to small family-owned shops in our cities — butcheries, tailor shops, shoemakers, and a myriad of repair outfits — walked in wonder through elaborate department stores with exclusively new goods, and covered shopping malls that seemed to us like small cities in themselves.

It was a journey of fascination and astonishment, of novel and exciting things. And if we forgot for a moment that we were living in the future, perhaps the year 2001, we were reminded by the news on car radios, on television, and in the newspapers; the space race had begun.

While we were still in the islands, Yuri Gagarin, the Russian astronaut, had orbited the earth on *Vostok*. "Vot you say to dot?" Werner had asked Patrick McGee, our American crewmate.

"All it means, buddy," Patrick had replied with a sneer, "is that before you know it, we'll be doing something even better."

And now, only about a month later, we heard it live: 'I believe this nation should commit itself to achieving the goal, before this decade is out, of landing a man on the moon and returning him safely to earth.'

"I can't believe he has committed to something so difficult," I proclaimed in surprise. "He'll look so bad in history if he can't deliver."

The lady who had given us a ride turned to face me in the back seat. "JFK will get it done," she declared. "He can do anything." Her confidence made her sound just like Patrick. But the more people we met, the more we recognized that this unfettered optimism was just part of the American way. No remotely realistic vision was put aside as mere fantasy. We were astounded by young children telling us that they were going to be space scientists and astronauts, or doctors and lawyers like their moms and dads. They were all going to college. That was taken as a given.

And their parents were still studying, doing Dale Carnegie courses on public speaking, and upgrading their skills as air force mechanics, or officers in the navy. It soon became clear to us that there was a keen awareness of the link between wisdom and opportunity. If you knew more, you were more valuable, and you could substantially improve your position. And I quickly gathered that know-how and ability were the criteria for promotion, rather than — what I had experienced — race, political affiliation, and age. It all made perfect sense.

One of the good motorists who offered us a ride was rushing to a night class. "What's it about?" I asked.

"History of the West," he replied. "Great stuff!"

"But how does that help you?" I asked. "Are you a teacher?"

"A welder," he shrugged. "But I love history. And I'm accumulating credits. Maybe I'll change to teaching one day. You never know." He told us that his "daddy," a senior citizen I gathered, occasionally took a class with him. "I'm sure it's the same in your countries," he said.

"No!" I disagreed. "In South Africa, people can't wait to finish school, or university, so that they can stop studying, be done with classrooms, homework, tests, and so on. They seldom go back."

"*Ja*, it's der same in Germany," Werner agreed.

But the Americans were a race of students, obsessed with education. And not only were they looking to get ahead, they were learning because they liked it. They had invented the Bomb, used cutting-edge technology to turn the tide on a world war, and magnanimously rebuilt the countries of their former enemies. Now was the time to do some equally important things at home, and in the process enjoy it.

They were living in the finest country in the world. These were the good times. And best of all, they knew it. And lest it briefly slip their minds, a generation of older folk fed them a barrage of reminders about the Great Depression, and World War II, and the ways that things had changed for the better — how many good jobs there were now, compared to the time when they were young, how much money was now in circulation, how much buying power the average wage earner now had, and how bright things looked for the future. Their unfulfilled dreams had come alive for their children, and they did not want any opportunity squandered.

We couldn't help but notice that Americans were different, that this was a country on the move, and the sense of it was invigorating. And we, in our small ways, began to adopt a similar frame of mind to those we met, an American-styled upbeat. I could feel myself changing, and I preferred my new self, by far, to my old. And in looking back I believe that, aside from the magnificent taste of freedom, my most precious gifts from the American people were the educational drive, positive attitude, and boundless optimism that rubbed off on me during those first months in the States.

The Civil Rights Movement

We had been dropped off along the road and were discussing, once more, the places we had chosen to visit. "Montgomery, okay, it's on our vay to New Orleans. But not Little Rock. No! Vot's dot for a place? Der's nothing to see. At least Memphis is on der Mississippi. Dot's fine."

But I wanted to see Little Rock Central High School where, a few years before, President Eisenhower had sent paratroopers, the elite 101st Airborne Division, to enforce desegregation at bayonet point. I had been told first-hand about the incident by a friend who, on a Rotary student-exchange scholarship, had been at school near there.

At the time I had related her thoughts on the incident to my dad, and mentioned her observation that it was a shame that it had had to be accomplished by the threat of such force. But in Pop's view, beyond Winston Churchill — whose mother, he often reminded me, was American — there were three people exclusively beyond criticism, Presidents Roosevelt, Truman, and Eisenhower, his war heroes. "Good for Ike," he had smiled, "he's a tough little sod."

"That's Irene's point exactly," I challenged. "He's tough and he probably overreacted."

But Pop was not about to be swayed. "Listen, Son," he offered firmly, "I don't know the details. But Ike wouldn't have done it if he thought he didn't have to."

"Vhy ve haf stop here?" Werner asked. "Dot's nothing but a lousy little town."

"It's where the Civil Rights Movement began," I said with more confidence than I felt. "A friend of mine was at school near here. This is where Martin Luther King, their equivalent of Nelson Mandela, made one of his first famous speeches."

"Ja, vot he say, sonny?"

"I can't remember," I replied. "My friend had some of his words written in her diary. Something like, 'The time comes when people get tired of being kicked around by the iron feet of oppression.'"

"Hmm. I haf read dot dis King also haf followed Gandhi."

"Yes," I affirmed, "his ideas on passive resistance. And talking about Mahatma Gandhi, did you know that he first tested his theories in South Africa, in 1913, leading a protest march from Natal into the Transvaal?"

"Where you fellas from?" the black gentleman asked us. We were in the back of his pickup, and he was speaking to us in a raised voice through the broken window panel of the cab.

"Germany," Werner replied. "Unt my buddy's from..."

"Australia," I interjected quickly, taking Annabel's advice.

He twisted to get another glimpse of us. "Long way from home," he smiled sympathetically. "I was stationed in Germany for a while."

"Not so nice as here," Werner offered cautiously.

"Not so nice? You got to be kidding me!" he boomed. "I loved it there! People were great, very respectful. Everything beautiful and green, and the country runs like clockwork. I didn't want to come home."

"Is home in New Orleans?" I shouted through the window. We were on its outskirts.

"Wish it was," he hollered back. "Wish my mammy had a place here. Expensive city, New Orleans. You'll find out for yourselves. But one thing I can tell you, stay away from the French Quarter!"

"French Quarter, ve stay avay," Werner promised. "Ve visit only vun place in New Orleans, Bourbon Street."

Our driver — 'Virgil,' he had introduced himself as — chuckled.

We drove on in silence for a while. "If you want to spend some worthwhile money," our friend suggested, "treat yourselves to some Cajun cooking, and some Dixieland. But in the back streets, mind you."

"Dixieland?" Werner exclaimed. "Vot's dot for food, sonny?"

Virgil let out a burst of bull laughter that had him sounding like the skipper. "Not food," he snorted. "Jazz, music of the South. You'll love it! And if you miss it, you will have wasted your time here."

I badly wanted to question Virgil on some civil rights issues, but Annabel's advice rang once again in my mind, the two topics of conversation that Americans are taught to avoid. However, Werner did so without hesitation. "Vot you sink, Virgil," he asked, "von Martin King?"

"Martin Luther King?"

"*Ja, ja,* Martin Luther King."

"He's a good man, but he's a troublemaker. JFK should have left him in jail for a while. What he really needs is a stint in the military!"

"But vot he says is right?"

"Yes, one-hundred-percent right, I won't argue with that."

"And you vill protest mit him?"

"I'm not into protest," Virgil said. "Protest can get a person hurt."

"But it's non-violent," I argued, itching to say something.

He laughed, and the exact pitch of it returned to me when, in the process of writing this book, I happened to read a paragraph in *The American Century*, by Harold Evans. It told of a black farmer, 70-year-old Hartman Turnbow, who had fought off white supremacists intent on burning down his home after he had registered to vote. Mr. Turnbow spoke to Howell Raines — *My Soul is Rested* — and mentioned a conversation with Martin Luther King Jr. shortly after the incident:

> Dr. King said to me right there he'd never 'prove of violence. And then I replied to him, I said, 'This nonviolent stuff ain't no good. It'll get ya killed.'

Mothers

*T*he man looked bored as he gawked past us from his box.

"How much for a room?" I asked, stooping to help my voice penetrate a lower Plexiglas panel with holes drilled in it.

"Twelve dollars an hour," he replied without even looking at us.

"Holy Moses, sonny," Werner exclaimed. "Twelve dollar an hour?"

His tone caught the man's attention. He sat up and craned his neck to get a better view of us. "You guys off the ships?" he asked.

"No," Werner replied. "Ve are off a sail jacht."

"And you're not gay? You're not, of course!" he said, answering his own question. "My apologies, gentlemen."

"We're just looking for a cheap place for the night," I shrugged. "We've got sleeping bags."

He shook his head and smiled. "You guys are in the wrong part of town," he said. "You got a car?"

Werner laughed. "Ve hitch-hike, sonny."

The young man's face softened and he suddenly looked like a different person. "You're German, right? And you're English?" he guessed, turning to me. "I'm Adam," he smiled. "Welcome to sin city."

We introduced ourselves and he went on. "Look," he said, "hang around for an hour or so. I get off at midnight. The place just starts to wake up then, anyway. I'll buy you a couple of drinks, and then you can bunk down at my place. No charge. I've done some hitch-hiking myself, England, Germany, all round Europe. People were mighty good to me."

"Really, sonny? You've been in Germany?"

"Yup," he said, "the Oktoberfest in Munich, one of my favorite places. Listen," he offered, "I'll be happy to show you around, at least a few jazz joints and some titty bars."

We left our bags behind his desk, collected him a short while later, and were soon mingling with a gathering crowd of tourists.

Adam jerked his head, and we looked up.

"Jees, sonny!" Werner swore, his eyes as large as saucers. A skimpily clad girl on a swing waved to us as she swept gracefully through a window. "Let's check dis place out. Vot you say, Adam?"

We made a move towards the entrance.

"Hey guys, don't go in there!" a doorman shouted from across the street. "This is where the girls are at. That's their mothers in there."

*W*e met another mother who left a lasting impression on us, in a town beyond New Orleans. Two female students had given us a ride in an old Volkswagen. They took us on a short tour of their high school, and then home for lunch. "This is my mom," Brenda smiled, showing her braces.

"How do you do, Mrs. Luff," I said, extending a hand.

"Please call me Deana," she invited. " 'Mrs. Luff' makes me feel so old and stodgy."

"Okay Deana," Werner replied easily. "Ve call you Deana, or Mrs. Luff, or voteffer you say, but you are not stoogey."

The girls laughed, but she curtsied playfully and replied. "Why thank you, kind sir." She was as open and unassuming as her daughter.

"We've invited them to lunch," Brenda announced. "They've just sailed over here from Africa."

"That's nice. And how did you-all meet?" she asked.

"We gave them a ride," Brenda replied.

Her mom raised an eyebrow, but nothing in her expression betrayed any hint of reprimand. I could just imagine my sister in the same position, arriving home with a couple of foreign hitch-hikers. My mom, nice as she was, would probably have had a fit.

"I can't believe how many high-school students have cars," I offered, eager to move from the topic of how we'd met. "It's unheard of in Africa."

"You'd be even more surprised if you knew how many worked to pay for them," Mrs. Luff said proudly. "They do all kinds of jobs."

"Now that's impressive," I exclaimed. I told her that I had not known of any white teenagers in South Africa who had worked at all while they were still in school. "And even at university," I said, "only a handful of students take jobs in the summers."

We talked on and on before Brenda's mom suddenly jumped up. "My goodness, look at the time," she exclaimed. "Let's eat. You, young ladies, must be getting back to school."

"I wish my mom could see your kitchen," I said as we ate.

"Oh, and why's that?" Mrs. Luff inquired with interest.

"All those newfangled gadgets you have," I smiled. "I'm not even sure I know what some of them are."

She happily showed us her collection, and I could not help but think that this was another side of the future — an electric range, a pop-up toaster, a blender, a washing machine and drier, and in a closet a Hoover vacuum cleaner and an electric polisher. Such items, no doubt, could have been imported into South Africa, albeit at great expense. But what was the point? The maid brushed the carpets by hand, and polished the floors on her knees, and did the laundry on a scrub board before hanging it on the line to dry. And if it took a little longer, who cared? Besides, clothes always smelled so good, my mom said, dried in the sun.

And our coal-burning stove helped warm the house in the winter. And in the summer, if it got too hot, the kitchen door could easily be closed; 'Lizzie did not mind the heat.' And what on earth would John do with a power lawn mower, like the one we spotted in Brenda's garage. He would probably ruin it. 'Bloody *kaffirs* are hard on machines.' I had heard it said a hundred times.

"I admire these American moms," I remarked to Werner later, as we stood by our packs waiting for our next ride.

"Vhy is dot, sonny?" he asked in surprise.

"I mean doing all their own work and everything."

"It's der same in Germany," he said, "but mitout all dose contraptions." He was silent for a moment, then his face brightened. "But Brenda's mom is unbelievable. I neffer see a mom like dot, a mom in blue jeans."

"And one who loves Elvis," I added, "and has all his records."

"Unt dis food vot she haf gif us, sonny, ve neffer can eat it all."

International Politics & Geology

We made it to a small town just across the Texas line. "I see MacDonald's," Werner announced joyfully. "I buy me a hamburger."

"What about all the food we have from Brenda's mom?"

He shrugged. "But it's a hamburger, sonny."

We both ate. "Dot vos so good," Werner sang.

We then ambled out into the twilight and slept in a field.

The next day a family of five picked us up in a big station wagon. It had wooden panels, perhaps simulated, of a type we had seen only in the movies. "Thank you very much for stopping," I breathed heavily, having run up on the vehicle. "We hadn't realized you were so full."

"Thank them," the mom smiled at her children, as they scrambled to make room for us and our packs.

We exchanged high fives with the youngsters. "We're off to our beach house. Would you like to come?" the little girl offered spontaneously. Her language skills, like Joy's at her age, seemed very advanced.

"Ve luff to come," Werner answered shamelessly.

Later in the day, Werner and I, and Ted, the dad, took a long jog along the beach. The sound of small waves lapping along the shore brought back memories of being at sea, and we told Ted a little about our trip. Dusk saw us back, as our host said, "just in time for dinner."

"What do you call this," I asked, "cooking outside like this?"

"A cook-out."

I laughed. "That's logic at its best."

"What do you call it in Africa?"

"A *braaivleis*," I replied. "It means, literally, 'a roast meat,' an occasion, I suppose, where meat is roasted over a fire."

" 'A roast meat,' that's funny," one of the children said and every-one laughed.

Ted informed us that he was intrigued by international politics, and when the children went off to bed he began talking energetically. He was ex-tremely concerned about the spread of communism that had taken place in the fifties. "From two countries at the beginning of the decade," I think he said, "to almost one third of the world's population by its end."

We offered no response to this, but I know that my face showed surprise.

"I see communism as a major threat in South Africa," he stated.

"Not really," I contradicted him. "The government there would like to have you believe so. But no!"

"But why would your government…"

I anticipated what I thought would be his question. "To justify its crackdown on the freedom movement. They've blown the threat of com-munism way out of proportion, and created a binge of hysteria, paranoia, amongst white South Africans. And in the process," I added, "they've got more people voting for them."

"I can understand that," Ted agreed before challenging me. "But you said that your government would like to have us Americans believe it. Can you address that issue?"

"Yes, sorry," I apologized. "You see, by attributing all political dis-sent to communism, the Afrikaner party believes it can divert the scrutiny of the west, and especially the United States, from its human-rights abuses. If it's only the 'commies' they're busting, that's fine."

"But the communists have a strong presence there," Ted argued.

"It's communism in name," I tried to explain. "But in reality I see it as no more than a left-wing movement, one that's more strongly opposed to apartheid than to capitalism or democracy. And I simply don't believe that it's controlled by Moscow."

"You portray it as non-threatening, possibly even benevolent?"

"No, I wouldn't go that far," I said. "It's complicated, and I don't claim to have all the answers. And I'm not trying to be soft on communism in general. But that's the way I see it in South Africa."

He nodded stiffly.

"And having said all that I did," I added, "it might sound like a con-tradiction when I tell you that I certainly wouldn't trust my life to them, the South African communists."

"And why's that?"

"They're communists," I shrugged.

"And your Nelson Mandela, is he a communist?"

"No!" I replied firmly.

My comments were clearly at odds with Ted's views on Africa, and he abruptly changed the subject. "And what do you think, Werner," he asked, "about our American troops still in Germany?"

"Ve like Americans," Werner replied. "But maybe is better if you vos leeft. Germany haf change, and maybe it's a vaste of your money to keep so many peoples der."

Ted laughed. "I think you might be right about that."

"Unt vot von politic in America, Ted? Vot you can tell us?"

He explained what he believed the States was trying to do, and told us about his strained days in Korea. "That was supposed to be war against communism," he said. "But it was the second war we'd fought in five years, and the government was never completely committed to it. And the war was never fully supported, not even by the military."

Werner asked him what he meant.

"For a start, our training was lousy," he complained. "Brutal, but lousy! Then they sent my unit off in tropical uniforms at the beginning of winter. Hell, it was tough enough just to survive, let alone fight a war."

He was lost in thought. Then he continued. "And in places like that where you're messing in other people's affairs, the locals are the last to appreciate what you're doing for them. So even if you win, you lose. And unless you stay there forever, they just go back to doing their...If we have to send a message to these small nations, we should just do what we're good at. Get in. Belt them on the nose. Say sorry. Then get the hell out, quickly. That's..." He tailed off, not finishing his second sentence either.

"Now we've got Special Forces in Vietnam, another half-committed protest against communism. It's dangerous and I don't like it! Besides, we're messing with their ancient customs and traditions. Nobody wants foreigners telling them how to live, least of all foreign invaders." He looked at the dying coals in the fire pit. "What I'm saying, I suppose, is that everybody wants their freedom. My father was a Scot and I grew up with framed words on our wall that were copied from a proclamation drawn up in Scotland in the early thirteen hundreds: 'We fight not for glory, nor riches, nor honours, but for freedom alone, which no good man gives up except with his life.' "

"Dot's nice," Werner said, "unt true! America too haf fought for her freedom, for her independence von Great Britain."

"And do you think you're heading for a war in Vietnam?" I asked.

"I was worried about that for a while," Ted replied. "But not with Kennedy. I don't think so. He fought in a war. He knows better."

John Fitzgerald Kennedy had just taken the oath of office, on 20 January 1961, and become the 35th President, and although he had won the election by only a narrow margin, everyone we met, who spoke of him, looked up to him. At best they were euphoric. At worst they respected him, his war record, his educated wife, his energetic and engaging style, his quick wit, and his apparent understanding of the big issues — like the nuclear threat.

*T*exas turned out to be bigger than we thought. "Things are getting tight," I remarked to Werner, as I checked off another precious day in my notebook. "People are just too nice. We keep getting sidetracked."

The judge was typical. "You boys ever seen an oil well?"

"No, but I'd love to, Judge. I'm a geology student."

"Interesting!" He left the road and glided into farmland.

Werner was grinning from ear to ear. "My first time effer in a Cadillac, Judge. I can hardly even feel der bumps."

The judge chuckled. "I sometimes forget what a good ride it is."

"Der's vun, sonny," Werner said, jabbing my arm.

"Can you figure it out, the counterbalance, the way it pumps?"

I said I thought I could, but the judge explained it anyway. "Let me ask you," he added a moment later, as I sketched busily in my notebook, "does the landscape around here remind you of anything; an area of South Africa possibly?"

"The Karoo!" I exclaimed at once.

His face lit up. He was uncommonly pleased with my response.

"How did you know?" I asked in surprise. It was clear from our lengthy conversation thus far, that he had not visited South Africa.

"I took an elective when I was in college, more than forty years ago, *Rocks for Jocks.* Our instructor had spent some time in South Africa. Chatting to you boys has brought it all back to me. Similar rocks and climate, he said, here as in the Karoo."

"Yes," I confirmed zestfully. "But I can't believe you still remember it. I'm sure I've forgotten half of what I learned less than a year ago."

"Memory is my forte," he smiled. "A judge lives or dies by his memory, you know. I remember Doc showing us a slide of the Karoo after some rain. It was full of flowers. I would have sworn it was taken in this part of Texas. The seeds seem to stay dormant, sometimes for years, waiting for that cloudburst that we get here every once in a while."

"It's the same way in the Karoo," I verified once more.

"Tell me, Ian, have they ever found petroleum in the Karoo?"

"Not that I know of," I replied, deep in thought. "But that's a good question. Perhaps the geological structure is not quite right — anticlines, domes, and the like — to trap the hydrocarbons."

"Or maybe they haven't looked hard enough," he said in his Southern voice, a certain fire in his eyes. "Could be your fortune, young man!"

I prickled with excitement. "I'll check into it," I promised, "first thing I do when I start studying again."

"Good," he said with a look of satisfaction.

We started back towards the highway. "Electives," I expressed after some thought, "law students doing geology. What a great idea."

"You don't have that in South Africa?"

"No, definitely not! If you study geology, all your courses are geology-related. I mean, you do some mathematics, of course, and physics and chemistry, but nothing that's fun, so to speak. There's no provision in the system to apply credit for a course in history, say, or law."

"That's too bad. What about Europe, Werner?"

"It's vorser," he said. "Ve specialize even on high school."

"Next stop, an oil refinery." The old man turned and winked at me. "You might see a few more one day, in the Karoo."

The judge caught Werner's eye drift to his watch. "Just one more stop," he promised, "then I'll let you go; after I take you to lunch."

Mexico

I paid in cash and, still complaining, walked across a bridge into Mexico. As a South African, apparently, I needed a visa. But cash was just as good — 'American dollar, no problem.'

We had barely made it before our passes expired, and we hoped that the Caribbean-type rules applied for getting back into the States. I would readily have turned about and tried immediately. But Mexico was Werner's domain.

"Seem like ve haf do more hike dan hitch," the German grumbled. But he had scarcely said it when a large tanker truck swung off the road, scattering gravel. Werner tossed his knapsack over his shoulder and tore off, with me in hot pursuit. *"Buenos dias,"* Werner grinned as he climbed up on the running board. *"Gracias.* Vhere you go, sonny?"

"No hablo ingles," the driver apologized with raised shoulders.

Unperturbed, Werner quickly produced a folded map of Mexico, one that looked as if it had been ripped from an old school atlas. The driver opened it, smoothed it out with an iron-like hand, and pointed to a spot halfway down the Gulf Coast — Tampico.

"Great!" Werner grinned, extending his hand, small and light-colored compared to that of the driver. The German announced his name and introduced me as Tom. "More easy for him to say," he explained later.

"Me llamo, Carlos," our driver said, tilting his Stetson-like hat.

We had not been in anything that large, and were enthralled by its bulk and power, the height of our seats, the small size of the lesser vehicles. Carlos reached out, twisted the fan mounted on his dashboard, and used his hand to test that we felt its cool breeze. This gesture, better than language, welcomed us aboard.

The windows were open and it was noisy, but to us it was the welcome sound of being on the move. We drove for many hours.

As evening approached Carlos pointed ahead to some white, flat-roofed dwellings, and began slamming down through the gears, double-declutching with considerable skill. There were some equally large trucks already parked there, and Carlos pulled up alongside them. He climbed out and ambled off, stretching his stiff limbs. But we called after him, and motioned him to lock the cab.

He waved aside our request.

"My· clothes," Werner said, tugging at his leather shorts and pointing at his bag inside the cab.

Carlos clearly understood, but gestured in a way that indicated theft was not a problem. He set off again, slightly ahead of us, and we were surprised to see a holster on his belt. It held what looked like a six-gun, of the type we had seen in cowboy movies. Werner caught up to him, grasped his arm and, with a questioning inflection of his head, pointed to the weapon.

"*Si,*" Carlos responded with a gold-toothed smile, "*para bandidos!*"

Everyone inside knew Carlos, and he introduced us as *amigos*.

Werner took out his wallet, and with a sweep of his hand and a drinking motion signified that he was buying a round for everyone.

The men cheered and nodded thanks, but with raised arms signaled that his offer was unacceptable. We joined a table and two cold beers were plunked down in front of us. "*Buena cerveza Mejicana!*"

Werner took a small sip, and swirled it as a connoisseur might do with a fine wine. All eyes were on him and he played his part well, understanding that in mime pause is as effective as action. Eventually he swallowed and beamed his thousand-carat smile. "*Gesondheid!*" he cheered in Afrikaans, and everyone applauded, "*salud, salud.*"

We were presented with chicken, beans, and rice, covered with a Chile-pepper sauce, hot but delicious. After dinner the men switched to some form of spirits, probably tequila, but we stuck religiously to beer.

Later into the evening we moved outside. A man who we took to be the owner appeared with his guitar and sang, and the party became more rowdy. We heard the word '*pistola*' branded about, and at one point, in response to some sort of bet, we supposed, the men began tossing bottles into the moonlight and shooting at them with their revolvers. There were not as many hits as we might have expected from men who took so freely to their guns. But when someone removed his hat and threw it in the air, it succumbed to a determined hail of lead.

I strained to see my watch — a diesel generator provided inside light, but flickering oil lamps barely lit our outdoor tables — and noticed that it was going on for midnight. I began to wonder about our plans, but a short while later the drivers started to move off. Carlos caught my eye, and waved in a manner that called on us to follow him. He led us up a staircase and onto a moon-drenched roof where there were two beds made up. He used hand language to indicate that this is where we would sleep. Then, with a warm *"buenos noches,"* he too was gone.

I did not expect, and was not ready for the contrast in lifestyles that existed between the United States and Mexico. We had fun both in Tampico and Mexico City, and the people were nice, indeed, more than nice. But I was anxious to be heading north.

Heading North

*W*e had traveled north by train, my idea. It was inexpensive and comfortable, and I would have been happy to continue, at least as far as *"Río Bravo del Norte,"* as a Mexican schoolboy on the train had said, and explained — he was referring to the Rio Grande, the border. But Werner was anxious to be back on the road. "You meet better peoples vhen you hitch-hike, sonny."

"You're right," I agreed. "If they weren't the best they wouldn't pick us up in the first place."

I awoke with a start, to the roar of a passing train. We had spent the night along the railroad tracks outside Monterrey.

"You look terrible, sonny."

I rubbed my rough chin, conscious of not having shaved.

"Your beard also, but you are dirty, sonny. Your face haf sleeped on something funny."

I wiped it with my sleeve. "How's that?"

"Vorser," he laughed.

I took out my geological compass and checked myself in its mirror. "Oh boy," I complained, "I badly need a bath."

*"I*f dis vun stop, I buy you beers for a veek, sonny!" It was a new Ford Thunderbird, a convertible with its top down, the potential ride of a lifetime.

It flew past us, but began to slow. "I think you're going to lose your beers," I shouted, lifting my backpack.

"Hi. We can take you as far as Dallas, Texas," a lady hailed us. She had long, blond, windswept hair.

"Dot vould be really great," Werner smiled. *"Eres muy bonita,"* he said, and added, "You are so pretty as der car!"

I shuddered as he killed our ride. But both she and her escort erupted into laughter — Werner had the flair for saying things like that without offending people. He had probably winked at the man.

"Think you can make it, guys? It's a little tight back there."

"Ve make it, no problem. If not, I leeft mine knapsack behind."

We introduced ourselves and sped off. It was too noisy to talk, but conversation was the last thing on our minds as we raced towards Laredo at more than one hundred miles an hour — we both periodically stretched our necks over the driver's seat to check the speedometer.

We stopped for a "cup of Joe," as Chuck called it, and an explosion of talk. We explained our predicament, the possibility of not being let back into the States.

"Don't worry, guys," Chuck reassured us, "you're as good as in! You're with us. There's no problem."

"Not for you. For us, alvays a problem. Alvays ve vorry!"

"Tell you what, buddy," Chuck advanced, turning to Werner, "you're my cousin. Look at us, a crew cut and we'd be brothers."

"You're right," the blond twittered. "And a woman should know."

"Listen, this is the way it is. You two are spending a couple of weeks with me before you meet up with your boat again. That joining-the-yacht thing is good, and this makes it even better." He took a notebook from his pocket and wrote 'Wernher.' "Wernher who?" he asked.

"It's 'Werner,' mit no 'h' in it."

"Oh, I thought it was 'Wernher,' like Wernher von Braun, the German rocket scientist."

"No," Werner said. "I've heard of him, of course. But for me it's 'Werner,' Werner Maier, von Heidenheim in der sous von Germany."

"That's all I need to know," Chuck said confidently. "For the rest, if they ask us any questions, we just tell the truth."

"Unt vot's der truth, sonny?"

"The truth is that our mothers kept in touch, but this is the first time we've met. You were in college in South Africa, joined the yacht and so on."

We came up on a line of cars at the border, and I braced myself for some Southern inhospitality. I was "ashen-faced," as Chuck told me later.

"Nice car," the immigration officer greeted us. "How did she do on the trip?"

"Went like a bird," Chuck responded lightly.

"That good," he said, "a real T-Bird then." As he spoke, he matched our faces to the passport photographs.

When he opened Werner's ID, Chuck said, "My cousin."

"How do you like it in the States, *Herr* Maier?" the officer asked.

"I luff it, sir."

Chuck had put my passport on the bottom of the pile. The officer crinkled his forehead as he examined it.

"He's British," Chuck said, "my cousin's buddy from college."

The officer gave him a questioning look.

"British Commonwealth," Chuck offered convincingly.

The man in uniform paged through the document slowly, then stamped it, closed it, and handed it to me. "Thank you, sir."

"Thank you, sir!" I smiled back, trying not to look over-pleased.

He dismissed us with a wave. "Have a nice day. And try to keep that bird down to a reasonable flight height."

*I*t was a tough call from Dallas. "You have got to go to Colorado," Chuck urged, "especially you, Ian. Cripple Creek, Silverton, Telluride. It's like a full-scale mining museum out there."

"Yes," I acknowledged, truthfully interested, "we studied the geology of the Rockies and the San Juans. And one of my professors mentioned Telluride. It's definitely on my list of places to visit."

Werner was all for it. "Colorado, California, der whole west coast, sonny, Alaska. Den home to Europe on der *Trans-Siberian Express*."

But it was my turn, my choice, and although I was tempted, I decided to be practical. I had a cousin — a real cousin — in Ohio, an orthopedic surgeon. 'Besides your Uncle Martin, look up Bunny, whatever else you do,' Pop had advised. 'He'll give you the time of your life.'

And from Cincinnati it was just a short haul to Cleveland, where Patrick McGee had told us, more than once, we could earn 'a ton of money' on Lake Erie. 'There's a ship that works the Lake every summer. It's full of college kids, and it's a blast. And in three months, if you're careful, you can save enough for a year in school.' It was just too big a package to pass up.

"Let's head for the Great Lakes first," I suggested.

"Okay, sonny."

We started waving our thumbs for Cincinnati.

"Sorry, but Dr. Braun is away at a conference," the lady said. "We don't expect him back until next week."

"So vot ve do, sonny?"

"We head up to Cleveland," I suggested, "and find out about Pat's ship thing. We'll come back here on a weekend when my cousin's at home."

We checked into a flophouse near the waterfront, and found the friendly atmosphere one might imagine of a small family-run prison. We slept in our clothes and placed the bed legs in our shoes. That was, no doubt, overkill. But, as Patrick had cautioned us, some care was clearly in order. "If you have sleeping bags," one of the inmates suggested, "use them. They may delay you getting crabs." We stood out like sore thumbs amongst the clientele, and were cannon fodder for their excess of humor. But they knew the tricks of subsistence survival, and we were grateful to learn from them.

The ship that Patrick McGee had recommended was still fitting out, but the chief steward, who did the hiring for the summer crew, was keen to take us on. "Have a seat in the mess," he said, "and fill out this paper-work."

We thanked him and borrowed pens, highly excited. But we were immediately bogged down — *Address* and *Phone Number, Social Security Number, Date and Place of Birth*... "We'd better get advice from someone at the flophouse," I suggested to Werner.

"I wouldn't mess with it," Vince hooted with contempt. "You'll be living aboard, working twelve, fourteen hours a day. And no drinking, buddy. Forget it!"

"But we can save good money," I explained, "for college."

He scowled and reached out. "Let's see the form." He studied it, running a finger slowly down the page. "Firstly," he cautioned us, "you don't even have a proper address. This place definitely won't cut it for a Social Security number."

"We met a couple of girls the other night, sisters. Maybe we could use their address and phone number."

His eyes returned to the form. "Yeah, that'd work. But what about this *'place of birth?'* If you don't put States-side, you raise a red flag. On the other hand, lying to the Coast Guard...I don't know. It's a tough call."

The American Dream — Denied!

There was a delay in processing our paperwork. "Ve should haf lied, sonny," Werner whispered, "said ve vere Americans born in der States."

"Come back in a week," the steward suggested. "I'll sign you on just as soon as I get a nod from the authorities."

But when we returned the following week there was a message for us to report to the immigration office.

Our meeting took off badly right from the start. "You boys are in trouble," the officer announced. His face held a severe expression.

"Why, sir?" I asked anxiously.

"You cannot work on a visitor's visa. You cannot even apply for work! These job applications are grounds for deportation!"

We explained that we were just trying to save some money to go to an American university.

He eyed us with displeasure. "Applications for college have to be made outside the United States," he explained. "And even if you are accepted, you still cannot work here!"

"Vhy is dot, sir?" Werner asked.

"Don't ask me why," he sniffed. "It's the law, that's why. It's the same in every country." His voice was cold and detached.

"No, sir," Werner smiled. "In Sous Africa I find easily a job."

"Then South Africa is different. Look boys, I really should have you out of here on the next flight. But I can see you have good intentions, so I'm going to cut you a little slack."

"Ve can stay?" Werner asked joyfully.

"No, I can't go that far. But I'm going to give you a break. Fifteen days to exit the country of your own accords. 'Voluntary departure,' we call it. This way, you leave, make the proper arrangements for college, and we issue you the appropriate visas."

"Is that the best you can do for us?" I asked, silently pleading for more.

"I'm afraid so," he replied, and sniffed again. "If I deport you, as I should, you get a free ride home, but we never let you in again. Know what I mean? That's it for you ever getting back into the US of A."

It was a sharp slap in the face and I was devastated. With a handful of sniffs and a few words of reprimand, years of dreams and months of my best planning had been laid to waste. My fine mosaic had been ripped apart. My long trip across the Atlantic had been for naught.

I had not come to the United States just for a visit. I had come to stay. I wanted some small part of the American dream, the smallest part, and I was prepared to work for it. But now it was being denied. It was a rude awakening, and I was drained, exhausted, and depressed — a dead pig. I began to sob in overwhelming despair.

It was the first time Werner had seen me in such a state of anxiety, and he tried to comfort me. "Ve sink von somesing, sonny."

I attempted to reply, but was inarticulate. It did not matter, I thought. Werner could not begin to understand. For him this was little more than an inconvenience, an annoyance that called for a change of direction. But for me it was catastrophic, a true disaster. There was only one place in the world where I wanted to live, and that had just been snatched from my grasp. I had no Plan B.

Perhaps it should not have come as such a surprise, I thought. For beneath the veneer of my cheerful expectancy, I had felt increasingly that things were not going my way, that my dream had been naïve, that I was immature and ignorant. What did I have to offer this great country? Nothing. I did not even have a degree. How could I possibly pay my way? But with my newfound optimism I had steadfastly stuck to the notion that something would eventually work out, as it had, with such convenience, to this point.

This is just a setback, I said to myself in a desperate effort to regain my cheer. I'll keep trying. They'll let me in eventually. But if the future could have been read, my old self would have laughed at my new, optimistic self — more than a decade still separated me from my dream.

The Great Lakes

*W*e did not dare wait. Cleveland, we quickly decided, was a place in our past. So bidding farewell to those friends we could find, and leaving messages for others, we started out around the Lake, heading for Canada.

"In Montreal ve find a ship. You come mit me to Germany."

"Thanks." I said. "But I'm worried about even getting into Canada, especially with South Africa no longer in the Commonwealth."

"Vot ve do, sonny, if dey say no?"

"I suppose we could go back to Cincinnati and see if my cousin can help us, or my uncle. But those would be our last resorts."

*T*he Canadian officials were lenient. We found a cheap rooming house in Montreal, and began what would turn into days of walking down the river-front, talking, or trying to communicate with seamen, sneaking aboard when we could get by security guards. Montreal, at that time, was one of the largest inland ports in the world, and ships crowded her docks.

"The Old Man makes the decision," an English deckhand informed us. "It's completely up to him. And you've got a better chance on ships heading into the Lakes. They need the help. Longshoremen are in short supply. This is only their third season for ocean-going shipping, and we're still doing a good part of the cargo-handling ourselves."

"What about your ship?" I asked. "Any chance of a passage?"

"We're Lake-bound, but no! British and American unions are too strong. Your best bet is with Scandinavian flags, I say."

On our fifth day out Werner picked up a German freighter, and I was left alone. We had not planned on separating, but quickly decided that, under the circumstances, it made sense.

I woke up early and scratched out Day 13 in my waterproof, geological notebook. Nagging superstitions haunted me as I pondered the frustrations of yet another fruitless day on the waterfront. Countless rejections had got to me, and depression had begun to claw at my soul. Perhaps I should take time out, I thought, climb the hill and visit McGill University. I remembered Professor King saying that it had a good mining program. Or maybe I should work for a few days, and then return to the docks with a fresh mind and a better attitude.

Unfriendliness was not the problem we — Werner and I, before he left — had been led to believe. 'Quebec, the *fleur-de-lis,* forget it,' someone had said. 'The *Québécois* speak only French. They won't talk to you in English.' But, as it had turned out, as soon as they established that we were for-eigners, not English-speaking Canadians, they readily accepted us. And we, for our parts, quickly learned to say *bonjour,* and thirty or so other French words that were much appreciated. And so, as in Cleveland, opportunities emerged, both for work and further adventure.

"Forget thees Germany thing, Yann," Henri suggested. "In two weeks Ah leave for Vancouver. It ees God's country, the Pacific Northwest. Why you don't join me?"

Henri reminded me of Gerry and I liked him. "How do you get there?" I asked.

"Ride the freights," he replied.

"The freight trains, people still do that?"

"Yes," he said with typical French-Canadian assurance, "why not?"

"I'll think about it, Henri," I said quite seriously. "I love trains!"

I scrapped plans for visiting the university, and took off to the li-brary to look at maps of the Pacific Northwest. But on the way I decided to drag myself down to the river, just for an hour I promised myself.

"Aye, let me introduce you to t' Old Man," the seaman offered. "A sailor jumped ship in Quebec City. I'm sure we hae need o' a hand t' replace him." His Scottish brogue was slight, but detectable.

"Yes," the captain confirmed, "we are undermanned. But we sail in two hours. Can you make it?" He had a balding head, bushy eyebrows, a pink face, spaced teeth, an agreeable smile and, other than no beard, a look not unlike Cap'n John's, that of a kindly old seadog.

"No problem, sir," I assured him, and tore down the gangplank.

I was soon back and aboard. We talked a little before the captain presented me with a form printed in Finnish. It had odd words blackened out, and some hand-written notations. "You sign this," he invited. "It is merely a formality. You agree to stay aboard until we reach one of our European ports, preferably Helsinki. We feed you, but no real pay, 100 *markka,* just enough to make it legal. We sign you on, I think the English would say, as a supernumerary."

"Thank you very much, Cap'n. You speak excellent English."

His face radiated pleasure. "And Swedish, without our awful Finnish accent, a smattering of French, and some Russian. Languages are my love, my obsession. But aboard you will not find much English. The First Mate speaks a little and, of course, the Third Engineer who you met, the young man with the Scottish burr."

"Yes, Cap'n."

"But thank you for voicing your opinion of my English. You your-self will manage with my countrymen, no doubt, and I will have a chance to further practice my English."

I offered my most cordial expression.

"Any questions, boy?"

I asked what I would be doing by way of work.

"You will be on deck, and I will try you at the helm. After all that yachting you claim to have done, I trust that I will find you adept."

"This is a large ship," I ventured hesitantly, forgetting my resolve to be more American, to 'think big,' to believe that I too could do practically anything.

"It is the same thing," he said, raising his head and drawing his mouth down. "And I am conjuring a plan for you in my mind. We have pilots aboard through the Lakes, and my men have trouble understanding them. If you can manage the helm, I will see about paying you."

"Thank you, sir. That would be much appreciated."

Someone called him and he cast his head to one side to dismiss me. "That's all, boy," he said. "Find Scotty and report to Bos'n."

The bos'n — boatswain, the supervisor of the deck crew — was a grizzled bear. He had a scarred face, a graying tangle of straggling hair, and only one eye in focus; the other shifted alarmingly and distracted me from looking him in the good eye.

Scotty introduced me. "Him," he said, pointing at me, "new man from Africa."

I smiled and made a move to shake the bos'n's hand.

But he disregarded my outstretched arm, and responded with a gruff, "Afrika Man work!" He motioned me to follow him.

"No Bos'n," Scotty said, bravely waving a finger in the old man's face. "First change clothes." He pointed to his shirt and shook it.

The bos'n lifted his head and rolled his good eye skyward, and I took this for a gesture of agreement.

Scotty steered me aft and showed me into a small cabin in the crew's quarters. There was a man lying on the lower berth reading.

I tried to greet him, but he ignored me.

"Do nae worry about him," Scotty said. He employed his index finger to make a circling motion next to his temple. "And he's a wee bit unsociable as well." He reached for my pack and heaved it up onto the upper bed, then led me down a steel passageway lined with asbestos-wrapped pipes and electrical cables, to a beautiful wood-paneled sauna, quite out of character with the rest of the ship. "The Finns love their steam baths," he said.

*B*y the time I found my boss again, we were ready to leave, and were soon bucking the flow on the immense river. And although it was away from Europe — we would steam more than three thousand miles before ever reaching the ocean — I was elated to be afloat and moving once more. But there was scarcely time to soak up the scene, for the next thing I knew I was being escorted to the mess for coffee, then back to the poop deck to standby for working mooring lines. We were about to enter the first of a number of locks that would ultimately raise us more than two hundred feet into Lake Ontario — our next link in the largest fresh-water chain of connecting waterways on the planet.

Beyond the fourth lock I was called to relieve the bridge watch.

"Two-three-two," the seaman said in a thick accent.

"Two-three-two," I repeated, stepping up to a wooden platform that let me look over the top of a varnished oak wheel, a giant replica of the one I had grown accustomed to on *Senta*.

"See that church spire on your bow, at twelve o'clock?" the pilot asked — the ship's master could not be expected to have pilotage endorsements for all the navigable channels of the seaway, and passage through these was the task of various pilots who joined and left the vessel at regular intervals; the captain, however, retained responsibility for the overall safety of his ship.

"Yes sir," I replied looking up from the binnacle.

"You can steer on that for the moment. Steady as she goes."

"Steady as she goes, sir."

"Get the feel of her, boy," the captain muttered without turning to face me. "Not more than one spoke at a time. If you over-steer you will have her weaving."

"Yes Cap'n, one spoke at a time, sir."

Things had happened so quickly that I'd barely had time to think about being scared, but now I could feel my heart pounding, literally thumping in my ribcage. These individuals must be crazy, I thought, entrusting a big ship like this to me. But I'm doing it. Somehow I'm bloody doing it.

I had already come farther upstream, I thought, than Jacques Cartier, the famous French explorer. I had learned about him in school, for although our history had been, in part, misleading about South Africa, we had been taught something more true-to-life of the world at large, and made to memorize much of it. I still remembered that, more than four hundred years before, Cartier had entered the gulf — of St. Lawrence — hoping to find gold and, with luck, a passage to the Orient. He had sailed inland, some six hundred miles from the ocean, before being turned back by the rapids we had bypassed at our first lock, *Rapides de Lachine*.

The waterway now was glass and I felt as if we were flying. But we were probably doing no more than about twelve knots.

"Okay, ease her to port."

"Ease her to port, sir."

"Easy now, easy."

"Easy, sir."

"What's your heading, sailor?

"Two-two-six, sir."

"Good. Steady as she goes, two-two-five. "Find yourself a mark ashore, and steer on it."

"The edge of that clump of trees ahead, sir, two-two-five."

I was slowly gaining confidence and was able to look about at farm-land, and listen to the conversation between the pilot and the captain. They were discussing a government plan to put icebreakers on the river the following winter, and keep the ocean passage to Montreal open year-round.

I had assumed that Scotty was joking when he had mentioned our cargo. But we were dockside and, sure enough, there it was, more cases of Scotch whiskey — 'whisky,' the Scots would have me spell it — than I could ever have imagined. We had put into Toronto, on Lake Ontario, and from what I could tell of the preparations that I was a part of, we were about to discharge a good portion of it.

I had been somewhat taken aback to come off my watch and be put straight back to work. But my partner hummed away merrily as we lifted yet another wooden hatch-cover and carried it to a mountain of others that we had already stacked up on deck. It was really tough work.

"Boy, am I beat," I complained to Scotty when we met in the mess.

"Hangover?" he asked.

"No," I smiled. "But I've been up since sparrow, stood my watch, then lifting hatch-covers for more than an hour. And what beats the heck out of me, is that the Finns seem to think it's fun."

"Aye, you would nae find them complaining about overtime; 'tis good pay. And anything t' do with cargo handling is a chore on the list o' 'Dangerous Work,' an added bonus."

"Ah-ha, now it begins to make sense."

"Aye, you'll see them scribbling on the backs o' their cigarette boxes, keeping a record o' how much they're making, how much they must give t' their wives, and what they can put aside for gambling. We'll hae some almighty sessions o' poker afore we reach Chicago. Do you play?"

"No," I replied.

"Too bad," he said. "But you can still enjoy some good whisky."

"Part of the cargo?"

"Aye," he confirmed. "You look carefully, you'll probably see Bos'n take out a crate today."

"Oh yes. How does he do that?"

"He's a maestro on the boom winch. He'll bang a pallet on the ship's side, an accident. Break a few bottles, but nae too many. What's left, or some o' what's left, is taken into bond. The rest goes t' the ship, officers first, then us. The loss is covered by insurance."

"And I suppose we do the paperwork?"

"Aye," he smiled, " 'tis a bonnie scheme."

We were offloading from two hatches. I was in a gang working Number 2, down in the hold, stacking cases onto a pallet in a net. A monstrous inclined boom, attached to a kingpost and held up by a topping lift, was swung over us. A seaman driving a large steam-winch lowered a heavy hook on a cable. We then rushed in, lifted the corners of a manila cargo net, and attached these to the clasp. Then Markku, our supervisor in the hold, gave a signal, crimping his index finger to his thumb. At this the sailor on deck above us — or the bos'n on Number 1 — took up the slack, tightening the net around the loaded pallet. Markku then made a circling motion, waving his hand above his head, and the winchman hoisted away.

As the load cleared the hatch, another man, on a smaller winch, swung the boom outboard, and lowered the precious cargo to the wharf below. Here Canadian stevedores detached the net, and the process was repeated. Trucks swung by now and then, and were loaded manually, leaving the nets and pallets for us to reuse. It was slow and labor-intensive, almost African I thought. But with the absence of shore cranes where we were berthed, I had to concede that it was a creative and practical operation.

When the ship was underway, Markku stood the eight-to-twelve watch, and he was my relief. He was not much older than me, and we had established the beginnings of a friendship. He commanded a vocabulary of about one-hundred English words, which meant that we could communicate after a fashion. To do my part I was anxious to learn some Finnish, and I approached Scotty on the matter.

"Aye," he said, " 'tis a good idea in theory. But Finnish is the hardest language you can imagine. Nothing sounds the same. You'd be better off practicing your pantomime, or trying t' teach him more Pidgin English."

"How many Finnish words do you know?" I asked.

"None t' speak o', a few swear terms. And afore you came aboard, I was scared that I was forgetting my English. You know, arrive home and say t' my dad, 'You my father, very good man!' And he'd hawk, 'Get the hell out o' here, Sean!' "

"Sean," I exclaimed in surprise. "Is that your name?"

"Aye," he acknowledged. "I'm 'Scotty' 'cause I'm a Scot, just like you're 'Afrika,' or 'Afrika Man,' as Bos'n says." His eyes lit up and he sniggered. " 'Afrika Man,' I just love it; makes you sound like an archaeological link between humans and the apes."

Our crew finished offloading first, secured the hatch, and we were dispatched to do some chipping and painting. Markku sent his usual partner, Jouko, to work with me on the after-deck stanchions, while he and the others set to painting a section of the hull that had been primed in Montreal.

After a stretch Jouko and I retired to the mess for some coffee — chicory might have been closer to the mark. But we had no sooner sat down when the bos'n stormed in. His face was red, the pupil of his lazy eye out of sight. "Afrika Man come!" he bellowed.

I took off at his heels, with Jouko following at a distance. I wondered what on earth could have happened to enrage him to such an extent, and what my part was in the matter. But when we passed Markku on the gangplank and he avoided making eye contact with me, I began to suspect something fishy.

The bos'n took a last step to the wharf, swung round and pointed amidships. And there it was, painted across the side of the ship in enormous orange letters: 'AFRIKA No. 1.'

"*D*id you hear what they did?" I snorted to Scotty later.

"Aye, and you should hae seen Bos'n's cockeye roll when he first spotted it. I thought he'd hae a heart attack."

I smiled at the thought.

Scotty continued. "But he soon twigged on. He's no fool. He knew you had nae done the painting."

Now my face flushed as a premonition began to dawn that the last laugh might be on me, rather than on the bos'n.

"And best o' all," Scotty quickly confirmed, "was your face when you saw what Bos'n was pointing t'. I never would hae thought that the old kook could've acted it out so well."

I smiled again, but this time weakly — a pricked balloon.

*T*he next time I saw the captain, he asked me what new tricks I had been up to.

My face blushed red once more.

He laughed. "There exists a perception," he said, "that we Finns are very dour folk. But as you see," he said proudly, "we love a good practical joke."

"Are they still all smiling at you?" Scotty inquired knowingly.

"Yes," I confirmed, "Bos'n included. And even my cabin mate gave me a toothless grin, although he didn't say anything."

"It's their way o' telling you they accept you, more probably even that they like you."

"Did they do the same to you?" I asked.

"Aye," he acknowledged, "something similar. I'll tell you about it some time."

*O*ur ship — with what remained of her blue-chip cargo — was now steaming full ahead. "I hope we put into Cleveland," I said.

"We do nae," Scotty assured me. "The rest o' the Scotch is for Chicago, more than a thousand miles still t' go."

As we left Lake Erie and entered the lower Detroit River, I was on the lookout. I had borrowed a book from Scotty, *Memories of the Lakes,* by Dana T. Bowen, master of a lake ship, and I wanted to see a special spot that the Captain had written about.

"What are we looking for?" Scotty asked.

"The Mamajuda Light," I replied. "It's on an island near here."

"Remind me o' the story again. I think I skipped that part."

"A young girl, Maebelle Mason, the daughter of the lighthouse keeper, rescued a drowning man here. Her father had gone to the mainland for supplies, so she took the skiff out alone, a rowboat. You can imagine how tough it was. Check the current we're bucking now," I said, pointing to the debris that was sweeping by us.

"How old was she?"

"Only fourteen."

"Aye, that's pretty brave."

"And the reason I'm so interested," I said, "is that Bowen tells the story by way of confirming the old saying that history repeats itself. The original event that he refers to concerns Grace Darling, a distant relative of mine."

"Ah hah!" Scotty exclaimed. He liked complex connections.

"I told you my Dad's family was from the north of England, a village close to the Longstone Light in the Farne Islands, where Grace's father was the light keeper."

"Aye," Scotty said in an interested tone. "I've seen the islands on a chart, "just south-east o' St. Abb's Head, past Berwick-upon-Tweed. I've sailed by there many a time, shipping out o' Edinburgh."

"Well, in 1838," I related, "a ship called the *Forfarshire,* bound for Scotland, was wrecked in a storm off the Light. And Grace and her Dad managed to rescue nine of her crew, in a skiff that I imagine was not that much larger than the one used here by Maebelle."

"That's an interesting wee bit o' family history."

I was pleased to hear him say so. "Yes," I continued, "and Queen Victoria, then only recently crowned, invited them to her Royal Court and presented them each with a gold medallion. We still have the medals in the family."

"How do you ken all o' this?" he asked, frowning. "I've next t' no knowledge about the history o' my family."

"Both my dad and my aunt are interested in it," I said. "And fortunately for us, quite a lot of it was recorded in the back of an old family bible."

"Aye, you're lucky, lad. And 'tis a really lovely story you told. Now, while we're still in the Detroit River, let me tell you something interesting."

I tilted my head enthusiastically, encouraging him to proceed.

"There's a wee boat comes out near here with post for the lake ships. She nudges her nose in and they do the transfer underway."

"How?" I asked, astonished. "Those freighters are gigantic."

Scotty laughed, happy, no doubt, that I appreciated the problem. "A sailor on the deck o' the cargo ship lowers a bucket on a line, just like you'd do on a yacht t' scoop up salt water for the dishes, and the postman stuffs it with what he has for the ship."

"Pretty smart," I smiled. "Will there be anything for us?"

Scotty shook his head. "Ours goes directly t' agents in places like Chicago. There'll be letters waiting for us there. But the Americans," he said, "want their 'mail,' as they call it, on a regular basis. I met one o' their lads in a pub last trip, and he told me that they even hae a postcode for the water service. Apparently it's been going for years. In his father's day, he told me, the delivery was made by rowboat."

The next day I did a double shift at the wheel. The crew had been on a whiskey binge and my partner had not turned to. "The AB is sick," I lied, referring to the Able-Bodied seaman who shared my watch.

The Old Man preferred it that way, Scotty had told me. He disliked writing up his men. "You're doing a good job," the captain smiled. "In Chicago, I shall put you on salary."

"Thank you, Cap'n!" I exclaimed happily.

"But hear me, boy, no more sandals on deck. It's dangerous! If you have no steel-toed boots, at least use what you are wearing now."

We turned at the strait that separates the lakes, and steamed south on Lake Michigan. And, eventually, there it was, Chicago in the early morning mist, a sight I shall always remember — a triumphant return to the States so soon, and my most memorable sight of a skyscraper, its pinnacle reaching through a fog bank, high above the Lake.

Jouko had hurt his shoulder, and the captain asked me to take his place as 'monkey.' I was jubilant. Monkey played a key role in docking the ship. I had studied the procedure closely, hoping I might get a shot at it. It involved a man standing on the bow railing, and swinging outboard on a knotted rope attached to a small swivel boom. It had to be timed so that he reached the wharf at precisely the time the bow pressed a kiss on it. The sailor would then put his feet down, run for the heaving line that had been tossed ashore, and use it to haul in a heavy mooring cable that he quickly attached to a bollard. He had to move at the double, and there was no room for error, because that single tether served as the spring that stopped the ship. However, with this attached the pressure was off, for all that remained to be done was to secure some additional ties, then help rig the boarding ladder. The final duty of the monkey was to attach the rat guards — big circular metal plates that prevented rodents from scampering aboard via the docking lines. When the ship departed, these tasks were done in more-or-less the opposite sequence.

If there were longshoremen available, of course, the monkey lost his job, and the danger pay that went with it.

"*Did* you see that cargo-handling setup we had this morning?" I asked Scotty.

"What do you mean?"

"I mean us working with those American stevedores. It was unbelievable; security guards down in the hold with submachine guns."

"Aye, I thought that's what Markku was trying t' tell me."

"Yes, I questioned one of them about the weapons. 'No disrespect,' the man said, 'but our client hain't taking no chances.'"

"That's a scream," Scotty laughed. "By the way, what are you doing t'night?"

"The Old Man has given me shore leave. I'm going to try and look up a family I met in the West Indies."

"A family with a bonnie daughter?"

"How'd you guess?" I smiled, taken aback by his acuity.

I telephoned the Halls and yes, they would love to see me. In fact, Mrs. Hall let on that they were having a small party, and that Annabel would be especially excited if I could stay the night.

I had left my suit aboard *Senta*, but I dressed as well as I could.

"Those shoes are just awful," Scotty said, eyeing the paint splotches. "Let me lend you a pair o' mine."

"Thanks," I replied with genuine relief. But when I tried them on, there was not the remotest chance of a fit.

"Like Cinderella's ugly sister," he taunted. "But never mind, I've an idea. Why don't you stop in at one o' the yacht clubs on your way t' the station," he advised. " 'Tis Saturday, everyone will be out sailing."

"Steal a pair of shoes?"

"Nae, borrow them," he grinned.

*C*hicago's upscale suburbs were spectacular, and so was Annabel. Caribbean shipmates of the Halls — their friends, the Vances — were at the party, and we relived the island charter with a lengthy slide show and lots of questions from dinner guests. It was a weekend in paradise, a window to an America I had not quite seen, and it solidified my resolve to one-day make the States my home.

Europe-Bound & 'Home' Again

We steamed from the big city slap into the center of the Mackinac Yacht Race, a three-day extravaganza sponsored by the Chicago Yacht Club.

Markku found me sitting on the poop deck, staring at the fading metropolis, sorry to be leaving it. He was short of breath. "Janne," he panted, "Captain say you to bridge."

I took the helm and it was chaos. "Hard to port!"

I repeated the order and, hand-over-hand, turned the wheel as quickly as I was able. I could see Bos'n below, on standby at the windlass, ready to drop anchor if he had to.

"Midships!" the pilot barked.

"Midships," I echoed and let the spokes spin.

"Half ahead."

"Half ahead," the captain repeated, and swiftly rotated the telegraph to the engine room.

A large yacht jibed towards our bow — in those days sail had exclusive priority over power.

"Full astern!" the pilot yelled, blowing a string of knotted blasts on the ship's horn. "And hard again to port!"

"Hard to port, sir."

"Midships, and steady as she goes. Half ahead, please Captain."

The pilot grabbed the loudhailer and stormed out onto the bridge wing. "Skipper," he shouted, "you and your boat were almost match sticks!"

"Sorry Cap'n," the yachtsman called back. "Sorry about that. But me and my boat got a race to win!"

Somehow we doglegged our way through the regatta, and made for the open lake. We were Europe-bound at last. We retraced much of our inbound passage, but this time passed Montreal and bunkered at historic Quebec City. From there it was still several hundred miles to the open ocean. However, as the river widened and became a gulf, and we frequently lost sight of land, we felt increasingly that we were at sea. Watches were now more arduous — a man was kept posted on the bow looking for shipping, and "other hazards," as the captain said.

"Do you think it is really necessary to have us out there in the cold and wet?" I asked Scotty. "It's miserable as hell."

" 'Tis hard t' say with radar as good as it is t'day. But the old *Empress of Ireland* collided with a Norwegian freighter about here and lost more than a thousand o' her passengers. Better safe than sorry, I suppose. And t' Old Man's toughening you up for the days t' come."

"The days to come?"

"Aye, our passage past the dreaded Banks. You'll hae t' stand a lookout there. More fog, and icebergs from the Labrador Sea."

"Icebergs this time of year?"

"Aye," he said, "come down from Greenland with the current; 'tis the smaller masses they worry about, the ones you cannae see well on radar, but that still can damage a ship, they say."

At last in the open ocean the captain was more relaxed, and he frequently engaged in conversation with me while I was at the wheel. "What are your plans, boy, when we reach Europe?"

"I'd like to get hold of a bicycle," I said, "and visit a friend of mine in Germany. We've talked about a cycling trip through Switzerland."

"And beyond that?" he inquired.

"Beyond that?"

"Yes, the future," he indicated.

"Well, by the end of the year I must find a ship to South Africa. I'm going back to complete my studies."

He asked me what I thought of the political situation in South Africa, and I told him — over several watches.

"And your ultimate vision is to live in North America?"

"Yes Cap'n, in the States, sir."

"Why the United States?" he asked.

"I love it there. It has freedom, and everything I'm looking for."

He nodded thoughtfully. "Yes, I have always liked the Americans," he agreed. "They are hard-working, and generous. But be sure to keep an open mind about Europe. It has a lot to offer — Finland, Sweden, the Netherlands, the British Isles."

"Yes Cap'n," I said. But the notion had never occurred to me.

"And remember, boy," the captain said, "that it was the Europeans, and especially the Scots, who made the United States what it is today."

"Did Scotland contribute a lot to American history?" I asked.

"It made an overwhelming contribution," he answered. "Nine of the original thirteen states had governors who were of Scottish descent, and an even greater percentage of all United States presidents have had Scottish blood. And if we started talking about famous engineers who were Scots, or Scot-Americans, we'd be here beyond the end of your watch. Go down to the engine room with Scotty tomorrow and see the natural feel he has. He might be rough in the mess but, like all the Scots I've met, he's a gentleman below deck with his engines."

On another day at the helm the captain told me about Finland. I had mentioned how much I had enjoyed Florida, especially Lake Okeechobee and the Everglades, and he said that a good portion of Finland was "an everglade, an enormous resplendent wetland. It's worth a visit," he encouraged me, "a country of many lakes, marshes and forests. Our ancient Finnish deities were gods of nature."

"I will put it high on my list," I said to please him.

"Yes," he encouraged, "you should. You want freedom, you want wilderness, a country with a future, come to Finland." He was quiet as he checked the radar, and when he spoke again I could tell that he had purposeful intent. "Consider making another trans-Atlantic trip on *Peter*," he offered generously. "Learn some Finnish and Swedish — I shall help you — and complete your studies in Finland. Education there is practically free."

I felt a stab of warmth. Here was a stranger, a man who called me 'boy,' offering me another passage on his ship, spontaneously bequeathing his country to me. I was moved and searched for the words to tell him so. 'Thank you for voicing your opinion,' he had responded graciously when I had joined his ship and commented on his good command of English.

"I appreciate your generosity, Cap'n," I said now. "I have never met anyone kinder than you. Your offer is tempting, and I shall think about it seriously."

He tilted his head and left it at that.

I was energized. This might be the break I was looking for. Perhaps I could start in Finland, and from there apply to a college in the States. At the very least it was a way to avoid the pain and embarrassment of returning home. I related the captain's proposal to Scotty.

"Aye," he agreed, "you cannae go wrong signing on for another trip with us. As little as you spend, you could save a heap o' coin." He paused and scratched his head. "But this whole thing o' studying in Finland, I don't know. Truly, 'tis a heck o' a language. I could nae do it."

We weathered some storms on the Atlantic, but these held none of the terror and fatigue of my yacht trip. For one I was on a big steel ship with lifeboats almost half the size of *Senta*. And without sails to tend, work was light by comparison. Our pleasant routine made time pass quickly, and I was almost taken by surprise when we fetched up the Scilly Isles off Land's End, cleared Lizard Point, and entered the English Channel.

As we converged on the Strait of Dover, one of the world's greatest concentrations of shipping, the captain never left the bridge. At one point I counted thirteen ships within sight, but according to First Mate the radar showed nearly twice that many.

We steamed ahead cautiously, rounded the North Foreland Light, lowered a Jacob's ladder off Sheerness, and took on our Thames pilot. We thumped on, and some way up the winding river we dropped anchor, launched a skiff, and I was put on duty as ferryman.

I rowed a good many of the crew ashore, and some hours later was dozing in the boat when laughter caught my ear and awakened me. I looked at my watch and reasoned that the pubs must have closed. Then I heard an inebriated shout. "Afrika Man!" It was Markku imitating Bos'n.

"Aye, where's the laird?" That was Scotty, also drunk.

"Here," I said, lifting myself and jumping to the dock.

Scotty was pushing a large porter's trolley that looked as if it belonged at a train station. "Look what we've got! Isn't it a beauty? Take the skiff over yonder," he shouted, pointing to a floating dock. "I think I can get it aboard from there."

"I don't think so! It's not going anywhere near this boat!"

But there were five of them, and they made it quite clear that they were not parting with their piano, "come hell or high water. Do ye ken?" Scotty slurred. "After all we've done t' get it here, 'tis going up on No. 2," he said. "And we will hae a concert — tonight!"

They boarded with a din and fired up the winch, and I was left alone with the piano slung across the sturdy rowboat, just aft of the oarlocks. A hook was soon lowered, with two dangling cables. I threaded these under the load and made them fast, and Markku began hoisting.

I gazed up, laughing silently, pleased to be rid of my unwanted cargo. But I must have had an intimation of disaster. I'd better get out from under it, I thought, in case something snaps. It was well that I did, for whoever hauled on the inboard winch — Scotty, I think it was — was a little hasty. The piano touched the railing and tilted, then slipped through the harness and splashed down into the dirty Thames, rather close to where I had been.

*F*rom England we were bound for Belgium, and then for Holland.

"I've agonized over your kind offer, Cap'n," I said, "and I've decided to pay off at Rotterdam. My father would be devastated," I half-lied, "if I did not return home to university."

The truth, of course, had I admitted it, was that I was afraid. The world was a big place in those days, and Finland, it seemed to me, was at the far and dangerous end of it, next to the hordes of Russia. And I lacked the confidence to go to a country that I did not know, and one that I could not speak the language of. My command of Afrikaans was mediocre, at best, I reasoned, after ten years of schooling. How could I hope to learn Finnish by the fall? And would it be as easy to get into Finland as the captain had indicated? Perhaps, but perhaps not. And was university there as inexpensive as he had suggested? I only had his word for it. Yet overall it was the best offer I had ever had. But it was still impractical, I decided.

I volunteered as watchman again in Antwerp, to save more money. Scotty had offered to give me a tour of the red-light district. He said it was his favorite, described a little of what I might expect, and sorely tempted me. But I wordlessly justified my decision, not only by what extra I could earn, but by what I might save. I consoled myself that it could very well pay for a bike and a month of touring.

Scotty went off alone that night, in a taxi, and that was the last I ever saw of him. He failed to return, and the ship sailed without him. The memory of it still haunts me.

"I have some good news for you," the captain announced with a dazzling smile. "I've found you a bicycle. Our agent in Rotterdam bought one to shed weight, but has given up on the idea. He said that you can have it for an attractive price."

"Thank you, Cap'n," I responded. But inwardly I cursed, for I visualized the typical Dutch bicycle, a trusty sit-up-and-beg, with upright handlebars, mudguards, and back-pedal brakes. I had been spoiled by British racing bikes, lightweights with gears, and that is what I intended to tour on, nothing less. But I need not have worried. It turned out to be an *Arbos*, a red Italian competition bike, the finest I had ever owned.

The Dutch agent advised me not to rush to Germany. "Go north first," he insisted, "to the island of Texel. Holland iss a country full of bicycles. You will luff it here!"

It was good advice. The Netherlands was a seventh heaven for cyclists. There were bicycle paths everywhere, away from the highways, across farmlands, along the tops of dikes, next to canals, winding through the great dunes that stretched along the shore. There were special ramps for bicycles onto the ferries, and lock-up bicycle sheds at the train stations, and special little traffic lights for bicycles in the cities. And there were beautiful girls touring on bicycles, in bikinis, and stopping at beaches along the way to swim topless. They were staying in the same youth hostels as me, and doing the rounds of the village bars and cafes in the evenings. And they were all eager to practice their English.

I stayed in Holland for as long as I dared — summer was slipping by — then pedaled alongside the Rhine into Germany, some 200 miles of river. I branched off to follow the Neckar, another meandering waterside route, and turned towards the Swabian Jura where Werner lived.

Our reunion was memorable. "Sonny," he shouted joyfully when he spotted me. "I thought I neffer see you again."

We shook hands and stared at each other, at a loss for words.

He was living for a while with his family, he said at length, and I should stay for as long as I liked. I was taken in and treated like a prince.

"Mein mother say she adopt you, sonny. So long you don't mind her being mit her granddaughter." The two were inseparable.

We took long evening walks in the forest, and a weekend ride on our bikes, and it seemed as if I never stopped eating. "Even mein niece can bake, sonny, and she's only eleven years old."

But Werner had started a new job and could not leave, so I slipped away alone. Someone photographed us outside his house. Werner had given me one of his sweaters. "You vill need dis in Switzerland," he said generously. "It get cold on a bike up in der mountains."

"I have no room for it," I protested.

"Tie it round your neck," he suggested, "over dot French maritime shirt vot Gerry haf gif you."

I dug into my carrier pack and hauled out *Senta's* tattered ensign that I had taken for the skipper. "Here, I want you to have this."

"Jees, sonny," he said with wet eyes, "I vill put it up on my vall and sink of you every day vhen I see it."

*M*y bicycle tour through Switzerland, and up through France, then back into England; my search for a ship, my new companions, my experiences in seedy ports on the west coast of Africa were epic, but followed the pattern of what I have already related.

"*I*'m back," I said into an ugly black telephone.

"Welcome," my dad replied. "We got your card from Angola."

"Good, so you expected me. We're only three days late."

"Not bad," he commented. "How are you — depressed?"

"You read my mind," I smiled. "It's like coming back into PE, the second time, on *Senta* in that storm. Only this is worse! But I'll be glad to see you. How are Mom and Joy?"

"Excited about your return. And we can't wait to hear your stories, of course. Do you want us to pick you up?"

"I could ride home," I answered. "I have a bicycle and only a handful of things, less than I left with."

"Wait where you are. We'll be there."

*W*e exchanged a kiss, a hug, and a handshake. Pop took my few belongings and stowed them in the boot, and I pedaled out through dockyard security, a small token of defiance. I was not going through immigration, and certainly was not paying customs duty on my bicycle.

Part 18

UNIVERSITY OF NATAL

The Copperbelt and Kat

Pete and I had been on the phone, briefly exchanging news. "Only one three-minute call," Pop had ruled. And that is all we had needed.

"What are you doing this summer, mate?"

"Whatever you suggest."

"How about mineral exploration in Northern Rhodesia? Prof. King says that outfits there are looking for students to run their field camps, so that their geologists can go home for Christmas. What do you say, mate?"

I said that I was with him.

"Excellent," he cried with a spate of passion. "We'll hitch-hike back through East Africa."

At that time — December, 1961 — the company we worked for had large concessions on the Copperbelt, as it was known, one of the world's most important reserves of copper-cobalt ore. The prospecting area we were assigned to was on the complex Lufilian Arc, near Kitwe and Solwezi, close to the remote Congo border.

Our exploration division had a special camp builder named André who, with his helper, Kat, would be dropped by helicopter at a likely spot, recruit labor from a local village, build a camp, cut a clearing for an airstrip, and then, still with nothing but *kazembes* — bush axes, as I mentioned, made from broken Land Rover springs — hack a path to the nearest road.

I relieved André that first summer in the bushveld, and with Kat now as my *Bas-Boy,* we erected the bridge previously mentioned, the one he had wanted raised in elevation because the weavers were building their nests higher that year.

When I met him, Kat had been living in the Federation of Rhodesia and Nyasaland for several years, having left the mines in *eGoli* after an *ngozi,* as he referred to it, an accident that claimed two fingers on his right hand. The advice of his father — urging him not to work on the mines — came back to him, he said, and forced him to leave.

André had a relapse of malaria that summer, so Kat and I worked together for the duration of my contract. Pete was assigned to a different camp and I saw him only once in all the time that we were there. He flew in unexpectedly with our bush pilot, in a little Cessna. He announced that it was Christmas the next day, which I had forgotten, having lost all track of time in the few weeks that I had been there. The four of us spent Christmas day together, tiger fishing on a nearby river. Kat, with a little wry smile, said he preferred our company to that of the other Africans in the compound. He was the only South African there he complained.

Shortly after New Year I was joined by three geologists and a helicopter crew, and our camp became a lot livelier. I was taken out by my colleagues, and taught the skills of stream sediment sampling and geological traversing, and the latter occupied most of the time Kat and I spent together that college vacation, and the next. The task involved a mapping and sampling exercise, with me promoted to the role of geologist, Kat as my lead man, and two African field assistants who walked through the bush in parallel with us, one to each side, helping to spot outcrops and things such as quartz float that were indicators of vein deposits.

I was required to sample each outcrop we encountered, identify the rock type, and any mineralization, if present, and plot its location on the aerial photograph we used as a base map. I would also, if appropriate, measure the strike and dip of the formation. Kat's primary function, far more difficult than mine I thought, involved, as I have already alluded to, the navigation of our crew by compass and pacing. He also had to stop every five-hundred feet and dig down about 18 inches for a soil sample. This he passed on to me to describe, bag, and label — samples were subsequently sent off for geochemical analysis. At each station, Kat would also call out the native names of the trees and plants, and I would record these in shorthand. Vegetation trends showed a good correlation with geology and helped us to delineate contacts, no easy task in that heavily covered area of bushveld and regolith. Furthermore, it had been found that certain plants, like one we named *die koper blom,* the copper flower, grew only in soils that contained above a certain threshold — parts-per-million — value of copper, and were, therefore, also indicators of what we were searching for.

That first summer in Rhodesia soon went by, working, fishing, and engaged in endless conversations with Kat. He was intrigued by my adventures in the States, and I, in turn, was fascinated by his life as a boy in the Transkei, and his subsequent career on the gold mines.

In late February 1962, when my contract ended, I flew into town, and Pete and I joined a Swiss land-surveyor and his wife who had planned their vacation in Dar es Salaam, the capital of Tanzania, the former Tanganyika.

Dar and the Cradle of Man

Although, by now, we should really have been heading back to college, Pete had set his mind on a detour through East Africa. He was highly interested in archaeology, and determined to visit Olduvai Gorge, a site that had revealed much about the beginnings of man.

However, for the moment we succumbed to the charm of Dar — the rhythmic clop of donkey hooves on the cobbles of winding alleyways; the elaborately carved doors of wealthy merchants; black men in turbans, *kofia* caps, and Arab robes; a market place milling with flamboyant Swahili dresses and smiles, on one hand, and on the other with coal-black *bui-buis* that hid female faces and gave a raven-like appearance to the wearers.

This unique corner of the continent is the melting pot of African and Arabic cultures. Visiting sailing dhows to Zanzibar and Dar — of extreme fascination to me — have plied the Indian Ocean trade route for more than 2,000 years, and over the years many Arab sailors have married African women and converted them to Islam. At the height of the slave trade, the Swiss couple informed us, the Sultan of Oman relocated his capital to the nearby island of Zanzibar and established a dynasty there. And it was the slave and ivory traders from Zanzibar, they said, who led European explorers like Livingstone and Stanley inland along their mercantile trails. I had heard a similar story from Ga. Her husband, who I never met, a well-to-do Englishman from Bury in Lancashire — but also with a farm on the Isle of Man — had served in East Africa in World War I, and she related much of what she had learned about the region to me.

Madiba had visited Dar only a month before us, on a tour of North African countries. Tanzania had just obtained independence and Madiba, to his pleasure, received an invitation to meet the country's new president, Julius Nyerere, who impressed the South African with his small car and simple lifestyle. Under a program of paternal socialism that everyone was talking about while we were there, Nyerere planned to reestablish a traditional way of life. Madiba had listened with interest, but was put out when the discussion turned to South Africa and President Nyerere suggested that he should postpone an armed struggle until Robert Sobukwe was released from prison — Sobukwe had been interned after the Sharpeville massacre. Madiba argued vehemently against this, but realized, for the first time, in what high esteem the PAC leader was held abroad.

We desperately needed a Land Rover to get to Pete's destination, and he managed to persuade our Swiss friends to move on with us to Olduvai Gorge. This site, near Lake Victoria, is one that Drs. Mary and Louis Leakey painstakingly worked to produce some of the oldest hominid remains ever found. And although our unsophisticated fossil search there revealed nothing of interest, we were elated, as Pete described it, "to be treading the same sacred ground as our distant ancestors, mate." Most scientists now agree that Africa was the cradle of our human origins, and that East Africa, in particular, holds valuable clues to humankind's early history. Pete had read up on everything he could lay hands on, and he was our source of information.

Madiba also knew something of the paleo-anthropological development of humanity in Africa, as did most people who had attended the University of the Witwatersrand. For it was one of that school's young professors, Raymond Dart, who stunned the world by describing the emergence of hominids in the form of a skull he named *Australopithecus africanus*. The fossil, a link between the apes and man — not, I reminisced, *Afrika Man,* me, as Scotty had quipped — was discovered near *Taung,* the 'Place of the Lion,' a small Tswana village north of Kimberley, a spot that Pete and I had visited with considerable interest.

Around a camp fire one evening our petite party fell to talking about Dart, and Thomas, our surveyor friend, asked Pete when the *Taung* child had lived. Pete said approximately two and a half million years ago. "It's old," he smiled in response to an exclamation, "but barely yesterday on a planet that's been around for about 4,500 million years. If the entire history of the earth was compressed into an hour," he went on, "the early hominids would have emerged only in about the last four seconds."

By this time our Swiss friends had warmed to Pete's archaeological zest. Elena, as it turned out, was passionate about everything in 'bizarre Africa,' as she referred to it, and began to question him on the details of Professor Dart's find. Pete explained that Dart had immediately noticed the small canine teeth in the *Taung* skull. These differed markedly from those of apes. Dart's attention, Pete said, was also drawn to the form of fossilized bones at the base of the head. These provided evidence of an upright posture.

*T*welve years after our visit to Olduvai, Donald Johanson, an American, would travel to East Africa and discover the partial skull and skeletal remains of an even older hominid skull, *Australopithecus afarensis.* I subsequently met Donald and asked him what had led to his finding of Lucy, as he named her. "Hard work," he laughed, greatly abbreviating the answer I had expected. He did, however, admit to a smile of fortune in securing so complete a skeleton. But the greatest element of luck needed no discussion between us. It related to a fact I had long pondered, that humanity had evolved at all.

The evolution of man is a poignant puzzle that still creeps into my mind today, oddly enough in the mornings when I go through my deep-breathing meditations, a routine I learned from Kat. I had seen him at the river at sunrise, sitting cross-legged and facing the rising sphere. He had a small bag cupped in his mangled right hand, and seemed to be drawing in the deepest breath I had ever seen anyone take. He then raised his head, and exhaled for even longer, slowly rounding his back and tightening his abdominal muscles to expel the last remnant of air from his body. I was fairly near him, but hidden in a thicket of trees. He repeated the exercise for a good ten minutes, then turned and looked in my direction — only eyes as sharp as his could have spotted me.

I approached him with my camera.

"No photographs of me," he said austerely, extending an out-stretched open palm.

My mind flashed to an American Indian I had wanted to photograph in Mexico; his forbidding protest had been even more adamant than Kat's.

I quickly put my camera away and asked what he was sniffing.

"The pure fresh air," he replied, reverting to his usual friendly tone.

"No," I said, pointing to his clenched hand.

He revealed a small net container. "*Buchu,*" he smiled, raising the aromatic leaves to my nose, "much healing power!"

But he explained that the leaves were really unnecessary. It was the deep inhalation of good clean air that stimulated the circulatory system, and its total expulsion that purged the poisons from the body. The *buchu* aroma, he led me to understand, had more to do with the mental process — sometimes he imagined inhaling the golden rays of the sun — of slowly saturating his brain, his heart, his intestines, every part of his body, he said, with the magical cleansing power of oxygen in the air.

"And you do this every day?" I asked.

"Everyday, and when I need to, *Bwana* Ian," he replied. Over the two years of our close friendship, Kat never addressed me as *Bwana Bula,* or called me any of the other names the local Natives used. Sometimes he would betray his little smirk and simply say 'Ian,' looking carefully for a reaction. But on this occasion he remained serious, explaining that for his deep-breathing revitalization to be effective, the mind must focus completely on the body. "It must not think!" he said, raising a finger for emphasis. And I knew that that meant even about my genesis.

South & North

When we turned and retreated south — by now we were already late for the beginning of the new term — Madiba continued north. He had traveled to Tanzania on a small charter aircraft that crossed the Zambezi at a point near the Victoria Falls, and then had nearly come to grief in ugly squalls over the mountains that lay ahead. He, like me in *Senta's* knockdown in the Doldrums, had thought it was the end.

From Tanzania Madiba flew to the Sudan, a peaceful place at the time. My grandmother had had a colleague at the university there, and told me much about what she had learned from him of the black Nubians. Her friend, she said, had participated in digs — sponsored by Harvard University — that successfully unearthed art objects dating to approximately 3,000 B.C., the probable height of Nubian culture. This, she said, was before the pharaohs of Egypt's Old Kingdom began construction on their soaring tombs, the pyramids.

Ga had an old photograph of a female figurine that had been recovered by the Harvard digs. "It shows a similar pattern of body scarifications" — scar body art — "that we still see today," she said. She also commented on the gender difference she had observed in both old and contemporary African art. Whereas men, she noted, were traditionally drawn to sculpting in rock and wood, and painting animals and scenes of the hunt, the day-to-day preference of women was, "and still is," she said, "on decorating their homes, their clothing, and themselves."

The skin-patterned female piece found by the Harvard expedition was presented to the famous Egyptian Museum. Madiba visited it when he was in Cairo and fulfilled a life-long dream, saying that as a student he had "fantasized" about traveling to Egypt.

Aside from the Sudan and Egypt, Madiba was also impressed by his visit to the legendary city of *Tombouctou* (Timbuktu), which lies on a bend in the mighty Niger River. My mother, and no doubt also his, frequently mentioned the name when I was young. In Africa, naughty children are often threatened with being sent to Timbuktu, and I came to regard it as a sort of nether world, an abode of the damned. However, in reality, Madiba learned, Timbuktu had been an important center of black learning, a place, my grandmother told me when I was older, where self-assured African scholars and merchants once rubbed shoulders with Arabs and Europeans. In the fourteenth century, Ga said, the entire country of Mali was extremely wealthy. It had gold mines, and was at the head of the Great Salt Road at a time when, according to her, "salt in the Sahara was paid for in gold."

Madiba was also roused by his visit to Ethiopia, where he was impressed by Haile Selassie, the Emperor, a man of many titles. Madiba knew of him as the Lion of Judah, but a Rastafarian I had met in the West Indies considered him a god, and referred to him as *Jah Ras Tafari,* Lord of Lords. The Emperor boasted a bloodline from King Solomon and the Queen of Sheba — Ethiopia, so my grandmother said, was the home of Ophir, the fabled location of King Solomon's mines.

Ga invariably had some unusual insight into matters that pertained to the Jewish faith, and told me that Ethiopians claim to have had in their possession, for the past three thousand years, the much-sought-after Ark of the Covenant, that biblical container of the Ten Commandments. The Ark was brought there, she said, by one of the Lost Tribes of Israel. She also mentioned that a sect of black Jews she had visited in South Africa claimed a link to Ethiopia, and so also to the Israel of old.

And besides what I had learned of Ethiopia from Ga, Pop had also mentioned it. Two of his tennis friends from the Wanderers Club had served in the South African 1st Division under Major-General Brink. This, at the beginning of World War II, had been part of a British Colonial contingency that decimated Mussolini's forces in Ethiopia and restored the Emperor to his age-old throne.

Gentlemen of Vision

Quite to our surprise, our late return to varsity appeared to do us more good than harm. "Welcome home, Mr. Watson and Mr. Aitken," Professor King said in class; we had presented him with our excuses the day before. "I'm pleased that your summer was such a productive one." He chose to totally disregard the fact that I had been away for a full year. "I visualize an A+ for your report."

He went on to say how pleased he was that we had taken the time to move on to Tanganyika, as he still referred to it, and increase our knowledge of Primates. "That's the spirit of adventure we want of geologists," he said.

He spoke for a good while about the merits of a well-rounded education, while we sat and attentively beamed as he offered us as fine examples of pursuing this objective.

"So they've missed out on the benefit of some academic instruction," he concluded, "and must catch up on their notes. But what does that matter in the big scheme of things, I ask you gentlemen, compared to what they have learned? You never know, in a more civilized world of the future archeological finds may be more in demand than gold, and these gentlemen of vision will not have to reinvent themselves from scratch."

'Gentleman of vision;' I loved the sound of it. But I was more like a klutz, I'd say, when I first met Leighan.

"Is your name Watson?"

"Is your name Watson?" she asked me.
I acknowledged that it was.
"I was just checking," she said.
I smiled helplessly, totally transfixed by her eyes, set widely apart and of dancing blue, her fine English accent, uncommon in Africa, her voice like a distant bell ringing on the wind.

She extended a slender hand. "I'm Leighan," she introduced herself — she pronounced it 'Lee-Ann' — "and I'm really pleased to meet you at last. You are all I seem to have heard about since term started. 'Watsie's back from the States.' 'Have you seen him?' 'Did he tell you about his trip?' "

I managed an impuissant shrug.

"But wherever I went," she continued, "I had just missed you."

In my mesmerized state I could only blurt that I was sorry.

"Not at all," she said, dismissing my response with a sweep of long fingers. "But I was beginning to think that you were no more than a figment of your friends' imaginations, like the ghost in Hamlet."

"You should have asked," I stammered.

" 'Them that asks no questions,' " she responded, " 'isn't told a lie.' " Most people I knew would, at that point, have left at that, this Rudyard Kipling quote — not that I recognized it as such. But this young lady simply straightened her back, raised her voice, and continued:

" 'Five and twenty ponies
Trotting through the dark —
Brandy for the Parson,
'Baccy for the Clerk;
Laces for the lady, letters for the spy,
And watch the wall, my darling, while the Gentlemen go by!' "

Her theatrical outburst caught the attention of my dinner group who were chatting in a cluster nearby. They turned and applauded.

I stood helplessly next to her, a furnace of embarrassment.

Leighan placed a hand over her mouth. "I'm sorry," she apologized quickly. "I'm a showoff, a total clown. Please forgive me."

I frantically searched for my voice. "You're an English major?"

"Close," she replied. "Theater, speech and drama to be exact. And that reminds me." She reached out and yanked Pete's academic gown. "Did you invite Watson to the play?"

Pete turned and finger-brushed red hair from his face. "Watsie," he said with a bow, "you're invited to Leighan's play, 'Ondine.' "

"When?" I queried.

"Friday evening. And no boozing beforehand, mate. The profs will be there."

"And all of you had better be there too," she said, shaking a finger at my friends. "No, 'I've got rugby the next day,' Mr. Bedford."

"Don't worry," Tommy laughed.

"And you'll be there, of course," I sputtered like an imbecile.

"I certainly hope so," she confirmed breezily. "I'm Ondine."

By this time the boys were slowly drifting off. "Come on Watsie, let's go," someone summoned me. We had arranged an evening at the *Eddies*, the bar at the King Edward Hotel, our waterhole. It was a boys' night out. The female students had a curfew. On weeknights they were locked into their residence at eight-fifteen sharp.

Leighan firmly shook my hand once more, and quoted the Immortal Bard, " 'When shall we thee meet again? In thunder, lightning, or in rain?' "

I was beginning to get the gist of her banter, and with a shred of rising confidence requested an appropriate reply.

She gave me a devilish look. " 'When the hurly-burly's done. When the battle's lost and won.' "

We exchanged a spontaneous chuckle.

"But seriously," she added, changing her expression, "I'd love to hear about your trip sometime."

"It was a year-long venture," I noted. "Sailing, hitch-hiking, bicycling; and more recently," I went on, "prospecting in Northern Rhodesia. Tell me where you'd like me to begin," I offered, "and I'll rehearse before I see you." I was happy with that. But there was no chance — as I was quickly learning — of having the last word with the drama department.

" 'Begin at the beginning,' " she said, raising her fingers to gesture yet another quote, " 'and go on till you come to the end; then stop.' "

My mind swirled, but I took a stab. "Shakespeare?"

She stifled a smile. "My goodness no, dear boy. Charles Lutwidge Dodgson, a lecturer in mathematics at Oxford University — Lewis Carroll in pseudonym." She picked up on my vacant look. *"Alice's Adventures in Wonderland,"* she whispered sweetly.

"She's one of us"

I was dragged off to the bar. 'Is your name Watson?' she had asked. Her vibrancy, her charm, the lucid enunciation of her English-language quotes, the keen interest she had expressed in hearing about my trip kept ringing through my head. She was more than a breath of fresh air, a lot more. "Who's dating Leighan?" I asked Pete over a drink.

"Nobody dates Leighan," he sneered. "She's one of us."

"What do you mean — 'one of us?' "

"She's one of the boys. You couldn't possibly date Leighan! She's way too much of a handful. Let me... Well, you saw her."

I nodded noncommittally.

"She's like a 'cat on a hot tin roof,' " Pete went on, quoting the title of a Tennessee Williams masterpiece to make his point.

"I thought she was a lot of fun," I argued with a shrug.

He swung to face me. "Don't tell me, mate! You really like her, don't you? I can see it in your eyes. You're absolutely bewitched."

I did my best to hide behind a mask of nonchalance.

"Listen, mate," he advised. "Don't get tied down. There's a million babes on campus, and they're practically all ours. We're no longer lowly freshmen. We've got rank now, mate, and the dolls know it."

*I*t was about two months later, and coming up for our Easter break. "So, mate, are you going to join us?" Pete was talking about a trout-fishing trip up to the Drakensberg.

"Yes," I replied.

"And Leighan?"

"She'll be with her mom and aunt at the beach cottage."

"And you weren't invited?"

"I certainly was."

"But you're coming fishing?"

I nodded and he shook his head.

"And what about next summer?"

"Back to the Copperbelt," I said, feeling my jaw tighten.

"Three bloody months! That'll be the end of it."

"I've got to take a chance on that," I said. "I really like her, I mean a lot! But the more time we spend together, the more scared I am of getting pinned down. I'm not here for good, you know."

I waited for a further taunt, but he backed off. "*Ja*, I know," he ceded quietly.

"**Y**es, I'm well aware of who you are. And what can I do for you, Mr. Watson?" She had the same theatrical voice as Leighan, and a similar intimidating manner.

Our assistant warden had advised me to get right to the point, so I did. "I'm sorry to bother you, Professor Sneddon," I started, "but my friend, Leighan, spends half her life caring for all the stray cats that live around the women's residence."

"Yes, and I'm grateful," she said, motioning me to sit. "I am very fond of Miss Nel, and I greatly admire her empathy for animals. But what, may I ask, does this have to do with me?"

"You're in charge of the hostel, Professor," I insisted, fully intent on standing my ground. "People say they need your permission to have the females spayed, to stop them breeding."

The old spinster gave me a slanted glance. "Look, Mr. Watson," she said, pointing an arthritic finger. "I don't believe in birth control." She paused as if to emphasize her point. "But if I was forced to make a move," she mocked with uncompromising humor, "I'd sooner have the males castrated!" She then waved me away like a busy teacher might do to a schoolboy. "That's all Mr. Watson, that's all."

Dismissed, I had little option but to rise and make my exit.

Intellectual Barbarian

*T*o my pleasant surprise I found myself enjoying being back at varsity. Leighan, of course, was a big factor. But another was that I had lessened my potential stress level by deciding to distance myself from politics. I was not about to place myself at risk again of losing my passport. We had learned that Jonty Driver, a former president of the National Union of South African Students (NUSAS), had had his confiscated while studying at Oxford. But at least he was out of the country. I was not.

Fortunately, as it turned out, the political front was tranquil, at least at the surface. "Why's everything so quiet?" I asked Chris. With his mind set on journalism, Chris kept himself well-informed on politics.

"Most of the leaders of the freedom fight are either in jail," he shrugged, "or have fled the country."

"Since Sharpeville?" I queried.

"Yes," he confirmed. "That was the start of it. And *Pofadder,*" he added, referring to the Prime Minister Verwoerd, "keeps things quiet with his ruthlessness. He swears that he will stamp out the resistance movement — 'terrorism,' he calls it."

"Do you think he will?" I asked.

He scrunched his face. "I think it's possible."

*A*nd yet another thing that contributed to the enjoyment of my being back was that the old judge in Texas had planted a seed with his talk of finding oil. And with my interest in geology broadening, as it had again over the summer, my grades improved. And although Leighan still referred to me as an "intellectual barbarian," I began to show a glimmer of original thinking, and my knowledge of the arts, nonexistent when I met her, began to flourish in a small way.

'I felt a certain power of color awakening in me,' Vincent van Gogh announced enthusiastically, as he put aside his drab palette and began to brush his canvases with the intense hues we love him for — his *Haystacks near a Farmhouse,* his *Terrace of the Café on the Place du Forum, The Bridge at Langlois*. I sensed a similar excitement within myself.

I sat for hours watching Leighan's rehearsals, and attended every play she was in. I even began reading a little Shakespeare, and studying some paintings, at least those of the Impressionists. "Is theirs good art?" I asked her.

"Good art," she replied simply, "is the art that you like."

I admired the way she expressed things like that, and told her so.

But she brushed my compliment aside. "I hope you're not doing all of this to impress me," she said.

I gave her a guarded look. "Why do you say that?"

"Oh, I don't know," she replied, her face showing its soft gentle lines, "I just feel sometimes that, like Mary Shelly's Frankenstein, I've created a monster, one that will return to irk me."

"You've lost me, as usual," I shrugged, and offered a gesture of despair.

She gave me an enigmatic smile. "Just stay the way you are," she said, kissing me lightly on the cheek.

Aside from her theatrical talent, Leighan was an excellent athlete, and she and I spent a lot of time together in the outdoors, jogging around the campus, swimming laps, and going to the beach. She would come and watch my tennis matches, and I would return the favor by attending her hockey games. At that time, hockey — field hockey — was the most popular team sport for females in South Africa.

In July of my first year back at school, Cliff Drysdale and I hitchhiked up-country for tennis 'intervarsity.' But my mind was on Ondine. I had invited her to spend the rest of our winter break in Fish Hoek — while I was in the States, Pop's long-requested transfer to Cape Town had been approved. It was my first experience of having a girlfriend stay overnight, and I was more than a little nervous about how things would work out with my dad. But I need not have given it a thought. Pop adored her. And years after we had parted, he would still, on occasion, address a young lady I took home as Leighan, quite unintentionally I am sure.

Even Joy took to Leighan, and she was pretty fussy about who I dated. Besides, the two of them had to share a room and Joy had not exactly been looking forward to that.

Two weeks in and about Cape Town had me gold-headed, seeing my home surroundings in an entirely new light. For although I was the host, she, with her boldness and dazzling energy, called most of the shots. 'Let's hit the beach.' 'Let's fly kites.' 'Let's climb Elsie's Peak today.' 'Let's make love.' 'Let's go over to Hout Bay and watch the fishing boats come in; I read that the *snoek* were running.'

She noticed everything. "See how the boats race to get ashore," she said. "The first to reach the harbor no doubt gets the best price for its catch." She, like Pop, loved the Cape fishermen, a hardy band, mainly Coloureds, as we knew them, mulattos — they had no counterparts in Natal where she had been raised. On the crowded wharves we milled with the white and Indian fish mongers bidding on catches. "Listen to the way the crews pander to sell their fish," she laughed. " '*Ja maaster*,' I'll give you the best price, *baas*.' All this 'master' and 'boss' stuff; you know they've got to be thinking just the opposite."

Part 19

MADIBA AND THE JEWS

What Might Have Been

"*T*he stupid sod should never have come back!" Pop spat heartily, if irreverently. His curse, on this occasion, was directed at Madiba, who, he muttered, "could easily have found a new home where he was safe and free." I agreed. When Pete and I had turned and headed home from East Africa, Madiba, as I described, had extended his travels northwards. He should just have stayed away, Pop said, continued to enjoy the company of other scholars; perhaps pursued research into what other eyes, ancient eyes, had pondered over millennia — the history and treasures of sophisticated black societies.

He could equally have led a fulfilling life in England. While he was in London, Oliver Tambo, his old law-firm partner, arranged for him to meet David Astor, of *Observer* newspaper fame. Madiba had apparently noted that the ANC was typically given less press than the PAC, and he thought that in a face-to-face encounter he could make a subtle case for change. The two met at Astor's house — with its fine view of Lord's cricket oval — and I learned that when David Astor questioned him about the two political parties, Madiba spoke up for the ANC, but gave liberal credit to his political rival, Robert Sobukwe.

I had always greatly admired both men, and hearing of Madiba's courtesy gave me pleasure. But, as time went by, I all but lost memory of the incident. It was an African sculpture by Fabian Madamombe that brought the spirit of it back to me. It showed two caterpillars in a forest about to do battle over a leaf that both had latched onto. Fabian's caption read something to the effect of: 'With so many leaves, why should we do battle over this one?' In a struggle the size of that they faced, Madiba had known there was no point in fighting over who had done what.

David Astor, impressed by Madiba's integrity, arranged a get-together with Member of Parliament Dennis Healy who, in turn, introduced Madiba to Hugh Gaitskell, leader of the Labour Party. It was soon apparent that a network of connections was at play and, as I would discover when I moved to London a few years later, people began to whisper excitedly about where it all might lead. "Nelson and Oliver could have set up a new law firm," a well-informed young British student told me wishfully, and went on to explain that a growing number of Blacks in London would have patronized it. Furthermore, London had become home to a sizable population of

South Africans in exile, and Madiba possessed the leadership qualities to unite them. He could have played a direct role in the struggle by strengthening the case for sanctions against South Africa and even, she thought, by presenting an argument for an armed British or North-African invasion.

"Yes," I concurred, "but in this game of 'what might have been,' I personally would like to have seen him go to the States."

"That also was a possibility," she added quickly, and told me that David Astor, with his large overview, had tried to persuade Madiba to do just that, to settle in Washington, D.C. "But Nelson," she lamented with open hands, "would have none of it. He simply thanked David Astor for his advice, and began his long journey home."

Today, of course, we understand the reason why. Certain lessons had been bred into him as a boy — 'in times of danger the good shepherd leads from the front' — and he had clung to their ineradicable pull.

The Mongoose & the Snake

*B*ack in South Africa, Madiba went into hiding. Government intelligence agents had followed his 'illegal' trip abroad. They suspected that he had sought military help for the struggle, and labeled him an outlaw.

After his exciting encounter with freedom, the day-to-day existence of a fugitive was painful for Madiba. He took some chances, and while driving home after a visit to Chief Luthuli — by then a Nobel Laureate — he and a white friend, Cecil Williams, were intercepted by security police. It was 5 August 1962. Pete brought the news to Leighan and me in the library. The apprehensions had taken place not far from where his parents lived, and Pete was shaken.

In court after his arrest Madiba announced that he would conduct his own defense. He had confidence in his legal training, and was aware of his allure in the courtroom; it was said that once his lion-like eyes locked onto you, there was no escaping their scrutiny. Others had their own perceptions of his magic, but all agreed on Madiba's hypnotic power. Wolfie Kodesh, a journalist who had once provided sanctuary for Madiba, and who was present at the trial, told author Anthony Sampson, in *Mandela,* that at one point Nelson stared at the magistrate and appeared to mesmerize him, like "a mongoose transfixing a snake." It took the justice nearly two minutes, he said, to fully regain his composure.

Madiba was charged on two counts, leaving the country without a passport, and inciting African workers to strike; in the previous year he had organized a three-day, stay-at-home protest. He knew the prosecutor from his law-practice days, but this was hardly an advantage. Unlike the Treason Trial, the charges, though seemingly trivial, were straightforward, and the state's case solid. Madiba recognized that there was not the remotest chance of an acquittal. It all boiled down to two questions: one, how harsh the sentence would be, and two, whether he could use the proceedings to salvage some small political advantage for his people.

We white students in Natal followed the trial as closely as we could by reading the left-wing press. We learned that whereas the prosecution had painstakingly paraded more than one-hundred witnesses, Madiba, when his turn came, stunned the court by announcing that he would not call any. The court adjourned until the following day when, under South African law, the accused was permitted to make an address — a plea in mitigation — before the magistrate delivered his sentence. Madiba had engineered it that way to present a political statement.

He started, we read, by entering the courtroom and crying out *"Amandla!"* Power! The eruption from the public gallery was a mighty roar of, *"Ngawethu!"* It shall be ours! The African section of the courtroom was filled to capacity.

Madiba's plea on the first charge, which we thought appropriate under the circumstances, was that in accordance with the laws of his culture he was guilty of no crime. Before the white man came to Africa, Madiba said, the land had belonged to his people. Africans were its guardians, and they moved about it at will. There was no need to carry passports.

On the second charge he explained to the court the democratic basis of the *Inbizo,* the Council that governed the Xhosa nation. He abided by the principles of the *Inbizo,* he said, and he rationalized how this justified his political struggle, at least his right to peaceful protest. He reflected on his deepest beliefs, conveying the point of view of an indigenous inhabitant, and attempting to have the court recognize some basic level of human rights, even for a black man. But his recital was in vain.

His sentence was severe, two years for illegally leaving the country, and three for strike incitement, five years in all. People in the chamber wept. But as Madiba was led away they managed to engage in an outpouring of spontaneous singing: *"Nkosi Sikelel' iAfrika..."* May the Divine One bless Africa...

Madiba was locked up in the grim Pretoria jail. But as miserable as prison can be, he was pleased to run into Robert Sobukwe, who, as mentioned, had been incarcerated after the Sharpeville massacre — under emergency powers, some 20,000 people had been arrested. While patching mailbags in the prison courtyard, the two held lively discussions. Madiba related the details of his journey through Africa, and spoke at length about the conflicting viewpoints of the PAC and ANC held by foreign politicians. Sobukwe, in turn, an expert on Shakespeare — as a lecturer in African languages at Wits he had translated Macbeth into Zulu — delighted Madiba with his intellectual views and insights on the arts.

A New Government Era

A new era of government repression and police tyranny had begun, and no one who opposed *apartheid* felt safe. A law promulgated on 1 May 1963 allowed the security police to detain any person, without charge, for a period of ninety days. But because the detention period could be repeated as many times as the police saw fit, the legal implication of a restricted time element was meaningless. In short, the law empowered police to hold suspects, without charge, for as long as they saw fit.

Within a short time of the law being put in place, dissidents began disappearing into a black hole of detentions. And it did not take long for stories of torture to be leaked by sympathetic wardens within the prison system.

And besides the elevated powers granted to it by the new detention law, the Special Branch — as the division of security police was officially known — was becoming more sophisticated and smarter. Major General van den Bergh, its new chief, was well educated and spoke good English. He dressed in fashionable suits, rather than police uniform, and looked more like the CEO of a large corporation than a policeman. He searched for and transferred into his division some of the best criminal investigators on the force. And to improve the image of the Branch, and increase its efficiency, he began recruiting college graduates.

But good looks and nice clothes did not deceive those, like my friend Chris, who had researched his past. The Major General and Mr. B. Johannes Vorster, the new minister of justice who had appointed him, had shared a prison cell during World War II, Chris said, when the two had been interned as Nazi partisans. Anti-*apartheid* politician Helen Suzman, leader of the liberal Progressive Party, also learned the truth, and publicly denounced the Major General, referring to him as, "South Africa's version of Heinrich Himmler." Mrs. Suzman, despite being subjected to frequent anti-Semitic slurs, dared to speak her mind in those oppressive times.

Rivonia: Arrests & Detentions

Madiba's sentence had been merciless, five years, a measure of the new *verkrampte* — hard-line — elements in government office, and their most recent crackdowns on freedom. But even its severity was relative. Shortly after their meeting in the Pretoria jail, Robert Sobukwe's prison term was up. However, instead of releasing him, the system continued to hold him without charge, then transferred him to Robben Island.

And in a separate case, Madiba's good friend, Walter Sisulu, was tried on a charge of 'incitement to strike' — the second count against Madiba — and given a sentence of six years. When the two met in jail, Madiba counseled him to appeal his sentence, then apply for and jump bail. He did, and went into hiding. Security police used the new Ninety-Day Act to arrest his wife, Albertina, a nurse. She was held in jail despite having no knowledge of her husband's whereabouts. The law permitted detention merely on the suspicion of possessing information, unwittingly or not, and however trivial.

Exhausted, humiliated, and afraid, the stress level amongst activists ran high. Even the students at my liberal university backed away from organized protest. We were scared stiff. But we continued to follow the political drama as best we could, studying free-thinking newspapers, and magazines like *Drum* that targeted black readers but had a large following by English-speaking students like ourselves.

*T*hen, one morning early in July 1963 — we were on our winter break, but I had stayed on to be with Leighan — Chris stormed into my room breathing like an injured gnu. "There's been a bust," he cried, "at a place in Rivonia, just outside Jo'burg. Seventeen people arrested. 'Big fish,' the security *ous* say."

"Was Mandela amongst them?" I asked, forgetting for a moment that he was already in jail. I corrected myself, but Chris ignored me; he had lost his composure and rambled on in a disconsolate way.

As the days wore on, press reports confirmed our worst fears. Disaster had struck veterans of the freedom movement. Those rounded up included Walter Sisulu and Govan Mbeki, Ahmed Kathrada of the Indian Congress, Rusty Bernstein, my grandmother's champion, and other prominent white *ikomunisi*, as Kat called them, former members of the banned South African Communist Party, the latter all Jews. The newspapers showed photographs of the Liliesleaf estate, described it as a communist safe house, and told of the scores of documents that had been recovered there.

Major General van den Bergh was in high spirits. The crux of the matter, he said, was that the revolutionaries were amateurs, but they, the security police, were professionals. Although boastful, the Major General's words had a special sting to them, because, in so many ways, they were the truth. The amateurism of the movement was undeniable. Incriminating documents that long since should have been shredded or burned, lay everywhere. For all of their achievements, the dissidents had blatantly ignored the first rules of an underground organization.

I remember how relieved I was at time, for not having been lured into their ranks. But friends of mine had, and to say that they were running scared was an understatement bordering on the ridiculous. The police, naturally, had not revealed everything they had found, and there was wild speculation about lists of names that might be in their possession. What we knew for sure was that the police had manuscripts in Madiba's handwriting, primers that would implicate him in planning sabotage. As we would subsequently learn, Madiba had specifically sent word to his colleagues to destroy these papers. But, evidently, this was not done.

Other material that would also prove damaging to Madiba was a collection of his old diaries that someone had decided to retain for its historical value. In the days following the raid the police retrieved this bundle, hidden in a metal trunk at the bottom of a coal-storage silo.

White activist Rusty Bernstein did his best to deal with the situation in jail. He and the others taken at the Liliesleaf estate were being held, without charge, under the new ninety-day detention clause. Confined alone in the depths of the prison, things were grim, not brutal as they were for his African colleagues, but harsh by the standards he was accustomed to.

Whereas the thrust of abuse aimed at Blacks was physical, its focus on white political prisoners was largely psychological. Nevertheless, as time wore on, Rusty, we would learn, began to break under its pressure. A part of the process, he said, was a cognizance of his mental deterioration, but an inability to stop its progression. On one of the many fronts of the mind game, an incident that stuck with me involved his warden issuing him a roll of toilet paper and barking that it had to last a month. In his nightmare of unstimulated time, Rusty took to unwinding and rewinding it, counting and recounting the perforations, and trying to estimate how much he could use each day. He attempted to stop, but the exercise was compulsive.

Acutely aware of this and other patterns of crazy behavior, Rusty entered into prolonged states of depression. He became increasingly nervous, his hands began to shake, he said, and he felt as if he was in a demon's world amongst the living dead.

Another white detainee, lawyer Jimmy Kantor — who was apolitical, but who had been caught up in a web of coincidences — also began to crack. Despite being described by one of his interrogators as "a tough little Jew," Jimmy experienced constant nervous headaches. In his book, *A Healthy Grave,* he offered an example of the type of incident that unnerved him. He described a man in a nearby cell receiving eight strokes of the cane, the sound of its connection with "human flesh," the cries "of agony."

With most of the known black leaders now in custody, Chris told me, the immediate fallout of the Rivonia raid was to move the spotlight, for a while, to white dissenters. Joe Slovo, Chris said, was suspected of playing a leadership role in the recently-commenced armed struggle, and declared Public Enemy Number One. But since he had fled the country and made himself a difficult target, the order went out to "get Mrs. Slovo" — in her own circle, Joe Slovo's wife, a journalist, went by her maiden name, Ruth First. I knew a fair bit about her, for, like Helen Suzman, Ruth had been another of Ga's heroines. "And it's not just because she's Jewish or, for that matter, that I know Tilly," she'd remarked. Tilly, Matilda First, was Ruth's mom. Like my grandmother and Hilda Bernstein, Rusty's wife, Tilly was also of European-Jewish extraction.

They came for Ruth on 9 August 1963, less than a month after the roundup in Rivonia. She was hauled off for questioning by two men in plain clothes. In her dramatic book, *117 Days*, the length of her subsequent detention in solitary confinement, Ruth outlined her ordeal.

In solitary confinement there was no news. And for someone like Ruth, Pop said, an intellectual energized by social interaction, lone isolation was "a bloody tragedy," as he put it. When I returned home on a college break, we talked a lot about Ruth. Both Pop and I remembered Ga telling us how stubborn she was, even as a child, and Pop said he thought she could hold out against police pressure and not tell too much.

Author Glenn Frankel astutely captured, in *Rivonia's Children,* the challenge that faced her, saying that the government had the "brutal tools" of the law, but that Ruth had her remarkable mental capacity and steadfast resolve. Her battle with the authorities would be "an uneven contest," he said, "but a contest all the same."

An endless list of deprivations added to Ruth's prison ordeal: besides no news, nothing to read, no pencils, no paper, no wristwatch, and no calendar. There was just an endless string of time, and dismal thoughts of abandonment, perhaps rotting in that foul hole for an eternity. She worried constantly about her family, especially her children. And there was always the unknown, the nagging possibility of torture. The unremitting state of stress made her feel nauseous and caused her persistent bouts of diarrhea.

Helen Suzman had repeatedly challenged the aspect of "psychological torture" associated with solitary confinement, quoting Stefan Zweig's account of its use by the Gestapo, "how it eats into and destroys one, this nothing and nothing and nothing."

Ruth did her utmost to cope. From time to time her inquisitors had her dragged from her cell for interrogation. But she remained defiant, refusing to answer questions, or make any statement that would incriminate her friends. She tried to keep up her appearance, no easy task without a mirror. She worked on her posture, knowing that it influenced her attitude. There was no toilet in her cell, and her dignity suffered when she had to pound on her door and yell for permission to relieve herself. The guards frequently ignored her cries — a form of torture.

But eventually it was the little things that began to play worst on her mind. She grew to hate the crash and echo of the steel cell doors that were slammed day and night throughout the prison. These would be unlocked and pulled open with a key — there were no handles. Then the metal gates were shoved shut with an earth-shattering clash that thumped through her body, vibrated through her brain, and made her shiver.

On the eighty-ninth day of her detention she heard the rattle of a key. A guard led her to a public room where, to her extreme delight, she saw Tilly and her daughters waiting to greet her. She was told that she was being released. Robyn rejoiced that her mom would be home for her tenth birthday party. After some warm hugs Ruth was allowed to change into the clothes she held for a possible court appearance. She was then taken to the charge office where her paperwork was pulled. A release form was elaborately stamped. She was given a property bag containing her purse and personal affects that had been confiscated when she was brought in. Then she was led to a side door and let out. She took a few jubilant steps before two men in suits intercepted her. "Mrs. Slovo," one of them called. He reached for her arm and she was re-arrested.

Rivonia: The Trial

Unlike their approach to the Treason Trial, the government was cautious with the Rivonia defendants. They charged only those they were sure they could get convictions on, eleven in all. Ruth First was not amongst them. She had eventually been released and, with Helen Suzman's help, would soon be granted a one-way exit permit to leave the country with her children. The politicians, ruthless as they were, "still lacked the stomach," Chris said, "to hang white-female political prisoners."

Yes, Leighan agreed, it would certainly not have made for good publicity abroad. Besides, the thought of an internationally-scrutinized trial, and "a multiracial one to boot," she said, was probably sufficiently messy without contemplating the inclusion of a "well-groomed white lady with a varsity degree."

The trial began on 9 October 1963. The defendants arrived in an armored police vehicle, four Whites in the front, seven Blacks in the back. The public gallery was jammed. The press dubbed the proceeding the most significant political case in South African history. Chris was there — his family lived in Pretoria — and we had a blow-by-blow account.

Madiba was the first accused. He appeared looking gaunt, his skin limpid. He had lost considerable weight since being in jail, and those who knew him shrank back in horror when he first entered the courtroom, stressed and sleep-deprived. He and his fellow accused, Chris said, clearly bore the scars of life in prison. Their self-esteem, he noted, was shattered.

Defense lawyer Bram Fischer asked Judge de Wet for time to prepare their case. He was granted a three-week adjournment, and reports described this as an important healing period for the prisoners; "a much-needed time," Chris said, "to restore their lost sanity."

*B*ack in court after their planning time, the defense chalked up some early gains, including permission for Madiba to wear a business suit; before the recess, he had been obliged, as a convicted felon, to wear prison attire. But the prosecution quickly regrouped and began to build a powerful case. As we had anticipated, the most damning evidence was the collection of documents seized at Liliesleaf.

I received a long letter from Pop telling me what I was already aware of. Madiba had been out of the country, he said, when much of the planning for an armed struggle had taken place at Rivonia, and when most of the recent acts of sabotage had been committed. So if the trail of paperwork that tied him to the others had been destroyed, he wrote, "Mandela would likely have walked free." — not quite, he would still have had to serve out the balance of his existing sentence.

However, as things moved on, a fear-filled atmosphere began to sweep over the defendants, and our early hopes for acquittals soon dwindled to a desperate wish just to have them stay alive. But even that started to look unlikely when, of all people, Mr. Vorster, the minister of justice, speculated on the likelihood of the gallows. He jested that the greatest mistake General Smuts had ever made was not hanging him — Vorster — for treason, when he had been interned. He avowed that his government would not make a similar error.

*F*ollowing the pattern of Madiba's previous trial, we read that the leading defendants had decided, against the advice of their attorney, Bram Fischer, that rather than a futile attempt to test the law, they would make the case a platform for their beliefs. They also resolved that, whatever the outcome, they would not appeal. Appeals, Madiba explained to a distressed Bram Fischer, would erode their moral stance.

Madiba's closing statement was the most moving of his career. As expected, there had been considerable talk about communism, and he explained that although he had embraced the help of men who admitted to being communists, he was no more a communist than Winston Churchill, or Franklin D. Roosevelt had been when they had entered into their wartime alliance with Joseph Stalin. Chris read the report to us, and his smile was like a sunbeam. "An excellent comparison," he said. "We'll see what the *Jaaps* have to say when that reverberates around the foreign press."

He read on about Madiba's speech; how he had dwelt on the indignities of *apartheid,* how he had stressed the need for political equality in the democracy that South Africa claimed to be, and of how he had ended his impassioned address with the much-quoted words:

During my lifetime...I have cherished the ideal of a democratic and free society in which all persons live together in harmony and with equal opportunities. It is an ideal which I hope to live for and to achieve. But if needs be, it is an ideal for which I am prepared to die.

Madiba then stepped back with his head held high, we learned, bolstering to a pinnacle the enormity of his character. He quietly sat down, and a hush fell on the chamber. It was broken only by the quiet sobbing of women in the gallery. Judge de Wet let the charged silence linger, Chris said, before filling it by announcing the verdict. The case against James Kantor, he implied, was flimsy, and the charges against him were dismissed. Likewise, Rusty Bernstein was released. The others were found guilty. Sentencing would follow.

On 12 June 1964, those convicted entered the courtroom for the last time. The judge called for the prisoners, Blacks and Whites, to rise, and stated that he had decided not to impose the supreme penalty.

There was a gasp of relief from the gallery. The excruciating suspense was over. Madiba and his friends turned to each other and smiled.

We rejoiced. "Where there's life there's hope," Chris whooped.

"I thought, dear boy, that you hated clichés?" Leighan teased.

But Chris knew better than to pursue that.

Part 20

MARINE DIAMONDS

Drastic Changes

The Rivonia Trial was followed by drastic changes in many of our lives. Ruth First and her daughters moved to London. In being granted her freedom Ruth could be said to have won her contest with the law. But for the security police the engagement was not yet over. They still held a trump card. They had the means to deal with anarchists in exile. But Ruth's children would be spared, and would move on to inspired achievements, including a brilliant movie, *Catch a Fire* — Shawn was the screenwriter, Robyn the producer — which astutely captured the intricate psychology of the *apartheid* era, and built on Madiba's theme of forgiveness in post-*apartheid* times.

Rusty Bernstein, on his acquittal, was placed under house arrest, but he and Hilda managed to execute an elaborate escape, also to London.

A few weeks later Bram Fischer joined his South African friends in London. He had recently been charged with participating in activities of the banned Communist Party, but had been released on bail to conduct preparations for an international patent case he was involved in. Like Madiba, Pop said, he should not have returned, but he did, and paid an awful price for it.

Madiba was banished to Robben Island, 'South Africa's Alcatraz,' as the London Sunday Times referred to it. He had first set foot there two years before when he was dragooned by rough Afrikaner guards shouting: *"Dis die Eiland! Hier gaan julle vrek!"* This is the Island! This is where you die!

And in December 1964 a large number of my friends and I graduated from varsity. Pete returned to the Copperbelt and in his first letter to me he enclosed a note from Kat. Kat's message was written in the calligraphic hand he had learned at mission school, and was beautifully illustrated with pen-and-ink drawings of animals and scenes of the wild; it urged me to think of returning to work with him.

Chris Cairncross found a dream job in Cape Town, and Leighan and I also moved there. Leighan was interested in teaching drama, and I had an interview with a company from Texas.

"You Like Boats...?"

"You like boats, and you don't get seasick?" It was the second time the senior executive had asked the question.

"I love being at sea," I said with genuine enthusiasm. "And I'm really interested in this ocean mining venture."

He let a thorny quietness hang. His eyes were flat. He wanted confirmation, I supposed, of my immunity to heavy weather.

I remembered my plight in that first storm on *Senta,* and I knew that the seas off South West Africa, where I would be working, were some of the roughest in the world. I had better be truthful, I thought. "Look," I stammered awkwardly, "I might be sick once or twice if the weather's really bad. But I'll be over it in a day or two."

His expression remained deadpan. "The last geologist we had, a good man, was chronically seasick. We had to let him go."

I searched for a way to break through his pessimism, his impassive standoff. Then suddenly an idea came to me. "Mr. Vartsos…"

"Socrates," he interrupted.

"Socrates," I corrected myself. "Try me. I'll sign on for my first prospecting voyage for no pay." I held my breath. He stared at me. I detected a twinkle in his eye and pressed my advantage. "I really want this job," I said. "I know I can help you."

Then, to my great relief, he raised himself from his high-backed chair and extended a hand. "You've got yourself a deal," he smiled.

"Yes!" I exclaimed with a flush of pleasure. I shook his hand.

"I'd like you to meet my colleague, Dave," he said, "and Hoffie, Mr. Hoffman, our chief geologist. He's the brain behind our side of the operation." He looked up at the clock in his office. "How about lunch?"

A week later saw me clinging to a stanchion, spewing my guts over the side of a converted tug that served as our prospecting vessel. "Here, try a swig of this," Bevin offered, extending a glass to me as I wiped my face on the sleeve of a damp Norwegian sweater.

"What is it?" I asked miserably.

"A hot toddy, mate. It'll slide down smooth as snake shit."

I downed the brew, but it barely touched bottom before I lost it.

The ship plunged into another sea and shuddered, shaking me to the core. We grabbed for the railing to steady ourselves. As the bow came up Bevin raised a glass in his free hand. "Cheers, mate," he toasted and drank. He looked at me again. "Maybe you should try a shot of rum — later."

"Yes — later," I agreed, immeasurably thankful to be offered some grace time. I tried desperately to collect myself, but my mind remained crowded by nagging doubts. What if I had reached a threshold in my resistance to motion distress? What if it persisted as a chronic complaint? I could clearly visualize myself sitting in that same chair opposite Socrates. 'Too bad, Mr. Watson. You had the makings of a good man, but I'm afraid we're going to have to let you go. Thanks for thinking of us.'

*B*ut by the next day the storm had eased, and I was fine. I leaned over the chart table, engrossed in the plotting of locations we proposed to work.

"Listen Zog," Bevin said, addressing our chief scientist by his nick-name, "why not forget these deep-water holes and move closer inshore?"

"Unfortunately, I can't," Zog replied. "Soc wants us in an offshore band of sediments. And this section here," he said, pointing to the chart, "is as shallow as we can go. It's the money game again. Hoffie has to decide whether or not to bid on the deepwater concession."

"The deepwater concession?"

"Yes, the sediments beyond that rock shelf that has been our sea-ward boundary so far."

"What's the story?" Bevin queried, his forehead creased.

"It's all about the source of the diamonds." Zog said as he inscribed a rough oblong on an overlay to the chart. "If we find diamonds anywhere here, detached from the inshore gravels, there's a good chance they're de-rived from Kimberlitic pipes offshore."

"So?"

"So they're not our regular alluvial deposits that have come from sources inland, brought down by ancient rivers. Those are what we're min-ing now."

"You think we'll find them out there, mate?" Bevin asked.

"We could," Zog replied. "We now know firsthand that seamounts like Vema are igneous and could contain diamond-bearing blue."

"I've heard of Vema," I said. "Remind me again where it is."

"It's west south-west of Oranjemund," Zog said, jogging my mem-ory, "on the edge of the Cape Basin. We were there on the *Emerson K* a few months ago. Ask Bevin about it."

"*Ja*, mate, I don't know about diamonds, but you sure could make a fortune on all the *kreef* there. The place is crawling with them. On my first dive I came up with a couple of five-pounders."

"You should have seen Sammy's face," Zog added. " 'Goddamnit,' he shouts to Bevin from the bridge. 'I spend a goddamned fortune on this expedition and my boy comes up with lobsters.' "

"*Ja*, that was good," Bevin chuckled. "Sammy almost crapped."

*S*amuel Vernon Collins, a Texan oilman and expert on marine pipeline in-stallations, had come to South West Africa to do a job for De Beers. They wanted a means of transferring oil from ocean tankers to their diamond town, Oranjemund. A harbor was too expensive, they reasoned, and the an-swer lay in a pipeline from an offshore mooring system.

While working along the desert shore, the *Sperrgebeit*, the forbidden territory, as the old German colonists named it, Sammy observed lucrative mining operations on raised beaches and in the surf zone. "Why aren't you working further offshore?" he queried.

"Our concession ends at the low-tide mark," a De Beers man told him. "We've not taken up the option to mine beyond that."

"Why not?" Sammy asked with Jewish curiosity.

"I think our engineers decided that the cost of offshore mining would be too high."

"Goddamnit," the little Texan declared with a rising sense of animation, "I think I can make it pay!"

He quickly set about raising the necessary capital, and established the Marine Diamond Corporation. Not long after that, on the strength of some early prospecting finds in Chamais Bay, off a stretch of coastline designated as Diamond Area 1, he began mining on a small scale. But his enemy soon emerged, the weather. The Roaring Forties push through Drake's Strait, periodically deflect northeastward and, with a fetch of the full Southern Ocean, throw the ultimate breaking waves on the Diamond and Skeleton coasts. It was not long before he lost his first mining unit, *Barge 77*. She was torn from her anchors in a storm, and swept high up on the rocks ashore to become yet another of the wrecked skeletons the coast was named for.

De Beers looked on with interest. In the world of diamonds they sat on the throne of high authority. And although their silent charter called for exclusive control, they were content to have people like Sam Collins do some of their dirty work. If the offshore operation proved cost-effective, De Beers would simply set about buying it out. If not, they would let the Texan take the rap for its failure.

The bottom-line objective of my fellow geologists and me was to ensure that Sammy did not take a dive, that his operation was successful. In the complicated hierarchy of business dealings, we were employed by Geoservices, Geological & Mining Consultants — and later, Collins Submarine Pipelines — and contracted to the Marine Diamond Corporation to conduct their exploration. Our formal mission, first and foremost, was to find new offshore deposits. Beyond that we were to improve the efficiency of Sammy's recently-expanded mining program.

After two weeks of heavy toil we had found only a single stone. "And that," Zog reported to Socrates by radio, "was probably a carry-over."

I was bitterly disappointed, but reminded myself that, for the present, learning how to operate the ship was just as important as finding diamonds. "What else do I keep an eye open for?" I asked. I knew that the next voyage would see me in charge of the technical operation.

"A million things, but you'll pick them up as you go along. You're doing just fine at logging the sediments. And you're positioning the ship really well. That took me a lot longer to get the hang of, especially using that bloody Hydrodist on the move."

The first order of business for the geologist was to lay an anchor spread. This facilitated dredging a series of locations along a desired prospecting line within the secured layout. Setting anchors was accomplished with the help of a surveyor ashore. He radioed horizontal theodolite readings from his beacon, and the geologist, in turn, employed each angle and a simultaneously-derived distance — obtained from a marine adaptation of the tellurometer — to plot the ship's location and call out courses to the helmsman. In an advanced configuration the first anchor was dropped inshore. The vessel was then turned and navigated to weather, and a second hook placed. The third was laid downwind to stabilize the ship's movement. Once held within this triangular anchor arrangement, large shipboard winches were employed to move onto each new sampling position.

"It sounded so easy when Soc first explained it to me," Zog smiled. "But the toughest thing, as you've already seen, is doing it all on the fly."

"Yes," I agreed. I could appreciate the learning curve for anyone without previous sea time, and especially for a scientist with no experience at the helm. One needed a marine perspective of the goings-on to execute the procedure properly.

"And anything else I should know?" I asked.

"One big worry is always the plant hands. You saw them this morning, throwing stones at the sea gulls. They're bored because we're not finding anything. And when they're bored, they get sloppy."

Bevin agreed with Zog. "*Ja*, that's a problem, mate."

"And another thing to contend with," Zog added, "is their honesty. We screen them as carefully as we can, and give them a good bonus for everything they find, but you never know."

"Stealing diamonds?"

"*Ja*. It doesn't matter too much on the rigs. But in prospecting it's critical! A handful of lost stones would completely upset our grade evaluation of an area. It might translate into not coming back to mine a potentially good spot."

"Or in this case," I said, extrapolating the problem, "losing an entire deep-water concession area."

"*Ja*, and our precious bonuses," Bevin put in.

"And you especially need to keep a keen eye on the sorters. They have the bad habit of popping diamonds into their mouths, so fast you can hardly spot them. They all do it, not necessarily to steal, just a sorters' tradition. It's a practice we're trying to break."

Bevin suddenly darted onto the bridge wing. "I thought I heard something," he shouted. "The pipe is bouncing. We're on bedrock."

"Bring her up," Zog called out to the deck crew.

"Ve do anodder hole?" Captain Emerich inquired. He had a can of tobacco in one hand, and with the other he had deftly extracted strands of leaf that he was busy rolling into a small sheet of rice paper. He raised the gummed end to his mouth, licked it, then lit it and inhaled the smoke.

"No," Zog replied. "We're done here, Captain, thank you. You can lift the spread and steam for Hottentot Bay at your convenience. We'll spend our last week there."

"*Hottentotsbaai*," the old man beamed, "dot's goot. Perhaps ve stop at *Lüderitzbucht* on der vay, check for post." He had spent a lot of time there, I had been told, the first harbor town in old *Deutsch-Südwestafrika*. In 1883 Adolf Lüderitz had acquired the Bay, and a five-mile radius of land surrounding it, and declared it a segment of a new German colony in Africa.

"He likes to get back," Zog said in a low voice when the old man had left the bridge. "Shake a few hands and speak some German. We purposely have the mail sent there between crew changes."

*T*he next day saw us rounding Diaz Point, about to enter Lüderitz Bay. I was immediately taken by the small town, in particular its old colonial architecture, towers and high-raked roofs — the Germans knew no other way to build — completely wasted in the desert.

Zog pointed to a spot ashore. "Granite," he said, "not unlike the Cape Peninsula Granite you see around Hout Bay."

"Interesting," I replied, my geological avocation aroused. "I'll check it out for some recreational entertainment. There doesn't appear much else to do." The only indication of life was the occasional fisherman mending nets, or tending crayfish pots aboard the small boats that we glided by.

"Don't be deceived," Zog smiled. "You'll find some places boarded up to be sure. But there's a road into the town, and a railroad, and even a small landing strip. And you'll be surprised how lively the bar is. We'll pop in for a shot or two. But I warn you, it's a free-for-all."

"You can say that again, mate," Bevin added. "No formal *apartheid* in these parts."

Zog turned to Bevin. "I was thinking," he suggested, "that we might go out to Kolmanskop and show Ian the old mining town."

*K*olmanskop, the first diamond mine in *Deutsch-Südwestafrika,* turned out to be a ghost town, half buried by an encroaching sea of sand.

"This place is absolutely fascinating," I called in delight. "And nobody to be seen."

"Yes, but can you picture the buzz here at the height of its boom days: nice homes and shops, a school, and a recreational club with a theater. Come, let me show you." He led me into an impressive-looking hall, and started into a popular rugby song that Bevin at once joined him in. "Do you get a feel for the fine acoustics of the place?" he asked.

"Yes," I replied appreciatively.

"Captain Emerich claims that the sound in here is up to the mark of any auditorium in Europe."

"I wouldn't be surprised," I said. "And if that's any indication of the efficiency of their mining operation, I can see why they were so successful."

"Too bad the Old Man couldn't come," Zog complained. "He's got some interesting yarns to spin."

"I bet," I said. "I must remember to ask him if he knows what happened to the old German mining companies that were here."

"Oh, I can tell you about those," Zog volunteered with a pleased expression. "They were dissolved when our troops captured South West Africa in the First World War. Smuts and a South African force of some six thousand landed right here...I say here, but I mean, of course, at Lüderitz Bay."

I bobbed my head, highly interested.

"Sir Ernest Oppenheimer, Harry's father, was quick to pounce on the German diamond interests here. Have you read much about the history of De Beers?"

"No," I admitted.

"You should," he advised. "It's absolutely fascinating!"

"I'll get some books from the library," I said, "when we get back. I'd like to know how they came by the De Beers name, and how Cecil Rhodes was placed in the diamond equation. I really only know of his work in building railroads."

We stepped through an arched doorway and entered a house that was half filled with dune sand. "It's incredible how quickly the desert takes over," I remarked.

"*Ja*, mate," Bevin agreed. "It's probably only thirty years, or less, since people lived here."

"I can also tell you about the De Beers name," Zog offered, returning to my comment. "You remember from school history that diamonds were discovered in 1871, in what is now the Kimberley area?"

I raised open hands to show affirmation; that much I knew.

"One of the first big finds occurred on a farm owned by the De Beer brothers. They soon sold out, but their name stuck."

"It's as simple as that?"

He answered with a nod.

"I remember having it drummed into me at school that the discoveries were made in *Voortrekker* territory," I tendered.

"True," he agreed. "But the treasure didn't help the *Boers* much," he asserted. "There's a dark side to diamonds you see, greed! It didn't take long for the word to get out, for the usual rush, for the European diamond brokers to dispatch their agents to South Africa, and for the British politicians at the Cape to see the Afrikaner lands in an entirely different light. In fact it took less than six months to hoist their jolly old Union Jack over the newly-found diamond fields."

"And when did Rhodes arrive there?" I asked, trying to tie the whole thing together. Both Ga and Pop had mentioned it, but I'd forgotten.

"Less than a month after the British flag," Zog grinned, "in November of 1871. They say he appeared hiking across the *veld* carrying a prospecting pan and a shovel, ready to join his brother on the diggings. At the time he was only a boy, eighteen years old, I think."

"And a few years later he owned it all," I sang. "Amazing!"

Zog smiled, delighted that I shared his enthusiasm for this geological side of African history. "What really absorbs me about Rhodes," he went on, "is that he managed to keep up with his studies, commuting between the diamond fields and Oxford. And what tickles me most of all," he offered with high spirits, "is that by the time he graduated, in 1881, he'd already established the De Beers Mining Company. He was a multimillionaire. I mean talk about paying your own way through varsity."

I shook my head, thankful that I was not completely in the dark about Rhodes, and pleased to be learning more. I took another bite on my sandwich. The morning fog had lifted, and we now sat in the shade of one of the ghost-town buildings. "I just can't imagine how he managed to swing that whole diamond deal," I said, prompting Zog to continue.

"Yes," he went on, "and gold as well. In 1886, when the Witwatersrand deposits were found, Rhodes used some of his diamond revenue to set up Consolidated Gold Fields." He glanced at his watch.

I wanted to hear more. Pop still owned shares of Van Dyk Consolidated Mines and I thought to ask about those, but for the moment I stuck to diamonds. "The big Kimberley find was igneous, not so?"

"Yes," he confirmed, "an intrusive mica-peridotite pipe. But with the big ingredient, carbon!"

"Not all of them have carbon?" Bevin queried.

"No," I was able to respond — my professors had impressed that fact on me. 'Don't think you've struck it rich just because you've located a Kimberlitic pipe,' Lester King, for one, had said. 'All you might have found is olivine, and a few subordinate minerals and opaque oxides. It's only the inclusions of carbon, if such are present, that are forged by intense heat and pressure into diamonds.' He always emphasized the word 'if' when referring to the presence of carbon.

"So at Kimberley," Zog repeated, "we had carbon and hence diamonds, and mining was easy at first. They could work the upper weathered section of the pipe, yellow ground, in much the same way they had the alluvial gravels along the Orange and Vaal rivers. Soon there were some 30,000 diggers working more than 3,500 claims. Can you picture it? They say that the Big Hole, Kimberley's octahedron heart, was like a pit swarming with ants. And the diamond settlement, of course, was a proverbial boomtown, geologists and miners lighting cigars with bank-notes, and girls of ill repute bathing in champagne."

"Lovely stuff," Bevin smirked.

Zog looked at him and laughed, then took a long draft from his army water bottle before continuing with his geological narrative. "But deeper into the pipe they found themselves in hard blue ground, Kimberlite proper. This required more elaborate mining and mineralogical techniques, and it soon became painfully clear that the days of small-time operators were over. Business-management minds were needed now, to consolidate the random mining efforts, to put order to the chaos."

"Enter Rhodes," Bevin cheered dramatically, sounding for a moment like Leighan.

"Yes," Zog acknowledged. "He was one of the big movers. But he didn't have it all at first. A number of smart operators had already stolen a march on him, Barney Barnato, a fellow Englishman, and Alfred Beit, a German, amongst ..."

"I read somewhere," Bevin cut in, "that when Beit and Rhodes first met, Beit said something like: 'Mein objective is vun day to haf control of der entire diamond business.' 'That's funny, old chap,' Rhodes shot back, 'so is mine.' "

"And we know who won that contest."

"Yes, but it wasn't easy. And it certainly wasn't cheap, the buy-out I mean. Barnato's share alone cost Rhodes a bundle. I've seen a copy of the check, dated 18 July 1889, in the amount of 5,338,650.00 pounds" — nearly $13 million — "a lot of loot in those days." Zog slapped Bevin's arm. "Can you i-bloody-magine?"

"*Ja*...I mean no, mate. I can't imagine it," Bevin said. "I think I heard that, at the time, it was the largest personal check ever written."

"And what about the link between Rhodes and the Oppenheimers?" I pressed further.

"That involved a generation gap," Zog began. "Old man Oppenheimer, Sir Ernest, was some 25 years younger than Rhodes. He only came to South Africa the year Rhodes died, 1902. And that, by the way, was a very big year! The Premier Mine deposit was discovered near Pretoria. And, as you probably know, that yielded some of the world's largest diamonds, including the *Cullinan*, 3,106 carats, presented to King Edward VII."

"Yes, the *Cullinan*. Some stone! I'd like to see something like that come bouncing down the oversize screen on the *Emerson K*."

"*Ja*. And if it ever does, mate, make sure your catch is good!"

"Anyway, as I said," Zog continued, "1902 was the year Ernest Oppenheimer arrived in Kimberley. He was twenty-two. He'd been working in London, earning twelve dollars a month as a diamond sorter."

"I'd always been led to believe," I said, "that the Oppenheimer empire sprang from Rhodes."

"It did, but in a somewhat indirect way. You see by the time Rhodes died he'd secured about ninety percent of the world's diamond production. But he'd always wanted more. He was obsessed with the idea that he couldn't make it really big just by mining diamonds. He had to have control of their marketing as well. Sir Ernest worked for De Beers, and when he ultimately became its chairman, he set about turning the Rhodes dream into a reality. However, that's a story in itself. And so is his establishment of the Anglo American Corporation in 1917. And so is the brilliant break-through in advertising by Harry" — Sir Ernest's son — "conning the Japanese into using diamond engagement rings."

"Give me a hint of the Anglo setup," I begged.

Zog peeked again at his watch. "Not now," he grinned. "It's time to hit the bar. I've got a thirst on me that I wouldn't sell for a gold sovereign."

*T*he next day dawned on a hung-over crew steaming for the prospecting spot Zog had previously chosen. Captain Emerich was personally at the helm. "Vot you sink von *Lüderitzbucht?*" he asked me.

"I love it," I responded. "The last place we saw was the old Lutheran Church, and a stained glass window donated by the Kaiser."

"Unt vot's dot for interest to an English boy?" he queried.

"I sailed to America a few years ago," I responded, "on a yacht built for Kaiser Wilhelm II, a boat called *Senta.*"

This news put a new slant on our relationship. He had seen *Senta* and been aboard her, and marveled that I had journeyed so far on her. "How she haf sail?" he asked with keen interest.

"Like an angel," I replied.

"*Jaa,*" he said lovingly, "beautiful wood boat. But I don't sink even der German can today build soch a *seevögel.*"

We talked at length about *Senta,* and about the skills of the old shipwrights who had built her. He told me a little about his experiences in World War II. Because he was German, he said, he had not been permitted to go to sea, and had worked ashore as a carpenter. He knew enough about woodwork, he declared, to appreciate fine craftsmanship. And *Senta,* as far as he was concerned, was the epitome of an expert's hand. And did I know, he went on, that the grandmother of Kaiser Wilhelm II was England's Queen Victoria, and was I ..."

And as often as our many prospecting voyages brought us together, he would talk about *Senta,* and about the Kaiser and his father, and he would tell me stories of his own sailing days — as a young naval cadet he had trained aboard a square rigger. He was probably well into his sixties when I knew him, but as sprightly as a man half his age. I still have a fine photograph of him, standing up on the high wood-capped bridge railing of the *Emerson K,* his German beret stretched over his head so that he did not lose it to the ocean, expertly placing his ship stern-to the mining unit *Diamantkus* to transfer supplies. The other masters in our fleet used the small boats to transship cargo. No one dared do what he did.

At the end of our prospecting trip, we steamed back to Cape Town where I had a week off. I stopped by the Coloured flower sellers off Adderley Street, and then dashed round to see Leighan.

But she lacked her usual striking radiance, and things were strained.

"Is something the matter?"

"This isn't going to work," she said, sounding tearful.

"What do you mean?" I blurted.

"This whole thing, dear boy, our relationship. I haven't seen you for a month. I didn't even hear from you."

"I was at sea," I stammered, but my mind flooded with guilt. I could so easily have telephoned her from Lüderitz Bay. I knew, and so did she, that the radio-telephone was another option. And writing letters was even less painful; she had written to me, several times. I searched her face, her noble beauty, awaiting a reprimanding quote.

But there was nothing but silence.

I was not getting off that lightly.

If only I'd had the humor and imagination of Oom Jan, or Ismael, and could have called her Lioness Leighan. But I did not, so I hove the helm hard down, and crossed her bow.

She countered easily. "Look," she said, "I know why you wanted this job; it's a stepping-stone back to the States."

"You can come with me."

I'm not going with you, Ian, I'm not! Cape Town was one thing, but not America. No!"

For almost three years we had successfully avoided the subject, but now, in a flash, it was out, piercing me painfully in the heart.

We talked on, matching each other in stubbornness.

We retreated downwind, and tried a different tack.

There was a hopeful lull. But fresh gusts bore down on us. We were close-hauled, and could make no meaningful headway. We lay to the wind.

"I'll miss you," she said finally, and if she'd added 'shipmate,' I thought stupidly, it would have replicated my parting from Pete, on *Cariad.*

Take Yourself a Raise

I would not have dared to go up to his office, as Zog had suggested, and introduce myself. But I had seen his photograph in the newspaper, and on my first day back in our corporation headquarters I recognized him in the elevator, the King of Diamonds.

"Mr. Collins," I said, extending a hand, "I'm Ian Watson, one of your new geologists."

"Sam Collins," he replied, clutching my hand firmly.

"How do you do, sir," I said, completing my introduction in the formal British way. I bit my tongue.

But he quickly put me at ease. "Have you been to sea yet?" he asked.

"Yes sir! I just arrived back yesterday, on the *Emerson K.*"

"And?"

I waited for him to complete his question, but apparently he had. "And, how did the trip go?" I stammered, trying to verify what I assumed he was asking.

"Yeah, how many diamonds you find, boy?"

There were muted sniggers from some of the occupants in the lift, but these quickly evaporated with my reply. "Seventeen," I said.

"In deep water?" he asked quickly.

"No, sir. But north of Chamais Bay."

"Nice going," he boomed with the hearty enthusiasm I remembered of Texans. "We need a back-up mining area. Take yourself a raise, boy!"

"Thanks," I called after him as he stepped out on his floor.

He turned. "We'll have lunch next time I see you."

I pressed the down-button, and the first person I ran into on the Geoservices floor was Bevin. "I just met Sammy," I reported in an energetic tone.

"What do you think of him?"

"He's great," I laughed. "He loved the news that we'd found diamonds. 'Take yourself a raise,' he said."

"And if you thought he was joking, I can tell you, mate, he was deadly serious. Go to payroll and tell them the story. You'll see an extra ten percent, or so, on your check next month."

"My check next month? There might not be a check next month. I don't even know for sure if I have a job yet."

"You found diamonds in *Hottentotsbaai,* and Sammy knows it. You'd better believe you have a job, mate. You've got employment coming out of your eyeballs!"

Part 21

Oliver, the Texan & Dr. Stiegler

Lofty Perch of Freedom

*I*t was five months later and I was back in the office. "Zog and Socrates are in a meeting," Bevin said. "They told us to take the day off."

"Yes, thanks, Soc left me a note. I've just popped by to drop off my prospecting logs. And by the way," I added, "I'm trying to get a few people together today to climb Table Mountain. What do you say?"

"Going diving, mate. Why don't you join me instead?"

"I've already set it up with Riana," I begged off. "She wants to see what Robben Island looks like from up there. See you tomorrow."

"How about tonight," Bevin suggested, "about nine, at the *Den?*"

I called Chris. "Would you like to hike up Platteklip today?"

"Sure," he responded. "Be a chance for you to meet a new sailing buddy of mine, Oliver. He's a Watsie clone, another bloody geologist. You two should hit it off like vultures on a kill."

*A*s Chris had predicted, I took an instant liking to Oliver. He was outgoing, smart, and humorous, and we enjoyed some invigorating conversation as we trudged upward through the city. "I say, I've never seen a place with so many good looking birds," he remarked, at one point, with a smile. "I swear, when it comes to women, Cape Town has the edge on London, Paris...even Stockholm, and that's sticking my neck out!"

"It's our immigration policy," Chris offered.

"That's a good one," Oliver said, and laughed quietly.

"No, I'm serious. In an attempt to increase the white population of the country," Chris explained, "the government has introduced a scheme that offers Europeans a free passage, a settling-in allowance, and guaranteed employment. You didn't know that?"

"No," Oliver answered. "I'd have applied for it myself."

"It wasn't intended for wealthy chaps like you," Chris smiled. "But it doesn't stop you from enjoying the results. As you see, it's attracted a bevy of beauties to Cape Town."

"I thought there were more females here than men. Perhaps the young ladies are more adventuresome, or less obsessed with establishing home-bound careers."

"Whatever," I said. "But the word's out; *eKape* is the place to be, the most romantic, the most scenic, the party capital of the world."

"They claim we're up to about five girls now, for every chap that's around," Chris went on.

"Well, I don't know what happened to my other four," I joked.

"How about your other five?" Chris cut back sharply.

I was about to smile, but the heavy hint of sarcasm in his voice caught my notice. "What do you mean?" I asked.

"Riana says she didn't hear from you last trip. You can't be that hard on her," he warned. "You'll lose her just as surely as you lost Leighan!"

I experienced another pang of conscience, but said nothing.

We tramped on in strained silence for a while, but when we finally left the last of the built-up area and began picking our way through pine-woods and *fynbos,* our mood shifted once more to a lighter vein.

Our hike thus far, although easy, had taken much longer than I had expected, and we were almost a half-hour late to meet Riana at the cable station. But she was not at all put out. "How'd I look?" she asked. She was wearing a cute Alpine outfit I'd not seen before, with long red knee-socks on long Nordic legs, and my heart skipped a beat.

"Stunning," Oliver offered before I could even introduce them.

"You're British," she observed.

"And you're neither South African, nor an English rose."

"How can you tell?" she asked in her charming way.

"Your accent is too good."

"And your accent, sir, hints of the West Country."

"That's brilliant. How on earth…"

"I did some of my thesis research in the Cotswold Hills."

"Your thesis?"

"Yes, *Design with Nature,*" she expanded, giving him the title.

"You're a civil engineer?"

"An architect," she corrected. "I'm interested in construction that employs natural materials: sandstone, slate, and the likes." She extended her hand to Oliver. "I'm Riana," she said. "I'm from The Hague."

She kissed Chris on the cheek, "Hullo Christopher." Then me, on the lips. "Do you love me?" she asked in her customary way.

"Yes," I replied, embarrassed to have to declare it in public. We had only been going out for a month. And, besides, I still had a soft spot for Leighan and hoped that relationship could be patched-up.

"Let's be off," she said brightly, striding like a general towards the switchback trail that led up to Platteklip Gorge. "You cannot imagine how long I've been looking forward to this climb."

"That's some set of *verkykers* you have there," Chris said, referring to the binoculars Riana had strapped to the outside of her backpack. We had just crossed a cascading mountain stream, and stopped for a breather at the intersection of the Contour Path and the trail to the top.

"Yes," she agreed, "I want to see if there's really a tennis court on Robben Island."

"And if there is?" I asked puzzled.

"I shall be writing to your Minister of Justice," she declared, "and requesting a game of tennis with Nelson Mandela. I need to see for myself that he's in good health."

We were flabbergasted, shocked into silence.

Chris was the first to gather his wits. "You're joking of course?"

"No," she stated poker-faced.

"Do you think Robben Island is some sort of holiday camp," Chris stammered, "with everyone sitting around chatting outside their *rondavels?* That might have been the way it was when the old Xhosa Chiefs were banished there at the end of the last century, but I assure you it's not like that now!"

"But Nelson Mandela is a political prisoner," she responded naively. "I cannot see any possible harm in him playing a game of tennis. The guards go back and forth between the docks and the Island. We could simply join them one Sunday to get there. What do you say, sweetheart?"

I winced, but could not find it in me to crush her spirit, to tell her how it really was. "Listen beautiful," I said. "If anyone could negotiate permission, it would be you. And if they say yes, I'll be more than happy to go along with you."

"And I'd like to play as well," Oliver piped.

"Good," she smiled, clapping her hands together gently, her long pink nails catching the sunlight. "Then it's all arranged. We have a foursome. I'll pack a picnic hamper. And Christopher can come and watch. Do you think they'll allow us to take wine?"

"It wouldn't hurt to ask," Chris said, now also playing along.

But Riana, in her enlightened way, was deadly serious. Being a Dutch girl, as she often described herself, gave her a special dispensation, she thought, certain privileges not accorded to others. After all, it was her countrymen who had paved the way for European settlement in South Africa and that, surely, must count for something.

Sweating, we welcomed a chilling breeze as we entered the shadows of the narrow gorge near the top. Eventually at the summit, and in the sun again, we stretched ourselves on a weathered sandstone ledge and began eating the snacks that Riana doled out to us from her backpack.

But she ignored the food, and leaning against a rock she had carefully chosen, she balanced her elbows on her knees and began scanning the Island with her binoculars. "I can see the harbor," she purled, "and part of the town, and a road out to the left. But that's it." She was clearly disappointed.

Chris and Bevin had once trained together as navy divers, and I asked Chris whether they had had a chance to exchange notes on Bevin's expedition to Vema. "Yes," he replied, "and that's the last time I saw the bugger."

I turned to an account of our recent diamond search, but Riana steered the conversation back to The Rock. "That ship of yours, the *Emmy K,* is pretty sturdy," she chittered.

I gestured accord and held my breath.

"I've seen boats like her weather North-Sea storms. I'm sure she could cross an ocean."

I once again indicated agreement, wondering what outrageous suggestion would follow this time.

She did not disappoint me. "I jogged to the top of Signal Hill and watched you leave for South West Africa," she remarked. "You were pretty close to the Island." She looked at Chris. "Bevin and yourself are familiar with the use of weapons," she said. "We could nip in there, rescue the prisoners, and just keep going."

The three of us turned to her and gaped, but it was clear that this time she was only daydreaming.

"I just feel so bad, so helpless," she blubbered, tears starting to trickle down her cheeks. "We sit up here on this lofty perch of freedom, while those poor souls down there suffer because they dared to stand up for what is right. Can't your government see it?" she cried. "If they liberate those men, they liberate themselves."

We were off the mountain, in the yacht-club bar. "I suppose that's the way it is," I squirmed unhappily. "I'm South African, so it's my government."

"You didn't like the way Riana put it?"

"No!"

"But she's right. That's how the rest of the world sees it."

"And that's why I've got to start thinking again of leaving," I said, rubbing my chin thoughtfully. "My bind is all this diamond adventure. It appeals to me, and I'm getting a little too comfortable again."

"Where are you planning to go?" Oliver asked.

"To the States," I said. "That's the reason I wanted this job so badly, to establish some contacts."

"And you'll transfer back to America with the Texans?"

"In a flash," I said. "But my real goal is college, get my masters, and maybe even a Ph.D."

"You should think of the UK for that," Oliver suggested, "IC, Imperial College, the Royal School of Mines."

"Is that where you were?"

"Yes," he nodded, "and Oxford before that."

"Chris said you're a geologist."

"Yes," he smiled. "But engineering geology is the way of the future, especially in the United States."

"Engineering geology?"

"Yes, geological input to civil engineering practice: foundation support for dams, bridges, high-rise buildings — everything that's built is founded on either soil or rock. Then there's seismic risk, routing of pipelines and railroads, dredging, hydrology...the list goes on and on."

I sat up, engaged. "That sounds really interesting!"

"Even more interesting," he informed me, in a rush, "is that they're starting a new program at the School of Mines." Oliver swigged the last of his beer, and then continued. "The person in charge of it is John Knill, the nicest fellow, and really brilliant, on his way to the very top they say. It's Knill, de Freitas and Fookes so far, a superb team."

Riana tripped back from the ladies' room and our attention shifted to her. "I redid my hair," she announced. "What do you think?"

"It was gilding the lily," Oliver bubbled.

The digression ended our discussion on geology. "We've got to split," Chris said a little later. "Oliver's wife is expecting us for dinner."

"You'll miss Bevin," I complained. "I forgot to mention it. We're all meeting tonight at the *Navigator's Den.*"

"I'll try to get back later," Chris promised. "You'll be there, no doubt, until daybreak."

"Probably," I laughed, "trying to sober up to drive to work."

If Vema was crawling with *kreef,* the *Den* was crawling with people from Marine Diamonds. We met English Jill, Hoffie's secretary, in the parking lot. "I didn't know you hung out in places like this," I teased her.

"I love the old harbor," she responded. "And this place is full of great characters."

"But you see them every day at work," Riana challenged.

"Not the blokes on the rigs," Jill clarified, "and they're some of the most hilarious."

"They scare me," Riana said with a look that betrayed an inward cringe. "They're such a rough bunch. And their language leaves much to be desired. But I agree with you on the charm of the old harbor. And its architecture is a treasure."

"Before I forget," Jill announced, "Wynn is having a party on Saturday, and you're invited."

"Wynn?"

"Yes, Wynn Harvey, the Section Manager for Sea. He's a sweetheart. And his parties are sensational. He has a penthouse flat overlooking Clifton Beach, the lordliest view."

Wynn's party was a typical American affair. Everyone was invited, from Sammy to the plant operators on the mining units. Greetings were on a first-name basis, and attire was strictly casual. Most of the Texans were dressed in what Riana referred to as 'cowboy outfits' — blue jeans or Sta-Prest Levi's over high-heeled boots, tailored shirts embroidered with Colt revolvers, longhorns and lone-stars, and broad-brimmed Stetsons.

Wynn Harvey met us at the door in his own version of western gear. Its centerpiece was a string tie, fastened with a clip of banded tiger's-eye.

Once we had introduced ourselves, I admired it. "Silicified asbestos," I said, "crocidolite, one of my favorite semiprecious stones."

"Would you like it?" the Texan offered.

"No," Riana spoke up quickly. "It wouldn't suit him. But it's nice on you. You're very generous to give your clothes away like that."

"That's what people are like in Texas," I advanced.

"Have you been there?" Wynn inquired with interest.

"Yes," I replied, "and I loved it." I told him about meeting the old Judge and of how he had aroused my interest in finding oil in the Karoo.

"And did you follow up on it?" he asked in an ebullient tone.

"I started to," I responded, "by looking into the literature."

Riana sensed the lively interest of the oilman. "Let Ian tell you about it," she said graciously. "I'll have a word with Jill. I see her there."

"There's not much to tell," I said, backing off.

But his steely eyes urged me to continue.

"There's been a lot of interest in the Karoo System," I said. "It was triggered by a seep into a coalmine. And some small oil patches have been intercepted when drilling water wells."

"Have they done any deep borings?" Wynn's absorption was now shimmering.

"Yes," I replied, "a few; one as far back as 1921. But disappointing! No petroleum to speak of, and even a sparsity of invertebrate fossils. Some say that the heat generated by the subsequent igneous activity in the region has burned off any large reserves of hydrocarbons that might have been there in the first place."

"Maybe they're wrong."

"You sound just like the Judge," I laughed.

"What do you think, Ian?"

"I think there's a good chance of finding something," I said. "But you've got to temper anything I say with the optimism that rubbed off on me in your country."

"Nothing wrong with optimism," he chortled in true Texan style. "If there was, we wouldn't be here right now."

"Mining gemstones in the sea?"

"Yeah," he confirmed with a satisfied grin.

He glanced over at Riana and changed the subject. "We'll talk about petroleum later," he said, "and I really want to! But before your friend comes back, there's someone I want you to meet. His name is Heinrich Stiegler. Sammy ran into him at a conference in Geneva and thinks he can help us. He's apparently an expert on marine exploration and dredging."

"I'd like to talk to him," I said.

"Good," he acknowledged, placing a strong hand on my shoulder. "I've given him some office space. And I'd sure appreciate it," he said, "if you'd swing by and say hi; spend a little time with him."

"Be·a pleasure."

"I don't see him right now," Wynn said, scanning the room. "He might be down at the Clifton having a drink with Sammy. You can't miss him. He's the only one wearing a suit and tie."

"I'll pop down to the hotel right now," I said, excusing myself.

"And don't forget to have a steak," Wynn shouted after me. "I had them specially flown in from Texas."

Wynn's apartment, as large as it was, could not have begun to accommodate everyone, so the jamboree extended informally to the bar and balcony of the Clifton Hotel, and to the beach below where a number of Mexican-styled blankets had been stretched between coolers.

I met Stiegler — 'Doctor-Professor Stiegler,' as he introduced himself — at the hotel, and arranged to drop by his office.

"We met at Wynn's party," I said.

"I remember," she smiled. "Do you want to see him?" she whispered, flashing her eyes at Wynn's door.

"No," I whispered back, thinking 'this whispering is contagious,' "Dr. Stiegler."

"I'd better tell him you're here."

"Don't bother," I said. I walked past her and rapped on his door.

"But he…"

Her protest was cut short by a guttural, "*Jaa,*" which rang with the irritable note of one being unnecessarily disturbed.

Perhaps I should have let her call, I reflected, catching her apprehensive expression. It was interesting how quickly one tended to forget these little formalities in a company run by open-door Americans.

I turned the handle and entered. Dr. Stiegler jumped to his feet with a suddenness that might conceivably have been complemented by a crisp heel-click and an impassioned '*Heil* Hitler.' Demoniacal eyebrows, fierce piercing eyes, and an approximation to a patch moustache added to the impression. I must remember he's Swiss, I thought — at the time I had no way of knowing otherwise.

"Mr. Watson," he proclaimed with a flourishing bow. "I didn't inspect you." He seemed put out by my unannounced call. "Iss de girl der? She didn't told me you vos here."

"Yes, she's there. I said to her not to bother. It's my fau…"

"But I tawled her…" he began in a rising stiletto voice, and then, sensing my embarrassment, checked himself.

"Sorry about that," I apologized.

"No, no, no, okay." He rushed to pull out a chair. I thought it was to shake hands and extended an arm. He saw it and responded.

I noticed, once again, that his handshake was weak.

"Sit, sit," he offered with all the fuss of a banker cavorting around a geologist who had just unearthed a second *Cullinan*. When he was sure I was comfortable, he seated himself and rocked back in his large pivoting chair, attempting to compose himself. "Soo," he said with a gold-toothed smile.

"I just popped by for a chat," I submitted uneasily.

"*Jaa, jaa,*" he began. Then smiling tightly in the silence that followed, he continued defensively, "You excuse mein English, *ja.*"

This disarming plea brought back memories of my own frustrations on the Finnish freighter. Language inhibitions could certainly explain why he appeared to be so ill at ease. "Before I forget," I heard myself ask, "do you think you could join me for dinner tonight?"

"Yes, sank you, yes," he smiled more genuinely. "At vot thyme ve meet?"

I could not help but notice that the pencils on his desk had been sharpened to a pinpoint and painstakingly arranged in descending order of length, and that the journals on his side-table had been stiffly arranged, *en-echelon,* to follow the curved line of the glass. The current issue of *Geotechnique* was in full view, while each succeeding text had been placed with its binding edge outward so that it could be immediately identified. "I'll pick you up here at five past six," I said. That will appeal to him, I thought. Perhaps six past six would have been better, or six and one-half past six better still.

Dr. Stiegler negotiated the small passenger-seat of my MG with amusement — he was portly — but dinner was a huge success. Riana, at short notice, served up the most exotic cuisine, Indonesian, but combining the Malay influence of both the Netherlands and South Africa.

"Delicious," Dr. Stiegler said. "Vot you call it?"

"*Bobotie,*" she replied.

It was all 'vunderful,' and 'wery fine,' and half a dozen Germanic superlatives. And where had Riana learned to speak 'soch' good German? Her accent was flawless, he declared.

A reasonably tolerable evening, I thought, as I drove him back to the Mount Nelson. There had been some pretty heavy name-dropping, all lost on me, but no mention of industry affiliations. He was an academic, it seemed, on sabbatical, enjoying some educational travel before returning to Europe where, he said, he had promised to teach a course at the *Technische Universiteit* in Delft, and serve as a consultant on the Zuiderzee and Delta Projects. When I had tried to lure him into some technical discussions, he had backed off sharply, understandable with Riana present. But I had been surprised at how quickly he had changed the subject when Riana, on impulse, had offered to translate some of his publications for 'the boys,' as she referred to us.

"I'm so glad we could entertain the Doctor," Riana smiled when I returned later. "He is such a gentleman."

The Good, the Grim, and the Ghoulish

*T*he 'good' was my next tour of duty: a further successful voyage on the *Emerson K;* then a visit to our shore party to find a suitable source of ground water, and help install a well for a proposed new base camp; and finally, a week on the mining units where, in one twelve-hour shift, the *Diamantkus* sucked up from the seabed 7,803 diamonds totaling 2,737 carats. I called Bevin, by radio, in a frenzy of excitement. "The grade ran as high as 87 carats a cubic meter," I reported.

"Mind-blowing," he replied. "But you sound as if you have a dose."

"A dose of what?" I asked, looking askew at the microphone.

"Diamond fever, mate," Bevin laughed aloud.

The 'grim' was arriving home and learning that Chris had run into Riana and Dr. Stiegler at the theater. And the 'ghoulish' turned out to be a weird encounter with Oliver.

I let myself into Riana's apartment, but she was out.

She arrived home late, in my MGA, apparently pleased to see me.

But I was on edge. "Let's pop down to the *Pig*," I suggested. The *Pig & Whistle* was a student pub not particularly frequented by our crowd, but I thought the lively atmosphere there might elevate my mood.

After some chitchat I turned the conversation to Stiegler. He had spent a few days in the mining area, I told her. "And besides my rising suspicions about his technical competence," I said, "I found him very tiresome."

"How can you say that about Heinrich?" she challenged with unusual firmness.

"Because he's a prick," I stammered. It was not the turn of phrase I would normally have chosen, but her use of his first name had made my blood boil.

"I think that's a childish thing to say," she scowled. "And it's simply not true. He knows everything about the diamond business, from the old

German companies that once worked in South West Africa, to what goes on in Europe today."

"And you find it all highly intriguing?"

She drew a sharp breath of displeasure. "Don't speak to me like a child, Ian. And don't be roundabout either. I have nothing to hide."

"But you've been out with him," I sputtered, almost choking on the anger that clogged my throat.

"I don't know about 'been out with him?' But yes, I've seen something of Heinrich," she admitted. "He asked me to do some translations, and I said yes. I was sorry for him…and I was lonely, Ian. I received only one letter from you in all that time. And those ghastly reports about the weather, and of that diver taken by sharks." She was crying softly. "It gave me nightmares," she sniffed, wiping her eyes.

"So where have you been, the two of you?"

"Nowhere in particular, to eat, the theater, the German Club."

I dropped all pretence of understanding. "Look," I said, turning to her with murder in my heart, "I'm going to forget that this conversation took place. But just don't ever go out with him again!"

She gave me an 'are-you-finished' look, and I sensed her steaming at my threatening tone. "Why not?" she asked in a harrowing voice.

"Because I say so," I cut back sharply, "that's why!"

She let my words hang.

After a stillness that seemed to ring, I continued in what I considered to be a more reasonable tone. "Look babe," I tried to explain, "if you go out with this fellow, my friends are going to see you."

"And?"

"And they're going to say, 'There goes Watson's girl with that Stiegler character.'"

She sucked in another deep breath and spat her next words like poisoned Bushman arrows. "My God, you're a blackguard!" she hissed. "I honestly believe you're more troubled by what those scoundrels think, than about any concern you might have for me."

"Listen Riana, I'm crazy about you. We've never fought before, and I can assure you I'm not enjoying this. Now I'll drop the whole thing, but I'm telling you not to see Stiegler again. Okay!"

"No, Ian. I'm not a child, and it's not okay!"

I felt my stomach knot. "Then that's it, Riana."

She rose from the table.

I fidgeted for my car keys. "I'll drive you home."

"No thank you," she quaked with dispiriting intonation.

I shook her hand, watched her leave, and suddenly felt empty. This job, I thought, is heavy on relationships. But it was not that at all.

*T*he next day I called Oliver. "I need a game of tennis," I said, "to help clear my head. And I'd like to learn a little more about that new program you mentioned at the Royal School of Mines."

"How about this afternoon for tennis? And if you're not doing anything this morning, swing by Hout Bay and join me in some sailing. There's a good Sou'easter blowing; it should be a blast. And no pun intended."

"Is Jacqueline going out?" I asked, not wanting to intrude.

"No, just you and me. Are you at Riana's pad?"

"No, Fish Hoek."

"Good," he said. "See you in a jiffy."

If I thought I was going to clear my head, I was wrong.

But our encounter began on a high note. He had brought me a book published by The Geological Society of America. "Read this," he said, "you'll enjoy it."

I looked at the title, *Applications of Geology to Engineering Practice*. Then turning to the table of contents, I scanned the page: 'The Geologist in the Engineering Organization, Geology in Dam Construction, Design and Construction of Tunnels, Geological Aspects of Beach Engineering, Geologic Engineering in the Petroleum Industry,' and more. "This is fantastic," I said, excited. "I'll take great care of it."

"It's yours to keep," he offered generously.

I carefully stowed it in my daypack. "Have you done much in the way of engineering geology yourself?" I asked him.

"No," he smiled cryptically. "I haven't done much of anything. I'm what you might call a geological tinker. I hate to admit it, but I don't think I've done an honest day of work in my life."

"What do you do for income?" I asked before I could catch my runaway tongue.

"Draw down the family fortune," he shrugged slowly. He then moved the conversation. "Chris said your friend Bevin has been promoted."

"Yes, he's now the marine superintendent on the *One-Eleven*," I confirmed, referring to one of our mining units, the *Barge 111*.

That set Oliver off on a tirade. "You know, I've been thinking," he sparked with breath-taking audacity, "just how easy it would be to make off with a huge heist of diamonds from the rigs."

I looked at him in disbelief, but remained silent.

We cast off from the dock, and Oliver, in his aristocratic way, began to outline the most elaborate scheme. "All you need is a couple of inside men. You set up a small shunt from the concentrate screens, and just keep siphoning off a portion of the goods. It wouldn't take long to build up a stockpile, a few months at the most. Then you stage a raid," he leered, "in a boat disguised as a Russian trawler. They're out there fishing all the time."

He paused, but I said nothing.

"And all the bulldogs would know," the Englishman continued, "was that one crew-change haul had gone missing from the *One-Eleven*. There'd be a lot of noise, of course, but insurance would pay up. They wouldn't want to provoke an international incident over such, quote-unquote, 'small pickings.' The whole affair would blow over quickly, and we'd be in the clear with our trove of treasure. What do you say?" he asked, brimming with confidence.

I blinked, trying to ease the discomfort that had begun to swell in my brain. I didn't know whether to laugh or cry, as Bevin often said. I had not seen this streetwise side of Oliver. He had to be joking. Yet, what if he was serious? I had to assume that he might be.

"I'll finance the whole thing," he went on, "and arrange for the rough to be bruted and cut. Be the highlights of our careers! And it's not as if chaps like you didn't find the fortune in the first place. Frankly, you'd just be taking something closer to your rightful share."

He had said it all before we even reached the breakwater, and my head spun with wild possibilities. One was that Oliver might be a corporate criminal. I'd heard of such people, although not in the field of geology. He had just admitted, probably in jest, that he had never done an honest day of work in his life. But one never knew. Yet the more probable scenario, I reasoned, was that he had been staked out by diamond security, to test me. He knew the diamond-business slang terms — the 'goods,' the 'rough,' 'bruted and cut' — and his use of its argot scared me.

"What do you say, old chap?" he asked again.

I decided to stay cool. "It's even crazier than Riana's plan to rescue Nelson Mandela." It was shallow, but it was an out if he needed one.

He ignored it. "Do you really think so?" he challenged.

"Look Oliver," I said with mounting agitation, "can we drop this thing? I know you're only kidding, but it's making me uncomfortable."

"Sorry, old chap," he apologized. "Let's get the sails up."

We carried on as if nothing had been said, pitting our skills against the weather on a boat that was state of the art.

I canceled our tennis appointment, and telephoned Chris as soon as I reached home. "What do you know about Oliver?" I asked breathlessly.

"What do you mean?" he queried.

"Do you think he works for De Beers security?"

"No," Chris replied in a tone of absolute dismissal. "What on earth gave you that impression?"

"He was sprouting off about a diamond heist…"

"Oh that," Chris laughed softly, " 'Operation Trawl.' It's pure fiction! Oliver might be an upper-class drifter, even an insufferable one at times. But I assure you, he's absolutely harmless."

Part 22

DIAMOND DRAMA

Diamond Tug Capsizes

"*T*he R150,000 sea diamond tug *Collinstar,* which capsized and sank with the loss of six men at Chamais Bay, 80 miles north of Oranjemund, last week, is to be abandoned as a total loss." So wrote the Argus Shipping Correspondent on 12 February 1965.

*T*he *Collinstar* had made a desperate attempt to prevent the *Colpontoon,* a mining barge, from being swept ashore in huge seas that came crashing into our dredging area without much warning. We estimated that rogue waves, at the peak of the storm, were running a good sixty feet.

The tugboat had been called in to tow the 250-foot barge further out to sea, where the swells were longer and less steep. But the operation had gone dreadfully wrong. In making her turn to pass a line, a wave of Brobdingnagian scale caught the ill-fated *Collinstar* broadside. She broached and turned turtle. Miraculously her bos'n escaped. He had been standing on the stern of the tug with a heaving line, and had managed to scramble over onto the barge as his vessel swept by the big mining scow, bumping her and tearing a hole in one of her steel plates, fortunately above the waterline. The nimble-footed bos'n had swung his head to see his ship, the *Collinstar,* capsize, her dark hull, like a great whale, being swallowed by the ocean.

Somehow five of his mates had also broken free, and made it to the beach where our land-surveyors had picked them up. But, sadly, the others perished. Our shore party had kept searching for survivors, scanning their spotlights into the bilious green spray along the surf zone. They'd found some battered bodies — torn by rocks, or mauled by sharks — that they'd pumped and tried to breathe life into; but in vain.

*B*uilt exclusively for mining, the *Colpontoon* had no engines, and without the tugboat to move her to safety, she now lay abandoned at her dredging location, precariously held in place by her deep-sea anchors. Aboard the *Emerson K* we heard the drama of her predicament play out over our radio, but could do nothing to help her. Our hands were already full, plowing 'slow-ahead' into the heavy seas with another mining unit, *Barge 111,* in tow off our stern.

"*One-Eleven* to the *Emerson K,*" Bevin had radioed us earlier.

"*Emerson K* back."

"Can you come in and pick us up?"

I had seen the captain nod. "Roger Bevin, we're on our way."

"Thanks mate. *One-Eleven* out."

We had done it in daylight, when we could see the swells and time our approach, and when other aspects of the rescue had been less arduous.

In hindsight it was clear that *Colpontoon* should also have drawn stumps then. But there was always pressure to keep dredging. 'Goddamnit,' Sammy would complain after downtime, 'we've gotten behind on our monthly diamond count.' And the marine superintendent on the *Colpontoon*, also a Texan, liked to keep his countryman happy.

So, in this storm, the super had no doubt figured that, with his over-sized anchors, he could keep working until the very last, then call for help, or ride it out. He had certainly not counted on the weather worsening to the extent it had. "Our only hope," the Texan now drawled to his leading hand, "is to keep our anchor cables from getting busted. I'll come down to the deck, and we'll see what Wincher" — the winchman — "is up to."

"Here, take a life jacket, sir," Sparks, the radio operator, offered.

"Life jacket, hell! What do you want me to do, scare worse crap into the men? I'll take this instead," he said. He reached into his pocket and cut himself a healthy chunk of chewing tobacco.

"That'll keep the coyote at bay," Sparks murmured.

"That's good Texas lingo," the Southerner grinned, and with the slam of a door he and the leading hand disappeared into the maelstrom.

A sudden jerk is what causes an anchor cable to snap. So, in seas like these, safety depended on the skill of the winchman. The trick lay in slipping the clutch, alternately releasing cable to move inshore on each big swell, then, once the wave passed, gunning the winch to take up the slack and regain position. Wincher now held the key to their uncertain survival.

We sat at the radio on *Emerson K* and heard some intervals of chatter as the *Colpontoon* updated her position — in the present dire circumstances she did this every ten or fifteen minutes. Then we heard the Texan again. "We're riding it pretty good," he said in his slow, lengthened tone. "Of course we'll eventually burn the clutch on the winch. But by that time, good buddies, the storm might well be over. Go ahead."

There were calls of good luck from the rest of the fleet — the *Emerson K; Barge 111;* a large salvage tug, the *Collinsea,* which was standing by another mining unit, *Diamantkus;* and two small anchor-moving work boats.

"*Shore Party, Pontoon.* Anton, any more survivors on the beach?"

"*Shore Party* back. That's a negative. Five confirmed dead. Only one not accounted for now. He might have gone down with the ship. Over."

"Bad news, but thanks. *Colpontoon* out."

"Good guy that Anton," the Texan remarked. "And we probably lost a few just like him."

Sparks nodded. He had donned a full wetsuit — in case, like the unfortunate *Collinstar,* his barge capsized — and he was sweating.

"Never really thought much about the people of Africa," the Texan went on, "not till I came out on this job. Might have wondered once or twice about the animals, big game hunting, know-what-I-mean? But not the people. Good guys though, some of these *Bores.*"

"*Boers,*" the radio operator corrected. "*Boers,* it means farmers."

"Yeah, *Bores* like Anton. I like Anton. No questions. No lip. Just does his job, cool as can be."

Nothing changed for a while, and Sparks became hypnotized by the alarming swing of a calendar hanging from a screw on the bulkhead. Then he heard the leading hand on the walkie-talkie, and held his breath. The Texan reached across the chart table for his set. "Yeah, go ahead."

"Wincher says the clutch has gone. He's thrown in the dog."

"Okay, the two of you come inboard. Could be recoils when those wires let go."

The next thing we heard aboard the *Emerson K* was that the *Colpontoon* was floating free. I said a prayer, and it was answered. Somehow the flat-bottomed scow — with her eighty men — remained upright in the hideous waves, and was swept up onto a stretch of beach with no further loss of life. To us it was nothing short of a miracle.

*B*y daylight the storm had moderated, and the small boats began recovering dropped and snapped anchor cables. We returned *Barge 111* to the mining area, and within a matter of hours she was back in production.

The ocean continued to settle, and we took a run as close as we dared to the surf zone to look for any sign of the sunken *Collinstar,* and better scan the stranded *Colpontoon* with our binoculars. The big barge had turned in her sweep ashore, and now lay with her accommodation dome facing the beach. She looked intact and, aside from her damaged bow plate, she appeared to be seaworthy. By contrast, all we could see of the wrecked tug was a section of her superstructure that had been torn off and now lay in the shallows, half-buried in the sand.

The captain's inclination was to capitalize on the turnabout in weather, and run a line inshore to the stranded barge. But we had been instructed to do nothing until Sammy arrived in the mining area. He alone would manage the salvage operation — for insurance reasons, we were told.

Sammy's Salvage

"ALL-OUT BID TO PULL GEM SHIP OFF BEACH. An all-out effort was made this afternoon to refloat the R1,200,000 diamond mining

barge *Colpontoon,* which went aground on a sandy beach near Chamais Bay, north of Oranjemund, on Thursday. With the assistance of helicopters, a messenger line — the prelude to the passing of a tow-line — was passed from the barge to the powerful Diamond Marine Corporation tug...."

This extract of updated news appeared in the Cape Argus two days after the grounding. The powerful tug in question was the *Collinsea.*

*T*he light-line 'messenger,' mentioned in the newspaper clip above, is attached to a heavier line, which, in turn, is employed to haul something still sturdier. This building-block operation proceeds, until, at last, a steel tow-hawser stretches between the vessels. But at some point in the progression, the product of impatience no doubt, the transition in size had been too large and the line had parted. "Goddamnit!" Sammy swore. "Get one of those choppers up again with another messenger."

But by this time a strong wind had come up again, and the helicopters were too small for the task. Sammy needed help.

"Sam Collins to *One-Eleven.*"

"*One-Eleven* back."

"Yes, get me that guy Bevin Blatchford."

There was an interval of silence, then Bevin's voice. "Sammy."

"Bevin, the boys here have been telling me how you often head up crew changes in rough weather, and that you sometimes swim the mail ashore to the surveyors. Go ahead."

"They're probably exaggerating, sir."

"I don't think so. Listen boy, do you think you could swim a messenger in? You saw how the chopper was battling in the wind. She couldn't do it."

"I'll give it a try," Bevin offered.

"Good. Be sure to wear a wet suit. Take one of your buddies and dinghy across to *Collinsea.* From there you can try to run a line into the shore. Use the *Zodiac* to get in as far as you can. But whatever you do, don't take the dinghy into the surf. The swell's up again and you're better off swimming there, with the line attached to a harness. What do you say?"

"*Ja,* that's a good plan, Sammy. I'll call you from the beach."

*W*e kept an eye on Bevin as he and his buddy left the *Collinsea,* and made their way inshore in an inflatable with a big outboard engine. They turned several times to negotiate towering swells bow-first, then followed these inshore with bursts of speed. We saw Bevin go overboard, and although he must have been buoyant in his wet suit, we lost sight of him in the surf.

But a surveyor ashore broke into a frantic radio commentary. "I just hope he can get through these *monsteragtige* waves...Here comes one now and he's NOT going to make it! ...No, he's turned and ducking under it;

honest to God, it would have killed him! ...Here comes another...And here he comes. The bastard's surfing... Unbelievable! He's making the drop. But it's going to dump him! No, he's got his hands down, and he's kicking... He's out and ahead! He's through! Here he comes. What a bloody body surf! *Ek het nog nooit so iets belewe nie!"*— I've never seen anything like it!

"Has he got the goddamned messenger?"

"*Ja! Ja!* Sorry Sammy. The slack has washed in ahead of him...he's got the line...he's made it! He's coming out backwards. Here he is, taking off his feet, I mean his flippers."

With a connection made, the men spun a line from the *Colpontoon* to the *Collinsea* and we, in turn, extended a towline to her. With two ships in tandem to pull, things began to look more hopeful for re-floating the barge.

About an hour before high tide Sammy gave the order to take up the slack, and slowly put strain on the hawsers. The tugs powered up to full-ahead, the tide peaked, but the heavy mining scow would not budge. A newspaper reporter mentioned the "vain bid" to salvage the barge, and sympathized with the fact that Sammy, "a human dynamo," had been on the job since early the previous morning; "without a break," the reporter noted.

"There's no goddamned time to sleep," Sammy barked, his eyes puffed with fatigue. He called for help from the fleet.

The wind had let up and the seas were down again, so several of us went across to the *Colpontoon* to see what we could do. We were asked to assemble in the mess, where Sammy began outlining his plan. "Wynn thinks we can help ourselves by getting some pipes over the side; know what I mean, start dredging ourselves a channel. He'll coordinate you mining guys, and you can start right away. The galley staff, Sparks, and the surveyors can proceed as usual. The rest of you will be in my gang. We need to lighten this goddamn scow substantially before the next high tide. For a start we'll get rid of all those drums of ferrosilicon," he said, referring to the heavy-media material that we used on the rigs to separate the light sediments, like quartz sands and gravels, from the heavy diamond-bearing concentrate. "Beyond that," Sammy continued, "dump anything else that isn't an absolute necessity. Any questions?"

"Aside from the ferrosilicon, what exactly do we toss?"

"Use your judgment, goddamnit! Anything else?"

"Yeah," Wynn said. "At low tide I need two engineers, volunteers, in the water with me, to check the welds on the bow-plate repair."

*J*ust after midnight, as the tide flooded to its peak, we set the strain again, and less than an hour later the *Colpontoon* was off the beach.

There was a hearty cheer on our vessel, and a cackle of over-talk on the radio, before Sammy's voice broke through, no longer tired, now a rhapsodic contralto. "Nice going guys!" he sang. "Take her well offshore."

252 / Diamond Drama

Then, with the same re-energized lilt, Sammy was on to us. "You can drop your hawser, *Emerson K.* You did a great job!"

His last call that night was to the *One-Eleven*, "*One-Eleven, Pontoon.*"

"*One-Eleven* back."

"Tell Blatchford to take himself a raise."

With the salvage done, the preparations to tow the *Colpontoon* to Cape Town were an anticlimax. Time began to hang heavily, and it was not long before there was some mischief.

"*Emerson K, Diamantkus.*"

"*Emerson K* back."

"Is your limey engineer there? I've forgotten his name, the one who can't stand Stiegler's guts."

"Fitzsimons."

"*Ja*, Fitz. Tell him Dr. Heinrich Stiegler wants to speak to him. And stick around on the bridge; you might get a grin out of this."

I asked the mate to give the chief a call and dashed off to roundup a couple of my shipmates who, I knew, would appreciate Mike's humor. He was up to something. He had been on the blower the day before, relaying a weather alert from Cape Town that, he said, predicted 45-foot seas by midnight. When the master of the *Collinsea* called back — in a panic — for confirmation, Mike said, "No, no, Captain, four-point-five-foot seas, not 45-foot. Where on earth did you get that from?"

The mate nonchalantly reappeared on the bridge and was followed by a sweaty Fitz, wiping his greasy hands on a piece of cotton waste. He turned to me. "Didn't know t' prick was up 'ere. Wha' 'e want?"

I shrugged, keeping my eyes steadfastly on the Hydrodist, pretending to be fixing our position.

Fitz reached for the microphone. "Chief on t' *Emerson K.*"

"Goot mornink. Ofver"

"Bloody 'ell," the chief swore, then depressed the 'speak' button again. "Yes, governor, wha' you want?"

"Iss dot der Chief Engineer, off der Chief Mate?"

Fitz clenched the microphone, "It's t' Chief Engineer! Over."

"Goot. Listen Chief, I haf thawght of a vay to mak-ed your engines go faaster. Ofver." Mike was a master of voice impersonation and his accent was excellent.

"Caw blimey, mate!" Fitz swore, turning to me in disbelief.

I drew up my face and twisted back to my instrument with a spasm of pain in the pit of my stomach.

"Vot vos dot?" Mike asked, continuing with his Stiegler mimic.

"Make t' engine go faster?" the limey spat. "What sort o' tripe is that, mate?" He released the speak button. "Blithering idiot!" he swore, shaking his head at me.

"I don't can understand. Plees say more sloowly. Ofver."

"Never mind. Carry on," the chief growled.

"Told me, Chief, how farr you hold der microphone from your mouse? Ofver."

The chief fought for control, his brown eyes darting with frustration. He turned to the mate who had his face buried in the scope of the radar. "Great guns, now what's 'e onto?" He depressed the speaker button. "'bout nine bloody inches. Why?"

"Vell, I don't can hear you goot. I sink dot you haf got mouse vater in der microphone. Ofver."

"Mousevater? What t' 'ell is 'mousevater?' Over."

"I sink, Mr. Chief, dot you haf SPIT in der microphone."

The chief had clipped the microphone into its bracket, while he once again wiped his hands and face with his scrap of sodden waste. His ruddy countenance, now livid with rage, was too much for my companions and they made their escapes. Meanwhile the chief reached out and tore the fragile object, bracket and all, from the bulkhead. But before he had time to explode, Mike's voice was on the air again. "Just kidding, Chief. Do you think you..."

"Put 'at bloody kraut on again!" the chief demanded.

At this point the mate gave up and also left the bridge.

"He's not here," Mike pleaded apologetically. "It was me. Mike. I'm sorry Chiefy. It was just a joke."

"Don't give me that, mate! Put 'im on! I'll break 'is ruddy..."

A Celtic Wench

"This is it," I said, easing myself into a pool in the rocks, "the sun heats it."

"It feels cold to me," she squeaked, dipping her pretty toes.

"Well it's not bath water," I admitted, "but it's not bad."

I pulled my broad-brimmed bush hat over my eyes and lay back against a rounded granite boulder. "This is the life," I breathed lazily.

When I looked up again, Katrina was slipping out of her tartan miniskirt. She'd already removed a white cotton blouse and her bikini top bulged on an otherwise slender frame.

"I thought you weren't going to swim?" I mumbled weakly.

"I'll do whatever you do, baby. Besides, if I get cold, I've got you to cuddle up to."

"Not here!" I protested. "This is precisely the time of day some old geezer will be taking his dog for a walk, or something."

"We aren't going to do anything," she purred.

A chic response evaded me.

"Umm-m," she cooed, rolling half onto me. I caught a whiff of her heady perfume as she plunged her pleasing mouth onto mine. She then pushed away and a moment later emerged from the water sputtering. "You know, of course, that I fancy you," she said with a devilish smile, her Irish eyes sparkling.

I heard the screech of a seagull, and the tumble of the sea, and if I had said something it would surely have been that I also fancied her. But I had not made public yet my rift with Riana. And there was still the wishful hope that Leighan might yet come to find me as indispensable as her poetry.

Katrina fixed her bornite eyes on me, iridescent, a rainbow of opalescent hues in the reflected light of the pool. "It's too bad your girl friend doesn't stay-put in Holland. It just doesn't seem fa-air."

I closed my eyes in a way that pleaded for a change of subject.

But she ignored me. "Chris said she saw me chatting you up at Wynn's party, and referred to me as a 'coquette.' "

"A coquette," I laughed, "what's that?"

"A flirt," she smiled impishly. "I looked it up in the dictionary."

"Well you are," I laughed again.

But she was not slighted in the least. "I know," she sparked piquantly, "but I'll give it up when you marry me."

We walked back slowly along the beach, and ambled up the slope to Bevin's house. "I should have brought my board," I said. "It's been a perfect day for surfing. Nice curls, not dumping, not too big. Just the way I like it."

"Oh, I forgot to tell you," Katrina said excitedly, "I've bought a surf board. I tried it out last weekend, at Muizenberg."

"And how did you do?" I asked with interest. I had never thought of her as a surfer.

"Not bad," she giggled. "I got two or three good rides, lying down, using it like a boogie board."

"That's the way to start," I encouraged her. "We'll have to go out together sometime."

She sat me down with a view of the bay. "You rest here *Bwana,* and watch the sunset. I'll cook up something for Simba."

Bevin had asked for the favor. 'Stop by if you have a chance, please mate, and give the hound a beer and something hot to eat. He looked like a sick bloody jackal the last time I got home. And if you get a chance, check that the canary hasn't crapped himself up against the bars. And give Gold-finger a bite as well.' — Goldfinger was an aquarium fish.

"This place is like a zoo," Katrina remarked with a smile.

"You should have seen St. Mungo," I said, referring to Bevin's previous pad on Clifton beach. "The first time I stayed there, I had to use the neighbor's bath. His was full of crayfish, all still alive."

"I'm glad I was spared that," Katrina said with a pulled-up face, as she handed me a glass-bottomed pewter mug.

"Cheers," I toasted, raising the flask. "I hope you realize you're drinking the best beer in Africa. It's brewed in Swakopmund. Wynn tried it last week, and is having someone drive down with a whole truckload."

"I can't tell, honey," she smiled, "I've mixed it with ginger ale."

"Mixed it," I cried in disgust. "That's sacrilege, woman!"

She spat back giggling. "Just kidding," she said. "But you boys and your beer are an absolute pain."

She disappeared to the kitchen, and returned on a more serious note. "Chris says you've been talking again about leaving?"

"It's just talk," I said to distract her.

But she placed herself next to me and put a long finger on my nose. "You know, I often think how alike we are."

"How so?"

"The way I've spent my whole life running away. A Celtic wench and I don't even sound Irish anymore. And you following in my footsteps. And here I am, having escaped all that religious drama, but right back in another war zone. And you could be too." Concern darkened her expression.

"What do you mean?" I asked suspiciously.

"Vietnam," she said. "You think you're going to America, but that's where you'll likely end up, a possible short step, I'm afraid, to annihilation."

It was 1965. President Johnson had ordered the bombing of North Vietnam and things were looking grim. Was she right? Was I stepping off the edge of one dark world and into another? I creased my brow, but said nothing. I could not face even thinking about that.

Then she was talking again. "But it's funny how life goes on despite the turmoil. We do our little jobs as best we can, and make love and enjoy ourselves. And so do the so-called enemy, everyone, that is, who hasn't yet been hurt or killed. And very few people really want to fight. And we wouldn't have to either, if it wasn't for a handful of politicians who start the downward spiral, and then, with crafty propaganda, suck everyone into the chaos."

"So what do we do about it?" I asked.

"Most people grit their teeth and bear it, or even join in the fight, or are forced to. Others, like the two of us, just move on."

"And you, my dear, moved to the wrong place."

"Yes, but it'll be to the right place next time. I guarantee it."

"And where might that be?"

"Look at you," she laughed. "I believe it's the first time I've ever seen you interested in anything I plan to do, surfing and now this. Twice in a day. Remarkable!"

"Where to?" I asked again, smiling at her sassiness, but recognizing the truth of what she said.

"Oz," she announced. "Somewhere near the Great Barrier Reef — Port Douglas. Or a place like Byron Bay where I can walk along the cliffs and see dolphins and whales, and go surfing every day, and lie around on clean beaches."

"You didn't like the beer bottles and the chicken bones down there?"

"It's uncivilized, a total disgrace! You won't find that in Australia," she said. "The beaches there are sacred. Why don't you come with me, baby?"

"No, you're not driving, St Croix," I said emphatically.

"Why not, Watson? Bakker does."

"Riana's different."

"And why is that?"

"Well, for one thing," I explained indelicately, "she's an architect, and if she writes it off she can afford to replace it."

Katrina pouted and I relented. "You can take it as far as the main road."

"Thanks," she cried with childlike charisma, doing a little jig. "I've never driven a real sports car, one without a roof."

She slipped her shoes off, slid the stick through the gears, and screeched the Michelins round the hairpin bends that lifted us from the beach at Llandudno. We felt the wind — the lower beach area had been protected — the Cape Doctor, the purifying South-Easter that rids the city of pollution, and drapes a tablecloth of cloud over the mountain.

Katrina stopped at the junction with the mountain drive, and we changed places with a kiss. A waxing moon had shown a partial face. "How romantic," she whispered, looking up at the loom of one of the Twelve Apostles that towered ominously above us.

"Your place or mine?" I asked without thinking.

She cast me a quick-witted glance. "If we're going to argue about where we do it, baby, let's just forget it."

I let her see the smile in my eyes.

"Fish Hoek," she cheered, "and eat at the *Brass Bell*, my treat! And later," she said, "I'll be a naughty girl, if you'll let me."

"We'll see about that," I responded eagerly.

I depressed my foot and we vroomed off, down a curving ribbon of silver.

Part 23

A DIAMOND HEIST

Some Stones Carry Curses

On my next return from sea there was a letter from Riana. I carried it round for a day before opening it. And when I did, I saw art masked by art. A typical product of her creativity, it was laid out on mauve, scented paper. Her elegant script began, 'My darling Ian,' at the center of the page, and spiraled outwards, round and round, to the edge of a circle where it ended, 'All my love, Riana.' She had accepted an assignment to restore the historic section of a town in the Netherlands. Visit me, she wrote, I'm dreaming up some lovely stories to tell you. I've named one, *The Enchanted Diamond Gecko*.

I sighed as I thought again about that awful night of our break-off. My whole approach to her had lacked even a facade of subtlety. But had I acted quite as childishly as she had implied? Was I really what she had called me, 'a blackguard?' I was unquestionably worse! Because, though in my heart of hearts I now knew better, I still stuck stubbornly to the absurd notion that our feud had all been her fault. I am immature and inflexible, I thought now, and certainly not a gentleman, and I suppose I deserve to suffer.

And, on the subject of suffering, I had also recently seen Leighan. She still emanated irresistible charm, but I learned that she was soon to become engaged to a medical student. Should I try to stop that progression?

And Katrina had left me a wily package, a message with two beautifully faceted gems enfolded in it, my birthstone, and one I took for hers. I uncrumpled the wrapping and knew for sure:

> If you cherish a love that's true,
> In Aquarius well you'll do;
> Please carry these gems of warmest hue —
> your Topaz and my Garnet.

She reminded me that the power of the topaz was 'fidelity,' and that of the garnet, 'loyalty,' and ended by saying that she was in Ireland visiting her parents, but would soon be off to Australia and hoped that I would follow.

It was a lot to swallow. I decided to get away from the memories and glitz of the city, and recharge my urban soul by seeking the quiet comfort of the *bundu* — in this case, the distant desert.

Chris and I applied for leave, and set out to drive through South West Africa. Each of us had our own expectations of what we hoped the trip would offer. Chris wanted a better journalistic feel for the politics of the vast country. The South West African People's Organization, SWAPO, founded a few years previously by a group of politically aware Ovambo workers in Cape Town, had started its own freedom fight, terrorizing white townsfolk and farmers in the north. And SWAPO guerillas trained abroad had moved into the Caprivi Strip, north of the Okavango Delta, a corridor to the Rhodesias. The police had retaliated, and Chris hoped to orientate himself for the long battle ahead, one that threatened to spread north into Angola, one that Cuba's Castro would ultimately enter with Russian weapons and advisors.

My primary interest was the geology. In the arid climate of the Namib Desert so much of it would be visible in outcrop. And we both wanted to see, amongst a list of things, the Augrabies Falls, the fabulous desert wildlife of the Kalahari-Gemsbok Park, and the mysteries of Sossusvlei.

The Augrabies Falls are on the *Garib,* as the Bushmen say, the Great River. Europeans know it as the Orange River after the Prince of Orange. In times of flood *Aukoerebis,* The Place of Noise, has more than fifteen individual falls that thunder into the deep granite gorge below. We spent some time there, then moved on to the Kgalagadi, rich in game, circled back, and drove north, in incendiary heat, to a soaring pinnacle of rock known as *Mukurob,* the Finger of God. This geological tower, an hoodoo, reached like a gnarled finger to the sky, an erosional remnant millions of years in the making. Incredibly, it toppled a few years after we saw it.

The weather stayed good, hot, but cool at night, and we spent two beautiful days at Sossusvlei. There, in times of flow, the Tsauchab River disappears into the Great Sand Sea. "You'd never know it today," I said to Chris, "but the Tsauchab and other streams in the area once flushed diamonds to the ocean."

"Flushed them from where?" Chris asked incredulously.

"From eroded Kimberlitic pipes and depositional plains inland."

"And moved them to the ocean through these?" His creased forehead showed doubt, as he pointed to the mighty dunes, some more than a thousand feet in height, that lay between us and the ocean.

"No, no! There were no dunes here at that time. All this sand has invaded more recently, and cut off the lower courses of the rivers here."

"So if you only knew where, in old geological times, rivers like this had their outlets to the sea, you'd probably find diamonds there?"

"Precisely," I said, impressed by his quick grasp of the problem. "Since joining Marine Diamonds," I went on, "a pet project of mine has involved using air photographs to map the dunes and resurrect the old drainage network. Like you say, if we can pinpoint the prehistoric deltas, that's where we'll find more diamonds, at least in the concentrations we need to make Sammy's venture 'economically viable,' as Lester King would say."

"So Chamais Bay, where you're working now, is an old delta?"

"That's right. And you, my friend, are in the wrong profession. You should have been a geologist." My praise was genuine.

"Zog and I have been studying the diamondiferous sediments," I went on, "and we're finding these to be characteristic of river-outfall deposits. Our map shows them skewed to the north."

"The strong Benguela current, I suppose," Chris smiled.

"Yes," I agreed. "But even more to the point," I added, "the long-shore drift is also to the north. When we reach the ocean remind me to show you the swash-backwash effect along the beaches. You'll be surprised."

"And you'll hopefully explain it at the same time. But let me see if I have the rest of it right. If rivers moved in straight lines, you could simply look at your air photographs and see where a river like this, the Tsauchab, meets the dunes. Then you'd project its course some sixty miles to the coastline, and that's where you'd find more diamonds?"

"Right again," I smiled. "You'd expect to find the gems in a similar hydro-sedimentary environment to what we've mapped at Chamais. And that's exactly what we're going to look for at Sandwich Bay; see if the bay offers field evidence of being the ancient mouth of the truncated Tsondab River, and therefore another likely source of offshore diamonds. We'll be there on Tuesday."

"I can hardly wait," Chris laughed. "I'm really getting into all this geological *bedrieëry*." — trickery.

On our second day at the *Vlei* we ate early, admiring the changing colors of the dunes as the sun set. Then, exhausted, we stretched out on our sleeping bags and looked up at the stars. The night sky in the heart of the desert is unpolluted by artificial lighting, and I was reminded of being at sea on *Senta* and, more recently, on Oliver's *Jacqueline*. "How's Oliver doing?" I inquired as his name came to mind. "I haven't seen him for a while."

"He's been in England for the past few weeks."

"Well that explains it," I said, and would have left it at that.

But Chris pressed on. "The last time I saw him, he was acting very strangely."

"In what way?" I asked with more than casual interest.

"I couldn't put a finger on it," Chris said, "but it was behavior with an eerie similarity to what I'd expect if he'd got his diamond heist."

I lifted my head and strained for his expression in the starlight.

Chris let out a nervous laugh. "It's probably just my imagination at play," he chuckled. "Even if he had 'the goods,' as he always referred to them, he'd still be at least a year away from converting them to hard cash."

"What do you mean?" I asked, now highly inquisitive.

"I mean," Chris responded in the near-darkness, "that Oliver might be crazy, but he's not stupid! He's well aware of the fact that diamonds, when cut, increase in value by a factor of at least nine. He'd never have sold them in the rough. Besides, uncut diamonds are hard to move!"

"Back up a bit," I said. I raised a hand half-paralyzed by my inquisitiveness. "What put you onto this in the first place?"

"Oh, I suppose it was all that rattlebrained talk of his, 'Operation Trawler,' or whatever? At the time I told you it was fantasy."

"I remember it vividly," I said, feeling myself shaking.

"So, between that and the way he has been behaving lately, I've begun to have some second thoughts."

"Behaving how?"

"For one thing, he bought a new car. I heard him on the phone before he left, talking to his brother in England. 'Good God, Charles,' he said, 'you don't test-drive a Rolls Royce! And you certainly don't ask what it cost, not if you're British. Buy it, I tell you! I can afford it.' " Chris had been miming Oliver's voice and mannerisms. He now raised himself and, leaning on an elbow, turned to me with a spurt of laughter. " 'I'm afraid I just purchased a new toy,' Oliver said to me. You know how pompous he can be at times."

"Don't remind me," I chortled into the silvery light that was beginning to envelop us — the moon was rising behind a dune. "And good luck to him, if what you suspect is true. I'm just glad he left me out of it."

"Why?" Chris asked with what I sensed was a glint in his eye.

"Good God, Christopher," I said, also imitating Oliver, "I can't risk an eminent geological career over a mere handful of diamonds."

"Likely more than a mere handful," he responded with a bent grin.

"*I* know diamonds are amongst the oldest treasures of nature," Chris said, "and that they have unique properties that make them widely sought after by industry, including the ultra high-tech sector. But the simple feature that sells most of the diamonds that I am aware of, is their alluring brilliance. What causes that?"

"Their high refractive index," I said. "And, of course, the way they're cut; the facets translate light into the sparkling play of prismatic color that women love so much."

"And what about that sparkling play of De Beers advertising, 'A Diamond is Forever.' Obnoxiously far-fetched, don't you think?"

I laughed. "It's not as misleading as you may think."

Chris snorted. "Come on Watsie, give me a break."

"I'm serious," I said. "Perhaps already more than a billion years old, and scoring a perfect 10 on the Mohs' scale of hardness, is as close to 'forever' as most people would want. Now you tell me something that I really want to know," I goaded him facetiously. "What does an English major think of diamonds?"

"That would be opening a Pandora's box," Chris smiled. "My dissertation was on diamonds."

"I know. Leighan said it was brilliant. I must read it some time."

"You'll think it total trash," he laughed. "It's about diamonds being brandished as symbols of romantic mystery, everlasting love, and royal power. Do you know, for example, that for the magic of a diamond to work, the gem must be freely given? Or that the chilling truth is that some stones carry curses?"

I almost doubled up.

"I warned you," he smiled.

I lay awake on the sand that night thinking about Oliver and all that he might have been up to, and about the theft and misrepresentation of diamonds in general.

Oliver's initiative, if the suspicions that Chris was toying with were correct, was an example of illegal activity somewhere mid-scale, but there is diamond fraud to be found at every level. A friend of mine, James, a gemologist, described what he referred to as a 'piggyback' diamond assemblage, a small swindle that the average person can readily identify with. It involved two diamonds, cut, superimposed, and mounted in a way that let it be sold as a single 7.78-carat stone of some elevated value — size and price follow an exponential relationship.

This specialist in gems went on to say that the individual components were not glued, but rather held in place by the mounting prongs of the ring.

I questioned him further on this and he explained that a paste would have reduced the reflective brilliance of the aggregation. "The setting was cleverly constructed with platinum filigree that hid the join," he spelled out.

He received the pear-shaped diamond ring from a client for a minor repair to the mounting. "But I'm so interested in diamonds," he said, "that I invariably spend more time than I can possibly charge for. For example, I always examine diamonds under my microscope."

"I have the same respect," I assured him. "I know how hard they are to find."

"Anyway, in this case my effort paid off, at least for my customer," he said. "He was able to return the ring to the jeweler he had purchased it from, and get a refund."

"And was he or she, the jeweler, the one who initiated the fraud," I asked.

"Probably not," he shrugged.

"So nobody takes a hit for it?" I was fired up now.

But James quietly soothed my indignation. "The diamond industry is a closely-knit group," he said, "a little like the Mafia when it comes to policing itself. Its people would take a pretty dim view of something like this that casts a shadow over their integrity. I believe they'd follow-up on it!"

I wondered what lay in store for Oliver.

*F*rom Sossusvlei we continued north. Sandwich Bay, as it happened, was disappointing; the blanket of sand there was too thick to assess the location's status as an old delta. So we moved on. At Terrace Bay I mapped the elevations of raised diamond-yielding beaches that had once been mined there, while Chris visited a dry river bed an old prospector led him to, to see a 'weird plant' as he, the diamond digger, had referred to it. "It turned out to be the famous *Welwitschia mirabilis*," Chris said, "a living fossil" — some plants are more than 2,000 years old — "found only in the Namib." He went on slowly, "This succulent, in reality a dwarf tree, has deep tap roots but, like other plants and animals in the coastal zone, derives most of its moisture from the sea mists that condense at night on its large curled leaves."

"How close did you get to it?" I asked.

"I was right on top of it," he exclaimed in a buoyant tone. "It was a miniature world all of its own, crowded with ants and other small life. Just wait till you see the photographs!"

I had not seen him that energized about plant life since we had spotted Tsamma melons that the Bushmen and the gemsbok survive on in times of protracted drought.

Anglo & De Beers

*T*he serious side of the research Chris had done, addressed the international diamond business. And one night, as we sat hunched over a bar counter in Swakopmund, I got him talking about the De Beers diamond syndicate, its ubiquitous struggle to preserve a marketing monopoly, and how it punished countries that tried to bypass the cartel.

"How on earth do they do it?" I asked with interest.

"In any number of ways," he replied. "A much favored method is to flood the market with diamonds in the offender's production size-range, say small stones, and then imply by advertising that no one but an absolute peasant would purchase a gem of less than half a carat."

"And when the culprit, Russia or whomever, sees the light?"

Chris raised his hands. "They simply back off and reverse their former publicity campaign, 'An anniversary ring of small stones that says you'd marry her all over again.'"

"Amazing!" I cried. "But it must cost them plenty in advertising."

"Many millions each year," Chris smiled, "and most of it appealing to the vanity of women. And speaking of women, and Russia," he added, "did you know that it was a female geologist who made the first big diamond discovery in the Soviet Union?"

"Really," I exclaimed. "Someone like Bakker would just love to have a fact like that at her fingertips."

"You can tell her," Chris volunteered. "I have her name jotted down somewhere in my office, Larissa someone-or-other. She made the find in 1954, in the wilds of Siberia. Riana will get a kick out of the story. She's big on the accomplishments of females."

"And on anything to do with the wisdom of nature," I added.

Chris showed vigorous agreement. "She's the only person I know," he said, "who comes out of a wildlife park where she's seen practically every-thing, and raves on about *inkuba-bulongo,* the flightless dung beetle."

I reached for her half-forgotten comments. "Remind me again."

"Oh, how the female beetle collects elephant poop, rolls it into a ball, and lays her egg in it; how the larva then feeds on the dung ball. 'That's interesting as hell,' I said to her. 'It's more than interesting, Christopher,' she scolded me. 'It's a lesson in recycling!'"

"Yes, yes, I remember now. How much we waste, the curse of our throw-away culture. True enough. But dung beetles?" I laughed out loud. "Riana would be more interested in the 'Little Five,' if there was such a thing, than in the 'Big Five.'"

But although I had brought it up, I was eager to drop the topic of Riana and return to our talk of diamonds. "What do you know, Chris," I probed, "about the tie between De Beers and Anglo?" I had asked Zog the same question, but our conversation, at the time, had been interrupted.

"I take it that you know about the origin of De Beers, and that An-glo American was set up nearly forty years later by old man Oppenheimer to take care of mining on the Far East Rand. Well, whereas Rhodes got his start with Rothschild support, most of the money for Anglo American came di-rectly from the States, people like J.P. Morgan, William B. Thompson, foun-der of the Newmont Mining Corporation, and Herbert Hoover, a mining engineer before he became America's 31st President. His wife, by the way, was a geologist he met at Stanford University."

"Hoover a mining man?" I exclaimed. "Not a lawyer?"

"No, a nice change," Chris said. "And his involvement in mining was more than superficial. Before going to university he worked under-ground, in Nevada, for less than two dollars a day. And then he moved on to the Kalgoorlie gold mines in Western Australia where, I imagine, he proba-bly wasn't paid much more. Tough guy, a self-made man, I admire him."

"Incredible! I must read up on him. But getting back to Anglo, you imply that gold was the impetus for setting it up, not diamonds?"

"Yes," he confirmed, "gold, and strategic minerals like platinum. But Sir Ernest's first love was always diamonds. He established CDM," Chris said, referring to Consolidated Diamond Mines, "and nailed most of the mines in South West Africa when South Africa invaded the country in World War I." — information I had already gathered from Zog. "So in 1929," Chris went on, "when Sir Ernest became chairman of the board of De Beers, he was well on the way to having control of everything."

"And Harry?" I prompted, wanting to know more about the man who currently controlled the Oppenheimer fortune. I knew that Chris had met him.

"Harry, of course, inherited it all from his old man."

"Yes, I know that," I said. "But what's he like, as a man?"

"He's an excellent chap," Chris replied, "a benevolent tycoon, another Oxford man, like Rhodes, and a war veteran. And when it comes to macroeconomics and finance, he's as sharp as they come."

He lowered his voice. 'The walls have ears,' he had cautioned me at the start of our conversation. "I'd like to have seen him as prime minister," Chris whispered now. He turned and looked over his shoulder. "If Harry had been persuaded to take the helm," he continued, "we'd be in a country with a future, instead of the bloody mess we're in today."

"Good businessmen aren't always good politicians," I remarked.

"True, but Harry was a good one. He proved himself as a Member of Parliament. But, of course, when Sir Ernest died he had to move out of politics and attend to the business. There was no one else to see to it."

"Too bad," I expressed in a sympathetic tone.

"Yes," Chris grieved, letting out a breath and reaching for his wine glass. "But anyway, to answer your question, today Anglo American and De Beers are more or less one-and-the-same outfit, at least as far as I can gather. It's a split only of convenience, tax shelters, loopholes in the law. And although the Oppenheimer Empire is now truly that, an empire, it still functions more like a family business than a vast multinational network, everything done on a handshake."

"You make it sound so casual," I said. "Why is it that whenever there's any serious talk about the big picture of how Harry runs things, I always get the impression of a cocoon of tight-lipped secrecy?"

"You're naïve, Watsie," Chris smiled indulgently, "a typical scientific wonk. What if I said that whichever way you cut it, De Beers is a monopoly and therefore illegal in the States? But, and here's the kicker, New York is the largest distributor of diamonds in the world, and Americans are their most ardent consumers? Do you see the need for some confidentiality?"

"I suppose," I admitted, "when you put it like that."

He picked up on my expression and laughed. "Don't worry," he assured me, "it's no cloak-and-dagger operation. It's big business and it's conducted at the highest level, and with discretion. No one in the States is going to think badly of you because you worked in an industry that is controlled by De Beers. In fact, 'quite the contrary, old chap,' as Oliver would say."

Rotten to the Core

Before leaving Swakopmund we visited the library, then took a swim and chatted to some good-looking local girls with German accents. We also unpacked our automatics, which we wanted handy as we headed closer to Ovambo areas with SWAPO trouble.

But other than a short delay caused by an elephant herd, our journey proceeded without incident, and we were happy to secure rooms at Namutoni, on the eastern end of Etosha Pan, an old *Beau Geste*-type fort constructed at the turn of the century — it was taken by the Ovambos in 1904, but quickly recaptured by the Germans; it served as a police post into the 1950s. There were hot showers there, a luxury I had not expected, and the ravenous smell of wild game cooking.

"What do you think of the Ovambos?" Chris asked over dinner — we had been given our own table in a quiet corner.

"I don't know much about them," I admitted. "De Beers, of course, employ them on the mines, and we have a few around our survey camps, but they're hard to get to know. All I can really tell you is that they're good workers if you leave them alone. But they definitely resent taking orders from white men, same as the Himba." To make my point I related an incident of a recent visit to Diamond Area 1, where, in the company of some senior De Beers officials, I had stopped to observe a work gang sweeping an exposed bedrock terrace for residual diamond pick-ups, the final step in the mining process. "Now you'd expect that with our arrival," I suggested, "they'd have worked harder to impress us."

"That's what I'd think," Chris acknowledged.

"But they did just the opposite." I shook my head and smiled. "They took a break. They sat for as long as we were there."

"Doing nothing?"

"Nothing," I confirmed. "Worse than nothing. Occasionally one of them would point to someone in our group, and they'd all laugh."

"Talk about being independent."

"Yes," I agreed. "As we pulled away I noticed them going back to work. 'That's the slowest part of our operation,' the De Beers chap complained as we drove off. 'Why don't you replace them with some sort of industrial vacuum cleaner, or something?' I asked. 'We've tried,' he said, 'and we find there's nothing more efficient than an Ovambo and his broom. We eventually sat down with them,' he continued, 'and hammered out a bonus system, and now everybody's happy.' "

"From what I understand most SWAPO members are Ovambos," Chris said. "I just hope our police take a lesson from De Beers."

Our kudu steaks arrived and my mouth began to water. I was famished. We ate in silence for a while, until, my immediate appetite appeased, I picked up again on our conversation. "Talking of police," I said, "I've been meaning to ask you; what do you think of our police?"

Chris checked my expression to see if I was serious, and satisfied that I was, he began speaking in his usual slow way. "They're a mixed bunch. Those up here, and in places like Rhodesia, are really good, more like soldiers than police. They belong to anti-terrorist, counter-insurgent units, whatever you'd like to call them. They're well trained, disciplined, and dedicated. And you've got to understand it's a tough job, defending borders, protecting farmers, patrolling on some pretty hair-raising fronts. They're up against insurgents trained in China and Russia, with decent weapons, AK-47s, grenades, land mines, and so forth."

"So to them it's just a war?"

"Yes, a guerrilla war if you like, but yes, a war. Most of the men in the field don't know much about the African struggle, the freedom fight. To them it's all about communist-inspired terrorists, a fight, at its roots, against Moscow and Peking. That's what they're told."

"And what do you think?" I asked.

"It's a bit of both," he said. "It's hard to draw the line. But I'll tell you one thing. Some of these so-called freedom fighters are completely out of hand, hacking women and children to death with *pangas,* and killing their own people. They're criminals and somebody's got to put a stop to them."

"And what about the reports we hear, of torture in the jails?"

"The prison crowd and some of the special ops," he spat, "I've got no time for those bastards, Gestapo types, goon squads. They're giving the whole country a bad name. They ought to be nailed!"

"So why haven't they been?"

"Ask the politicians that, the people at the top, our uncompromising white-supremacist leaders. They're the ones who establish policy."

"And the army?" I pried further.

His expression changed. "Mainly top notch," he said with emphasis in his voice. "And there are some smart people coming up through the ranks, fellows close to our age, Meiring, a physicist, and Chris Thirion, a geographer who grew up right here in South West Africa."

"So what you're saying is that we're generally in good hands?"

"I wouldn't go that far," he said. "I know zilch about covert operations, and like I say, the political end of it is rotten to the core!"

Part 24

SPANK THE HUN

Sinking of the Emerson K

We were in the news again: *"24 ESCAPE AS TUG HEELS OVER."*

She capsized slowly enabling us to scramble, like rats, onto her hull, and then make our way astern to where the men of the harbor tug *T.S. McEwen* hauled us inboard.

"What I can't understand," Sammy bawled to whoever in his office section was listening, "is how any goddamned guys can sink a goddamned ship in the goddamned dry dock."

*"C*aw blimey, mate, I'm glad that's over."

"Me too," said the captain, still looking gaunt.

We had tied up the day before in the Duncan Dock, the newer section of the Cape Town harbor. Both the old man and the chief had been under considerable pressure since the accident. In transshipping supplies for the mining rigs in rough weather, one of the Corporation's steel tenders had been lifted on a freak swell and slammed down on the *Emerson K,* tearing a dangerous gash in her side. On the captain's orders we had stuffed blankets into the split to stem sporadic inflow. Then, by pumping our portside fuel to the starboard tanks, the chief had induced a sufficient list on the vessel to cut away sections of the ripped plates, and weld a patch onto the damaged high side of her hull.

We had sailed and arrived home without further mishap. Relieved to be on *terra firma,* we had disappeared to the *Den.* But on returning to the ship at dawn, the watch was asleep, the pumps were not running, and the ship was well down on her marks.

When the captain arrived from home a little later, he called in the harbor tugs to help us bridge the half-mile gap from the new dock to the old, no big issue, or so we thought. And we were almost there, at the very entrance of the Robinson Dry Dock, when one of the tugboats nudged our Achilles' heel, the chief's quickly-welded patch. It gave way and we began to take on water at an alarming rate.

The car screeched to a stop and two men leapt from half-open doors. The shorter one was immediately lost in the crowd, but their weaving path could be followed by the progress of a white Stetson worn by the taller man. They elbowed their way through half-caste fishermen in old felt hats, their thread-

bare clothes blooded and splotched with slime and scales, burly black stevedores in overalls and knitted ski caps, and a few bare-headed white men. By
the time they reached a vantage point, the small man was panting profusely,
and sweating despite the crisp morning air. The throng made room for the
conspicuous arrivals. A barefooted boy, dressed in shorts and what appeared
to be the discarded jacket of a full-grown man, nudged the Texan and extended a dirty finger in the direction of the *Emerson K, "Die skip sink,*
maaster." That ship is sinking, master.

Sammy fixed a somber eye on the bearer of this unwelcome news
and the boy slunk back into the crowd.

An explosive whoosh of quenching steam brought a temporary lull
to the wharf, and Sammy took advantage of it. "We need some lines on
her," he screeched. "Fifty bucks for everyone who helps."

He pulled a roll from his pocket and began peeling off banknotes
that he handed to the men around him. "Find me some monkey fists," he
shouted with authority. "And you," he called to a big stevedore wearing a
tattered sweater with our corporation letters, 'MDC,' embroidered onto it,
"do you work for Marine Diamond?"

"No, *Baas.*"

"Well you do now! You're hired! Get me some volunteers to swim
over to the boat. A big bonus for anyone who attaches a line."

"Fifty bucks, sir?" the man asked, tearing off his clothes.

"A hundred and fifty, if you get a line aboard."

In short order the ship looked like a wasp caught in a spider's web.
Wynn's Stetson was bumped off and trampled on. And it was not long before his suit was torn, his knuckles skinned, and his hands greasy. The veins
in his neck bulged as he uttered a loud, "He-e-ave!"

A thunderous, "Ho-o-o!" echoed from the work gang.

Wynn felt his back wrench, and winced. "Too durned long in the
office," he swore. He then took the strain again like a desperado.

Having escaped from the sinking ship, we had joined the gathering
of helpers on the wharf. And one of our big seaman now fought his way
through the crowd, snorting and hissing curses as he labored backwards,
dragging a big steel block. *"Bliksem!"* he swore as he backed into Sammy. He
reeled about, *"Jou don..."* In the sickly instant that he recognized his victim,
he managed to catch his words, but not his savage elbow.

Sammy doubled up.

Blood drained from the sailor's face. "I'm sorry Master Sammy,
Master Collins, I mean Mr. Collins, sah!"

"Who're you?" Sammy rasped.

"Bos'n, sah. Hendrik, sah. Boatswain on the *Emerson K,* sah."

"Carry on," Sammy croaked weakly. Then, as his voice regained something of its usual ring, he repeated with a Gulf-state boom, "Carry on! You're doing a great job, Bos'n! You're kicking butt just like a Texan!"

It took eight days of round-the-clock labor to salvage the ship. Every available company person was on the waterfront, and this translated into a stint of comradeship and good humor. I had not seen much of Zog since we had begun alternating shifts on the *Emerson K,* and it was bracing to be back in his good company. And it was even more enlivening when Bevin, on his break from the rigs, joined us a day or two later.

"I saw Katinka and she's getting fat," one of the bargemen remarked to Bevin, teasing him about his current 'squeeze,' as he called her.

"She's not fat, mate," Bevin spat. "She's just too lazy to shit."

I related his remark to a gathering at the *Navigator's Den* that evening, but changed the names to protect Katinka's identity. But she complained all the same. "That's typical of the sort of comment I'd expect from Bevin," she whined. "I just hate to think what he says about me."

*C*olin J. Fitzsimons, our cockney engineer, was also at the *Den* with a story. "I got a story, mates."

Zog raised a hand. "Fitz has a story."

Fitz waited for some semblance of quiet. "I'm down at t' docks, see," he said, "wandering round like a lost fart in a bottle."

"And why's that, Fitz?"

"Why, 'cause I don't 'ave an proper ship t' work on, do I mate?"

"What about the *Emerson K?* Plenty of work on her."

"We're not allowed t' touch 'er, mate, not 'til our man from Lloyd's 'as seen 'er."

"And who's our man from Lloyd's?"

"Ah, that's my story, matey," he said. "See, I get this message from Sammy: ' 'Ightail it up t' my office,' 'e says. 'You need to be briefed by my lawyer.' 'I'm in an overall,' I try t' explain. 'An overall? What's that?' 'e asks. 'A boiler suit,' I tell him. 'Do you want me t' change?' 'Goddamnit, no!' 'e 'ollers. 'Just get your skinny li'l ass up 'ere in an 'urry. We've got some guy from Lloyd's of London flying in tomorrow.' "

"So what's your story, Fitz?"

"I'm getting t' it, young fella, keep your 'at on." He glared at Zog. "I get to t' office, see, and t' bird tells me 'e's waiting for me in t' conference room. In I go, and there's all sorts o' seats; but do you think 'e offers me one? Not on your life, mate. 'Don't touch anything,' 'e says, 'you'll 'ave grease on it.' Then it's all Oxford accent and Eton superiority; 'e's a Limey see, like me, only 'e's from t' upper classes."

"The story, Fitz!"

"I'm getting t' it, mate. I'm getting t' it. 'Well, Fitzsimons,' Sammy's man says t' me, 'we seem to have landed ourselves in a spot o'...er trouble, t' night o' t' ...er accident.' 'What's your point?' I asks 'im. 'When you're with our man from Lloyd's,' 'e says, ' 'e'll want t' know what's what. You mite like t' mention your navy days,' says 'e. 'I beg your pardon?' says I, all polite-like. 'Your war record, man,' 'e blurts, as if it's 'urting 'im t' say it. 'Tell 'im something o' your...er, distinguished service in t' navy.' Now, that's a fine how-do-you-do, thinks I. But I don't say it, see."

Fitz paused and gave us a taunting look of mischief — one he might well have given Sammy's lawyer. " 'Well t' wye I sees it, governor,' I let 'im know. 'If I says t' right fings, mate, mite be worf a bit o' money t' you. Mite be worf somefing t' me as well.'

"You should 'ave seen 'is face, mate. It was an angry color. Green, I'd say, or near enough; 'e couldn't even speak. But then 'e's up and on again, all in an 'uff. 'Why my good man,' 'e stammers, 'that's what's commonly known as bribery and corruption.'

" 'Don't care what you calls it, mate,' says I. 'So long as you know 'ow it works!' "

Fitz slapped the table. And while we laughed heartily, he almost choked on his drink. " 'e was green again, mate. Green, I tell you." Tears of delight ran down Fitz's cheeks. "Green as a ruddy Irish navvy on St. Patty's Day."

In the end the *Emerson K* was determined to be too expensive to refit. Sammy decided to cut his losses and invest in a new prospecting vessel. He took what he could get from Lloyd's, and lodged a claim against the South African Railways and Harbours for the outstanding value, as he saw it, of the old ship, and for the time he had spent in removing her from the dry dock. And Fitz must have got his bribe, Bevin said. "I was at his flat the other night, and he offered me a Scotch. 'T' Sammy's good health,' he toasted. That's all he would say. But there were two boxes of Chivas Regal in the corner of his lounge."

A Blizzard of Misinformation

It took almost a month for Wynn's contact in Zürich to trace Heinrich Stiegler to a company in Germany, and bridge the gap between it and the *Deutsche Diamanten-Gesellschaft,* the original diamond mining syndicate in old *Kolonial Deutsch-Südwestafrika.* Stiegler, Wynn's agent revealed, was an imposter. Worse than that, he was an industrial spy.

The Texan passed the news on to me.

"The bastard," I swore. But the disclosure, in a way, was a relief, and I felt a brief rush of satisfaction at hearing it. I had set the ball in motion by expressing my suspicions about Stiegler's technical credentials. Since then, however, I had sweated, wondering if I had set him off on a wild mongoose chase.

Wynn handed me a telex. "Take a look before I shred it."

I reached for it with an unsteady hand. The communication — stamped 'FOR YOUR EYES ONLY' — was a bombshell. In the decade that followed the discovery of diamonds at *Kolmanskuppe*, near *Lüderitzbucht*, more than five million carats had been mined in the *Sperrgebiet*. However, with the loss of the German colony, Wynn's attaché noted, Stiegler's company had reverted to its old business of cutting and retailing diamonds in Europe. But it had not, apparently, forgotten its lucrative former holdings in Africa. Heinrich Stiegler, the detective suggested, was a player in an elaborate plot to reclaim these. And the man, she added, was neither Swiss, nor an engineer. He was German and a lawyer. And nothing could be found to support the title he claimed of 'Doctor-Professor.'

"Does that tell you the story?" Wynn asked.

"Yes," I responded, although it didn't. There were a million things about 'the story' that I still wanted to know.

"Good," Wynn said.

"I suppose he had a reason for making his move now," I advanced. I was groping in the dark. I knew there was something bigger in the works, but I was not at all sure what. And I was not about to ask, at least directly.

"You mean him doing it at this point in time?"

"Yes."

Wynn's face creased in an askance grin, but he said nothing.

"And how much damage did he cause?" I asked, still probing.

Wynn had bent down to pick a pen up from the floor, and now glanced at me over his shoulder. "Nothing that can't be undone," he replied casually. "Fortunately," the Texan smirked, "the Germans lost the momentum of their early initiative by bickering over details." His intonation retained its customary right-stuff edge, but I could sense his pleasure as he delivered his exposé, as confusing as it was to me.

But I did not let on. "So you received the information in time?" I said, continuing to prod.

"Yeah," he smiled. "Thanks to you." He shook his head. "It's all so obvious to me now," he said. "I can't believe I didn't see it from the start."

I was wondering what next to say — by now I was exasperated — when Wynn suddenly leaned forward, and lowered his voice. "Let me tell you something in the strictest confidence," he whispered. "We're negotiating the sale of our concession, and Stiegler's cartel is in the loop for a slice of it. With what we've just learned from our Swiss policewoman, we suspect that they retained information on undisclosed reserves, and see the offshore concession as a way of getting back into their old mining game."

"And could they do it?" I asked in a flustered voice. I was astounded by his revelation, not so much the news about Stiegler's cartel, but the sale of our concession. I'd had no inkling of it.

"It's a moot point now," Wynn replied. "But at the start, before all this blew up, Sammy thought they had a good shot at it. Their top men are well-connected, *diamantaires,* all former German and Russian Jews. That's where a big power base lay in diamonds, and it's still a force to be reckoned with."

"But it has no clout in this part of the world, surely," I said. "It's been Rhodes and the Oppenheimers here, British and Christian."

"Yes, but both are relatively recent phenomena," he smiled. "We're talking old connections, very old bonds, where blood ran thicker than water. And go back just one generation on the Oppenheimers, you'll find that Sir Ernest's father was a Jewish merchant in Hamburg, home to some of the world's most prestigious diamond brokers. Sammy tells me that Jewish guilds in Europe have been in the trade for at least five centuries."

"Five hundred years," I exclaimed. "Are you serious?" But I was just going through the motions. For despite my recent preoccupation with diamond history, this information about the Oppenheimers had fallen on me with only moderate impact. My personal absorption at this point lay in knowing what fate awaited my adversary. "And Stiegler?" I inquired, still stinging from the part he had played in contributing to my split from Riana. "Do you expose him and have him prosecuted?"

Wynn focused on me through narrowed eyes. "You'd think we would."

"But no?" I questioned, raising my hands in disgust.

Wynn shrugged.

"So what do you do?" I demanded.

He smiled shrewdly. "We stall on the sale of the concession, and we start feeding him a blizzard of misinformation." He paused, then went on in a tone that held an edge of unmistakable delight. "It's been a good few years since we did it last, and it's time again to spank the Hun!"

Part 25

DE BEERS

Rockeater

*E*vents took off and moved at the speed of light. Bevin married Renée, 'the Bat.' She worked with us, and we all loved her, Pop in particular. He knew her dad, a lighthouse keeper, and I fancy that he regarded Renée as a sort of Grace Darling — our distant family heroine from Longstone Light, the young lady I had told Scotty about.

And the next thing I knew I was invited to an interview with the Anglo American Corporation of South Africa. It was suggested that I might be interested in joining their mineral exploration division. Marine Diamonds had been taken over, I was told, and was now a wholly-owned subsidiary of De Beers.

Our letterhead, I soon noticed, had been stamped, and now clearly showed H.F. Oppenheimer as Chairman of the Board. S.V. Collins (U.S.A.) was still listed as a Director, but he no longer held the high spot. Wynn Harvey, I learned, would retain his position in a consulting capacity. But our top three geologists would receive golden handshakes and be phased out in a timeframe yet to be decided. The latter news was a blow to me, and I was further saddened to learn that Zog had decided to move on. But he did not get away easily. Like Cookie's attempts to hold me in Miami, we kept him around with a series of engagements.

By contrast, Stiegler's disappearance was abrupt. One day he was there — in what appeared to be normal circumstances — and on the next he was gone. And a day later, in a rare display of one-upmanship, Wynn smiled at me across his desk. " 'Stupid Americans,' the goddamned kraut referred to us in one of his dispatches. Well I can tell you, buddy, we'll show him who's stupid!"

I leaned forward, keen-eyed and attentive. I desperately wanted to hear more. But Wynn said that he was sworn to secrecy.

*T*here was some time to kill while I waited for my formal interview with Anglo. Katrina had just left for Australia, surfboard and all, and to keep myself from brooding I decided to do something for my academic soul, some geological mapping. I selected a scenic coastal section that Charles Darwin had observed from the survey ship *Beagle* in 1836. The geology was marked by an unconformable contact that separated the underlying Cape Peninsula Granite of Namibian age, from a thick overlying sedimentary sequence the deposition of which had begun some 500 million years ago. It was an exciting project for me. It also had a structural-geologic aspect in that the entire sequence was laced by a pattern of high-angle faults that dated to the break-up of Gondwanaland, and the split of Africa from the Americas.

I had good access to the section from Chapman's Peak drive, a narrow winding byway ingeniously hewn into the steep mountain face. From the road I could scale the cliffs above, or traverse down to the ocean below me. But the roadway was so cramped and stopping so difficult, that I planned from the start to bicycle there each day from Fish Hoek. It was no more than a forty-minute ride.

However, what I hadn't counted on was a troupe of baboons that roamed that section of the mountain. On my second day out, a big, menacing male, ignoring my shouts and a raised arm clutching my geological hammer, closed in on me and drove me from my position; then grabbing my backpack he loped off with it. He had no doubt been attracted by the smell of food. Fortunately I had my precious Stanley compass — the British equivalent of an American Brunton — in a leather pouch on my belt.

I quickly retreated to where I had hidden my bicycle, and was relieved to see that it had not been tampered with. I had visions of the apes being attracted by its bright red color or shining alloy, and making off with it, or hurling it over the cliff. I tied it down after that and carried my automatic, and although I thought I appeared less threatening with a hand on my holster — than I had waving my geological pick — these intimidating primates kept their distance. 'Perhaps they didn't like your food,' Katrina commented in one of her letters.

I attended my interview in a new suit that Pop's Malay tailor cut for me, and was ready to jump on Anglo's offer of employment. By this time Chris had convinced me that if one worked in diamonds, De Beers was the colossus and, like some medieval guild, was the magic name to have on one's résumé.

"What do you think you're worth?" an executive asked me.

"Whatever you think is fair," I replied. "Salary is not the issue. I'm just happy to have the chance to work for you."

The men around the table smiled, and one of them mentioned a number that was considerably beyond my expectations. I stood up, on impulse, and shook their hands, and they promptly dispatched me to an in-house conference in Johannesburg, to learn more about their organization and, as it turned out, what they were doing in the fascinating world of gold.

It was a time of great stimulation for me, a quantum jump from what I had learned as a student in *eGoli*. I was now exposed to the thinking behind the project. I saw how it could take years and many millions of dollars just to open a new mine, before the first ounce of gold was processed. And I observed in more sophisticated terms the enigmatic contrast that characterizes deep mining in South Africa, the ultra-sophisticated technology that goes into developing the mine and, as I had seen, the hard manual labor that subsequently wins the gold.

I reveled in the fine treatment that my new employers lavished on me. And what added still further to my pleasure was Pop's favorable reaction to my progress. "I'm proud of you, Son," he beamed in delight, "you're working for a first-class outfit!" But more than its reputation for being one of the leading companies in the world in my field, I fancied that he was most impressed by the fact that Harry Oppenheimer had taken a stand against *apartheid.* "He's a good man, just like his father," Pop said. "Make sure you shake his hand and tell him so, when you meet him."

My first Anglo work assignment, after what had seemed like an extended working vacation, was to a sophisticated new prospecting vessel, *Rockeater.* For a young geologist with my interests, operating a ship like that and using the results to direct mining operations, was like a dream come true. I would willingly have done it for no pay at all.

"Welcome aboard," said Des O'Shea. Like Zog on the *Emerson K,* Des broke me in. I was impressed not only by his knowledge of the ship, but also by his familiarity with the entire Anglo-De Beers establishment. He was clearly poised to climb the corporate ladder, and I could not have wished for a better partner.

My training commenced with the finer points of the ship. "For our needs, this is the Rolls Royce of rigs," Des said with zeal, and I soon saw that he was right. By contrast with the *Emerson K,* which, in hindsight, had been little more than a jury-rigged dredge, *Rockeater* was a proper drill ship, with a derrick over a center-well built into the hull. Sampling twenty feet of sediment, down to bedrock, could be done in less than a third of the time I was used to. And the metallurgical process was a replica of that used on the rigs, complete with heavy-media separation.

It was also apparent that a similar commitment to the detail that had gone into her design at Scripps, had been extended to appointing the ship's company. And, as with Des, I hit it off immediately with her master, Captain C.J. Harris. He had spent a lifetime at sea, and a segment of his career, I soon learned, had been spent in the Seaward Defence Force — before it became the South African Navy.

The discipline of the navy showed in the way CJ did things, his dedication to safety for example. My first lifeboat drill was a rude awakening. Past experience had been limited to donning a lifejacket, and then half-heartedly mustering at a deck station for a mock roll call. But CJ had us lower the boats in stormy weather, and row.

"Are you sure the Old Man's not drunk," I complained to Courtney, the first officer, as we pulled on the oars, waiting to be called in.

"You ought to see fire drill," Courtney smiled crookedly. "The only thing we haven't done yet," he said, rolling his eyes, "is set the confounded ship alight. And I'm expecting that any day."

I acknowledged his wit. But I soon learned that he had probably not been exaggerating to the degree I had at first surmised. For on about the third tour of duty on my new ship, while we were on station prospecting, CJ unexpectedly reached for the mining-area radio. "*One-Eleven, Rockeater.*"

"Yes *Rockeater.*"

"This is Captain Harris. Tell your marine and mining supers that there's a fire drill, starting now, at 13:23. One of your generators is alight and we're coming alongside to assist you."

"Yes Captain. I'll relay your message, sir. *One-Eleven* out."

We stopped drilling without completing our hole, lifted our spread as fast as we could, and under CJ's stopwatch bore down on the barge with fire hoses at the ready. When we were within range, he called for the pumps.

One-Eleven was completely taken by surprise, and we soon had bargemen, as Courtney said, "bum-sliding around the decks."

"Hey! Ease up there, men," CJ yelled over his megaphone. "This is not a war, for Pete's sake. It's a fire drill! Keep those hoses trained on Number-2 generator!"

But he laughed about it later in the mess. "That will teach those landlubbers a bit of seamanship. What do you say, Ian-boy?"

"I agree," I replied. "But that lifeboat drill the other night, in rough weather...a bit dangerous, don't you think?"

"Well, ships don't sink in good weather, my boy." His comment was accompanied by a look that let me know that that part of our conversation was over.

I soon observed that CJ spent most of his free time writing, and when I got to know him better I commented on it.

"I'm writing a book," he revealed.

"What about?" I asked.

He elaborated. "The history of the mailships between Britain and South Africa, the Union-Castle Line. I once worked for the Clan Line that merged with them, and I got interested in the exciting legends and fluctuating fortunes of the UC Steamship Company. "

"Is there enough to write about," I asked, "I mean sufficient to fill a book?"

"More than enough, the seamen, the ships, the passengers, the ports of call around Africa, the intrigue since 1857. You'd better believe there's enough to write about, too much in fact."

"Give me a for-instance," I encouraged him, "something you're writing about right now."

"As you are no doubt familiar with," he began, "the ships carried both passengers and cargo, but the basis of the service was the mail contract." He sipped his tea. "And its timely delivery," he went on, "was a matter of high priority for the master mariners of the fleet."

I enlarged my eyes to indicate my interest.

"On one occasion a mailship captain, outward bound from Southampton, found himself in the middle of a Royal Navy exercise, steel muscle about to repel attacking torpedo boats. He was unaware of it until he received a desperate message from the flag officer, saying that the passage of his ship was impeding the business of His Majesty's fleet. In a flash the old man dictated a reply. 'And you, sir, are impeding the passage of His Majesty's mails.' "

"That's good," I applauded. "So what happened?"

"The Navy halted the maneuver and let him through."

"It'll be a great book," I predicted.

"And you, Ian-boy, did you ever travel on the mailships?"

"Yes," I replied, "and you don't want to hear about it."

"Come on," he encouraged me.

I told him of how we, as students, had stowed away, to and from college.

"And your parents weren't aware of it?"

"No. They thought we were going by train. They'd have flogged us for even thinking of it."

"Well, it couldn't have been easy?" CJ smiled.

"It was," I contradicted him. "We did it only at the beginning and end of term, when the ships were alive with students. It took some daring, but no skill."

I could tell from his expression that he wanted to hear more.

"The only hard thing about it," I explained, "was mustering enough nerve to stay aboard when the call came for visitors to disembark."

"And where did you sleep," he asked, "in the lifeboats?"

"No, no, none of that," I assured him. "We had sleeping bags, and we just bunked down on the cabin sole with some of our paying companions. There was no need to hide. The ship was literally crawling with students, and we simply mingled with the crowd. The only place we had to stay away from was the dining saloon. Like cabin assignments, that's where they checked names again, before placing you at a table."

"So how did you eat?" CJ inquired.

"Our friends brought us a few snacks. But it really wasn't a problem. You see, we'd board at PE, and the next day we'd put ashore in East London. Then it was just another night's hop to Durban."

"And you were never caught?"

"We had one close shave," I admitted, "but that was through sheer stupidity."

He curled his fingers, urging me to reveal the details.

"I'll be reading about it," I protested. "And worse still, so will my dad."

He broke out into a short peal of laughter. "It's not that kind of book, I assure you."

"To be fair," I began, "rather than blame my friend, Pete, I'll put it all down to duty-free beer. We'd had this big party, see, and one our mates told us that the cabin next to his was empty. 'Why *kip* on the floor,' he said, 'when you can have nice clean bunks?' Pete thought it was a great idea, and I, like a fool, eventually gave in.

"The next morning we were awakened by an irate cabin steward demanding to know what we were doing there. He probably heard us snoring. Anyway, Pete had this flash of inspiration. 'Sorry, mate,' he said, 'we must have been drunk and wandered in here by mistake.' 'But, you slept here,' the steward cried, 'I'll have to inform the purser.' "

"That's trouble," CJ smiled, still amused, but by this time, no doubt, wanting the short version of my narrative.

"Well, suddenly the cabin door next to us swung open, and out staggered some of the guys on our varsity rugby team. 'What's all the noise about?' my friend Tommy asked. 'We slept in here by accident last night,' Pete explained, 'and this *ou* says he has to inform the purser.'

"Big Jocko, the nearest, grabbed the cabin steward by the shoulder pads, and slid him up the bulkhead. 'You woke me up, you little shrimp,' he stormed, 'with all that palaver. Now are you sure you have to inform the purser?' 'I don't have to inform him,' the steward stammered. Big Jocko let him go, and he crumpled under his own weight. But he was quickly up again, trying to straighten out in his jacket. 'Could you please excuse me, then?' He received a nod and was off."

"And that was it?"

"Yes, luckily. And that was also the last of stowing away. Too close a call for my liking."

And my lingering in South Africa was also becoming too close a call, on a far more critical yardstick. *Apartheid* was showing an increasingly hostile face, and the long-simmering draft threatened ominously. The consequences of delay could be enormous. So despite my anticipation of a promising future with De Beers, I decided it was time again to make a move.

Part 26

TWO DESTINIES DIVERGE

God-Awful Politicians

*M*adiba had not seen his aging mother since the Rivonia Trial, more than two years before, and he was worried about her failing health. As her only son and eldest child he felt responsible for her, and could not help but bear a strong sense of guilt for the prolonged anguish he had brought upon her.

He was also beside himself with concern for his wife, Winnie, who was being systematically persecuted by the government, her every move scrutinized by secret agents and spies. From the day he had stepped onto Robben Island, the letters he could receive from her were limited to one every six months. And even then, Madiba says, the wardens would withhold mail.

He had seen Winnie the year before, but then only briefly. It was a strained and frustrating meeting, without their children. They had spoken through a glass window under the watchful eyes of prison personnel, and were forbidden to communicate in Xhosa, or to discuss anyone outside of their immediate family circle. It would be two more years before he would see her again. Within that time he would lose both his mother and his son, Thembi, who was killed in an accident in the Transkei. His spirits were at an all-time low.

*I*n the spring of 1966 the Island prisoners noticed a slight letup in the iron-clad discipline that had been the rule until then. But Madiba remembers that this reprieve was short-lived. A return to the former harsh regimen came with the death of Prime Minister Verwoerd. As mentioned, Dr. Verwoerd had survived an assassination attempt six years earlier, but on this occasion, perhaps at the zenith of his power, severe stab wounds proved fatal. His assassin, Dimitri Tsafendas, was a parliamentary messenger and, as it turned out, a past student of my Catholic high school in Johannesburg.

But despite Dr. Verwoerd's base treatment of Africans, those in custody on the Island did not celebrate his passing. And Madiba, with his good breeding, found the words to write, in *Long Walk to Freedom,* that the Prime Minister's death had not given them any pleasure. Political assassination was "a primitive way of contending with an opponent," he said, not something he, or the ANC, had ever condoned. And his diplomatic statement did not end his discretion on this matter. Some three decades later, when Madiba became the country's leader and publicly forgave those who had persecuted him, he took the spirit of reconciliation a step further and paid a social call on Mrs. Verwoerd, then in her nineties, and with dignified formality viewed a statue erected to the honor of her late husband.

Under succeeding Prime Minister B. Johannes Vorster, a keen golfer, some had hopes that *apartheid* might soften. But fanatical attitudes persisted, and extremist politics continued unabated. In 1967, just as I was about to leave South Africa, a typical government communication was issued. Pop quoted it:

> No stone is to be left unturned to achieve the settlement in the homelands of non-productive Bantu at present residing in the European areas.

"Non-productive persons were listed," Pop said, "as the aged, the unfit, widows, and women with dependant children."

It was a continuation of the gruesome plan, already outlined, to drive millions of Africans from their homes, racial insanity that pushed Pop over the top.

"We don't want to see you go, Son," he said in a husky voice. "But you can't keep living here. Our God-awful politicians are charring the country into wreckage."

"I know," I responded, sensing the shame he felt for his once-proud country.

He looked up at the ship's brass clock on a bulkhead. "We'll miss you."

"I'll miss you too, Pop," I croaked, "you, and Mom, and Joy."

He shook my hand. "If your mother and I were younger," he said, "we'd be joining you."

The Entire Apartheid Catastrophe

I was on one of the grand ships of the Union-Castle Line. The call went out for visitors to disembark. I stayed, but this time without the worry of being a stowaway. I was leaving my country once more, on my way to London. The thought reoccurred to me that Madiba had been in that historic city before his most recent arrest, and that if he had stayed I would soon be joining him there in freedom.

I had climbed Table Mountain for the last time the day before, and said a prayer for him and his companions. Then under heavy clouds that raced across the southern winter sky, my thoughts had reached out, beyond the immense view, to Madiba's white friend Bram Fischer who, less than a year before, had been sentenced to life imprisonment. They badly mistreated him, and "hounded him even in death," Madiba would write, in *Long Walk to*

Freedom, referring to the fact that the government seized the ashes after his cremation and refused to release these to Bram's family.

I had shivered as I sat quietly on the ancient sandstone, and contemplated the recent death of Chief Luthuli. He had been killed under suspicious circumstances, hit by a train while on an exercise walk near the mission station that had become his home.

I knew I was doing the right thing in leaving, but wondered what lay hidden from me in the darkness of the future. My mind flashed to those in exile — as I soon would be — Rusty and Hilda Bernstein, Oliver Tambo, and Thabo Mbeki who would become South Africa's second black president; he had left South Africa in 1962, a year after my exodus on *Senta,* and would not return until 1990.

There seemed to be scores of people to see me off, and although I was sorry to be leaving their good company I felt the relief that comes from escape being close at hand.

It was more than five years since I had departed South Africa on *Senta,* and I now had the confidence that came from having done my homework. I had a degree, and money, and permission to study in Great Britain. Letters of recommendation from Oliver and Wynn — "You write it, I'll sign it," the Texan offered — had helped to secure my acceptance to the Royal School of Mines.

And best of all I had been told on good authority that it was less difficult to enter the United States from the UK, than from South Africa. Both Sammy and Wynn had promised to help me, and I hoped to be in the States within eighteen months — as it turned out, it would take three times that long, but I would eventually get there.

The crew slipped our moorings. The Blue Peter was lowered from the yardarm. And as the ship drew slowly from the quay, the thin colored streamers began to snap, severing the last links between passengers and those ashore.

I glanced astern, past a two-toned funnel, the vermilion — beneath the black — shining with exaggerated brilliance. I had no mates aboard, no one to speak to, and as I stood there in my khaki field clothes I began to reflect, with deep nostalgia, upon my good times in Africa. But it was difficult to relate, in a friendly way, to a land I was leaving.

There were three reverberating blasts from the ship's horn, a maritime farewell. Then, as the lovely lady moved slowly ahead, I squinted back at the wharf, trying to distinguish my family and friends. But they now merged into a faceless throng, and I was suddenly overwhelmed with the fear that I might never see them again. I tried to tell myself that I was on the threshold of another great adventure, but deep within me I felt betrayed and frightened.

A harbor tug bade us a cheeky send-off — Vip! Vip! Vip! Passengers waved their last farewells. With the flat-topped mountain as a backdrop, we slipped imperceptibly from the harbor and began narrowing a moat of shimmering water between Robben Island and ourselves. I am a survivor I thought in a brief moment of optimism, but at the closer sight of the forbidding prison my mood shifted again, plunging into depression. The dark notion occurred to me that Madiba was there because of my apathy, and that I was responsible for the entire *apartheid* catastrophe.

Then, as we steamed on, our African destinies diverged, his to become the Father of the nation, mine to deal with the torments of a runaway.

THE LIONS PREVAILED

Afterword

*T*he afterword of my saga begins with five majestic years of academic life in Great Britain — that global epicenter of knowledge, culture, and democracy — a year of blissful employment that followed in the high mountains of Greece, with a girl who would later become my wife, and then a move, at last, to the States, my finest times. But some of my most wretched years were still to come. I had successfully got out of Africa but, as it happened, could not get Africa out of me.

I corresponded endlessly with family and friends there, gathered every scrap of news I could lay hands on, and when I thought I was not keeping up with what was happening, I boarded an aircraft and went back to see for myself. As so, as the epilogue of my story progressed and the political situation in my old country went from bad to worse, distress continued to tear at my soul. Then, when at last the government finally began to choke, and I thought that my pain soon might end, Amy Biehl was murdered near where I had lived, and I plunged once more into an abyss. I tried to claw my way out, but was dragged back in by the Commission findings — the hideous truth of the *apartheid* past, far worse than I had ever dared imagine.

Amy Biehl

*T*he story of Amy Biehl, for me, epitomized the full tragedy and confusion of *apartheid*. From childhood Amy had been intrigued by Africa — just as I had been about the States. As a political science student at Stanford University, she had read extensively about the subcontinent, and eventually, in the early 1990s, as a young adult, she set about getting there. She was thrilled when she learned that her Fulbright proposal had been funded to do research in South Africa. Her plan was to immerse herself in its controversial politics and culture, and compile data for a doctoral dissertation. She was well aware of the dangers she faced there; she had kept herself abreast of the recent history of the country.

Founded on a dream of exclusive white — Afrikaner — control, *apartheid* had become a house of horrors. Since I had left, the United Nations had declared it "a crime against humanity." The world had condemned it. The United States had imposed economic sanctions against South Africa in the hopes of pressuring its leaders to abandon it. But in the years leading up to Amy's visit, heads of state, with their backs to the wall, were enforcing their malevolent policies with unrelenting fury. And the liberation front, for its part, had long since put aside passive Gandhi vignettes and lashed back with *pangas* — long-bladed knives — bombs, and land mines. The country was in a state of undeclared war, and by the time Amy arrived there casualties had climbed into the tens of thousands.

Amy dared to think that she could help to change things. She approached her task with a tirade of devotion and, despite setbacks, began to emerge as a small oasis of hope in a vast desert of despair. She was open, and honest, and led by example. And with gifts of dialogue and debate, her bold initiative paid off. She made a difference.

Amy was sympathetic to the African cause. During her stay she befriended many black people and was extremely generous in her dealings with them. She had every good quality. She was a courtly ambassador of her great country. She was a sweetheart. Everyone who knew her loved and respected her. She was a tireless intermediary between contending Blacks and Whites, a diamond of radiating light in a country under a cloak of dismal gloom. Amy's encouraging message was that *apartheid* would soon end, and that a process of reconciliation would take place. She predicted that Nelson Mandela would emerge as a strong and successful leader, and that he would create a grand model for African democracy.

On the day of her farewell party, shortly before her scheduled return to the United States, Amy offered to drive some black friends to their homes in a township outside Cape Town. On the way they encountered a crowd of youths throwing rocks at passing traffic. This was a relatively common practice at the time, but Amy was unfortunate enough to have a missile shatter her windscreen and strike her on the head.

She staggered, bleeding, from her vehicle, expecting that when the mob saw how badly she was hurt they would offer to help her. Instead, a scene emerged that was reminiscent of biblical martyrdom; the crowd began stoning her. She tried to deflect their barbaric salvo of rocks, but her efforts were futile. Jagged edges tore into her.

Her African companions sprang fervently from the car, waved their arms at her frenzied attackers, and screamed that she was a friend. Dazed and bleeding, Amy herself appealed to the unruly mass for mercy. Those nearest dropped their stones, began *toyi-toying* — weaving in an aboriginal war dance — and chanting slogans. And for a moment the tension appeared to ease.

But a disorderly outer throng pushed through the dancers like a pack of wild dogs. They had not heard the pleas for compassion, and the only thing this new wave of rabble could focus on was Amy. She was white.

Amy paused, a precarious angelfish cornered by hungry sharks. In this medieval nightmare the maniacal beasts also circled short and gawked, baring their rotten teeth. Amy recoiled in horror, her pulse pounding. Her primal instincts beckoned survival. Her eyes searched desperately for a refuge. Then, through a blurred vision of terror, she spotted a gas station. She braced and began an adrenaline-induced sprint in its direction. The fractious multitude swarmed after her, breaking step to hurl rocks. In a few furious moments she was struck again and again. But she bravely faltered on, reeling and nauseous. Some of the older boys caught up to her. One later testified [*Truth and Reconciliation Commission (TRC) Report of South Africa*]:

> We chased after her and I tripped her, and she fell down next to a box with the name 'Caltex' inscribed on it. I asked one of the persons in the crowd for a knife. I got the knife and moved towards Amy Biehl as she was sitting down in front of the box facing us... I took the knife and stabbed her once, in front on her left-hand side. I only stabbed her once. Seven or eight others armed with knives also stabbed at her.

It all happened very quickly, on a sorrowful Wednesday in 1993.

*F*our young men were extracted from the blameworthy mob and convicted of Amy's murder. Each was sentenced to eighteen years of imprisonment. Because Amy was American and a Fulbright Scholar, and I — now a US citizen and a professor — was on a student Fulbright committee, I had been following the case very closely, and was exceedingly relieved to hear this befitting news.

However, some four years later the boys applied for amnesty. Their burden of responsibility was to convince a tribunal that their crime had been triggered by a political objective. It was argued on their behalves that under the ravages and decimation of *apartheid* they had been coerced into their action. At their hearing — I was in South Africa at the time — prosecuting lawyer Robin Brink described the assault on Amy Biehl as "mindless and savage." He gave little leeway in his questioning of the amnesty applicants, wanting to know how the killing of an "unarmed, defenseless woman" could possibly have advanced the aims of their organization. It was no more than an act of "wanton brutality," Mr. Brink said. The youths, he suggested, had behaved like "a pack of sharks smelling blood. Isn't that the truth?" he asked. The boy being questioned denied the charge. "We are not such things," he answered.

Eventually the hearings wound down, and after exhaustive deliberation it was rationalized by members of the Commission that the applicants had been caught up in a delirium of mob violence. Overloaded with stimulation, they had perceived Amy as a 'white settler,' and in that drugged moment she had loomed large as an enemy of their cause. Her death, the boys had thought, would send a political message to the government. The killers of Amy Biehl received amnesty.

I did not want it that way. Amy had been cruelly murdered by the very people she had gone to help. The decision added to my emotional pain and confusion, and I could only stem my depression by telling myself repeatedly that Amy was a saint, and that her parents were saints. A strong mitigating factor in granting freedom to the youths was that Linda and Pete Biehl, who journeyed from the United States to South Africa for the hearing, did not oppose the pleas the boys made for their freedom.

Naturally not everyone could be that forgiving. Marius Schoon, a white anti-*apartheid* activist, fled the country to escape arrest. In exile with his family in Angola, he suffered the heart-wrenching loss of his dear wife and beautiful young daughter. They were torn to shreds by a parcel bomb mailed to them by the South African security police. Katryn, his daughter, was only six years old when she met her vicious death. As Amy's parents had done, the distraught widower returned to South Africa for the amnesty hearing.

He had been lecturing at a university in the Angolan town of Lubango when the mail bomb arrived — I had followed the reports. In a scratchy voice he described the abhorrent sight that met his eyes when he came home. "One wall was covered with blood," he said, "that had been Jenny (his wife). On the floor, there was a little pile of flesh and blood; that had been Katryn."

The inquiry into their deaths was held some fourteen years after the devastating incident, but Marius Schoon was still consumed with anger. As it turned out, his wife and Craig Williamson, the man who had built the bomb that killed her, had been colleagues at the University of the Witwatersrand — the school Madiba, and my old school friend, David, also had attended. Unknown to Jenny Schoon at the time, Williamson had been a student spy for the security police. The Schoons had entertained Williamson in their home, and the deceit that surrounded this misrepresented friendship made the ghastly incident all the more macabre. Marius Schoon's visible agitation in court reflected the loathing that Williamson inspired.

Although the hearings that Marius had returned for were targeted, in part, at achieving reconciliation, he was not moved. "There is no feeling of forgiveness in my heart," he cried. "There is no constitutional duty placed on me to forgive."

The Commission

Like Marius Schoon, I also could not forgive, though my suffering was a fleabite compared to his. I was happy of course when, in 1994, *apartheid* ended, and my old country returned to democracy. But I was still plagued by the notion that if *apartheid* had not been allowed to happen, Katryn Schoon and Amy Biehl would still have been alive, and so would countless others who died in the freedom fight. And all that suffering would not have taken place. Madiba would not have spent most of 27 years on an Alcatraz-like rock and who knows what he might have accomplished.

And in 1997 — I was visiting the new South Africa — I experienced a revived wave of anger as I heard fresh testimony presented to the Truth and Reconciliation Commission. This, a multiracial delegation, had been set up by the Mandela government, and charged with the daunting task of unraveling the painful past. In exchange for the truth, it was empowered to grant amnesty to those who, like the killers of Amy, had committed crimes, however gory, provided that the latter were politically motivated.

The early stages of the hearings were swamped by the wounded. In anguished tones they laid bare their souls about the loss of loved ones, and about the stony paths of pain and depravity they had trodden in the shadows of *apartheid*. Many wept openly in the hearing chambers. Their strained faces reflected the gnawing grief that had tormented them over the years.

However, on the perpetrator side, despite the promise of amnesty, the executioners of heinous deeds refused to come forward. If their response alone was the litmus test, it was as if no crimes had been committed. As weeks turned to months, Commission chairman, Archbishop Tutu, suffered an agony of frustration. He may well have seized on the words of the Stratford Poet, as exasperated prosecutor Jackson had done at the Nuremberg trials following World War II, when prominent Nazis refused to admit to any wrongdoing.

'Say I slew them not,' the bloodstained Gloucester pleaded.

And the Queen replied in ridicule: 'Then say they are not slain. But dead they are.'

And so it was. The lifeless bodies existed of countless young freedom fighters, like Steve Biko, slain in police custody. Dead they most certainly were — we had grieved their loss. Yet no one would assume responsibility for these martyrs of *apartheid* terror.

The solidarity of the security police reigned supreme. Records had been destroyed and tracks carefully covered. A conspiracy of silence hung over the hearings like a bank of impenetrable fog over the African veld. The situation appeared hopeless. But Madiba, Archbishop Tutu, and other savvy lions in the new government pride were too cunning to be blocked by this impasse. In a half-century of precarious survival they had triumphed over far worse setbacks. They were scarred and wily veterans of the savanna, and they instinctively began to work the mist to stalk their quarry. The predator-prey relationship had been reversed.

*P*rior to the start of the Commission hearings, a fleeting shaft of light had pierced the drape of police cover-up. A black security policeman, about to be executed for murder, called for a judge and swore under oath that he was an *abasocongi,* a 'neck-twister,' a member of a police killing squad. He pleaded for the government immunity he said had been promised him for atrocities committed under orders. No one believed him.

But the light sharpened and the haze began to lift when Captain Dirk Coetzee, 'the Jackal,' a disgruntled white policeman from the same unit as the condemned man, fled the country and, from a safe venue, confirmed reports of death-squad activities. In a statement to a South African newspaper he disclosed intimate details of police torture, executions, and bombings. I read his account, and although I had long suspected something of what it revealed, I was ill-prepared for the full force of it.

The Jackal also implicated, amongst others, a high-ranking officer, Major Eugene de Kock. Following further investigations the Major was arrested and bought to trial, and the latter stages of his case proceeded in parallel with the hearings of the Commission.

Madiba and the Archbishop stuck to their Xhosa instincts: *umnxeba wakubhabhisa awubimkhulu,* the cord used for the snare need not be thick. They turned to the Major's trial and set their delicate noose, a slew of far-reaching witness indemnity incentives. Then these royal kings of the hunt retreated into the tall grass and waited with infinite patience. Soon others began to follow the Jackal's lead, and break the ranks of silence. When *'Slang'* — 'Snake' — van Zyl, a Johannesburg detective, hinted at the existence of a secret counter-insurgence unit, Major de Kock began to stir nervously.

The big cats sensed a change in the air. The brume had lifted and all but disappeared. Their keen eyes narrowed from dilation. They raised their limber bodies and stealthily crept forward, probing for weakness. They were tantalizingly close when a sudden shift of wind revealed their scent. The edge of the herd spooked.

The first to take flight were five white policemen. Fearing implication by de Kock confessions, they sprang for the cover of the Commission. They pleaded for amnesty in exchange for the truth on some forty death-squad murders. It was a token offer in the big scheme of atrocities, a lame calf in the herd. But the formidable lions jumped on it and clasped their powerful jaws to its throat. It was small, but by this time they were ravenous; it was the first real breakthrough they had achieved in more than six months of Commission work. And their attack and kill, they knew intuitively, would trigger a stampede.

In the months that followed, the claws of incrimination spread and clasped at the highest levels of the *apartheid* government. A screed of nervous truth began to unravel. It revealed perniciousness and savagery of the most shocking dimensions. The grim acts of inhumanity that were brought to light were not those inflicted by an invading army. One might have attempted to understand those. But these, like the persecution of the Jews in Germany, were nauseating crimes against its own people, genocide, a government systematically murdering its own citizens. My grandmother had been right when she had cautioned me about what the country's leaders might be capable of.

The pattern of human rights abuses that had been outlined in the de Kock trial began to be echoed by the affirmation of others in the security police. Major de Kock himself decided to testify to the Commission. By now a criminal court had sentenced him to life imprisonment, and he had nothing to lose. The international news media were in a state of hysteria as they geared up for his appearance. They had jumped on the nickname 'Prime Evil' given to him by the men of his former police unit, and the sobriquet appeared on every headline. He was widely labeled as a psychopath, but the Major vehemently fired back, saying that he had derived no pleasure from his killing sprees. He had just been doing his job, he claimed, under orders from the very top.

An interesting slant on the unscrupulous nature of *apartheid* emerged with the opening statement of the five policemen who first sought amnesty. It revealed something of the propaganda of fraud that was leveled at young Afrikaners of the day, and it provided an insight into the origins — faith and trust were the spurs — of their twisted beliefs.

> We were brought up to believe in apartheid. We were made to believe that apartheid was sanctioned by God through the church. We were made to believe that our participation in the security forces was justified to uphold apartheid. We were made to believe that black people were inferior and that the needs, emotions and aspirations of black people differ from ours. We were made to believe that we were superior and that these differences justified apartheid — *Truth and Reconciliation Commission (TRC) Report of South Africa.*

The findings of the Commission unveiled or confirmed what most people, I believe, now accept as the truth. I'd had the framework of it presented to me as a child, but most Whites had not, and they were victims, for the better part, of indoctrination and deceit. But even I, as it turned out, had known very little of what actually had happened — the extent and horror of the internal violence, the high death tolls that had resulted from over-the-border raids against guerillas in places like Botswana and Mozambique, the intensity of fighting in Angola. The Commission findings made it painfully clear that in the end, to a greater or lesser degree, all South Africans — and many of our neighbors — were poisoned by some sinister aspect of *apartheid*. Even the quiet lifestyles of the Himba were affected by it.

As the few illustrations that follow will show, in the closing days of National Party rule, the system, in crisis, generated behavior of the most obscene kind. I learned, for example, that police units were routinely deployed to terrorize and, if need be, eliminate suspected dissidents. William Harrington was only eighteen years old when he graduated from Police Training College. He testified that in his less than three years in the police force he and his colleagues had assaulted more than a thousand people. He did not know how many of these attacks resulted in death. The police, he said, would set homes alight and toss people from their vans into rivers; he did not look back to see whether these persons survived. Harrington was brought to trial and sentenced to eight years. His prison term was subsequently extended to eighteen years. In 1997 he applied for amnesty, but this was refused.

Brutality in police custody was apparently commonplace. Captain Benzien, a bull-necked security policeman in Cape Town, looked into the shocked eyes of Commission members and stated blatantly that his manner of interrogation was torture. A means extensively used by him, he testified, was the 'wet-bag method.' He explained that the procedure he followed in applying this degrading technique was to strip the victim naked to humiliate him, blindfold him to disorientate and psychologically terrorize him, and then place a wet bag over his head and repeatedly suffocate him to the point of death. Benzien liked this practice, he said, because it left no incriminating marks.

In the cross-examination of a victim who had survived this form of torture, Benzien was called on to demonstrate the procedure. He appeared untroubled by this unusual request, and offered a vivid commentary as he bent over a volunteer in the courtroom.

At another point in the hearing, Benzien was chastised by the judge for not answering a question properly. But the torturer remained defiant. "Sir, if I said to Mr. Jacobs I put electrodes in his nose, I may be wrong. If I said I attached them to his genitals, I may be wrong. If I (said I) put a probe into his rectum, I may be wrong. That is why the specific methods I used could have been any one of those three."

Commission advocate Chris de Jager, pleading the cause of those ill-treated, immediately challenged him on his response. "Did you, during your service, use all three methods?"

Captain Benzien responded that he had.

Benzien's hearing went on and on, ever shocking to its end. In all, 188 pages of testimony were recorded. I checked to see if he was granted amnesty. He was. It was concluded that the 'anti-terrorist' unit he was attached to, had regarded information, and the retrieval of weapons, matters of extreme urgency. It stated that Benzien's acts, "arose out of the conflicts of the past between the State and the Liberation Movement." "There can be no doubt," the Commission concluded, "that his action related to a political objective." Benzien went free.

*T*he police were a law unto themselves. And many of those who, for one reason or another, left the police force, often integrated a self-styled lawlessness into their civilian lives. A case in point involved two former policemen, Johan van Eyk and Hendrik Gerber. They were both sentenced to long terms of imprisonment for the grisly murder of Samuel Kganakga, a black co-worker they had suspected of theft.

Mr. ·Kganakga was transported at gunpoint to an abandoned gold mine near Johannesburg. There the ex-cops bound him hand and foot, suspended him upside down from the branch of a tree, and went to work on him with an old police torture machine. Electrodes were "affixed to various parts of the deceased's anatomy, including his sexual organs and shocks were applied." The men took turns at hand-cranking the generator, but the victim continued to deny the crime he was accused of.

He was left hanging from the tree for most of the day. A witness said that the former policemen, and a friend, embarked on an entertainment of sorts, drinking brandy, and from time to time questioning their prisoner under further duress. At one point a fire was lit on the ground beneath his head. As evening approached, the trio, by this time frustrated and drunk, applied even more pressure. But their unfortunate victim, already in pitiful shape, bleeding and with protruding eyes about to pop out of the sockets of his grotesquely swollen face, still mumbled innocence.

With darkness the men debated taking Mr. Kganakga away with them, but, according to evidence, "Johan did not want to get blood in his *bakkie,*" his pick-up truck. So, instead, they murdered him at the mine. They then doused his broken body with gasoline and burned it. The next day van Eyk returned to the scene to see if the body was identifiable. One of the arms of the deceased had not been completely burned, so van Eyk hacked it off and took it with him. The men were denied amnesty.

I was pleased to learn that women were a special group that the Commission singled out for sympathy — for their suffering under *apartheid.*

In powerful testimony an elderly black lady, Evelyn Zweni, expressed the frustration and pain of an 'ordinary' African woman trying to avoid trouble at a time when police harassment was rife, and when the movement of Blacks even between neighboring towns was restricted. "Which South Africa are we going to live in?" she asked rhetorically. "If you go anywhere, you are told you are trespassing."

She described how she had been assaulted by policemen — who she referred to as '*Boers*' — slapped across the face, punched and kicked. She told of how, after a police raid, she had attempted to extract a bullet from her husband's shoulder. She could not take him to the hospital, she said, because doctors were afraid of treating those who police might identify as 'rioters.' "I tried to take the bullet out myself, I did everything myself." She testified that after another police encounter, she and her friends had buried the bodies of perhaps twenty people.

She was visibly emotional and clearly angry as she recalled her hapless past. The Commissioners, following their compassionate style in addressing the injured, soothed her frazzled nerves and shattered confidence by treating her with the utmost respect. They addressed her endearingly as 'Mamma.' "Thank you, Mamma, we thank you very much...Thank you for your bravery."

As she spoke, Evelyn Zweni's eyes flashed to a white Commissioner, Dr. Wendy Orr, who, in the worst years of brutality, had courageously challenged the police system in the courts. One sensed a bond between strong women. Mrs. Zweni concluded her testimony by praising the white ladies of the Black Sash, an anti-*apartheid* woman's organization. "They are my parents," she said wiping tears from her eyes.

*D*r. Sheila Meintjes and Ms. Beth Goldblatt, of the University of the Witwatersrand, prepared a gender report for the Commission. It notes that, in confinement, not only men but also "...women were brutally beaten; slammed against floors and walls; flung around on beams; deprived of sleep; forced to stand and to sit on imaginary chairs for hours; teargassed; held in solitary confinement for months on end and forced to endure days of interrogation and even killed." — *TRC Report of South Africa.*

*I*t will never be known how many people died under police interrogation — numbers were estimated to be in the hundreds. To confirm some doubtful incidents the Commission exhumed the remains of fifty victims.

One of these, a case that threw me into yet another bout of misery, was that of Phila Ndwande, a young mother and dental student from the province where I had attended university. Labeled as a dissident with widespread connections, Phila was pursued by the police. Fearing for her life she escaped to neighboring Swaziland. Security agents abducted her there and smuggled her back across the border to South Africa. She was taken to a remote police house, held naked in a small concrete dungeon, and relentlessly grilled. But she courageously resisted her inquisitors, refusing to implicate any of her companions.

The Commission learned of her final moments. A young security policeman, Laurence Wasserman, had been given the order to eliminate her. "Once she was outside," he revealed in his testimony, "I rendered her unconscious with a heavy blow." He said that he and a colleague then carried her to a grave dug in amongst the trees and placed her "half way, sort of half way in. I then fired a single shot into her head," he said.

But the bodies of most victims could not be recovered. Joe Mamasela, an *askari* — a black policeman — confessed to the killings of more than three-dozen victims. Ten of these had been boys, recruited, under false pretences, for training as revolutionaries. They were driven to a quiet location, he said, and dynamited into oblivion.

And I heard Captain Dirk Coetzee describe how he and his colleagues had helped dispose of a young African, Sizwe Kondile, who had been severely tortured by security police in the Eastern Cape — a distant political backwater, or so I had thought when I lived there. After months of suffering the dying youth was dragged out like a mad dog and shot. His twisted body was then burned to conceal evidence of his maltreatment. "The burning of a body on an open fire takes seven hours," Coetzee said. "Whilst that happened we were drinking and *braaing* next to the fire." Mrs. Charity Kondile, the mother of the dead boy, was told by police that her son had been released and was probably in hiding. She spent close to ten years in a frantic search for him, only to learn at last of her cruel deception. She referred the men who had murdered her son as "barbarians."

Testimony revealed that the remains of other fatally-tortured victims were often fed to wild animals. One of these was Stanza Bopane. His body, the Commission was told, was dumped into a crocodile-infested reach of the Komati River, near the Mozambique border.

As the Lions had predicted, a rush of security policemen ultimately came forward to testify, and hopefully secure amnesty. They were terrified of being incriminated by their colleagues, ever mindful of the 212-year sentence Major de Kock had received in criminal court.

And with mounting evidence it was soon apparent that gross human-rights abuses were not restricted, as former President de Klerk had suggested, to a "handful of operatives," a few "mavericks." Rather, it became increasingly clear that the pattern of inhumane behavior had been condoned at the highest levels of government.

The Commission fell short of legally carrying the blame to the very top. But overall, I believe, it succeeded handsomely in meeting its primary objective, that of unearthing a large volume of truth. This, in turn, helped lay to rest what Nobel laureate Tutu referred to as "the ghosts of the past," the haunting memories of *apartheid* days. However, as President Mandela had emphasized from the start, the truth could not bring back the dead, nor could it address, in a satisfactory manner, the suffering of survivors. Yet it contributed, as the Lions had sensed it would, to the process of reconciliation, and to the rehabilitation of a traumatized nation. And that, in and of itself, was a task of formidable proportion. Commission chairman, Desmond Tutu, was my — but, as we shall see, far from everyone's — hero.

A distinguished lecturer at the University of Cape Town, I.J. Mosala, described Archbishop Tutu as *'Mwan' Envu,'* Son of the Soil. I concur, but I see him as even more; to me he is — like Mrs. Biehl — a living saint. I felt his spiritual power calm me when his large hand first clenched mine. "All of us in South Africa are wounded people," he once said, and although I no longer lived there, I included myself amongst his injured. For all the psychological pain that I endured — the cogency that has powered this story — I would be worse off without the Archbishop's truth probe, for it is helping me to symbolize closure on the *apartheid* system and on the far-flung evils spawned by it.

But for all the favorable things I have observed about the Archbishop, there were, as I have hinted at, strong criticisms leveled against him. One revolved around amnesty, and an alleged recklessness in granting it. Even I had a problem with that. However, the fact was that an offer of amnesty was the very pivot that shed light on the truth. Moreover, some instances of official pardon were unavoidable; President de Klerk had insisted on a forgiveness clause in negotiating a transition of power. Madiba had accepted it, knowing that compromise was necessary for a timely transfer of government. Highly acclaimed author and Oxford scholar, Martin Meredith, wrote, in *Coming to Terms,* that: "Amnesty therefore became the price for peace."

And the bottom line on the issue of pardons was that of the more than seven thousand applicants who filed for absolution, only some two percent were successful. "This," said the Archbishop, "could hardly be described as an avalanche of reckless decisions."

And in addition to the condemnation that the churchman and his delegation received whilst in session, their final report attracted still further faultfinding and censure, and not only from Whites. But that, to my mind, was the price they had to pay for disclosing the full truth; for, in addressing issues of human rights, the Commission, to its credit, did not favor one group over another. There was only one goal, and that was to reveal the truth. We looked "the beast of the past in the eye," said Desmond Tutu.

A powerful black faction tried to block publication of the Commission report, condemning it for being too harsh on incidents that, many argued, were justified in the battle for freedom. 'It is too critical of us, *Baba*,' they complained. But their endearing *Baba* — Father — did not appease the eminent *Mwan' Envu.* "I have struggled against a tyranny," he thundered. "I did not do that to substitute another...I didn't struggle in order to remove one set of those who thought they were tin gods and replace them with others who are tempted to think that they are!" The contending delegation cringed in the face of his wrath.

Despite heated attacks and enormous pressures on all sides, Chairman Tutu stood strong, and President Mandela extended his full support to the Archbishop. The five-volume report was submitted in its original form. History, I believe, will honor these two great men for their steadfast courage in promoting the truth, for their projection of a new value system — racism, bigotry, and torture are unacceptable — and for their determination to breathe new life into all South Africans, those who stayed, and those like me who fled.

The lions had prevailed. They had relentlessly stalked, then pounced upon and choked the last life out of *apartheid*. They could have roared and trampled upon their kill, but they chose not to. These two majestic kings simply stretched and let the African jungle rest for a while.

Was There Another Way?

The greatest tragedy of *apartheid* is that it was ever allowed to happen. Bucking the trend of progress on human rights — that followed World War II — was the beginning of madness. But given South Africa's turnaround in politics, in 1948, was there another way?

"It has always been my view," Oom Jan said, "that in a multi-ethnic society the Swiss canton system is the best form of government."

"But Swiss politics date back to 1291," I argued. "Wouldn't their system be too sophisticated to implement in Africa?" I knew that amongst his many credentials Oom Jan was a history major, and I was keen to get his opinion on this matter.

"Not at all," he responded, shaking his head.

I nodded in a way that must have implied some doubt.

"Listen," he said, raising his spectacles, "not every solution is as simple as providing hand pumps for the Himba."

I smiled, but quickly resumed my serious composure. "It would take a strong leader," I said, "to institute the process, to split the country fairly, to relinquish his or her federal power base to the individual provinces or states, twenty six I think there are in Switzerland."

Oom Jan studied my expression. He could tell from my demeanor that I was not all-together opposed to his fundamental premise, that perhaps I even supported it. "It would certainly take someone with a lot more than just words," he said. "Talk is cheap, but it's action that pays for the brandy."

The thought suddenly occurred to me that Prime Minister Verwoerd could so easily have furnished the action. Timing is everything in instituting change, and he, certainly, had had the window of opportunity. And he had possessed the energy, and the qualities — the brains, the political charm, the hardheaded drive — needed for the task.

Oom Jan and he had attended the same university, and I wondered if the same introspection had ever flashed through 'Uncle' Jan's head. I was tempted to ask him, but guessed, from similar questions I had posed in previous conversations, what his answer would be. 'You'll see it all in my next book,' he would say, 'and it'll ruffle a few feathers.' And if I'd inquired about his writing progress, he would surely have said: *'Stadig en met krag,'* Slowly and with power, the same words he used in advising me how best to drive in difficult off-road terrain.

The Great West Window

I recently attended a service in the Church of England — I am an Anglican — conducted by Archbishop Emeritus Tutu. He and I had studied in London at the same time, and after the mass we talked about our happy student days there, and laughed about the fact that we might even, inadvertently, have waved to each other — at that time we had not yet met — as motorcyclists were accustomed to do in those days.

Later, I toured the church, St George's Cathedral in Cape Town, to look for changes within its walls of striking Table Mountain Sandstone. I could find nothing of note, and finally returned to admire its Great West Window, the most recent acquisition that I was aware of. Its center panel contains a black Christ, and the window itself is dedicated to the memory of Earl Mountbatten of Burma. South African ex-service men and women, who had served under him in World War II, sponsored it. I stared, mesmerized by the stained-glass masterpiece, and thought about the words of Nosipho Rapiya — at the service in 2001 to mark the centenary of the Church and the completion of the Window — a message that reflected on the victims of the World Wars. He mentioned the "forgotten dead," and the "countless coloured and black South Africans who fought for world freedom only to find their own freedom systematically denied them in the years that followed those wars."

I was suddenly overcome with memories of childhood conversations with Ga and Pop — my dad too had passed away by this time. They would readily have identified with Rapiya's words. And I thought also of Kat. I had learned only much later that he had served in uniform, in World War II. He had written to tell me that *'Bwana* Pete' had died in the Solomon Islands, and that he, after taking so many chances with his own life — the context of his mention of the War — was thinking about returning to the

Transkei to raise cattle. But, sadly, this also would not be; he was killed in an accident before he left the Copperbelt.

My focus blurred on the colored blocks of the Window as I thought about my old friends of *apartheid* days. Many, like David, had moved abroad, as had my mom, and Joy and her family; others, like Pete, and Kat, and Chris — though dead — lived on, the way they were, in a recess of my mind. I had shared a student house with Chris in London. He had lived with me while building a boat alongside the Thames, near Tower Bridge with its indestructible skeleton of Cornish granite, and writing his book, *Ferrocement Yacht Construction,* and we had kept in touch when he returned to South Africa. But tragically, a few years ago, he was washed overboard in a Cape storm while sailing single-handed; incredibly his yacht remained afloat and was recovered. Had he not advanced to a higher world, the two of us would surely have enjoyed some further African adventures.

My university friend Ian Knight stayed on in South Africa and he and his wife, Bev, continue to do much for the country, and as I gazed on at the Window I experienced a glow of pleasure at the thought of seeing them later in the week. They have purchased my old family home — with the King's bath — in Fish Hoek, and Ian and I have enjoyed nostalgic climbs up Table Mountain, and heavy-weather sailing out of Hout Bay. I have also been sailing with Bevin, but have not heard from him of late and think that he and Renée might have moved to London to be closer to their children, Leighan and Ian — my son is named after Bevin. I ran into Cliff Drysdale, not so long ago, at a tennis event in the States, and a mutual friend has promised to set up a game of doubles.

And although a true raconteur would not untie any of the threads of a story once these had been knotted, I call on poetic license to say that shortly after a preview release of this book — while I was studying coral on the Great Barrier Reef — I received the devastating news that Oom Jan had been ambushed and murdered in Namibia, savagely speared to death. My gut lurched and I felt the bile rise in the back of my throat. But I managed to calm myself and not give too much utterance to my anger, and write to his dear wife and family: 'I see his spirit roaming free with his much-cherished wildlife, forever loved and remembered.'

And a short while later I received word that Jan junior, Oom Jan's son, was embarking from Cape Town on a yacht bound for Miami. I look forward to seeing him and hearing about his great voyage.

Now and the Future

And what of things now — at the time of writing — and in the future? In these still early post-*apartheid* years history has not yet been written. But at least that evil era is over, and I am elated about that! I only wish that I could be as forgiving as Madiba, and others who suffered so appallingly. I am working on it. One might have thought that for me it would be easy — someone who was little more than inconvenienced by *apartheid*, and in many ways even gained by it. But it is tough. I still seem to have its scars imprinted on my soul. And I cannot even begin to comprehend how, for example, Madiba finds it within him to spread his message of forgiveness and love, or how his friend Ahmed Kathrada, could write in such an unembittered way about the Island Rock where, together, they endured so much. Ahmed's words appear on a wall at the Old Harbor in Cape Town, near where the *Emerson K* went down.

> While we will not forget the brutality of apartheid, we will not want Robben Island to be a monument of our hardship and suffering. We would want it to be a triumph of the human spirit against the forces of evil; a triumph of wisdom and largeness of spirit against small minds and pettiness; a triumph of courage and determination over human frailty and weakness; a triumph of the New South Africa over the Old.

I think about their physical, emotional, and psychological battering — lesser men could not have survived the aftermath — and I admire these imposing figures all the more. Unfortunately I am not as strong and, like Hilda Bernstein, I entered the New South Africa with a "lasting feeling of anger." She also was excited that the country was back, more or less, to where it had been all those years ago, except that, as she implied, and as I have already mentioned, Nelson Mandela was then a relatively young man, except that Amy Biehl, Steve Biko, Ruth First — killed in 1982 by a parcel bomb — and so many others had not been so brutally murdered, except that so much suffering had not taken place. Hilda said more, expressed it a little differently, and presented it so well that I feel amiss for not quoting her in full. And I myself could certainly write a lot more, but I know I have already said too much. One of the arts of telling a good story, Oom Schalk Lourens — a Herman Bosman character — said, in *Mafeking Road,* is to "know what part of the story to leave out."

My American friend Annabel impressed on me that two topics are taboo — politics and religion — but I, to my horror, have addressed both, and politics at length. Perhaps, instead, I should have kept a diary, and confined my writing to that. As ten year old Iris Vaughan, a young South African lady, put it so delightfully, in *The Diary of Iris Vaughan:* "Every one should have a diery. Becos life is too hard with the things one must say to be perlite and the things one must not say to lie."

And I know that, like Iris, I shall have to pay the piper for not confining my thoughts to a 'diery,' and, instead, trying to tell the truth as I see it.

She wrote indignantly about what happened to her when she attempted to tell the truth. A family friend had told her that she was his "little sweetheart," and she had protested with a firm "NO," because, as she explained to him, he was "an ugly old man" with a beard. "For what I was sent to bed," she said, "without any more dinner, even jelly and had a good jawing about perliteness."

There is certainly a time for 'perliteness,' but too much of it can often sidetrack the truth. Douglas Brinkley, professor of history at the University of New Orleans, had this to say about another young lady who told the whole truth: "Antjie Krog has rendered the world a great service." It took high courage for Antjie, an Afrikaner, a journalist who so brilliantly covered the hearings of the Commission, to write, in *Country of my Skull,* what she did about a former Prime Minister, P.W. Botha, who many in South Africa still regard as *Die Groot Krokodil,* The Great Crocodile. She said he was "not senile, or old, or suffering from the effects of a stroke." He was "a fool." And South Africans, she noted, had "been governed by this stupidity for decades."

Antjie's words inspire me to rant on about the past, and deliver a tirade on the future — the urgent need to address crime in the new South Africa, and so on. But before I invite more of a 'jawing' than I already anticipate, let me end with a brief review of three telling questions.

Firstly, could the *apartheid* era have occurred under any other political party than it did? Perhaps. But it did not! So National Party politicians, and those who supported the Party, must squarely take the blame for what happened, not in the least for misleading an entire generation of their own young people. Madiba did his part by spiritually liberating all South Africans, enabling us to express regret with honor. I accept my share of the blame, and apologize for not having done more to combat the evil.

Secondly, what can we, and the world, learn from the tragedy that occurred? I believe it is to be vigilant! Regardless of where one lives, one should, I suggest, have a healthy skepticism for the politics and ideology of the day, and for what is bantered as the truth. And one should question everyone in authority — politicians, religious leaders, the police, business people, teachers, and parents — and make them accountable. And this should apply especially in times of crisis. It is all too easy to hide human rights violations behind the need to protect citizens from the foe of the times, be it communism, terrorism, Islam, or Christianity. The happenings of Abu Ghraib, for instance, are unacceptable in my America. And one should constantly work to separate church and state, a creed the United States, historically, has tried to adhere to, and one, it seems to me, that has particular merit in the troubled world of today.

And thirdly, with *apartheid* now behind us, is there hope for a bright future in South Africa? In my opinion, yes there is. One cannot choke the spirit out of Africa; it is too old. I should like to have been able to hug Amy Biehl and tell her so, and congratulate her on all she did for us. And I should love to have seen her vibrant smile when I told her that now there is even a majestic flower named after Madiba, a hybrid of *Strelitzia Reginae,* Bird-of-Paradise; it is called 'Mandela's Gold.' Perhaps in *mputu* — Kat's term for 'the world beyond' — I shall be able to present her with one, and thank her for the seeds of hope that she and fellow martyrs planted. These have borne a far greater harvest than she, and they, ever might have imagined.

I am still, as I said, incensed about the past, but I have the strongest feeling that things will work out for the future. My most recent visit to South Africa was to write the concluding sections of this book there, close to the places that held memories of my childhood. Towards the end of my stay I took a customary break and went out for an exercise walk along the ocean-front in Fish Hoek where I had enjoyed so many happy years — the village is not far from Cape Town, which still remains the cultural heart and soul of the country.

At low tide the beach there is broad and flat. I saw a black student reach up and catch a ball in a game of touch rugby. He tore off and scored, his white colleagues spontaneously applauded, and I forgot — for a minute — that *apartheid* had ever existed. I stopped again to look into a small pond a child had dug with her beach spade. There were tiny critters swimming furiously within its enclosure. The little girl and the old man — me — stood there for a brief moment in silent observation. She then turned and lightly touched me. "I saved these fishes," she announced with the impromptu grace of her age.

I had seen schools of the small fry swimming in the shallows as I walked. Every now and then a wave would throw some of them up onto the sand and retreat, leaving a handful stranded, jumping, easy pickings for the seagulls that noisily pounced on them. "You're a good little environmentalist," I heard myself say, and then set about wondering if a little black girl of barely school-going age would even begin to comprehend what I was trying to convey to her.

But I need not have given it a second thought.

"Do you think so?" she smiled with a curious note of pride.

"Yes," I confirmed and walked on towards the river. There is hope for this country, I thought. I have the strongest sense of it.

ISBN 141208093-2